RE-MEMBERING
AND SURVIVING

RE-MEMBERING AND SURVIVING

AFRICAN AMERICAN FICTION OF THE VIETNAM WAR

SHIRLEY A. JAMES HANSHAW

MICHIGAN STATE UNIVERSITY PRESS | *East Lansing*

⊗ The paper used in this publication meets the minimum requirements
of ANSI/NISO Z39.48-1992 (R 1997) (Permanence of Paper).

Michigan State University Press
East Lansing, Michigan 48823-5245

Library of Congress Cataloging-in-Publication Data is available
ISBN 978-1-61186-371-0 (paper)
ISBN 978-1-60917-645-7 (PDF)
ISBN 978-1-62895-406-7 (Epub)
ISBN 978-1-62896-407-3 (Kindle)

Book design by Charlie Sharp, Sharp Designs, East Lansing, Michigan
Cover design by Cover design by Erin Kirk
PFC Milton L. Cook (Baltimore, MD) from Company C, 1st Battalion, 5th Mechanized Infantry,
25th Infantry Division, near the Filhol Plantation, Republic of Vietnam, 1967. Courtesy Wikimedia Commons.

Michigan State University Press is a member of the Green Press Initiative and is committed to developing
and encouraging ecologically responsible publishing practices. For more information about the Green
Press Initiative and the use of recycled paper in book publishing, please visit www.greenpressinitiative.org.

Visit Michigan State University Press at *www.msupress.org*

*To the Brave Black heroes
who served in Vietnam
and the Brave Black heroes
who refused to serve.*

*Also to the ancestors,
and in memory of my father and mother
Mr. T. J. and Mrs. Mary Alice Gillespie James
whose moral values shaped me
and gave me the desire to learn and teach
and the will to survive.*

Contents

ix   Preface

xv   Acknowledgments

1   Introduction

19   CHAPTER 1. Historical and Literary Background

59   CHAPTER 2. Untangling a Paradoxical Web for the Black Warrior: The Anansean Motif in *Captain Blackman*

89   CHAPTER 3. Reading the Signs: Re-Membering the Legacy of Voodoo as Path to Empowerment in *De Mojo Blues*

121   CHAPTER 4. Playin' It by Ear: The Jazzerly Sound of Survival in *Tragic Magic*

167   CHAPTER 5. Transcending Abstractions by Re-Membering Self in *Coming Home*

211   Epilogue

227   APPENDIX 1. Literary Representation of the African American Experience in Vietnam

231   APPENDIX 2. Visual and Musical Representation of the African American Experience in Vietnam

239   Notes

257   Bibliography

281   Index

Preface

I believe in the Prince of Peace. I believe that War is Murder. . . . I believe that the wicked conquest of . . . darker nations by nations whiter and stronger but foreshadows the death of that strength.

—W. E. B. Du Bois, *Independent Magazine* (October 1904)

While completing course work for a Ph.D. in English, I took a course titled "Literature of the Vietnam War." Little did I know at the time that it would cause me to open a chapter in the book of my life that I thought had been closed, especially since I lived through that era and lost numerous high school and college classmates in the war. As a student in undergraduate school during some of the most furious fighting in Vietnam, I did not realize the emotions that would surface when we began discussing the literature of that era. One of the course texts was a collection of poetry titled *Dien Cai Dau* by Yusef Komunyakaa, a Vietnam War veteran who was the first African American male to win the Pulitzer Prize for poetry for his 1994 collection of poems, *Neon Vernacular: New & Selected Poems, 1977–1989*, when he also won the Kingsley

Tufts Poetry Award. A war correspondent (and later an editor) for *The Southern Cross*, a military newspaper (1969–70), he earned a Bronze Star for his service. Komunyakaa's poetry appealed to me because of the painterly imagery he creates and the stark, almost reportorial commentary he makes on interactions between Black and White soldiers, as well as among them and the Vietnamese. Also, the innovative and intellectually stimulating approach the instructor used to discuss the poetry kindled in me a desire to search for other literary representations of the Vietnam War era by Black writers. My interview of Komunyakaa later resulted in my first book, *Conversations with Yusef Komunyakaa* (2010).

Since narratives by White writers mention only tangentially, or completely omit, the experiences of Blacks in Vietnam, early on I set out on a mission to determine the extent to which Black writers had produced literature about the war. My initial research resulted in five novels, two oral narrative collections, an anthology, three autobiographies, and a collection of poetry. In the intervening years, however, I have uncovered a literary corpus of African American representation of the war consisting of over thirty-five novels, eighteen oral narratives and autobiographies, nine collections of poetry, and an anthology. This corpus is an unprecedented literary canon of Black war-related literature (see appendix 1), and in that respect, it is significant enough to warrant serious scholarly attention. Additionally, I have compiled numerous musical compositions and films by African Americans about the Vietnam War and its aftermath (see appendix 2).

I came to this project trying not to have preconceived notions about literary representations of the Black war experience in Vietnam. After deciding to concentrate only on fiction, I also assessed each of the novels on its own merits rather than attempt to make all of them conform to a particular paradigm. I then asked myself: "Who am I, a woman, to be writing about Black masculinity and war?" However, my literary mentor, who is a fellow university professor, literary critic, and a Vietnam War veteran, responded to my query with "Why not you?" I considered his response literary license to proceed, and the rest is history.

At the outset I wondered why there was a paucity of fiction by Blacks about the Vietnam War, especially during the seventies when there were many novels and film adaptations by Whites. During the course of my research, however, I learned that one reason, according to Mel Watkins a *New York Times* book reviewer in 1981, was that many of the editors at major publishing houses who had sought and supported Black novelists during the 1960s and 1970s later left the publishing business. Black writer Barry Beckham's contribution to Vietnam War novels is *Runner Mack* (1972), which was selected as one of best books of the year by the *New York Times*. However, the editor to whom he was assigned left the publishing company. Then despite his subsequently having signed two contracts for nonfiction books, "both publishers subsequently turned down the manuscripts" (3). George Davis, suffered a similar fate. Though his novel *Coming Home* (1971) did not initially receive critical acclaim, it was later touted as not only one of the "finest" but also "most underrated novels to be written about the Vietnam experience" (Watkins, "Introduction" xxi). His editor also left his publishing company prior to publication, and afterward the company was not interested in publishing other fiction. After finding another publisher, he later published several works of nonfiction.

A second reason for the nonpublication of Black war novels had to do with the unwillingness of many publishers to accept manuscripts from Black writers, several of whom presented an antiwar stance, or at least questioned American involvement. Yet another reason was the U.S. government's denial of visas to Black authors, journalists, and news correspondents desiring to enter Vietnam. Such was the experience of acclaimed author John A. Williams, an honorably discharged Navy veteran of World War II, whom the Pentagon denied permission to enter not only Vietnam but also Cambodia. One notable exception to Black journalists being denied entry into Vietnam was Philippa Schuyler who unfortunately met an untimely death there under mysterious circumstances in 1967. She was only thirty-six years old. The book that she traveled to Vietnam to write, *Good Men Die*, was published posthumously in 1969.

After the war ended, two writers, Stanley Goff and Robert Sanders, were able to interview Black veterans for their book, *Brothers: Black Soldiers in the Nam* (1982) a collection of oral narratives that chronicles the Black experience in Vietnam and captures the immediacy of the war as well as the angst of the Black soldier. In the foreword, Clark Smith tells how this oral history captures the universality of the Vietnam combat experience and provides a "unique documentation of the *ambiguities of heroic action* and its consequences" (xiii; emphasis added). He expresses the sentiments of any number of Black Vietnam War veterans who, as opposed to veterans of earlier wars, either speak reluctantly about or entirely refuse to relate their experiences about the war. Then two years later Wallace Terry published another book of oral narratives that was as compelling, if not more so. Titled *Bloods: An Oral History of the Vietnam War by Black Veterans* (1984), it made the list of New York Times Notable Books. According to Terry the Black veteran "illuminates" in his own words his "own *humanity* as well as racial perception [that] will help complete the missing pages of the American experience" in Vietnam (emphasis added). As a result others can understand how the experience for Blacks differed from that of other soldiers ("Introduction" xvi).

Perhaps adding to the circumstances of nonpublication of Black novels was the dilemma of being a Black man fighting a war for White America against another people of color, which was too taxing emotionally. Additionally, for the Black veteran it is doubly hard returning home given the unpopularity of the war. Several questions were likely on his mind. After risking his life to become a war hero, will he be accorded the same accolades as his White counterpart? Will he be rewarded at all? What about the aftermath of war when he comes home to under-/unemployment resulting from the same systemic racism that existed when he left for Vietnam? Will friends and relatives hail him as a hero or as a traitor to the civil rights and Black power movements? What is the fate of the Black man who takes a stand and conscientiously objects to the war or becomes a deserter from the battlefield? Answers to these questions and more are found in the Black literary corpus of Vietnam War literature. During the course of my research for this book, I performed several interviews, including A. R. Flowers, author of *De Mojo Blues*; Yusef Komunyakaa, author of *Dien Cai Dau*; several of my colleagues and friends; and relatives, including two brothers, John A, and Louis E. James, and a cousin, Willie B. Hampton, all of whom are Vietnam War veterans. Their insights helped me place into perspective the incidents discussed in the novels explored in this text.

I began my research several years ago when very little information about the African American experience in Vietnam was available. Since that time an excellent online resource has been established at the African-American Involvement in the Vietnam War website. Chronicling information about those who served, those who protested, and those who refused to go, it includes a sizable collection of full-text articles, papers, other documents (including government documents), web links, sound files, photographs, speeches, poetry, and film references, as well as annotated bibliographic citations.

As appendix 1 reveals, more Black novels about the Vietnam War were written during the 1980s than any other decade, and they are still being written into the new millennium. I can only speculate why. Perhaps those who participated in the war needed adequate time to process their experiences to allow necessary distancing from the harsh realities of the double whammy of racist treatment the Black soldier experienced "in Country" (Vietnam) coupled with the less-than-welcoming reception upon his return to "the World" (America). Perhaps such writing continues because America did not "win" the war,[1] and Vietnam veterans in general, and Blacks in particular, were treated with condescension and disdain upon their return, a fate that was perhaps too psychologically taxing to place the events of the war in a fictional framework immediately after the war ended in the seventies. Even now during the twenty-first century, post–traumatic stress disorder has not released its grip on the Vietnam War veteran, as America has been plunged into another war, the justifications for and the escalation of which are horrifically similar to events during the war in Vietnam. On Memorial Day in 2012 during his second term in office, President Barack Obama was the first, and only, president to issue an official apology to the veterans of the Vietnam War for the less-than-honorable reception they received when they returned home. Below is a brief excerpt from his oration as he gathered with Vietnam veterans at the Vietnam War Memorial on the National Mall in Washington, DC, on the fiftieth anniversary of the Vietnam War:

> Fifty years later, we come to this wall—to this sacred place—to remember. . . . And one of the most painful chapters in our history was Vietnam—most particularly, how we treated our troops who served there. You were often blamed for a war you didn't start, when you should have been commended for serving your country with valor. (Applause.) You were sometimes blamed for misdeeds of a few, when the honorable service of the many should have been praised. You came home and sometimes were denigrated, when you should have been celebrated. It was a national shame, a disgrace that should have never happened. And that's why here today we resolve that it will not happen again. (Applause.)[2]

At this writing, however, under the Donald Trump administration yet another war continues to rage in Afghanistan, and by all accounts it has the dubious distinction of surpassing the length of the Vietnam War. Touted as the longest war in American history, it has no end in sight, as a writer for *The Nation* attests, despite the current president and his military leaders being under the delusion that America can win.[3] Furthermore, as British antiwar protester Jeremy Corbyn reports, fifteen years after protests against the then impending war in Iraq during the George W. Bush administration, peace is still farther away than ever as war atrocities in Iraq continue, according to a recent article in *The Guardian*.[4] Dr. W. E. B. Du Bois's prophetic words in the epigraph accurately assess this present situation. One can only wonder what literary representations will result from the experiences of

Black soldiers in these wars and others that have occurred since the Vietnam War. Unfortunately, the more things change, the more they remain the same.

Hopefully the reader will find in these pages a way to assess and appreciate the pivotal role that the African American fighting man played during his service in Vietnam. Chapter 1 provides a historical overview and literary background on the Black war experience, addresses the Black presence in mainstream literature of the Vietnam War, examines nonfictional narratives of Blacks in Vietnam, and compares the nature of myth and heroism from an Afrocentric and a Eurocentric perspective. The second chapter, focusing on Williams's *Captain Blackman*, is devoted to narrative adaptations of the paradoxical trickster hero, a crucial figure for understanding the Black soldier who fights to defend America despite the inherent contradictions of his service. Also, because of the broad overview it provides concerning the history of Black involvement in all of America's wars, *Captain Blackman* functions as an archetypal example of the Black war experience. Chapter 3 examines how the African American oral tradition has contributed to the spectrum of Black legendary heroes, as evidenced in Flowers's *De Mojo Blues*. Brown's *Tragic Magic*, which is the subject of chapter 4, explores the improvisational energies of the Black vernacular within the context of a jazz/blues paradigm stylistically and thematically. Chapter 5 discusses Davis's *Coming Home*, a signal example of the ways in which conflicting world views can confuse and either hinder or advance the Black hero on his quest for wholeness prior to his reconnection with vernacular culture. The epilogue concludes and recapitulates, as well as expands on the quest of the Black hero in additional representative novels. Finally, appendix 1 lists fictional, nonfictional, and poetic literary representation, while appendix 2 provides a listing of representations in music and film. The musical selections include blues, soul, R & B, gospel, and classical compositions.[5]

Acknowledgments

am grateful to God, the Creator and Sustainer of the universe, and to my ancestors for a legacy of survival. I am also grateful to the Michigan State University Press editorial staff for assisting me in bringing this book to fruition. Attainment of this goal has been a long journey fraught with many personal and medical challenges that I have been able to surmount with encouragement from a cast of supporters.

I am indebted to Jerry Ward Jr. who recommended sources related to the African American experience in Vietnam that contributed to my formulation of a theoretical/critical design for this book. His sage advice, scholarly insight, and encouragement sustained me. I thank Judson "Jay" Watson III for providing the "spark" that lit the flame of my curiosity to pursue literature of the Vietnam War. I am also grateful to Yusef Komunyakaa, who graciously consented to an interview, the text of which is included in my first book, *Conversations with Yusef Komunyakaa* (2010). Additionally, I thank Ethel Young-Minor and Donald Cole, as well as the interlibrary loan staff, at the University of Mississippi.

I appreciate the assistance of David Willson, former editor of *Viet Nam Generation Journal*, who supplied copies of several out-of-print and limited edition Black novels of the Vietnam War. Thanks are also in order for literary mentor Ousseynou

B. Traore, founder and editor of *The Literary Griot: International Journal of Black Expressive Culture Studies,* for his encouragement and scholarly guidance as well as his invitation to present a paper based on my research at the First International West African Research Association Symposium in Dakar, Senegal. Moreover, I have benefited from the support, both collegial and financial, of Richard Raymond, former English Department Chair at Mississippi State University (MSU). Thanks are also in order for a host of others, including Jerry Gilbert, former Provost at MSU. His office supplemented departmental funds for my travel abroad to perform research and present scholarly papers, resulting from invitations by Coralia Ditvall, at the University of Lund, Sweden, and Mark Heberle, at the University of Hawaii, Manoa.

I appreciate the collegiality of many in the African American professional community who gave scholarly advice and/or provided publishing opportunities for my research. These scholars include, but are not limited to, Howard Jones, Joyce Jones, Abioseh Porter, Al Young, Georgene Bess Montgomery, Tom Spencer-Walters, and Bertis English. Through the years I have also benefited from the work of several graduate assistants during my tenure as an English professor at MSU, including Kristie Cole, Jalesa Parks, Antoinette Hayden, Aaron Grimes, Greg Marcus, and Elizabeth West.

The Vietnam War exacted a heavy toll on my generation, as I lost many class-mates from my all-black high school and my historically black undergraduate school. Consequently, I am grateful to God that two of my five brothers who served in the war, John A. and Louis E. James, came back alive, as well as my cousin, Willie B. Hampton, who was wounded. I thank them all for their service. Moreover, I appreciate the sacrifices of my uncles, maternal and paternal, who served in World War I, World War II, and the Korean War. I acknowledge also the support of my eight siblings, three of whom succumbed during the production of my book. I thank my two children, Nneka T. H. Breaux and Okera Sekou Hanshaw, for being my cheerleaders through the years as I wrote and completed my manuscript and for being my raison d'etre. Finally, in memoriam I thank my parents, Mr. T. J. and Mrs. Mary A. Gillespie James, both of whom succumbed during the course of my research, but whose spirits guided me to its completion. I am most grateful to my Mother who, by her example, taught me to be a virtuous, strong woman and a survivor.

Introduction

Our life is a war.
   —Ralph Ellison, *Invisible Man*

Black Americans, despite fragmentation of body, mind, and spirit, resulting from the Middle Passage and forced enslavement, have preserved a high degree of their "African character" at the much deeper and more fundamental level of interpersonal relationships and expressive behavior.
   —David Dalby, "The African Element in American English"

By calling themselves to remember Africa and/or the racial past, black Americans are actually re-membering, as in repopulating broad continuities within the African diaspora.
   —Melvin Dixon, "The Black Writer's Use of Memory"

Heroism is simply survival.
   —Walter Mosley, "The Black Man: Hero"

I n April 1975 the last U.S. military helicopter left Vietnam, bringing an end to a war that by many accounts was the most controversial of America's military engagements during the twentieth century. The Vietnam War was not only the longest (i.e., prior to the current war in Afghanistan) but also one of the most divisive wars in American history, and Muhammad Ali aptly sums up the attitudes of many African Americans, within and outside the military, when he says: "I ain't got no quarrel with them Viet Cong. . . . No Vietnamese ever called me a nigger" (Tischler 5). The Vietnam War caused lines to be drawn: according to military involvement, between hawks and doves; according to class, as sons from white-collar families often got student deferments or fled to Canada, while those from working-class families were often drafted disproportionately; according to region, with much of the cosmopolitan Northeast being in favor of disengagement, while the rural and poor South (home to most military installations) generally favored involvement; and, most importantly, according to race, as Blacks were not only drafted disproportionately to Whites but also more often placed on the front lines of battle, thereby sustaining more casualties (Mooney and West 279).

Lines also separate narrative representations of the war. Because of their different ethnic histories, Blacks and Whites had different perceptions relative to their involvement in the war and therefore used different strategies to develop narratives about it. The dividing line of institutionalized racism influenced the definition and depiction of heroism; consequently, heroes in the Black expressive and discursive traditions (for example, Ananse the Spider, High John de Conquer, Shine, Railroad Bill) are not even recognized as such in mainstream literature. The strategies for representation differ because historically the White hero, whose identity is often based in the myth of what Richard Slotkin calls "regeneration through violence" (5), has survived at the expense of peoples of color. Survival for the Black hero, on the other hand, is based on strategies of recollection by culture bearers, which the Black writer uses, according to Melvin Dixon, "to transmit an Afrocentric wholeness" (19), to counteract the fragmentary, stereotypical representations of Blackness dating back to enslavement in America. By remembering the African past and mining its rich resources of oral tradition, myth, and folklore, Black writers are therefore "re-membering" (21), or practicing *Sankofa*, that is, looking to the past to determine the future.

As far as narrative representations are concerned, since the 1960s Black writers have produced over thirty-five novels about the Vietnam War. (See appendix 1 for listings of fiction as well as nonfiction, plays, and poetry.) Despite diversity in technique and theme, however, this literary corpus has not enjoyed the same popularity as that by mainstream White writers,[1] nor has it received adequate scholarly critical attention despite good reviews in major publications, such as the *New York Times Book Review* and *Publishers Weekly*.[2] This study aims to address that critical neglect, and it will focus on four novels: *Captain Blackman* (1972) by John A. Williams, *De Mojo Blues* (1985) by A. R. Flowers, *Tragic Magic* (1978) by Wesley Brown, and *Coming Home* (1971) by George Davis.

In each of the four novels that are the focus of this analysis, the protagonist experiences a rite of passage in a real or vicarious war zone during which he goes through what Linda James Myers calls "nigrescence," or the process of "becoming Black and developing a positive identity" (84). Having acquired a positive self-concept and inner security, he then becomes committed to improving the quality of life for other Blacks as well as for other racial groups who are similarly oppressed. Discovering his identity on the quest is a consequence not only of realizing his connection with other African Americans but also identifying with the Vietnamese, another people of color dealing with oppression, colonialism, and imperialism. This common plight becomes a common denominator, evoking empathy with the so-called enemy despite his fighting as a soldier in America's military.

Interestingly, most of the novels about the Black experience in Vietnam foreground the search for identity. This connection between self-knowledge and bravery undergirds heroic quests in most cultures; however, for the hero of African descent, whose sense of self-worth is constantly undermined by racism and emasculation in American society, this connection is more a determinant of whether or not the quest for wholeness will be fulfilled. His psyche fragmented by racist treatment before, during, and after the war, the Black protagonist in Vietnam War fiction seeks wholeness of self and connection with the Black community to survive. Consequently, my analysis of selected novels will demonstrate that the extent to which the Black hero in African American fiction of the Vietnam War is able to re-member or (re)connect with Black cultural memory determines his ability to survive not only the war in Vietnam but also the effects of racism upon his return home.

Remembering is of the highest importance in African culture, according to Huberta Jackson-Lowman, who has extensively studied the relationship between African proverbs and cultural transmission, and she points out that of the many African proverbs relating to memory, one equates forgetting with discarding: "To forget is the same as to throw away" (80). Therefore, if you forget you fail to appreciate the "strength and wisdom" of the African forebears, and as a consequence, you are ill-equipped to survive. The Black Holocaust known as the Middle Passage, according to Jackson-Lowman, "signaled the beginning of our *maafa*, a disaster beyond comprehension—ruptur[ing] the spirits of Afrikan peoples physically, mentally, emotionally, and socially" (78). Consequently, Africans in America are continually in a process of re-membering, that is, recuperating from the fragmentation of self-identity by recouping the preslavery African heritage to survive.

Moreover, remembering is significant for Africans in America because, unlike immigrants of European descent who came willingly to America and built monuments such as the Statue of Liberty and the Ellis Island Memorial Museum as tangible memorials to their deliverance from tyranny, no monuments existed as signposts to the deliverance of African Americans from the horrors of institutionalized slavery and postslavery lynching. In recent years, however, a number of initiatives have been taken to correct this critical neglect. For instance, in 2006 those of us who are members of the Toni Morrison Society created a historical memorial called the "Bench by the Road Project" to commemorate and set aside significant sites in the struggle for civil and human rights across the African American/African Diaspora.[3] As a result of the society's efforts, bench emplacements can be found in the following states: Delaware, Georgia, Louisiana, Massachusetts, Mississippi, New York, Ohio, Pennsylvania, South Carolina, and Washington, DC. Interestingly, a Black soldier of Guadeloupian descent named Louis Delgrès provided inspiration for the first international Bench by the Road emplacement that was dedicated to his memory. On November 6, 2010, in the 20th Arrondissement in Paris, France, Toni Morrison met with the society when it dedicated the bench to Delgrès—outstanding insurgent and revolutionary freedom fighter—for his stalwart determination to prevent the reenslavement and dehumanization of Guadeloupians by Napoleon Bonaparte's military in 1802.[4]

More recently, on September 24, 2016, the preeminent monument to the struggle and achievement of African Americans was established with the grand opening of the National Museum of African American History and Culture (NMAAHC) on the National Mall in Washington, DC, by President Barack Obama, the first African American president of the United States. Worthy of note is that Black soldiers initiated this effort a hundred years ago. According to Lonnie Bunch III, founding director of NMAAHC, this monumental event was the culmination of a "laborious process that began in 1915, when African American Civil War veterans first began the push for a national museum to tell the African American story."[5]

African Americans also have less tangible ways of codifying memory through stories handed down from generation to generation as an aid to remembering the trials as well as the triumphs of the past. The task of the Black writer has been to translate this expressive cultural form for discursive purposes. Indeed, a great deal of contemporary Black writing is "a meditation on remembrance," according to Charles Johnson (qtd. in Pederson 48) whose novel *Middle Passage* attests to the power of the imagination to interpret that devastatingly memorable event, the *maafa*, to contemporary audiences. Toni Morrison assigns the utmost importance to memory in the craft of writing when she says that Black writers have a "responsibility" to revive the past because the "act of imagination is bound up with memory" (qtd. in Fabre and O'Meally 5). With her personification of memory in the form of the eighteen-year-old titular protagonist/apparition in *Beloved*, Morrison attempts to "heal the psychological disruption of identity" (Dixon 23). In like manner, by remembering heroes from the African American vernacular tradition, Black authors of Vietnam War novels are involved in the process of healing the psychological wounds caused by the war and the Black soldier's ongoing struggle with racism and emasculation in the military and in American society.

Though Black representation of the Vietnam War runs the gamut from non-fiction to poetry to oral narrative to fiction, I chose fictional narrative for my focus as I set out on a mission to answer the question, How have Blacks represented the Black experience in Vietnam during the war and in its aftermath? Fiction, which is essentially storytelling, appealed to me because traditionally in African and African American culture storytelling has encoded the passing on of cultural values and survival strategies from generation to generation. Fiction also allows experimentation with narrative technique not afforded by other genres. Out of the oral tradition emerged the African American novel, which Bernard Bell calls a "hybrid narrative derived from . . . indigenous roots of Black American folklore and literary genres of the Western world" (xii).

Because of the historical dialectic between Eurocentric and Afrocentric culture in the United States, I agree with Bell that the following concepts developed from the writings of W. E. B. Du Bois are crucial to an understanding of the Black novel:

- double-consciousness [that] signifies the biracial and bicultural identities of Afro-Americans and
- socialized ambivalence, the dancing of attitudes of Americans of African ancestry between integration and separation, a shifting identification

between the values of the dominant White and subordinated Black cultural systems as a result of institutionalized racism. (xiv)

Neither double-consciousness nor socialized ambivalence should be viewed as psychopathological responses. Rather, they signify both the "sociopsychological process of acculturation of Black Americans—the will to realize their human and civil rights—and the sociocultural relationship of colonized people of African descent to colonizers of European descent," as Bell rightly points out (345). In other words, these are healthful rather than pathological adjustments to the reality of institutionalized racism in America and elsewhere.

This double vision regarding the racial consciousness of Black Americans results from a unique set of experiences shared by no other racial or ethnic group in America: being forcibly taken from their indigenous homeland in Africa; surviving the horrors of the Black Holocaust known as the Middle Passage; and experiencing the "peculiar institution" of slavery, as well as emancipation, Reconstruction, "Jim and 'Jane' Crow" (West, "40 Years"), the Great Migration from the South to the North, and urbanization. These shared historical circumstances have produced a "residue of *shared memories*" (B. Bell 5; emphasis added), or what we know as cultural memory. Consequently, Robert O'Meally and Geneviève Fabre's observation, in *History and Memory in African-American Culture*, that African Americans are "'born knowing' that there is a wide gulf between America's promises and its practices" (3) emanates from this reality of a shared cultural memory resulting from institutionalized racism.

Comprised of the positive values of African cultural retentions on the one hand and the negative fragmentation of racism on the other, a shared cultural memory gives rise to a common quest. Historically for Black Americans this quest has been for "life, liberty, and wholeness—the full development and unity of self and the black community," as Bell observes (12). This quest is exemplified in Black discursive art, particularly the novel, as well as in Black expressive culture. David Dalby corroborates this view with his observation in "The African Element in American English," that Black Americans, have retained a deep level of African character and "expressive behavior" (173). The modern Black novel represents the "sophisticated continuation of African storytelling conventions," as well as other expressive cultural practices, in "dialectic tension" with discursive Western forms of narrative as evidenced in the novel (B. Bell 17). Though African American prose forms have historically followed similar trends to those of the mainstream, certain innovations within the African American fictional narrative tradition reveal the uniqueness and importance of memory and double-consciousness as survival strategies.

In *The Afro-American Novel and Its Tradition*, Bernard Bell discusses the development of the African American novel, as well as similarities and differences between it and the American novel. The early African American novel, during the period 1853 to 1917, exploited the conventions of historical romance and social realism. This era was followed by a period of experimentation in novelistic form, which sought to recapture the folklore of Africa and the African American past through the uses of poetic realism, genteel realism, folk romance, folk realism, and satiric realism during the Harlem Renaissance into the mid-1930s. Naturalism, also pervasive in Western narrative, was dominant in the Black novel from 1937 to 1952, but with a slight difference (151). Whereas scientific and economic determinism in the mainstream American novel usually led to despair, to the contrary, in the African American novel a generous helping of the double vision occasioned by double-consciousness led to "a glimmer of hope beyond despair that concedes life's limitations while celebrating its possibilities" (81). Bell observes further that from 1952 to 1962 many Black novelists moved away from naturalism and began to rediscover and revitalize the practices of earlier Black writers by using "myth, legend, and ritual [from African and African American culture] as appropriate sign systems for expressing double-consciousness, [and] socialized ambivalence" as aids to their application of modernism (189).

From 1962 to the early 1980s neorealism, particularly critical realism (B. Bell 246), dominated the fiction of Black writers. From the mid-1980s to the present Black fiction has been dominated by modernism and postmodernism in conjunction with other features that hearken back to African expressive culture. However, despite the hybridity that exists between novelistic approaches of African American and mainstream American writers, a distinct difference is apparent as far as postmodernism is concerned. For many mainstream novels of the Vietnam War, the predominant literary/critical theoretical approach for analysis has been postmodernism. One of its tenets is that conventional elements in fiction are "exhausted" and that the foundation of a "new fictive reality" can be found only "either in the individual perceiving mind or in the act of perception" rather than in the world that exists outside the novel, a view that, according to Bell (283), often neglects social issues and celebrates fragmentation. Also it is noted for placing emphasis on literature that has no center, or "meaning [and] that its meaning exists only in our consciousness," which makes it self-referential (B. Bell 282). For these and other reasons, therefore, postmodernism is ill-equipped as a theoretical/critical paradigm for analysis of African American fiction of the war. As Bell notes, the few Black novelists of the Vietnam era who are postmodernists differ from their White contemporaries by "rejecting their arrogance" while "rediscovering and reaffirming the power and wisdom of their own folk tradition: Afro-American ways of seeing, knowing, and expressing reality, especially black speech, music, and religion" (284).

Bell's historical analysis of Black fiction reveals the diversity of narrative approaches through the various literary periods of the African American novel. Such diversity, in thematic approach as well as subject matter, is evident in the work of Black fiction writers during the Vietnam War era.

The novels under review exploit several the above novelistic conventions: naturalism (*Coming Home*); critical realism through the use of myth, legend, and ritual (*Captain Blackman* and *De Mojo Blues*); and neorealism (*Tragic Magic*). Two Black novels about the Vietnam War experience that can be considered postmodernist are *All-Night Visitors* by Clarence Major and *Runner Mack* by Barry Beckham. Depictions of the Black hero in the above novels are testaments to Black survival and heroism in the tradition of Black vernacular culture and historical memory.

However, the image of the Black hero in American culture has been sullied by America's irrational fears of the Black male, a position that filmmaker and cultural critic Michael Moore takes in many of his films, including *Bowling for Columbine*, which he discussed as a guest on *The Oprah Winfrey Show* where he referred to White America's irrational fear of Blacks as a "mental illness."[6] Moore goes on to say that racial fears are "manipulated" by media, such as television and newspapers, which "feeds our fears of black people." A White male himself, Moore contends in his book *Stupid White Men . . . and Other Sorry Excuses for the State of the Nation* (2001) that White America is in such a state of fear because the people it has classified as "the other" are perceived as a threat. Those groups, or people who differ racially, ethnically, and/or culturally from people of European descent, are marginalized, and little effort is made to understand them or their culture(s). One of the somewhat benign aspects of this process is the effort to assimilate others within hegemonic American culture. A more malevolent result of designating whole groups of people as "cultural other," according to Marimba Ani, is that it "allows Europeans to act out their most extreme aggression and destructiveness, while simultaneously limiting their collective self-destruction on a conscious level" (xxv).

Significantly, Moore's appearance on Oprah's show was during one episode of her antiwar series that was broadcast from early November 2002 until March 2003.

As a result, Oprah was vilified and received hate mail that according to her was "like 'go back to Africa' hate mail" for having the audacity to ask if war were the only answer during the time leading up to the Iraq War.[7]

"Othering" an entire group of people simply because they are different breeds irrational fear and contempt. These are the sentiments also of Barry Glassner, author of *The Culture of Fear: Why Americans Are Afraid of the Wrong Things*. During his appearance on the *Oprah Winfrey Show* episode with Moore, he attributed the fear of Black men in society to the reality of White America having "no sense of the everyday lives of black men," especially from looking at TV, because of the scarcity of positive images portrayed. Because of the negativism surrounding the image of the Black male in media, it is necessary to supplant those with positive images that already exist in Black creative literature. Critical analysis from a Black perspective is necessary to explore the richness and diversity of themes.

As far as Vietnam War literature is concerned, currently the only full-length critical study of Black fiction about that era is Norman Harris's *Connecting Times: The Sixties in Afro-American Fiction*, which was published in 1988.[8] That no other full-length work and few critical articles have appeared in the intervening years since the war officially ended in 1975 speaks not only to the paucity of critical attention to this important corpus of Black war literature but also to the need for further study.[9] I use the foundation that Harris laid in his pioneering critical analysis of Black fiction of the Vietnam War to provide a basis for my present study.

Harris's critical method is an extension of the "Black Aesthetic" of the sixties.[10] The Black Aestheticians provided for African American literary study what Thomas Kuhn would call a "paradigm shift" from principles in art based on an integrationist cultural approach to an assertion of the essential "'Negro-ness' or 'Blackness' of an expressive work" as being a "fundamental condition of its 'artistic-ness,'" according to Houston Baker Jr. (*Blues* 77).[11] This change in focus for African American literary-critical and literary-theoretical study ushered in an era of Black expressive culture studies that is reflected in the writings of literary theorist Robert Stepto, who considers all phases of culture, whether lived experience or artistic endeavor, to be directed by "certain desires or quests." For African Americans the quest is for "freedom and literacy (ix)." In his discussion of the African American tradition, Gates uses the trope of "repetition and revision" for the Black discursive process that is accomplished through signification, or improvisation (*Signifying Monkey* xxv). Therefore, through the processes of "repetition and revision," that are fundamental to Black artistic forms, Harris "signifies" upon Stepto's theory by defining "freedom" as "knowledge of the racial memory" and "literacy" as "application of the racial memory as dictated by the confluence between personality and situation" (*Connecting Times* 6).

My analysis of Vietnam War novels then revises and extends, or signifies upon, the foundation that Harris set forth through my use of vernacular theory, a treatment of Black expressive culture in the context of modern discursive practices. Vernacular theory is based on methodologies focusing on the "blues matrix" set forth in Houston Baker Jr.'s *Blues, Ideology, and Afro-American Literature: A Vernacular Theory*, and on the study of Black myth and ritual as codified in Black language that Henry Louis Gates Jr. explores in *The Signifying Monkey: A Theory of Afro-American Literary Criticism*. The masculinist experience in most war novels, and particularly those in this study, includes a type of language that linguist Geneva Smitherman, in *Talkin' and Testifyin': The Language of Black America*, refers to as Black Semantics and Black Idiom, some of which can be regarded as profanity. Such language, according to Smitherman embodies and is part of a certain cultural world view (60). While such language is not central to the Black Semantic lexicon, its use is a sensitive matter; consequently, this critical analysis uses quotes directly from the novels to maintain the integrity of the original. My theoretical methodology, therefore, comports with the theoretical/critical foundations expressed in the work of Stepto, Harris, Baker, Gates, and Smitherman, which exemplify various aspects of the "blues matrix" that, as Michael Chaney notes, is "recognized as a central, shared component of a widely divergent body of late twentieth-century African-American writing loosely dubbed the 'New Black Aesthetic.'"[12]

Of the four novels that are the focus of this study, each is viewed as a specific manifestation of Black expressive culture within the New Black Aesthetic: *Captain Blackman* by John A. Williams and the African trickster myth of Ananse the Spider; *De Mojo Blues* by A. R. Flowers and African spiritualistic practices of Vodoun/ voodoo/hoodoo; *Tragic Magic* by Wesley Brown and the improvisational musical tradition exemplified in jazz; and *Coming Home* by George Davis that juxtaposes Afrocentric and Eurocentric world views exemplifying the Du Boisian double-consciousness conundrum. Only three of these writers are veterans of the Vietnam War, and they made their debut into publishing with their Vietnam War novels. The fourth, John A. Williams, was a veteran of World War II who had already established a reputation as a writer prior to penning his Vietnam War novel..

John A. Williams was born in Mississippi; however, his parents moved to Syracuse, New York, before he turned one year old, and that is where he was reared. The eldest of the four writers, he was also the most prolific until his death in 2015 at the age of eighty-nine. In some scholarly circles referred to as the Dean of Black Letters because of his long and distinguished career, Williams was most recently heralded by critic James L. de Jongh in the *New York Times* as "arguably the finest Afro-American novelist of his generation" (qtd. in Grimes). Although he did not publish his first novel until he was thirty-five, according to John O'Brien who interviewed him for *The American Scholar*, Williams produced a sizeable literary corpus, the number and variety of his books being unmatched by many writers of his time (489). Unfortunately, critical response to Williams's work has been mixed and at times unbalanced. William Grimes holds a similar view, referring to Williams as "an underrated novelist who wrote about Black identity" in his *New York Times* article that announces Williams's death (15). I agree with O'Brien who argues that critics have been so concerned with Williams's treatment of racial, sociological, and political themes that they have often overlooked the "philosophical and psychological" ideas that underlie those themes (489). The anger expressed in many of his writings reflects the rage that is often a response to racism in America and abroad.

A three-time African American Literature Book Club "Best-Selling Author," Williams was inducted into the National Literary Hall of Fame and was the recipient of numerous awards, including the American Book Award (once for fiction and once for poetry), Richard Wright-Jacques Roumain Award, New Jersey State Council on the Arts Award, the Carter G. Woodson Award, and the Phillis Wheatley Award for Invaluable Contributions to African American Letters and Culture, to name a few.[13] As a journalist and author adept at articulating the racial problems in America, he persisted in exposing what mainstream publishing companies would rather leave hidden. Seemingly with great urgency and working at an indefatigable pace, Williams produced an oeuvre consisting of works that span a variety of genres: thirteen novels, two volumes of poetry, seven nonfictional works, seven anthologies, five film and television scripts, and two plays. Published in rapid succession, his novels are *One for New York* aka *The Angry Ones* (1960), *Night Song* (1961), *Sissie* (1965), *The Man Who Cried I Am* (1967), *Sons of Darkness, Sons of Light: A Novel of Some Probability* (1969), *Captain Blackman* (1972), *Mothersill and the Foxes* (1975), *The Junior Bachelor Society* (later adapted to the television movie *Sophisticated Gents*) (1976), *!Click Song* (1982), *The Berhama Account* (1985), *Jacob's Ladder* (1987), and *Clifford's Blues* (1999).[14]

In addition to being an author, Williams also had a distinguished career as a professor at various universities, including City University of New York, New York University, and Rutgers. In 1987 the John A. Williams Archive was established at the University of Rochester. Additionally, he was a news reporter, working for papers such as the *Chicago Defender*, the *Pittsburgh Courier*, the *Los Angeles Tribune*, the *Village Voice*, and the *Syracuse Herald-Journal*. A voracious reader, he wrote book reviews for the *Washington Post*, the *New York Times, Essence, American Visions*, the *Quarterly Black Review*, the *Multicultural Review*, and the *Med Press Review* from 1946 to 1993.[15] His extensive travels, both domestically and abroad, gave him a unique perspective on the plight of peoples of African descent around the world. He was African correspondent for *Newsweek* and *The Nation*, and he was European correspondent for *Ebony* and *Jet*. Additionally, he worked for both CBS and NBC television networks.

Although best known for his fiction, Williams also produced numerous non-fictional works. These include *Africa: Her History, Lands, and People* (1962), *The Protectors*, with Harry J. Ansliger (1964), *This Is My Country, Too* (1965), *The Most Native of Sons: A Biography of Richard Wright* (1970), *The King God Didn't Save: Reflections on the Life and Death of Martin Luther King, Jr.* (1971), *Flashbacks: A Twenty-Year Diary of Article Writing* (1973), *Minorities in the City* (1975), *If I Stop I'll Die: The Comedy and Tragedy of Richard Pryor*, with Dennis A. Williams (1991), and *Flashbacks 2: A Diary of Article Writing* (1991).[16]

Williams's extensive travels as well as his stint in the U.S. Navy, where he served during the Second World War in the Pacific from 1943 to 1946, perhaps provided some of the perspective he needed to write *Captain Blackman*, his Vietnam War novel that takes the reader on a panoramic journey of Black military involvement in all of America's wars from the American Revolution to Vietnam. Despite his military service, his expertise as a journalist, and all of his scholarly accolades as a renowned writer, however, the Pentagon denied him a passport to travel to Vietnam. Not to be deterred Williams, who had originally intended to interview Black soldiers in the field so that he could write a nonfictional account of their experiences, decided to write a novel instead. In an interview with Earl A. Cash, he relates how he approached magazines that were interested only in "war stories told by white guys" (qtd. in Muller 100). He attempted to raise the money himself to go to Vietnam, but unsuccessfully. He said if he had been able to go, he would have gone first to the stockades because "that's where the truth always is, in the jails" (101). Having been rebuffed by the magazines for funding and the Pentagon for clearance, Williams devoted his creative energies to penning a fictional Black military epic, *Captain Blackman*, that provides a holistic view, through flashbacks, of Black soldiers in every war fought on behalf of America.

Like Williams, A. R. Flowers, author of *De Mojo Blues*, was born in the south. A Memphis native, he later moved to Syracuse, New York, where he currently serves on the English Department faculty at Syracuse University teaching in the master of fine arts program. He has been executive director of the Harlem Writers Guild and cofounder of the New Renaissance Writers Guild and the Pan-African Literary Forum. Flowers made his contribution to the Black literary corpus about the Vietnam War in 1987 when he published *De Mojo Blues*, his first novel. Wesley Brown says in his review of Flowers's book that it is "not only a compelling tale of several young Black men fighting in a war on behalf of ideals that are not honored in the country where they are not espoused, but also a meditation on tradition, destiny, and the exercise of mojo (power) as a healing force in a world poised for destruction."[17] Flowers's mentor and former professor John Oliver Killens expressed his appraisal of the novel more succinctly: "*De Mojo Blues* is a resounding success. . . . Walk, run, get to the nearest bookstore and buy this book."[18]

A blues-based performance poet who considers himself literary heir to both the Western written and the African oral traditions, Flowers has been called a modern-day griot, in the tradition of African culture bearers who, from ancient times, have passed on the history of their people to future generations through orality and performance.[19] Using spellbinding performance poetry, he often accompanies his presentations with African instruments. Infusing his writings thematically with the ancient African spiritualistic practice of Vodoun, he is self-described Hoodoo Man "Rickydoc."[20] Combining romance and journey between two lovers, his 1993 novel, *Another Good Loving Blues*, signifies upon Zora Neale Hurston's novel *Their Eyes Were Watching God*, replete with a cameo appearance by Hurston herself. Patricia Schroeder observes that this second novel continues the theme developed in *De Mojo Blues*: "that connections to African-derived cultural traditions are essential to the spiritual health of African Americans and the survival of the race" (263).

In addition to his Vietnam War novel, Flowers has produced an eclectic oeuvre ranging from juvenile literature to autobiography to performance poetry. Written in 1997, his book *Cleveland Lee's Beale Street Band*, a tribute to the birthplace of the blues, is written for young audiences. In the online journal *ChickenBones: A Journal for Literary & Artistic African-American Themes*, literary critic Ishmael Reed describes Flowers's eclectic nonfictional work *MoJo Rising: Confessions of a 21st Century Conjureman* (2001) as a fusion of various fields of study, including history, autobiography, and philosophy. Additionally, renowned literary and cultural critic Houston Baker Jr. calls *Mojo Rising* "a brilliant, honest, informed, energetic meditation and memoir from the heart of a 21st century conjureman. . . . 'Rickydoc' shows us the way to black empowerment—the longgame for our souls' survival."[21]

I See the Promised Land: A Life of Martin Luther King, Jr. (2013) is a graphic novel in which Flowers provides a panoramic view of the African American struggle from enslavement to the time of Dr. King's leadership in the civil rights movement. Apropos of his collaboration with Manu Chitrakara, a Patua scroll painter from Bengal, India, who boldly illustrates the book, Flowers discusses the influence of Mahatma Gandhi on Dr. King's philosophy of nonviolent struggle for human rights. In a recent interview for her *Words with Writers* blog, Marissa Toffoli asked Flowers why he chose this collaboration for a graphic novel.[22] He responded that he was performing readings at the Jaipur Literary Festival in India, when Gita of Tara Books asked him about collaborating with a Patua artist on the life of Rev. Dr. Martin Luther King Jr. Admitting that he knew "nothing of Patua art at the time," he was nevertheless intrigued by the idea, as he later learned that these artists went around to villages listening to and performing stories, sometimes to the accompaniment of music. In effect, this practice of storytelling with musical accompaniment is similar to what griots in Africa do and what Flowers does; consequently, he said, the chance to do a collaboration with an Indian artist "spoke to me."[23] Also being a Memphis native who experienced Dr. King's civil rights work there firsthand, Flowers wrote this book in tribute to his legacy.

Published by Tara Books in Chennai, India, *Brer Rabbit Retold* (2017) is Flowers's most recent book. In this retelling for a contemporary audience of the stories that the enslaved brought to America from Africa, Flowers collaborates with illustrator Jagdish Chitara, a ritual textile painter from Gujarat. In the book is a CD with a musical spoken-word performance in collaboration with a group of young Indian musicians. A limited edition book, it also comes with a short film. Described by the publisher as a "genre defying cross-media project [that] pushes the boundaries of narrative art," it combines sight, sound, and text.[24] These collaborations with international spoken-word and visual artists are divergences from writings such as Flowers's Vietnam War novel *De Mojo Blues* written earlier in his career, and they are examples of his constantly evolving eclectic artistic talent. Additionally, through his blog—*Rootwork the Rootsblog: A Cyberhoodoo Webspace*—which offers "Timely Observations on Politics, Literature, Culture, Struggle and the Hoodoo Way," Flowers has recognized the need to adapt to modern audiences by "making use of information technology for Black liberation," according to Nathaniel Turner.[25]

Like Flowers, Wesley Brown is also a superior storyteller; instead of blues, however, his writing is informed by jazz that serves as a subjective correlative in his writings. I agree with prominent literary and cultural critic Jerry Ward Jr. that Brown is "one of our national treasures."[26] In my discussion of his Vietnam War novel *Tragic Magic* (1978), I examine characteristics of his writing style in which the text "sings" on the page, like a jazz composition, producing what I call the jazzerly text (a play on Gates's "speakerly text" [*Signifying Monkey* 170]). Carrie Golus describes in a similar way the musicality of Brown's text in her assessment that instead of merely quoting music, he draws from "the trick chords of Thelonious Monk and the unresolving rhapsodies of Charlie 'Birdland' Parker . . . transcrib[ing] jazz into prose."[27] During a recent interview for his new collection of eight short stories, *Dance of the Infidels* (2017), Brown tells Colin Harrington of *The Berkshire Edge* that jazz appeals to him because of its "democratic form of communication" in which the individual, or soloist, works in concert with the ensemble to produce a harmonically pleasing composition.[28] Hearkening back to the 1920s and 1930s in New York at the Savoy Ballroom where jazz legends, such as John Coltrane, Cab Calloway, Dexter Gordon, Billie Holiday, and others, gather in an interracially convivial atmosphere, *Dance* improvisationally presents a society where these real musical giants interact with fictional characters.

Tragic Magic was Brown's debut novel, and it portrays a protagonist named Melvin Ellington who defies the draft during the Vietnam War by declaring conscientious objection, after which he is sentenced to prison for three years. After serving a year and a half, however, he is released. The action in the novel occurs during the day of his release when he is reunited with his childhood friend Otis, an alter-ego figure. Suffering from post–traumatic stress disorder and the loss of a hand while in Vietnam, Otis is a marine who self-destructs when he returns home. The novel juxtaposes Melvin's virtual war experience in prison with Otis's actual war experience in Vietnam. Brown takes pains to explain that action in the novel is totally fictional. The reason, perhaps, is that he became a political prisoner for refusing the draft in Vietnam, serving eighteen months of his three-year sentence. A man of principle who puts his beliefs into action, Brown fought for civil rights with the Freedom Democratic Party in Mississippi and later joined the Black Panther Party. In an interview with *Home News* he traces his interest in writing back to the period of the sixties: "the writing came out of my involvement with the civil rights movement. It seemed as if I could explain, at least to myself, then I would have more of a handle on my life and not be at the mercy of things."[29]

Similar to Williams and Flowers, Brown writes in a variety of genres. After *Tragic Magic*, he published the following fictional works: *Boogie Woogie and Booker T* (1987), a play; *Imagining America: Stories from the Promised Land* (1991), a multiethnic anthology of fiction coedited with Amy Ling; *Life during Wartime* (1992), a play; *Darktown Strutters* (1994), a novel; *W.E.B. Du Bois: A Prophet among Them* (2001), a play; *Push Comes to Shove* (2009), a novel; *Dark Meat on a Funny Mind* (2014), a play; and *Dance of the Infidels* (2017), a short story collection. His nonfictional works include *W.E.B. Du Bois: A Biography in Four Voices* (1996), a PBS documentary segment; *The Teachers and Writers Guide to Frederick Douglass* (1996); and *Visions of America: Personal Narratives from the Promised Land* (1992), a multiethnic anthology coedited with Amy Ling.

Adept at writing historical fiction, Brown captures in his work the zeitgeist of various eras from the nineteenth through the twentieth centuries: *Darktown Strutters* (novel), the period immediately preceding and beyond the Civil War through Jim Crow; *Boogie Woogie and Booker T* (play), the Reconstruction era; *Dance of the Infidels* (short story collection), 1920s era of jazz musicians and Harlem Renaissance artists; *Tragic Magic* (novel), 1960s era of civil rights, Black power, and the Vietnam War; and *Push Comes to Shove* (novel, with action sequential to that in *Tragic Magic*), radicalism extending from the end of the 1960s to the mid-1970s. Brown deals with each of these time frames in an extraordinary way with his facility for making the words sing on the page. For instance, in *Darktown Strutters* where the partial narrators are Jim Crow and his son Jim Crow Too, he provides a view of minstrelsy seldom seen in mainstream literature by revealing the interiority of these characters who are often portrayed as one-dimensional stereotypes. Though Spike Lee's film *Bamboozled* was inspired by *Darktown*, I agree with Ward's assessment of the different results of their satirical treatment: "[Brown's] fiction informs a consciousness of American class and caste formation; Lee's film trivializes that consciousness and cashes in on entertainment values."[30] Although Patricia Spears Jones thinks *Darktown* "may well be Brown's best work,"[31] I place *Tragic Magic* at the top of his oeuvre. Regardless which of Brown's fictional narratives one considers "best," we can all agree with James Baldwin that he is "one hell of a writer."[32] Currently Brown is working on a play about Baldwin.

Similar to Brown's *Darktown Strutters* inspiring the movie *Bamboozled*, George Davis's Vietnam War novel *Coming Home* is credited as providing the basis for the award-winning movie of the same name starring Jane Fonda. Depicting the thoughts of the protagonist and his fellow air force comrades in Country and their significant others back in the World, the novel is written completely in first-person point of view. Dramatically bringing the war home with a narrative that can be described as cinematic, Davis allows the reader to experience the air war from the perspective of an air force officer who has reached the pinnacle of success in academia (Harvard) and the military (Officer Candidate School), but who nevertheless struggles with his identity as a Black man in a racist society determined to diminish his personhood. This dilemma leads him to question his own motives for fighting the war against another people of color, ultimately prompting him to desert the U.S. military and to flee to Sweden for asylum. I agree with Mel Watkins, who wrote the introduction to the 1984 edition, that "because the author's vision permitted him to look beyond the actual combat and the specific moral and political questions that arose from that particular war, it is a novel that is still pertinent" in today's society (xxiv). *Coming Home* was reissued as the 40th Anniversary Edition in 2012 with a new introduction by the author himself. Davis's adeptness at capturing the angst of a Black air force pilot is unparalleled, owing perhaps to his own service in the air force as an officer who flew more than forty-five missions during the Vietnam War. Describing himself as an "idealist," Davis tells Alison Sussman of *Contemporary Black Biography* that he flew refueling/reconnaissance rather than strike missions "because I did not want to be involved with killing there, but I wanted to be close enough to it to write a book that would be so true it would stop the war."[33] Of course, his book did not produce his desired result; however, the impact of it is as real and poignant today as forty years ago.

Davis, similar to Williams, Flowers, and Brown, has been in academia a number of years, having served as professor at City University of New York and Rutgers University. He has also been a staff writer and an editor in the Sunday Department for the *Washington Post* and the *New York Times*, respectively. Having published in a variety of genres, he authored *Coming Home*, his debut novel, in 1971 when it was judged Notable Book of the Year by the *New York Times Book Review*.[34] Davis has also authored another fictional work, *The Melting Points: A Spiritual Spy Novel* (2012). His nonfictional works are more numerous, including *Love, Black Love* (1974), *Black Life in Corporate America: Swimming in the Mainstream* (coauthored with Glegg Watson, 1982), *Soul Vibrations: Astrology for African Americans* (coauthored with Gilda Mathews, 1996), *Love Lessons: African Americans and Sex, Romance, and Marriage in the Nineties* (1998), *Branches: The Human Spirit in Search of the American Dream* (1999), *Barack Obama and the World* (2011), and *Spiritual Intelligence* (2012).

In addition to writing fictional and nonfictional narratives and serving as journalist for two major newspapers, Davis has also been a contributing editor to two major magazines: *Essence*, a Black women's magazine, and *Black Enterprise (BE)*, the premier guide to financial empowerment for African American businesses. Each year *BE* publishes a listing of the top 100 Black businesses, highlighting CEOs and presidents of their own companies as well as those at the helm of major American corporations. As a result of his experiences at *BE*, Davis and his coauthor Glegg Watson were prompted to interview over 150 Blacks and Whites in corporate America to compile research on the experiences of Blacks in management for the book that would be published as *Black Life in Corporate America: Swimming in the Mainstream* (1982). The book was so well received that it became a national bestseller. As a result major business schools, including Harvard and Wharton, invited Davis to develop and teach a course based on it to help students better understand the landscape of corporate America where a racist environment, alienation, and exhausting work assignments often make the workplace unendurable.[35]

A major contributing factor to the discontent that Blacks in corporate America experience, according to Davis, is that many are from "spirit-oriented backgrounds"; however, they find themselves having to "learn to operate in the kind of spiritual vacuum that exists in major corporations."[36] Deeply invested in spirituality and the way in which it has enabled African Americans to survive through the centuries, Davis created the Spiritual Intelligence Project that aims to "explore what is fortunate, for both the African American individual and American society as a whole, about being black in America," according to Alison Carb Sussman.[37] Davis's most recent book, *Spiritual Intelligence*, sets forth the tenets of this exciting exploration of what he calls the "greatest gift" of Africans in America to American society.

CHAPTER 1

Historical and Literary Background

Racism is traumatic, causing a "severe fragmentation of the self."

—Toni Morrison, "Unspeakable Things Unspoken"

"In the front lines abroad! In the back lines at home!"

—Robert Sanders, *Brothers*

Send me no flowers, for my grave that I was born in

Send the President my flowers cremated and scented with
The odors
Of my brothers' napalmed flesh and my sisters' bombed
Out skulls
Send me no flowers man, send me no flowers.

—S. E. Anderson, "Junglegrave"

Early Wars: Literary Representation

Since the time of the Revolutionary War, Black men have fought for the right to fight in America's wars and to be a part of its military services. Distinguishing themselves in the American Revolution were outstanding Black soldiers such as Peter Salem, Salem Poor, Caesar Brown, Prince Hall, and numerous other heroes, some nameless and faceless, who performed deeds of valor in the service of America. Kai Wright discusses other less well-known Revolutionary Black heroes such as James Forten, Lemuel Haynes, "Black Samson" of the Battle of Brandywine in Delaware, Jack Sisson (aka "Tack Sisson"), and Boston King, to name a few, in *Soldiers of Freedom: An Illustrated History of African Americans in the Armed Forces* (12–19). At the beginning of the Civil War, President Abraham Lincoln denied Black men the right to enlist. However, "military necessity" finally caused the Union Army not only to enlist but also to arm Black soldiers (Jay and Crane 36). Shortly afterward, Congress passed an act in 1862 providing for the enlistment of Blacks. Emboldened by this gesture, Frederick Douglass said, optimistically: "If the black man could prove his equality on the battlefield, he would no longer be a second-class citizen" (qtd. in Jay and Crane 53). Little did he know that in the second millennium many Blacks in the military would still be seeking the same unrealized dream.

One of the earliest fictional accounts of African American participation in war is Frances E. W. Harper's novel *Iola Leroy; or, Shadows Uplifted* that was published in 1892. It portrays action during the Civil War. The heroine, an orphan, is its titular character who discovers immediately prior to the Civil War that she is biracial. Light-skinned enough to pass for White, Iola has been living as a White woman until her discovery that she is Black. However, unlike those who pass for White to seek a better life, she makes a conscious decision not to. Unfortunately, Whites who are aware of her African ancestry take retribution by separating her from her family and selling her into enslavement. Through a fortuitous circumstance Union soldiers rescue her from the plantation; and after the war ends, she sets out to find and reunite with her Black family.

Providing one of the earliest examples of Black heroism in fictional war literature, Harper's novel "embeds the narrative trajectory of maternal quest and [family] reunion, simultaneously feminizing war narrative and using this literary form to represent the importance of maternal and familial structures in the black community," according to Elizabeth Young in "Warring Fictions: *Iola Leroy* and the Color of Gender" (274). Then there is Pauli Murray's nonfictional *Proud Shoes,* published in 1956, which documents her grandfather's service on the Union side in the Civil War. It is the remarkable true story of slavery, survival, and miscegenation in the South from the pre–Civil War era through Reconstruction. Though written much later, in 1966, Margaret Walker Alexander's historical novel *Jubilee* follows the life of heroine Vyry before, during, and after the Civil War.

After the Civil War ended, Black units were disbanded. In other words, Black men had outlived their usefulness as soldiers for America, despite having put themselves in harm's way along with Whites during the war. And so they were disarmed perhaps because they posed a potential threat to Whites who feared they would seek retribution by attacking plantation owners and others for crimes committed against Blacks during and following enslavement. Revenge, however, was not uppermost in the minds of the enslaved, most of whom just wanted to be free and treated as human beings rather than chattel (a euphemism for cattle). Many Blacks moved from the South to the West seeking better lives after slavery was legally abolished. Many of them joined the rodeo circuit, two of the most famous being Nat Love (aka Deadwood Dick) and Bill Pickett (K. Wright 96–97). In 1866 the federal government felt that African American soldiers could be useful in the Indian Wars.

According to Kai Wright, the army after Emancipation was reshaped, reducing it to "ten cavalries, forty-five infantry regiments, five artillery units, and the US Military Academy" (96). During the Plains Wars, the U.S. Congress created four all-Black regiments that became known as the Twenty-fifth Infantries and the Ninth and Tenth Cavalries, whom the Native Americans called the Buffalo Soldiers, a name Black soldiers adopted and wore with pride (Jay and Crane 92). Wright cites two possible explanations of how the Buffalo Soldiers acquired this moniker:

> Some say the Cheyenne dubbed the Tenth Cavalry Buffalo Soldiers in 1867 following an incredulous two-day battle near Fort Leavenworth, Kansas. A mere ninety cavalrymen held off eight hundred Cheyenne attackers in that fight, losing only three men in the process. Others say the Tenth earned its nickname during an 1871 campaign against the Comanche. (99)

Whichever story bears the true origin of the name, one thing is certain: the Native Americans in general greatly admired the Buffalo Soldiers for their fighting skill and their tenacity, indicating that their hair resembled that of the prized buffalo of the plains. Later, Black men also served with valor in the Spanish-American War and won many laurels in 1898. However, despite a great number of them performing heroic acts, only three received commissions: Benjamin O. Davis Sr., John Green, and John Lynch (K. Wright 118).

An early writer of war fiction was F. Frank Gilmore whose novel titled *Problem* was published in 1915 (B. Bell 78). Having a plot line that deals with a case of mistaken identity, this novel is a celebration of the Black soldier's valor in the line of duty during the Spanish-American War. Later, Claude McKay, who gained fame during the Harlem Renaissance as a poet and novelist, represented the Black war experience in *Home to Harlem* (1927). A World War I novel, it deals with a soldier's desertion from the army, after which he goes abroad (a theme George Davis treats in the Vietnam War novel *Coming Home* from the perspective of an air force officer). As the novel opens Jake, the protagonist, returns home from the war. In Harlem he experiences a series of adventures and misadventures while engaging in various escapades and working at any number of odd jobs. Characterized by episodic and sometimes gratuitous violence in the interests of revealing wartime America at its worst, the novel focuses on the blue-collar city dweller and penetrates "the surface vitality of his struggle to survive" (B. Bell 117) in the wake of Jake's disillusioning experience in the military.

When World War I broke out, few Blacks were inducted in 1917. Shortly thereafter, the Selective Service Act was passed, enabling all Americans between twenty-one and thirty-one years of age to enlist. However Black soldiers and sailors, who were fighting alongside their White counterparts to "make the world safe for democracy," endured verbal and physical abuse, as well as lynching by their "fellow [White] Americans" when they returned home from the war (Jay and Crane 109). W. E. B. Du Bois was optimistic about Blacks fighting in the war at its outset; however, by 1919 he had become pessimistic and embittered by the treatment of Black soldiers, stating in the 1919 issue of the NAACP's *Crisis Magazine*:

> This war has disillusioned millions of fighting white men. . . . with its frank truth of dirt, disease, cold, wet, and discomfort; murder, maiming, and hatred. . . . But the disillusion of the Negro American troops was more than this, or rather it was this and more—the flat, frank realization that however high the ideals of America or how noble her tasks, her great duty as conceived by an astonishing number of able men, brave and good, as well as other sorts of men, is to hate "niggers." (qtd. in K. Wright 123)

The Selective Service Act of 1940 contained an amendment that forbade the military services from discriminating against Blacks in drafting and training. Despite the announcement in 1945 that Blacks would serve in an integrated unit to fight against Germany in World War II, however, racial discrimination persisted. Because of the maltreatment Black soldiers received upon their return to America after World War II, militant Black protests broke out at Fort Bragg, Camp Robison, Camp Davis, and Fort Dix, as Black veterans defiantly resisted discriminatory and racist treatment.

The effect of racial apartheid in the American military during the World War II era is poignantly revealed by renowned Black scholar and author John Hope Franklin, who in recent times headed the advisory board for President Bill Clinton's Presidential Commission on Race.[1] He shared his World War II experience with an audience in Chicago at a reading and book signing during a live broadcast from the Printers Row Book Fair on June 3, 2000. Excited about what appeared to be an opportunity to fight in the first integrated military, Franklin volunteered for the army in 1942. He was denied enlistment, however, despite his excellent academic record, his ability to "run the office" at his library job, and his adeptness at taking shorthand. Intimating that he was overqualified to be in the army, the commanding officer told him that he had everything going for him except "the right color." Apparently Franklin felt that the best revenge for this racist denial of his service was success. Consequently, he went on to receive a master's degree and then later matriculated at Harvard where he earned a Ph.D. in history. His bad experience with the military was part of his impetus to write in 1947 what has become a classic in Black history, *From Slavery to Freedom: A History of Negro Americans*, so that, according to Franklin, "the world could know what blacks have accomplished in American history," including heroism in the military. In the audience at Franklin's book-signing event was a Black retired air force pilot who related a story of how he was also turned down by the army during World War II because they "had their quota of blacks." Later, he joined the air force where he served honorably for thirty-three years.

And Then We Heard the Thunder (1962), a World War II novel by John O. Killens, also stands out in this tradition (Couch 181). Killens uses irony to explore the vicissitudes of Black heroism. Ironically, according to Bernard Bell, Black soldiers had to "wage a double war for freedom during World War II: one overseas against foreign fascism and the other at home against domestic fascism" (250). In a symbolic gesture of comradeship, Black soldiers often greeted each other with the "double V," raised fingers on each hand forming a "V." The protagonist in Killens's novel is deluded into thinking that his middle-class upbringing, his education, and his military accomplishments will earn him respect among his fellow White soldiers only to discover that the opposite is true. He soon comes to realize, after coming home from the war, that as far as the White populace is concerned, issues of race and fighting for one's country are separate. Consequently, wartime foxhole brotherhood does not translate to brotherhood in America with Whites. The novel ends in a race riot in Harlem.

Worthy of note is that the first American hero of World War II was a Black sailor named Dorie Miller who was below deck doing the laundry on the *USS West Virginia* when it was attacked by the Japanese at Pearl Harbor. Like the fictional Shine, protagonist of the legendary toast "Shine and the Titanic," Miller was ignored (because he was Black) when he warned the crew that they were under attack. As a lowly mess attendant, he was not allowed to be in combat on the upper deck. Only after it became obvious they were in danger, after the ship's captain was killed, did a White lieutenant enlist the aid of Miller in helping him to fire on the Japanese. Even though neither he nor any other Black soldiers had been trained to use weaponry because Blacks were forbidden, Miller, manning the fifty-caliber antiaircraft machine gun, "shot down between two and four Japanese aircraft (the number is in dispute) working the gun until he ran out of ammunition and was ordered to abandon ship" (K. Wright 155). Despite Miller's heroism, however, Lt. Cmdr. Doir C. Johnson, the White officer who filed a battle report, mentions all the sailors by name involved in the battle, except Miller whom he refers to merely as "'a colored mess attendant' who was 'a powerfully built individual'" (K. Wright 155). The honor for his bravery would not be forthcoming until over six decades later. In 2016 Navy Rear Adm. John Fuller spoke of Miller's heroism, at the unveiling of a plaque honoring him in Hawaii, thusly: "Miller went topside, carried wounded on his shoulders, made several trips up and down, wading through waist-deep water, oil-slicked decks, struggling uphill on slick decks."[2] Sammy Davis Jr.'s autobiography, *Yes I Can*, relates his experience of discrimination for the first time when he went into the armed forces during World War II (131).

Vietnam War: Literary and Visual Representation

Unlike their situation in earlier wars, Blacks had ample opportunities to fight in the Vietnam War, and many enlisted. Since Vietnam was touted as the first fully integrated war,[3] at the outset of the conflict in Vietnam many were supportive of the war effort, anxious to win the respect of American society for their patriotism as they had attempted to do in all prior wars. Even popular music of the period reflected Black optimism (see appendix 2), and in the early sixties the lyrics to several songs idealistically supported America's Black soldiers whose desire to contain communism undergirded their patriotic spirit. One example is "Soldier Boy," the Shirelles' number one hit in 1962 (M. Ellison 57). "Marching Off to War" by William Bell, "I'll Be True" by the Orlons, "Please, Uncle Sam" by the Charnelles, and "Greetings (This Is Uncle Sam)" by the Monitors also reflect the mood of those in the Black community who were enthusiastic about going to fight in the war.

However, in 1966 Project 100,000 was implemented, supposedly to give Blacks an opportunity to be trained for various trades. The Department of Defense implemented Project 100,000 to "reclaim the 'wasted' one-third of the draft pool," according to Milton Bates in *The Wars We Took to Vietnam: Cultural Conflict and Storytelling*. Its promoters viewed it as a way "to solve one social problem with another"; however, its critics viewed it cynically as "a device to generate cannon fodder—a total of 320,000 soldiers—for the war" (57). In theory this project would remove young men from female-headed households and then teach them "pride and marketable skills in the armed forces," which would supposedly return them to the United States as productive citizens (58). By all accounts this project failed. The Pentagon later admitted the real purpose was only to increase the military manpower pool (Foner 203).

Needless to say, there was great disappointment among the Black ranks that the promises of marketable skills that they hoped to use upon their return to the World were not forthcoming. Additionally, casualty rates for Blacks continued to mount and were disproportionate to those of Whites. Also, job opportunities were scarce for the first groups of returnees home from the war. Sol Stern, a writer for *Ramparts Magazine*, provides examples of such soldiers, one of whom was Charly Cato, who garnered the job of "tunnel rat" in Vietnam because he was small and agile. He risked his life on many occasions to seek out Vietcong who lived in these tunnels to avoid detection by the American military. His skills, however, were not transferable because no jobs existed in civilian life back in the World for Cato's trained specialty. Therefore when he returned to the United States he had to eke out a meager existence "collecting $33 per week in unemployment insurance" (216). When questioned, however, he was not bitter about his Vietnam experience.

Opinions about the war experience among Blacks run the gamut from acceptance to dissatisfaction to protest. A Black war veteran named David Tuck, unlike
Cato, was greatly embittered about having been drafted because of the atrocities
he witnessed in Vietnam even though he was able to get his old job at the U.S. post
office after the war. His dissatisfaction with the Vietnam War experience provided
impetus for his testimony at the Bertrand Russell International War Crimes Tribunal
in Copenhagen. As a result, he vowed never to fight on foreign soil for America
again (Stern 217).

Reenlistments among Black soldiers were high, attesting to greater opportunities for them in the military than in civilian life, especially for those uneducated or
undereducated. In 1966 alone, according to Stern, "60.5 per cent of Negroes in the
Army on first term enlistments decided to re-enlist"; however, this reenlistment
rate came at a tremendous price:

> In Vietnam between 1961 and 1966 Negroes accounted for more than 20 per cent of
> Army fatalities even though they represented only 12.6 per cent of Army personnel
> in Vietnam.... Statistics show that the Negro in the Army was more likely than his
> white buddy to be sent to Vietnam in the first place; once there, was more likely to
> wind up in a front-line combat unit, and within the combat unit was more likely
> than the white to be killed or wounded. (220)

John A. Williams represents fictionally in *Captain Blackman* a similar situation
of failed job opportunities for the Black protagonist after his return to America
and some of the deleterious consequences of his army reenlistment when he is
wounded in action.

Later in the decade, the civil rights and Black nationalist movements gained
momentum following the assassinations of five major civil and human rights
leaders within just five years, 1963 to 1968: Medgar Evers, June 1963; John F.
Kennedy, November 1963; Malcolm X, February 1965; Dr. Martin Luther King Jr.,
April 1968; and Robert F. Kennedy, June 1968. Within the same time frame, the
FBI, as a part of its infamous Counter-Intelligence Program (aka COINTELPRO),
stepped up its efforts to eliminate organizations that J. Edgar Hoover deemed a
"threat to national security." At the top of his list was the Black Panther Party, a
revolutionary organization whose headquarters the FBI strategically raided in
1969 in three major cities—Chicago, Illinois; Oakland, California; and Hartford,
Connecticut—assassinating several leaders and wounding/imprisoning many

members, thereby effectively crippling the organization that later disbanded (Junne 235). Hoover, the mastermind behind COINTELPRO, ordered numerous covert operations to dismantle the Black Panthers. He collaborated with police departments and used paid informants to infiltrate the organization and to get information that the FBI then used to mount calculated attacks against the group in several states. George H. Junne Jr. reports that "the FBI encouraged local police departments to raid local Panther headquarters and spread rumors and lies about its members" (235).

The FBI also purposely lied to the Panther membership in letters stating that the leaders had taken their money and set up Swiss bank accounts. Then they stirred up enmity between the Panthers and another community organization called US in California headed by Maulana Ron Karenga, according to Junne, who also provides the following statistics:

> "In 1969 the FBI conducted thirty-one raids on Panther offices and spied on meetings, rallies, and members. In the late 1960s twenty-eight Panthers were killed." … Hoover believed that if Black groups got together they would form a 'Mau Mau' revolution in America. He also warned against the rise of a 'messiah' who would galvanize that movement, a role that he feared Dr. King might play. (235).

On December 4, 1969, the Chicago police, urged by the FBI, raided an apartment in Chicago, firing a barrage of bullets and assassinating Fred Hampton and Mark Clark, according to media reports. One of the seven survivors of the "bloodbath" was Harold Bell, a fellow Panther who testified at the "People's Inquest," which found Chicago U.S. Attorney Edward Hanrahan and fourteen policemen "guilty of pre-meditated murder," according to David Smith's article in *The Black Panther* (7). Though the FBI claimed that Hampton and Clark fired first at them from their apartment at around 3:00 a.m., the inquest revealed that all forty bullets were incoming.

By 1967 Blacks were being drafted disproportionately to Whites, and Wright provides the following statistics: "sixty-four percent of eligible blacks were drafted while only thirty-one percent of eligible whites went to war" (241); many Whites were draft dodgers who fled to Canada or received exemptions because they were from well-to-do families. In 1968, the same year that Dr. King and Robert Kennedy were assassinated, both of whom had spoken out vehemently against the war, there was a major buildup in the war abroad. It culminated in the Tet Offensive, which has been described as the "decisive event" of the enemy forces against the American military. Tet is a celebration of the Vietnamese New Year, and during the celebration on January 31, 1968, communist forces, in a skillfully coordinated effort, "simultaneously attacked urban areas, military installations, and government facilities throughout South Vietnam," according to James J. Wirtz (qtd. in Mooney and West 169). Within twenty-four hours, reports Douglas Kinnard, "North Vietnamese and Viet Cong forces had attacked 36 of 44 provincial capitals in South Vietnam, 5 of the 6 autonomous cities, and the capitol, Saigon" (26).

Gen. Vo Nguyen Giap, the North Vietnamese commander, desired to score a psychological victory against the American people, whose military advisors had convinced them that America was winning the war, as Philippa Schuyler discovered during her sojourn in Vietnam in the 1960s (documented in her book *Good Men Die*). Many of the Black recruits who swelled the ranks of the U.S. military in Vietnam during the buildup were former participants in the civil rights and Black power movements. Several also marched in demonstrations against the Vietnam War, and they brought their militant attitudes to the war with them. Some commentators have referred to 1968 as "the fulcrum year" because even though the Tet Offensive was called a "military victory for U.S. forces" in Vietnam, it was a "shocking political defeat at home" (Zaroulis and Sullivan 151) because the Vietcong had won a psychological victory over the United States.

As the war effort escalated, Black war casualties became disproportionate to those of Whites, and the "spirit of foxhole brotherhood dissipated" as Black and White soldiers were pitted against each other in a "double battleground" (Terry, *Bloods* xvi–xvii). Therefore, optimism changed to ambivalence, cynicism, and militancy. This militant mood is also reflected in the lyrics of popular songs at the end of the sixties and the beginning of the seventies (see appendix 2). Some examples are "This Is My Country" by the Impressions in 1968; "I Don't Wanna Go to Vietnam" by Johnny Lee Hooker in 1969; "Dam Nam [Ain't Goin to Vietnam]" by Leon Thomas in 1970; "War (What Is It Good for?)" by Edwin Starr in 1970; and "What's Goin' On?" by Marvin Gaye in 1971 (M. Ellison 57–58). Jimi Hendrix's "Machine Gun" and his rendition of "The Star-Spangled Banner" (perhaps more appropriately called the "Scarred and Mangled Banner" because of its cacophonous, discordant adaptation of the original) musically portray the angst of the younger generation, Black and White, whose minds, bodies, and souls were being ripped apart by the war and its effects at home and abroad. (See appendix 2 for an additional listing of songs that gauged the mood of Blacks during the Vietnam War era.)[4]

Mainstream Film and Narratives

Significantly, the Vietnam War has been the subject of more literary works and movies than any of America's previous wars. A large number of Vietnam-related novels, oral narratives, and poetry collections have appeared in the past five decades (see appendix 1). Public acceptance of the images popularized in mainstream fiction and film has led to the perception that the Vietnam experience was the same for all of America's fighting men. However, most of these literary works and movies ignore the Black soldier altogether or deal with him stereotypically or tangentially. One writer who takes issue with this observation, however, is Perry D. Luckett, who defends White literary representation of the Black soldier, arguing that claims of Blacks being misrepresented in mainstream narratives and popular culture are "purely exaggerated" (1).

As evidence of his claim, Luckett selects for discussion Black characters in *Going After Cacciato* (novel) by Tim O'Brien, *The Boys in Company C* (film), *Dispatches* (part memoir/part novel) by Michael Herr, *Platoon* (film), *F. N. G.* (novel) by Donald Bodey, *Fields of Fire* (novel) by James Webb, *Apocalypse Now* (film), *A Piece of This Country* (novel) by Thomas Taylor, *Parthian Shot* (novel) by Loyd Little, and *The 13th Valley* (novel) by John M. Del Vecchio. From this corpus, he concludes that depictions of Blacks in Vietnam War narratives "often illustrate the black man's prowess in battle and powerful loyalty in relationships—with blacks or whites." Furthermore, he feels that these mainstream works "take seriously the special trauma of Black soldiers who must reconcile their combat service with the lack of basic freedoms in their own society" (25). Beyond these conclusions, however, I am unconvinced of Luckett's assessments, especially since he attempts to dismiss the stereotypical depiction of Sgt. Oscar Johnson in O'Brien's *Going After Cacciato*. O'Brien's description of Johnson, who "speaks of raping and looting and cracking heads with a sledgehammer, wears dark glasses even at night, [and] has black skin and eyes" (qtd. in Luckett 2), is stereotypical and one-dimensional. Luckett, however, views this description as nothing more than an example of "magical realism" in O'Brien's narrative technique.

Tyrone Washington, a marine who was formerly a drug dealer in the film *The Boys in Company C*, is another character Luckett discusses. He considers Washington such a strong character because he "believes completely in his own ability to survive" (3)—but only after his lieutenant (who is White) convinces him that "group survival" is of foremost importance. His commanding officer tells him he must become involved in "teamwork" and urges him to turn away from his drug-dealing ways. Such a depiction is contrary to the "camaraderie" and "brotherhood" prevailing among Black soldiers that Arthur Flowers says was a major factor in their survival. *Bloods: An Oral History of the Vietnam War by Black Veterans*, by Wallace Terry, also attests to this brotherhood and camaraderie among Black soldiers. They needed no urging from their commanding officers. Additionally, the movie conveys the message that, for Washington, being a soldier is a "natural outlet for his violence and an opportunity to enhance his worth as a man" because of his "natural aggressiveness," according to Luckett (4). This depiction conforms to the "black brute" stereotype discussed below.

Furthermore, Luckett implicitly justifies the practice of assigning Blacks to the dangerous position of point man while "humpin' the pig" (the M-60 machine gun) and carrying the equally heavy M-79 grenade launcher. He attributes the Black soldier's "natural affinity" for such duties to his huge size and his weight that ostensibly make him well suited for the tasks despite the inordinate amount of danger he faces in comparison to that of his White counterparts who very seldom are put on point. One wonders whether or not Luckett would have considered large White soldiers to have an "affinity" toward such hazardous duty as well.

Then there is the example of Day Tripper, in Herr's *Dispatches*, who is described as a "*big bad spade* gone wrong somehow, and no matter how mean he tried to look something constantly gentle showed" (qtd. in Luckett 25; emphasis added). Regardless of how heroic Luckett views this character, "spade" is neither a term of endearment among Blacks nor one befitting a hero. Its negative connotations are quite the opposite of terms Black soldiers use to refer to themselves, such as "bloods" and "brothers." As "mean" or fearless as he is supposed to be, Day Tripper acquires this name in *Dispatches* because he is "afraid of the dark. . . . He was always volunteering for the more dangerous patrols, just to make sure he got in by dusk" (Luckett 25). Stereotypically, Day Tripper says that when he goes back to the World in Detroit, he will "take mortar fragments" and reassemble them to "blow up the police," if necessary. Such dialogue reflects the paranoia of some Whites who have used their power to mistreat Blacks for so long that they depict Black characters using their war skills in retribution for past and present discriminatory treatment in America. Though Luckett unsuccessfully argues for balanced, unstereotypical treatment of the Black soldier in selected novels and films by Whites, to his credit he does show how novels such as *A Piece of This Country* and *The 13th Valley* "deal honestly with the peculiar difficulties of black career soldiers whose commitment to service and aspirations for advancement conflict with their awareness" (25).

These are just a few examples of how the corpus of widely accepted mainstream Vietnam War literature and film fails to address covert and overt issues of racism as well as imperialism. William Couch Jr., citing examples of war novels from Stephen Crane's *Red Badge of Courage* (to Joseph Heller's *Catch 22*, concurs: "Nowhere in our celebrated war novels is there a hint of the connections between modern warfare and racial exploitation" (178). In view of America's past as the only nation in modern history to institutionalize slavery, Couch observes further that through the omission of the Black soldier from America's early war fiction by Whites, the "compelling" implication, "both historical and psychological," is that Blacks are not a part of America's heritage (178).

On the other hand, there are some exceptions to the above mainstream Vietnam War movies in which Blacks play significant, positive roles rather than stereotypical ones. Although they neither directed nor wrote the screenplays, Black performers do have major acting roles. One of the earliest films is actually a documentary titled *No Vietnamese Ever Called Me Nigger* (1968) that documents an antiwar march from Harlem to the United Nations in 1967.[5] Director David Loeb Weiss, with camerawork by Michael Wadleigh, interviews three Black veterans—Dalton James, Preston Lay Jr., and Akmed Lorence—who discuss their experiences in Vietnam. Also included are shots of the April 1967 Spring Mobilization to End the War, which occurred after Rev. Dr. Martin Luther King Jr.'s delivery of "Beyond Vietnam: A Time to Break Silence" at the Riverside Church in New York, when he questioned the disproportionate percentage of Black soldiers dying in combat in Vietnam and urged Black ministers to declare conscientious objection to the war. A year later Bill Brodie directed a documentary about a Black war deserter. Titled *Terry Whitmore, for Example* (1969), the entire hour-and-a-half film depicts Terry Whitmore, a twenty-one-year-old Black marine who was wounded in Vietnam and later received a medal for heroism. After being treated for his injuries in Japan, however, he becomes a deserter from the U.S. military and finds asylum in Sweden. In fact, the tagline for his film is "The Vietnam War Hero Who Was Personally Decorated by the President and Deserted." Whitmore's autobiography about his experiences is discussed below.

Other mainstream films with positive portrayals of African Americans include Ronald Ribman's *The Final War of Olly Winter* (1967) that was touted by *New York Times* reviewer Jack Gould as a "poignant championing of human dignity and compassion, whether in the cruel war environment of the Vietnam jungle or in the oppression of the underprivileged at home . . . the most moving original television play of the season" (59). Made for television's *CBS Playhouse*, it portrays a Black war advisor (played by Ivan Dixon) whose empathy with the Vietcong leads him to try to protect rather than destroy innocent villagers. One of the earliest films juxtaposing injustice in America for Blacks with that in Vietnam, the film ends with the protagonist, despite all his efforts to be a force for change, unfortunately being killed. Another made-for-TV film broadcast on ABC television is *Green Eyes* (1977), winner of the Peabody Prize for its compassionate depiction of the anguish an African-American veteran (portrayed by Paul Winfield) experiences when he goes back to Vietnam after the war ends searching for the child he fathered by a Vietnamese woman, both of whom he left behind when he returned to his Chicago home as a wounded veteran after the war ended in 1975. Arriving in Saigon he finds the mother (now married with another child) who tells him that his baby has died; however, he refuses to give up searching. To his dismay he searches with no success among the squalid conditions of numerous orphanages where untold numbers of Amerasian children have been left, discovering that his child who had a disease has indeed died.

With amazing verisimilitude *Platoon* (1986) is one of the most realistic portrayals of the Vietnam War in film, probably owing to the screenwriter and director, Oliver Stone, being a Vietnam War veteran. Portraying in brutal detail the in-fighting among America's own officers and fighting men, as well as the slaughter of innocent villagers in the war against the Vietcong, it is a scathing antiwar film. In addition to starring roles by White actors Willem Dafoe, Tom Berenger, and Charlie Sheen, the film features Black actors Forest Whitaker and Keith David in positive roles. A year later, *Hamburger Hill* (1987) was released and is based on an actual battle on a mountain near the Laotian border where as many as six hundred men went up to fight the Vietcong, but only a third of that number returned. Because of the senseless number of heavy casualties in such a short amount of time, this battle typifies the wastage and futility of the war.[6] Apropos of its title, it depicts the blood and gore of some of the fiercest fighting during the Vietnam War, as footage from actual battles in Vietnam are woven into the film. Black actors Courtney B. Vance, Don Cheadle, and Michael Boatman also play major roles. Then there is *Bat*21* (1988), based on a true story about U.S. Air Force Lt. Col. Iceal Hambleton (portrayed by Gene Hackman) who, as a career pilot, has been fighting the air war. However, he is forced to experience the grit and grime of the ground war when his fighter jet is shot down over enemy territory. Capt. Bartholomew Clark, a Black pilot (portrayed by Danny Glover), is sent on a dangerous search-and-rescue mission during which he locates and rescues Hambleton. Yet another is film is *Cadence* (1990) in which Larry Fishburne plays a major role.

African American Films and Nonfictional Narratives

I classify Black films as those not only featuring Black actors but also having Black directors and/or writers (see appendix 2). The earliest of these, *The Bus Is Coming* (1971), explores a theme treated in several of the novels, that is, a Black veteran returning to America and finding racial unrest at home, therefore trading one battlefield for another. In this instance, the protagonist returns to Los Angeles where he discovers that racist policemen have killed his brother. A Black nationalist group is up in arms and therefore solicits his assistance to avenge his brother's death and to deal with the perennial problem of police brutality. Although the cast does not include well-known actors, it is written and directed by Wendell Franklin, a Black pioneer in the movie industry. According to Zeinabu Davis, who interviewed him for the Directors Guild of America, Franklin epitomizes the proverbial rags-to-riches story, having worked his way up from parking cars on the NBC lot to eventually becoming "the first African-American member of the Directors Guild of America. He was also the first to be assigned a feature film, assisting George Stevens on *The Greatest Story Ever Told*."[7] Davis's biography of Franklin chronicles his struggle to overcome racism in the film industry, not unlike the racism that Franklin depicts in his Vietnam War movie.

Another Black film that deals with the war brought home is *Gordon's War*. Released in 1973, it stars Paul Winfield, with Ossie Davis as director. Rather than depicting the carnage and atrocities of battle, as do many of the mainstream movies, it focuses on the effect of the war on family and friends back home. After returning to Harlem from Vietnam, Gordon discovers that his wife, unable to cope while he was away, has succumbed to drugs and died of an overdose. Distraught and angry, he teams up with three other Vietnam veterans, and they set out on a mission to rid Harlem of drug lords using tactical skills and intelligence procedures learned in Vietnam.

The setting for another movie, *The Walking Dead*, is 1972 Vietcong territory in the Vietnam jungle. Black director Preston Whitmore II released the movie in the spring of 1995. Starring Allen Payne, it portrays the visceral as well as the psychological aspects of warfare (Gregory 62), as a group of Black marines have been sent on a search-and-rescue mission to what they are led to believe is a cold landing zone (LZ) to bring home prisoners of war. However, quite the opposite is true, as they discover the LZ is hot when they are surrounded by Vietcong who ambush and engage them in a brutal firefight in which they lose several men. Kevin Thomas, in his review of the movie for the *Los Angeles Times* says *The Walking Dead* is "marked by passion and sincerity . . . a conventional war picture but with a key difference: It depicts the Vietnam experience from an African American point of view."[8] All the characters tell their stories through flashbacks, providing the viewer a retrospective of the soldiers' reasons for going to war and their disillusionment with the way they were used as expendable cannon fodder by military leaders and America's power structure.

Though not billed as a Vietnam War movie as such, *Jason's Lyric* (1994), starring Allen Payne, Jada Pinkett, Bokeem Woodbine, and Forest Whitaker, can be included in the genre of Black movies about the Vietnam War because the action of the film proceeds from an incident precipitated by Vietnam veteran Maddog, Jason's father (portrayed by Forest Whittaker), who has lost a leg in Vietnam and suffers from post–traumatic stress disorder (PTSD). Though prior to going to Vietnam Maddog has been a loving companion to both his children and their mother, he becomes a morose, almost demented hermit when he returns. Succumbing to alcoholism, Maddog becomes obsessed with the idea that the mother of his children rejects him because he has only one leg. In a drunken stupor, he attempts to propose marriage to her but ends up beating her instead. Jason, a mere adolescent at the time, shoots and kills his father in defense of his mother. The remainder of the movie deals with Jason's feelings of guilt and remorse as well as his search for love (embodied in his girlfriend, Lyric), and his obligation to take care of his younger brother who falls prey to a life of crime. *Jason's Lyric*, similar to *The Walking Dead*, also has a Black director, Doug McHenry.

A more obscure but nevertheless important film is *Georgia, Georgia* (1972). Unique in the canon of Black Vietnam War films, it has the distinction of being written by a woman—Maya Angelou—who also scored the music. Though her professional reputation rests on her autobiographical series of books and her poetry, Angelou was a multitalented artist who gained acclaim also as a singer, dancer, and actress. In this debut as a screenplay writer, indeed the "first black female screenwriter" to make a feature film according to *IndieWire*,[9] Angelou depicts a Black

American female singer who has been booked for a series of concerts in Sweden. The titular protagonist is portrayed with a stellar performance by the beautiful and talented actress/singer Diana Sands.[10] Conflicted about her acceptance by the European audience as well as the censure of some Blacks who reject her Swedish boyfriend, Georgia is constantly ill at ease as she struggles with self-doubt and anxiety. Accompanying her on singing tours is an older Black woman, a companion and mother figure, who encounters a group of young Black soldiers from the American military who have deserted the Vietnam War seeking asylum in Sweden. They try to convince her to allow them access to the singer so their plight can be made known to the world at one of her performances. So as a screenwriter Angelou not only deals with the pathology of racism from a woman's perspective but also expresses the antiwar sentiments of Black deserters in this film. It is conjectured that the film did not get wide distribution or availability as a DVD with commentary by Angelou because she felt that the Swedish director, Stig Bjorkman, distorted the vision she intended for the film; therefore, she was unhappy with the ending wherein the Black mother figure kills the protagonist by strangulation.[11]

The Vietnam War is often referred to as the first televised war, and as Michael Mandelbaum points out, this was not only the first war to reach us by television but also the first war that America lost (157). Many historians believe that the first was a cause of the second. As people at home watched the visceral images of incessant bombing of villages, innumerable body bags and coffins being brought home for funerals, and the daily body counts on the news, this reality contributed to turning the tide of public opinion against the war. Since previous wars had been fought prior to the majority of Americans owning televisions, the enemy had seemed more remote; consequently, the impact of the destruction and loss of life was more distant, not as real. Perhaps this "Hollywood" image of the war contributed to Ethiopian filmmaker Haile Gerima's portrayal of two young African American males—both aspiring movie actors, one of whom, Ned Charles, is a Vietnam War veteran—struggling to survive in postwar America. This 1982 independent Vietnam War film is titled *Ashes and Embers*.[12]

The hauntingly beautiful music of the opening and closing soundtrack, "American Fruit with African Roots," in Gerima's film provides a melodic soundscape, as the lyrics chronicle, panoramically, a view of Black oppression from the time of enslavement to the present, underscoring the displacement and angst that the protagonist feels as he attempts to reestablish his place in society and to heal himself from the wounds of war. That one-word description, healing, is the term that appropriately describes the theme of *Ashes and Embers*.[13] Evocative of Billie Holiday's emotional rendition of "Strange Fruit," Gerima's theme song, reprised throughout the film, conjures up images of not only physical but also psychic death resulting from constant struggle against insurmountable odds in a racist society intent on efforts to control those who are considered a threat to the status quo by virtue of race. Imperialism, grounded in racist and genocidal motives, formed the basis for America's annihilation of the "other" through its incursion into and sustained assault against Vietnam, with flamethrowers that decimated entire villages and napalm that denuded thousands of acres of otherwise arable farmland leaving in its wake untold devastation, to win a so-called decisive victory against the ostensible enemy despite substantial evidence to the contrary.[14] In S. E. Anderson's poem "Junglegrave," which Manning Marable refers to as "an ode to the black soldiers overseas," the poet paints graphic images of the death and destruction: "Even if I am headless or faceless, keep my casket open . . . Send me home, no matter how far I am strewn across this rice-filled land" (113). The poem also conjures up images of the Emmett Till murder, underscoring the racist and genocidal motives of America in Vietnam.

Filmed a year after *Georgia, Georgia,* and nearly a decade after the end of America's involvement in the Vietnam War, *Ashes and Embers* is a story of loss, displacement, and reconnection to family in the journey toward restoration of self. For Ned Charles the trauma of war leads to his struggle with alcoholism, personal demons, and loss of direction in the midst of a society that, despite its efforts to empathize, lacks the tools to help Vietnam War veterans generally, but African Americans particularly, deal with PTSD. Similar to many fictional narratives about the Black experience in Vietnam, the action in this film begins after the soldier returns home to America. The opening frame is a surrealistic foray into the mind of the protagonist who appears boxed into a garish, flaming inferno, with loud, screeching noises that give him no peace. The timeline is neither chronological nor linear; rather, the action cuts back and forth—from past to present to future and back again—to simulate the instability of the protagonist's mind. Furthermore, *Ashes and Embers* connects the experience of the Vietnam War and its aftermath to the global struggle against racism and colonialism for peoples of color, as it is punctuated with vignettes of world revolutionary leaders such as Malcolm X; Kwame Nkrumah, first prime minister and president of independent Ghana; and Patrice Lumumba, first prime minister of the independent Democratic Republic of the Congo. In that regard, Gerima's award-winning film presents the struggle and coping mechanisms of a Black war veteran as a microcosm of the identity crisis that the Black veteran of the Vietnam War continues to experience in a seemingly endless battle to bring closure to the psychological trauma of war and to reclaim his identity through reconnection with his African American past.

Ned Charles returns home from Vietnam, but he brings the war with him to America. Tormented by his role in the destruction of innocent Vietnamese, including women, children, and the elderly, he wanders aimlessly from Los Angeles to Washington, DC, to rural North Carolina trying to find peace from the burning images of death and destruction in his psyche. This panoramic view of experience coincides with Gerima's attribution of three important characteristics to environment in film narrative—physical, psychological, and sociological (Gerima 336). Environment and character are intertwined; therefore, each of these settings has symbolic and metaphorical meaning on the protagonist's journey to recovery and survival in postwar America. Because of this holistic treatment of the war's effects on the Black veteran and its juxtaposition with struggles against oppression by peoples of color globally, I consider *Ashes and Embers* the archetypal film of the Black experience in Vietnam. (See appendix 2 for other films.)

As devastating as the Vietnam War was for all of America's fighting men, Black and White, it exacted an even heavier toll on America's Black soldiers, physically and emotionally. Just how did the Black soldier fare in Vietnam? Perhaps the most reliable nonfictional record of that experience is the Black soldier's own words garnered from oral narratives and autobiographies. Interviews have been compiled in several collections of oral narratives, two of the most prominent of which are *Bloods: An Oral History of the Vietnam War by Black Veterans* (1984) edited by Wallace Terry, a Black correspondent for *TIME* during the Vietnam War, and *Brothers: Black Soldiers in the Nam* (1982), edited by two Vietnam veterans, Stanley Goff and Robert Sanders. In his review of *Bloods*, A. R. Flowers notes that regardless of rank in the various military services, from grunt to the highest ranking officer, one common theme pervades the oral narratives: "the conflict [that] blacks experienced as they began to realize their ambiguous role as an occupying army, colonizing another colored race" ("For Blacks" 115).

Representing soldiers from all branches of the military, with rank ranging from private to general, both of these narrative collections present personal reflections revealing a variety of responses to the war and the role of the Black soldier in it. Some discuss their compassion toward the Vietnamese who were victims of atrocities, including rape, mutilation, and castration (Terry, *Bloods* 73,

99; Flowers, "For Blacks" 115–16). Others, mainly those serving in the officers' corps or other high-ranking positions, philosophically view the experience as a job that had to be done, and so they made the best of it. However, most express anger and ambivalence toward America, which discriminated against them but still expected them to fight the war, while the putative "enemy," the North Vietnamese, waged a campaign of psychological warfare directed at Black American soldiers. For instance, the Vietcong often dropped leaflets in the jungle with such statements as "'Blacks get out, it's not your fight'; and 'They call us gooks here and they call you niggers over there. You're the same as us. Get out, it's not your fight'" (Goff and Sanders 131–32). Sometimes they even scrawled such messages on the walls of bombed out buildings.

In addition to the personal devastating physical and emotional effects of the war, other narratives focus on racism within America's military ranks among Black and White soldiers and officers. Consider, for example, the interviews of William Harvey and George Daniels, in *Black Marines against the Brass*,[15] who were brutalized by officers and imprisoned for their vocal opposition to the war. Jack Foner also notes the following occurrences following Dr. King's assassination in 1968: "At Que Viet, a navy installation, whites wore makeshift Klan costumes to celebrate the black leader's death, and at Da Nang confederate flags were raised. On the day of national mourning for King, whites burned a cross and hoisted a confederate flag in front of navy headquarters at Cam Ranh Bay" (213).

The titles of these two narrative collections, *Bloods* and *Brothers*, are Black vernacular expressions attesting to solidarity and camaraderie, prompting Flowers's comment that

> "another common thread" in these war narratives is the growing sense of racial awareness and commitment that developed amid the ambiguity of their role and the external and internal pressure of combat. In Vietnam, officially sanctioned racial discrimination was life-threatening. For black soldiers, racial solidarity became a matter of *survival*. ("For Blacks" 116; emphasis added)

Historically, the Black folk tradition has served to promote solidarity among the group as well as to provide a shield against external forces arrayed against it. The oral narratives contained in these two collections provide ample evidence of the survival of the Black folk tradition. For example, the pervasiveness of Black male bonding rituals, such as "the dap," was part of what Flowers refers to as an "extensive system of survival tactics that contributed to a decrease in the rate of black war casualties from 23 per cent early in the war to 14 per cent later" ("For Blacks" 117).

Other nonfictional accounts about the Black experience in Vietnam include autobiographies, the earliest of which is David Parks's *G.I. Diary* (1968). Son of famous photographer and playwright Gordon Parks, he provides examples of how some White officers abused power through racial profiling in assignments to KP duty. For instance, in his entry dated March 4, 1966, Parks complains about a White sergeant who continually harassed him and another Black recruit, assigning him to KP three times in one week when the usual assigned time for "pulling KP" was once every two weeks. Then, complaining that this sergeant "doesn't like the way I dress, stand, walk or talk," Parks tells how one morning during formation this same sergeant singled him out and told him he looked as if he "just came off the block in Harlem." Then he said: "I know your kind. . . . You're all the same" (23). Afterward, he ordered Parks to do numerous push-ups.

In his January 31, 1967, entry Parks mentions that Blacks and other nonwhites were typically given the most dangerous assignments, one of which was forward observer (FO) whose job is one of the "hairiest in a mortar platoon." Since there are only three FOs to cover "sixteen squads," this person is constantly on the go. The White sergeant in Parks's squad "hand-picks" only Blacks and Puerto Ricans for FOs, which prompts the following response from Parks: "It's a bitch. If only the Souls and Puerto Ricans could tell the world what really happens to them in this Man's Army. We do receive more than our share of the shit" (76). Some of the incidents he relates concerning the maltreatment and ordering of Black soldiers to dangerous assignments in Vietnam at this early stage of the war find fictional representation in several novels by Black writers. In Flowers's *De Mojo Blues*, for instance, Jethro, a Black soldier from rural Mississippi, always gets assigned the position of point man, despite exhaustion after being on maneuvers for hours. He is eventually killed in action.

Another nonfictional work early in the war was penned by an African American woman, Philippa Schuyler, whose book *Good Men Die* was posthumously published in 1969, following her untimely death at age thirty-six on May 9, 1967. It is an insightful and well-written account by a foreign correspondent in Vietnam who viewed the war as a futile cause because she felt that the U.S. government was not willing to do what was necessary to win; meanwhile, idealistic American soldiers were paying the ultimate price with their blood. In addition to being a musical genius, Schuyler was a gifted writer who used her skills around the world as a foreign correspondent for publications such as the *New York Daily Mirror*, the *Manchester Union Leader*, *United Press Features*, and the *National Review*.

Inquisitive and precocious from her earliest childhood, Schuyler as a gifted journalist went beyond mere reportorial style in her articles, as she traveled all over Vietnam getting the story behind the story.[16] Indeed, providing vivid detail she was adept at capturing the feel of the places she visited and the mood of the people in Vietnam, as some of her chapter titles illustrate. For instance, in part 1, "Da Nang," she titles chapter 1 "A Short Course in Hell" to describe the School of Landmine Warfare that she attended with a staff sergeant who taught American soldiers about weaponry used by the Vietnamese. There she learned about such dangerous and potentially lethal weapons as the innocuous looking coconut shell mines, shotgun shell mines (that the Vietnamese creatively crafted from spent American munitions), satchel charges (that were made to look like a peasant's thatched basket), bullet mines (made from rat traps), booby traps, and the deadly punji sticks/holes. Colin Powell was a victim of the dreaded punji trap after only six months in Country. According to K. Wright, when he stepped on the camouflaged sharp stick in a hole, "the pole drove into Powell's sole, straight through his foot, and back out the boot top" (235).[17] The reader can almost feel the pain as Schuyler describes these holes that were camouflaged with weeds or bamboo, inside of which were "wooden blocks that would turn over when stepped on, and a person's foot would go down into rusty nails that transfixed the leg" (18–20). Covered with poison or buffalo dung, the punji sticks would give the unfortunate victim an injury and an infection that could be fatal.

Well read, often quoting from writers of national and international renown, Schuyler was also extremely clever and quick-witted. She invariably saw through "officialese," the official language that the military officers would use to give the impression that Americans were winning the war when they were actually losing. Adept at using language figuratively, she derisively describes a meeting she attended where the top brass, with a penchant for doublespeak, gave a report that "had the precision worthy of one of Winston Smith's creations in Newspeak for the MINISTRY OF TRUTH in the Oceania of [George Orwell's] *1984*" (54). Sarcastically, she describes how the report is full of euphemisms: "'Structures damaged' by bombing raids meant we hit some huts. 'Light casualties' on our side meant we suffered moderate casualties. But if the report said 'moderate casualties' that meant our forces were mauled" (54).

Part 6 of *Good Men Die*, "The Final Dispatches," seems an eerie prognostication of Schuyler's untimely death. The last chapter in the book, chapter 16, "Failure in Vietnam: A Sea of Futility," discusses some of her harshest criticism of America's failure in Vietnam. With her usual penchant for questioning the difference between appearance and reality, she ponders: "What is really happening in Vietnam? Official statistics released to the American people make it seem that we are winning. Statistics released by the North Vietnamese government to their people 'prove' the Viet Cong are winning" (244). Prior to this chapter, Schuyler notes her discovery that wherever she travels in Vietnam the CIA is following her and that her apartment is wiretapped. She has also been chided by a Col. Stark for writing articles that are too critical of America's role in Vietnam (253). Being constantly harassed and under surveillance by American intelligence, who feign concern for her safety, Schuyler has also had limitations placed on her movement in Vietnam; consequently, with the aid of one of her Vietnamese friends she dresses in the conical hat and the traditional dress called an *ao dai* and passes as a Vietnamese woman, as she is fluent in several Vietnamese dialects. Blending into the crowd, she is able to freely go into places that are restricted to Americans. Exasperated at the restraints on her freedom of movement and on the censorship of her articles, she exclaims:

> This is why "intelligence" does not want a shrewd observer to really get around the country. They do not want to protect me, the blocks are not caused by concern for my welfare . . . [but] are erected to keep me and anyone like me from finding out about the extent of the failure. Up till now our war has not won here. It has failed the massive expenditure of lives and money and has not produced victory, but failure. (223)

Daniel Lyons, who wrote the foreword and edited *Good Men Die* for publication, reports that Schuyler had traveled to Vietnam, the second of two trips in a year, to perform classical music concerts for the troops and to write this book. Apparently the latter act was her undoing, as she met an untimely death, under suspicious circumstances, only a few weeks after performing a concert on South Vietnamese television in 1967 and shortly after writing the manuscript for her book. Schuyler was a very compassionate person who, according to Lyons, was not only an intellectual and musical prodigy but also a "genius in her love and kindness for her fellowman" (Schuyler, *Good Men Die* 4). She was concerned about the plight of Vietnamese orphans, especially Amerasian children who were often mistreated. So even though she had completed her tour, she extended her time in Vietnam to help evacuate Vietnamese orphans from Hue. This otherwise routine army helicopter flight to Da Nang included her and fifteen other persons, some of whom were military. The weather was clear, with temperature in the eighty-degree range, and the wind was calm. Lyons reports, however, that "the helicopter was only ten minutes from its destination, forty miles from the point of takeoff, when it inexplicably disintegrated in midair" (5).

At first it seemed as though there were no casualties. However, closer inspection revealed that everyone survived except three people: Schuyler, a little Vietnamese boy on her lap, and an American soldier. Before they boarded the aircraft in Hue, according to her biographer Kathryn Talalay, copilot Toews said he heard someone say to the pilot Capt. Hosey, "If you can convince her [Philippa] not to come back, we will get you anything you want." Some of the personnel laughed, as if this were said in jest (4). The mysterious circumstances that surround Schuyler's death have yet to be solved. Tragically, two years after her daughter's death, Philippa's mother took her own life by hanging.[18]

Several other works of nonfiction, including at least eleven Black autobiographies (see appendix 1), have appeared since Schuyler's book and Parks's narrative, including Terry Whitmore's *Memphis-Nam-Sweden*, which was published two years after Schuyler's book. The account of a Black deserter, this tragicomic view of discrimination within and outside the military sheds light on the reasons Whitmore and others chose to desert the military to the uncertainty of life in a foreign country rather than return to the certainty of racist treatment in America and on the battlefield in Vietnam. Whitmore chronicles in his account how the Japanese underground, Beheiren, assisted him and other American soldiers to escape the horrors of an unjust war, thereby revealing international involvement in the peace movement and the extent to which other countries were involved in antiwar efforts. Bill Brodie captures all the nuances, seriousness, and levity of Whitmore in his film that he made of a lengthy interview titled *Terry Whitmore, for Example*.

These early narratives were published against all odds. Though by the 1990s the market had been flooded with Vietnam War–related literature, such was not always the case. In the late 1970s one writer reported how it was virtually impossible for a first-time novelist of the Vietnam War experience to get published. This situation resulted in great part from the unpopularity of the war among publishers. A sixteen-year veteran of the publishing industry said in 1985 that any number of the novels turned down by editorial boards in the 1970s ironically ten years later were nominated for and/or won "first novel awards" (Searle 2). In light of the difficulty that White writers experienced getting their narratives about the Vietnam War published, it is little wonder that Blacks experienced even more difficulty. Wallace Terry, for instance, was rejected by 120 publishers, according to Timothy Lomperis (qtd. in Searle 2), before *Bloods* was finally published in 1984. Of two hundred journalists in Vietnam in 1969 (two years after Philippa Schuyler's untimely death), Terry was the only Black. During his stint there, just two short years from 1967 to 1969, relationships between Black and White soldiers deteriorated. After interviewing over a hundred Black and White soldiers in the field in Vietnam, Terry was initially unable to land a publishing contract. Later, after reorganizing the material he had collected into "a sort of oral history" consisting only of interviews of Black veterans, he published the resulting manuscript as *Bloods* (Hillstrom and Hillstrom 40).

Additionally, in all the military services Black promotions were few, stockade incarcerations for minor infractions were legion, and Black soldiers were more often wounded or killed disproportionately to their White counterparts. As an example of the disparities in rank and disproportionate numbers of Blacks assigned to combat duty, Manning Marable cites the following statistics:

> In 1967 in the Marine Corps, 9.6 percent of all enlisted men were black, while only 0.7 per cent were officers; in the army, 13.5 percent of all enlisted personnel were black. Afro-Americans comprised one out of every seven US soldiers stationed in Vietnam, and because blacks tended to be placed in "combat units" more often than middle-class whites, they also bore unfairly higher risks of being killed and wounded. (*Race, Reform, and Rebellion* 111)

Consequently, Black soldiers became more restive, militant, and less willing to fight in the name of "freedom and democracy" for a country they felt was denying them both.[19] Some of this militant resistance came on the heels of Muhammad Ali's refusal to be inducted into the army based on conscientious objection (having been converted to the Muslim faith and having changed his name from Cassius Clay) after being drafted in 1967. This refusal caused him to suffer a double penalty. He was sent to prison, and the World Boxing Association stripped him of his title as heavyweight champion. Undaunted, Ali took his case all the way to the Supreme Court. In June 1971, the court issued an 8–0 decision in Ali's favor, finding that the Justice Department had misled Selective Service by advising that Ali's conscientious objections were "neither sincere nor based on religious tenets" (Zaroulis and

Sullivan 229). Ali later succeeded in regaining the heavyweight championship crown. Ali's conscientious objection had the profound effect of elevating him to heroic status among Blacks all over America as well as those already fighting in Vietnam.

The skepticism, disillusionment, and sometimes militant resistance that resulted is thematically presented in an anthology of fiction, nonfiction, and poetry by Black writers that Clyde Taylor compiled. Similar to the oral narratives and autobiographies, this anthology, titled *Vietnam and Black America: An Anthology of Protest and Resistance*, further clarifies the difference between Black and White opposition to the war. In his assemblage of representative texts that reveal Black intellectual as well as physical resistance, pointing out the war's racist and imperialist implications (xx), Taylor has produced the definitive anthology of Black literature about the Vietnam War. The text consists of nonfiction excerpts from oral narratives, press releases, editorials, and interviews as well as essays from Black journalists and theorists such as Samuel Yette and Robert Browne,[20] and statesmen such as Representative Ronald Dellums of California and Representative Julian Bond of Georgia.[21] The book also includes speeches by Black leaders Rev. Dr. Martin Luther King Jr. and Malcolm X, both of whom were assassinated after speaking out vehemently against American involvement in the war in Vietnam.[22]

In Dr. King's speech at Riverside Church in New York, he castigated America for being involved in a war that was about everything else but freedom and democracy:

> The war in Vietnam is but a symptom of a far deeper malady within the American spirit. . . . We as a nation must undergo a radical revolution of values. . . . When machines and computers, profit motives and property rights are considered more important than people, the giant triplets of racism, materialism, and militarism are incapable of being conquered. ("Beyond Vietnam" 92–93)

Prior to this occasion, King's involvement with issues related to Vietnam had been minimal, as he did not want to lose the momentum gained in the civil rights struggle on issues of racial justice. Subsequently, he decided that the human rights of peoples of color in America and Vietnam were integrally related, and therefore broke the silence. One wonders if his stance could have contributed to bringing about his untimely demise. This speech was delivered on April 4, 1967, exactly one year before he was assassinated.[23] I agree with John Lewis, U.S. Congressman and civil rights activist, who said that this "was his greatest speech" (Schulke and McPhee 237).

Euro-American Myth: The Heroic Ideal

In addition to nonfiction, Taylor's anthology includes long and short poetry, short fiction, and excerpts from novels, all expressing the zeitgeist of Black America during the Vietnam War era. The positive images of real African American heroes in his book thwart the negative images of Blacks that White America has perpetuated in its "culture of violence" that Michael Moore and Barry Glassner discuss, which is an outgrowth of American myth from an idealization of the frontiersman, a conqueror at the expense of others who are invariably peoples of color. According to Donald Ringnalda, most mainstream Vietnam War novels are based on such American myths of "righteousness and innocence." For more than two hundred years before the war, America had prided itself with a "unique identity" as a "City on a Hill" whose avowed "mission," also referred to as "manifest destiny," was to "save the rest of the world—usually violently—from itself" (22). Mardena Creek concurs with this view in her assessment of responses to the Vietnam War by some White writers: "The America they discovered in Vietnam, [was] an America that had been disguised by myth and rhetoric [cf. *Apocalypse Now*]" (29). Therefore, in its attempt to destroy an outer evil America discovered its own inner evil.

This innate will to destroy, or inner evil, has evolved from the American frontier myth dating back to the time that European colonists settled this country. In *Regeneration through Violence: The Mythology of the American Frontier*, Richard Slotkin says this myth, with destructive consequences, developed because the first settlers viewed their experience in the New World as a chance to recoup their riches as well as to regain political power and religious hegemony. However, to achieve their aims, such "regeneration ultimately became the means of violence" against the people who were already inhabiting the land, namely, Native Americans, and, later, peoples they forcibly brought from Africa (5). As the "structuring metaphor" for the American experience, regeneration through violence has also been the guiding myth for America's incursion into and declaration of war against other countries, including Vietnam and, more recently, Iraq and Afghanistan.

The premises for such cultural myths that encode America's idealization of itself can be found in books such as *The American Adam* by R. W. B. Lewis and *Redeemer Nation* by Ernest Lee Tuveson. Purporting a myth of innocence, America, as "Adamic man," has been cut off from his history, or his sins of the past, and is therefore "morally superior" to other cultures. I agree with Creek, who characterizes this view as "idealistic innocence become destructive solipsism" (108). *Redeemer Nation* contributes to this ideal of moral superiority through its premise that America has a mission to exert its will over others, mainly peoples of color (who Eurocentrists designate "the other") and to supplant their culture. Among White Vietnam novels, Robin Moore's *The Green Berets* extols this "American warrior mythos," according to Phillip Beidler, and Norman Mailer reverses it in his parody titled *Why Are We in Vietnam?* (35). Both books, similar to those by Moore and Glassner, point to the innate proclivity toward violence in White American culture. Writers of Vietnam War novels were not necessarily aware of the underlying cultural myths that promoted the American ideals of innocence and mission; rather, as Creek points out, they knew and "reacted" to these myths on the "unconscious level on which people respond to the *Zeitgeist* of their culture" (42). American idealism, buoyed by such myths, contributed to America's failure in Vietnam.

John Clark Pratt feels that novels published after the Tet Offensive in 1968 project a postmodernist vision, often depicting characters who have problems separating "fact from fiction, illusion from reality" (141). Confusion resulted in part from the great impact that the well-orchestrated, surprise attack on Tet, the Vietnamese New Year, had on the American psyche. Steven Wright's *Meditation in Green*, for instance, though not published until 1983, was set in 1968. It "blends fact with fiction" in a surrealistic narrative (Pratt 145). Pratt's own contribution to Vietnam War fiction, *Laotian Fragments*, is a "hyper-realistic" novel set in a time frame of the year after Tet. It depicts characters who have difficulty separating "fact from fiction" (146). This decentering of experience also is an expression of American myth in general.

Kathleen Puhr concurs with the view that many novels about the White experience in Vietnam project a postmodernist view. She points to a sense of overwhelming "waste," "futility," "bewilderment" (5) as a way of distinguishing novels about the Vietnam experience from those about previous wars. She notes also that the "surrealistic" quality of television shows and movies about Vietnam is even "more concentrated" in the novels (8), one of which is Tim O'Brien's *Going After Cacciato*, which blends "realism and fantasy." Many of the novels that were set during the years 1964 to 1968, while President Lyndon B. Johnson was in office, express rage and the brutality of the battlefield along with a proliferation of profane language. Such memoirs as Larry Heinemann's *Close Quarters*, Phillip Caputo's *Rumor of War*, and Michael Herr's *Dispatches* are in this category.

In many mainstream narratives about the Vietnam War, not only the Vietnamese but also other peoples of color are marginalized and often treated with contempt.

Many Euro-American participants in the war as well as some who wrote about it seemed intent on destroying difference. Lt. Gen. William R. Peers, who headed the Peers Commission that investigated the My Lai Massacre, notes that some of the soldiers "never referred to the Vietnamese as anything but 'gooks,' 'dinks,' or 'slopes'" (qtd. in Mooney and West 194). Such racist attitudes were also reflected in the writing. In the same vein, "Blackness" in mainstream novels and movies most often symbolizes evil. Such is the case in *Apocalypse Now*, with its references to Joseph Conrad's *Heart of Darkness* to characterize the protagonist's madness as the "dark side of consciousness" (120). Robert Stone's *Dog Soldiers* suggests a connection between the "darkness and license" within American culture and "the war itself" (121). Additionally, Puhr points to the proclivity of some White novelists to portray Black characters stereotypically. One example is James Webb's *Fields of Fire*, which presents a character who does not have a presence in Black narratives, that is, a Black soldier who thrives on killing others, seeing in it a certain "nobility" that enables him to grant his "*natural ferocity* its whims" (qtd. in Puhr 195; emphasis added). Such characters are more a product of Euro-American imagination than African American myth.

Mainstream writers often express misogynistic attitudes, in addition to racist images, in nonfictional and fictional narratives, as Phillip K. Jason reveals in "Sexism and Racism in Vietnam War Fiction" (126). He notes that in some novels women become both "enemy and weapon," as in Gustav Hasford's *Short Timers* where a recruit makes love to his rifle, Charlene. Similar misogynistic references are in the film *Full Metal Jacket*. Also, the husky, "grunt" American soldier often views the Vietnamese, who is of smaller stature, as effeminate (126). Women in some of these mainstream Vietnam narratives are viewed with disdain similar to the Vietnamese. For instance, the short-timer's "calendar" depicted in Hasford's novel is actually a "big-breasted woman-child cut up into pieces like a puzzle. Each day another fragment of her delicious anatomy is inked out" (qtd. in Creek 115).[24] Jacqueline E. Lawson's article "She's a Pretty Woman for a Gook: The Misogyny of the Vietnam War" provides numerous examples of misogynistic references in the memoirs of Tim O'Brien, Ron Kovic, and Phil Caputo, to name a few. Rape, sodomy, torture, and even murder were commonplace heinous acts against Vietnamese women throughout the war, largely resulting from such attitudes. Lawson is quick to point out, however, that war did not create misogynists; rather, many soldiers had a "predisposition" to misogynistic behavior because "violence against women is built into the very fabric of American culture" (17), a fact that is proven by the emergence of the current "Me Too" movement.

On the other hand, misogynistic references are rare in Black narratives about the Vietnam War; and, in some cases, it is the Black soldier who intervenes on behalf of the victim during atrocities against Vietnamese women and villagers in general.[25] Also in many Black novels are positive portrayals of Black women, such as Mimosa who is confidante to the protagonist in *Captain Blackman*, aiding him in his identity quest. In *Tragic Magic* the female friend of protagonist Melvin helps him to readjust to society after he is released from prison for being a conscientious objector to the war. Yet another example resides in *Cohesion*, Thomas D. Williams's novel in which the Black protagonist meets and falls in love with a Vietcong woman. They not only help each other survive the war but also become deserters from their respective armies. These empathetic portrayals are not to suggest, however, that Black soldiers were immune from committing acts of violence against the Vietnamese. In some accounts they participated in rape and other atrocities. However, the preponderance of evidence, from accounts of Black and White writers, supports the notion that treatment of the Vietnamese by the Black soldier was more humane, which finds representation in Black novels about the Vietnam War. (See listings of other Vietnam war novels by Black writers in appendix 1 as well as summaries in the epilogue.)

Historically, peoples of color have been victimized by White heroism, and Blacks are no exception. When the White hero goes into the wilderness to ostensibly "civilize" the inhabitants, the people he conquers there are invariably of a darker hue. According to W. E. B. Du Bois, these Anglo-Saxon descendants have a heroic legacy that consists of men whose preoccupation has been "war and preparation for war" (qtd. in Van de Burg 28). He goes on to say that they are masters of deception, with "meanness of spirit." Furthermore, they extol and deify the "self," which is a type of "individualism gone berserk . . . at the expense of human brotherhood." Their credo is "might makes right." Du Bois felt, optimistically, that the Black heroic tradition could provide a "corrective" to what he characterized as "Anglo-Saxon hardness" (qtd. in Van de Burg 28).

During the days of European conquest and settlement in the New World, the colonizers were known for their rapaciousness, brutality, and cruelty. People of African descent who accompanied them (for example, the Spanish Conquistadores) possessed their share of cockiness, anger, and rebelliousness. However, these "darker-skinned patriots" possessed a "sympathetic, nurturing humanity which contrasted greatly with the hard-hearted ruthlessness and greed of the European adventurers," according to Van de Burg (59). Du Bois hoped that in his revelations of the differences between African American and Euro-American heroes in the literature, the Black heroes could have a "humanizing" effect on the brashness of White heroic models that ultimately would effect a "cultural synthesis and a reciprocal world order" (qtd. in Van de Burg 27).

In America's early literary history, White writers devised stereotypical and demeaning images that became an integral part of American popular culture by inventing so called Black characters that were figments of their imaginations. Unfortunately, these caricatures continue to exist throughout mainstream American popular culture. One is the "tom," the socially acceptable "good Negro" character whom Donald Bogle discusses in his groundbreaking study of Black stereotypes in film, *Toms, Coons, Mulattoes, Mammies, & Bucks*: "they are harassed, hounded, flogged, enslaved, and insulted, [but] they keep the faith, never turning against their white massas while remaining submissive, generous, stoic, and selfless . . . endear[ing] themselves to white audiences." (2). "Loyal servants" were Black household retainers during slavery, who—like Uncle Tom (titular character of Harriet Beecher Stowe's novel)—sacrificed their dignity, and sometimes themselves, for Whites. This type was submissive to his own detriment and that of his people (Van de Burg 31).

Yet another type was the "comic minstrel" who possessed an "innate" ability to evoke side-splitting laughter at a moment's notice. As such, this stereotypical buffoon serves as a "mechanism of social control and as an agent of white psychological security" (Van de Burg 34). Then there is the coward who was afraid of everything, from graveyards to haunted houses to funeral parlors. Too weak-willed to be adventuresome, he is "inept in freedom . . . and cowardly in wartime" (36), for example, the character Day Tripper in Herr's *Dispatches*. Bogle classifies this type as "the coon," the Black man as amusement object and buffoon of whom he says there were three categories: "pickaninny," "uncle remus," and the "pure coon." The pickaninny was the silly little easily excitable wild-eyed child whose hair stood up on his/her head when frightened, exemplified by Buckwheat in the Little Rascals (the female corollary being Topsy) cartoons (5). Then there was Uncle Remus, the comical old retainer on the plantation, usually with head lowered and hat in hand, who engages in comical "philosophizing" that evokes laughter and pity at the same time (6). A source of amusement, he is not a threat to the social order. Third in this series of demeaning caricatures were the pure coons who Bogle characterizes as "no-account. . . unreliable, crazy, lazy creatures good for nothing more than eating watermelons, stealing chickens, shooting crap, or butchering the English language" (5).

Two types ascribed to Black females, almost exclusively, were the "tragic mulatto" and the "mammy." The former was doomed by "Cain's curse"—one drop of Black blood (Van de Burg 35). Bogle describes her as "a light-skinned black who passes for white. Most often a female character, she is made likeable—even sympathetic [because of her White blood, no doubt]—and the audience believes that the girl's life could have been productive and happy if it were not for her one drop of black blood" (9). Related to the coon, the mammy usually speaks in broken English and is big, overweight, and cantankerous. Whereas the tragic mulatto is sometimes portrayed as oversexed, the mammy is sexless (9–10).

Yet another stereotype consisted of "brutes." Often called "savages," some were brutal by nature, ostensibly because of their "African blood" (Van de Burg 37). Others were brutal by "nurture"; that is, having been brutalized by the oppression of slavery, they meted out the same brutality to their own people. Bogle categorizes the brute into two groups: (1) Black brutes, barbaric Black men out to raise havoc, subhuman and feral, always engaged in physical violence; and (2) Black bucks, big, "baadddd niggers," oversexed and savage, violent and frenzied, lusting for White female flesh (10–15). These two categories of the Black brute type are portrayed in some mainstream Vietnam War novels and films.

All of these stereotypes of Black people are portrayed in D. W. Griffith's racist movie, *Birth of a Nation* (1915) that was adapted from Thomas Dixon's racist novel *The Clansman*. Together they indelibly imprinted these despicable stereotypes on American popular culture, and with their glorification of the Ku Klux Klan, as Bogle points out, "Griffith seemed to be saying that things were in order only when whites were in control and when the American Negro was kept in his place" (10). He also reveals the insidious nature of the "brutes, the bucks, and mulatto" stereotypes, all of whom wore "the guise of villains" (14). Moreover, these opprobrious caricatures have flourished in American cinema, television, and popular culture through the years, as Bogle points out:

> During the 1920s audiences saw their toms and coons dressed in the guise of plantation jesters. In the 1930s the types were dressed in servants' uniforms. In the early 1940s. . . entertainers' costumes. In the late 1940s and 1950s, they donned the gear of problem people. . . [and] in the 1960s as angry militants. (14)

In other words the images of Blacks were of one-dimensional types rather than well-rounded characters. In fact, during the early days of American cinema, Blacks were portrayed by Whites in blackface. In Griffith's *Birth of A Nation*, for instance, all the roles for so-called Black characters (men and women) were played by White men in blackface. These stereotypical images were intended to impede the development of a Black heroic tradition in American mainstream culture despite the existence of an African American heroic tradition that has its basis in African culture. Unfortunately, these stereotypes have continued through the years and still exist, as witnessed by the resurgence of such degrading images as blackface on college campuses and in American popular culture.

African American Myth: The Heroic Ideal

To counteract such opprobrious images, Black scholars and Renaissance men such as W. E. B. Du Bois and Carter G. Woodson at the turn of the twentieth century established research organizations, one of which was the Association for the Study of Negro Life and History, to document examples of Black heroism throughout history, in Africa and America. To advance this cause they, along with other Black scholars, wrote and presented pageants and folk dramas with the avowed purpose of debunking negative, stereotypical images, particularly those promulgated by minstrelsy in the early 1900s (Van de Burg 39). During that same time frame, they also initiated Negro History Week (renamed Black History Month during the 1960s) to provide a forum for information and to present skits about heroes/ heroines such as Gabriel Prosser, Frederick Douglass, Sojourner Truth, Nat Turner, Harriet Tubman, Crispus Attucks, and Benjamin Banneker, to name a few. Other larger-than-life figures represented on stage were Paul Robeson, Father Divine, and Marcus Garvey.

These human luminaries were not the only heroic models portrayed in Black culture, however. Derived from the West African oral tradition, a pantheon of Black heroes became a part of the African American vernacular tradition. Though a variety of models exists, three types that have a significant presence in Vietnam War fiction are the "moral hard man" (Levine, *Black Culture* 420), the trickster, and the heroic bad man. An example of the moral hard man is the legendary steel-driving John Henry, a manual laborer who triumphed over the steam engine (which symbolized the rise of industrialization and mechanization) though losing his life in the process. His martyrdom is a testament to his "strength, courage, and ability to flout the limitations imposed by white society" (Levine, *Black Culture* 420). A gentle man, he lived by a strict moral code. His strength, perseverance, and tenacity in the midst of seemingly insurmountable odds served as a testament to the indomitable will to survive. However, he did not exploit others to accomplish his heroic deeds as was the case with certain Anglo-American heroes such as Daniel Boone whose model developed from the "regeneration through violence" philosophy and whose modern-day counterpart is John Wayne.

Also originating in the West African tradition are the trickster tales, sometimes referred to as the "Jack/John" tales. By whichever name he is called in Black folklore, Jack or John is usually a trickster who uses "indirection" and wit to survive and "live to fight another day" (Van de Burg 52). John A. Williams adapted characteristics of the prototypical trickster from the West African myth of Ananse the Spider for use as an organizing principle in his Vietnam War novel *Captain Blackman*. The trickster uses "guile, wit, cunning, and deception—[and sometimes physical strength—to best better-equipped, higher-status foes" (Van de Burg 47). Though in an alien environment in America, Africans were able to adapt these innate qualities to suit the circumstances of their new existence and thereby survive its harsh realities. Combining the qualities of the moral hard man and the trickster is the legendary hero High John the Conqueror (better known in the vernacular as High John de Conquer).

According to cultural critic Julius Lester, "Ol' John was the first slave brought to America and he's been here ever since" (19). Similar to John Henry, he is a larger-than-life hero as well as a "master teacher." "'Old Aunt Shady Ann' said after Emancipation that High John 'put it in the heads of the white folks to give us our freedom'" (qtd. in Lester 19). Because his name means "power," the enslaved said they would not have made it through all the "trials and tribulations" if High John had not been around. A peace-loving man, High John de Conquer did not like to fight, and he was the kind of man "you'd have to argue with before he'd fight off a cold" (19). These are the characteristics with which the hero is imbued in A. R. Flowers's *De Mojo Blues*. As the case is with most tricksters, however, High John de Conquer is duplicitous. A paradoxical character, he can be both kind and mean, qualities that the protagonist possesses in John A. Williams's *Captain Blackman*. Consider this tale from Levine's *Black Culture and Black Consciousness* that relates the complementary, or "bad man," side of High John's character: "High John eloped with the Devil's daughter. The Devil pursued them and, when they met, High John tore off one of the Devil's arms and almost beat him to death with it. Before he left Hell he passed out ice water to everyone" (403).

Such tales of exaggeration are characteristic of the third category of Black hero legends—"the bad man" or what John Roberts, in *From Trickster to Badman: The Black Folk Hero in Slavery and Freedom*, calls the "bad man as outlaw hero" (171). But bad does not necessarily mean evil or no good. Words in the vernacular must be taken in context of a certain world view. For the enslaved person, for instance, being labeled as bad, or a thief, for taking food because he was hungry flies in the face of considering the slaveowner, who had stolen him and his family from Africa and deprived them of the bare necessities, as following any kind of moral code. Who is the real thief, or bad person, when one weighs the morality of the situation? As Geneva Smitherman notes in *Talkin' and Testifyin': The Language of Black America*, African Americans have a language that exists at a level outside the mainstream, or "the Black Semantic level," within which words can have any number of meanings based on the context. In this respect she provides examples of bad being used in a number of ways, noting that for most folk, Black or White, it suggests "negativity." On the other hand, on the Black Semantic level it can also have positive connotations, such as "good, extraordinary, beautiful. . . . I *got a bad cold* means the same thing to blacks and whites, but *He is a bad dude* would suggest to whites the idea of an undesirable character, whereas to blacks it would indicate a highly desirable person" (59).

According to Smitherman, this linguistic reversal process, that is, "using negative terms with positive meanings, is present in a number of African languages—for example, the Mandingo *a ka nyiko-jugu*, which literally means "it is good badly," that is, "it is very good" (*Talkin' and Testifyin'* 44). When it comes to the bad man as hero in African American culture similar rules apply, as he can be a person who takes care of business by standing up to the White establishment, purposefully defying their laws that are inimical to him and his people. Lawrence Levine, in *Black Culture and Black Consciousness: Afro-American Folk Thought from Slavery to Freedom*, puts it this way: "When the *a* is prolonged," the meaning of the word changes and becomes "*baaad*." This transformation of the word when applied to the Black hero becomes one of approval and admiration for those who had "the strength, courage, and ability to flout the limitations imposed by white society" (420). It is from this tradition of the hard or bad man that the legend of Railroad Bill emerged.

The story goes that Bill Slater (aka Railroad Bill) was a turpentine worker in rural Alabama who had come into town after working hard all week to unwind at a local juke joint. However, a racist White policeman accosted him for no apparent reason (other than the fact that he was Black) and demanded he give up his gun.

When Slater refused the policeman's order, they struggled; and in the ensuing fracas the officer was killed. To elude his pursuers, Slater jumped on a passing train and for years eluded all attempts to capture him, hence the moniker "Railroad Bill." According to Roberts, "Bill was a deadly shot and killed as many as a dozen men during his career. And the longer he remained at large, the bolder and more daring he became. In one story, Bill even robbed a train carrying a posse sent to capture him (*From Trickster to Badman* 172). In the online forum TeacherServe, Trudier Harris tells how Railroad Bill, a compassionate hero, went through the crates and boxes on the trains for years, taking canned foods and other goods and then leaving them along the railroad tracks for Blacks who lived in the vicinity to take for their benefit.[26] In other words, similar to other heroes in the African/African American tradition, his deeds were in the interests of the community while in defiance of the societal order that kept them all oppressed. Legend has it that Railroad Bill eluded all attempts to capture him because he was actually a conjure man (shapeshifter) who could transform himself into any kind of animal; consequently, even though the White sheriff says he captured and killed Railroad Bill, the Black folk say he is still out there roaming the forests transformed into an animal.

Yet another legend of the "bad man as hero" is that of Staggerlee (aka Stagolee/ Stackerlee). Embodying toughness, he is naturally skilled at surviving the worst personal tragedy. Molefi Asante characterizes Staggerlee, the prototypical bad man, as a "symbol of uncensored, unself-conscious force, pulsating with unpredictability" (*Afrocentric Idea* 118). Black literary artists often use the image of the "bad man hero" to portray the character who will do whatever he has to do to resist oppression, whether Whites like him or not. In his book *Stagolee Shot Billy*, Cecil Brown indicates that his legend began in the late 1800s coterminous with the origin of the blues. He calls Stagolee "a metaphor that structures the lives of black men from childhood to maturity," as the story of his exploits is passed down from generation to generation orally (2). Its revolutionary message was "appropriated" by Black Panther Bobby Seale. The legend continues today as "a symbol of the enduring black male struggle against white oppression and racism" (3). Moreover, the Staggerlee legend in modern society symbolizes defiance and resistance to the hypocrisy of American society, which uses Black men as cannon fodder in its wars then denies them true manhood rights when they return home. The characters Otis in *De Mojo Blues* and Childress in *Coming Home* epitomize this character type.

Peculiar to oral Black masculinist expression is the "toast," or what Bell refers to as the "ritualized black vernacular contest," a variation on the "bad man" theme that provides a means of sublimating feelings of anger and aggression in response to racism and emasculation in American society (21). In an interview on *The Tavis Smiley Show*, Cecil Brown defines the toast as an "oral narrative, usually with rhymed couplets or end rhymes," about legendary Black heroes such as Shine (of "Shine and the Titanic" fame), the Signifyin(g) Monkey, and Staggerlee. Often recited in a company of other Black men, toasts project powerful images of Black masculinity. Because they are rhymed, being passed down orally from one generation to the next, they aid in the memorization and the "performance." Toasts are often a part of a young Black man's rite of passage during male bonding rituals in barbershops, on street corners, or other places where men congregate, usually exclusive of the opposite sex and beyond the contact of Whites. Bell refers to "Shine and the Titanic" and other toasts as myths of "self-discovery in the midst of chaos" (114) offering a sense of hope in the struggle to survive. It is little wonder, then, that several Vietnam War novels by Black writers, including *Captain Blackman* and *De Mojo Blues*, use the toasts "Shine and the Titanic" and /or "The Signifying Monkey" structurally and metaphorically as part of the story line.

Van de Burg assesses the Black pantheon correctly with his observation that despite the diversity in their characteristics (and in spite of the trickster's outlandish behavior), one quality that connects these Black heroes is their "humaneness." Even the strong, stalwart steel-driving man John Henry had a heart as "soft and tender as a woman." Also, High John de Conquer was a peace-loving man, despite his master's boast during slavery time that he was the "strongest" man in the county. Another characteristic of the Black hero, from antiquity to modern times, has been his interdependent relationship with the Black community (60).

African American and Euro-American Heroic Quest: A Comparison

Derived from African cultural memory, the Black hero in Vietnam War narratives is a part of African American myth, one of the most important functions of which is to demonstrate control "over circumstances" rather than control "over nature," the latter being a characteristic of Euro-American myth. The Black hero has a "mission," therefore, to "surmount any obstacle in the cause of peace, love, or *collective harmony*," according to Asante (*Afrocentric Idea* 112; emphasis added). Moreover, As Clyde Ford illustrates in *The Hero with an African Face: Mythic Wisdom of Traditional Africa*, myth was traditionally a means of "healing self and society by helping people bring the circumstances of their lives into harmony with the larger concerns in the society and the cosmos" (5). In carrying out this mission, the hero with an African face will have achieved wholeness of self and harmony with the community.

Euro-American myth does not emphasize communal harmony or wholeness of self in its depiction of the hero, according to Marimba Ani, who points out that in the Eurocentric world view the mind is trained to "dichotomize" experience. Reason, or the rational mind, is separated from emotion, and a higher valuation is placed on the rational over the intuitive. Such valuations inevitably lead to imperialistic, racist behavior. A similar kind of dichotomization is applied to people and whole cultures. One group is imbued with negative qualities and is therefore considered inferior; while another, the dominant group, evokes positive connotations and is therefore considered superior. The terminology for such dichotomization is "binary opposition," a type of thinking that eschews harmony (35).

In the Afrocentric world view, on the other hand, the African principle of "twinness" predominates. Consequently, contrasting terms such as negative and positive are conceived as complementary, both of which are necessary to constitute the whole, that is, "both/and" rather than "either/or"; and that is why the trickster character in African myth can be villainous yet compassionate, altruistic yet selfish. In the Afrocentric world view, "harmony is achieved through the balance of complementary [sometimes opposing] forces" (Ani 35). This aspect of the Afrocentric world view African philosopher John Mbiti designates as "paradoxical complementarity" (32). These definitions of binary opposition, paradoxical complementarity, and harmony are necessary to understanding the differences between the hero in an Afrocentric universe as compared to a Eurocentric one in the novels discussed below.

Harmony is important because the "hero with an African face," according to Ford (90), is dependent upon the community for victory on his quest to self-knowledge and identity. In the Afrocentric world view the "individual cannot and does not exist alone, but owes his/her existence to other members of the 'tribe,' including the ancestors and the yet unborn," as Linda James Myers points out (20). In African societies communalism is highly valued. Consequently, this notion of interdependence between the individual and the group is encoded in many African epics, such as *Sundiata* and the *Mwindo Epic*, and myths such as "The Myth of Ananse the Spider." In contrast, Western mythological traditions, Ford rightly points out, primarily focus on "the individual to the exclusion of the group" (71).

The hero in Western culture, consequently, prides himself on accomplishing magnificent feats of heroism alone, as the "autonomous," "rational" self, and sometimes in spite of rather than in conjunction with the community. The "painful isolation and alienation" that their solitary existence precipitates tends to either incapacitate these cultural participants, according to Ani, or "makes them extremely efficient competitors, aggressors, and technocrats" (47). The protagonists in Wesley Brown's *Tragic Magic* and George Davis's *Coming Home* initially experience such incapacitation because at the beginning of their heroic quests they have not yet discovered the importance of interdependence between the individual and the community. This discovery later in their quest for self-knowledge and wholeness, however, enables them to survive.

From the corpus of novels about the Black experience in Vietnam, I have selected four with a common theme: the protagonist's search for identity. Ben, the protagonist of Davis's *Coming Home* (1971) becomes so frustrated with having to justify killing people who are not his enemy, while having to answer to those who are, that he goes AWOL. Similar to the real-life experiences of Whitmore, Ben prepares to start a new life, to "find himself," in Sweden after becoming a deserter from the Vietnam War. His decision to "hit the road" is symbolically similar to "catching trains," the classic response of the Black liminal figure to impossible situations (Harris 128). The protagonist of Williams' novel *Captain Blackman* (1972) attempts to benefit from his status as an officer in combat after he returns to civilian life at the end of his first valorous tour of duty in Country. However, experiencing discrimination in search of a job, he reenrolls and finishes college. After getting a history degree, he reenlists in the army and teaches a course in African American military history to fellow soldiers in Vietnam. Later wounded in action, Blackman lies in a semiconscious reverie as he takes the reader on an allegorical journey through the past, present, and future of deceptive and discriminatory practices America has meted out to Black soldiers in all its wars, from the Revolution to Vietnam.

Melvin Ellington, a character reminiscent of Ralph Ellison's protagonist in *Invisible Man*, is the hero in *Tragic Magic* (1978) by Brown. A conscientious objector, Melvin refuses to be inducted into military service and is thereby sentenced to serve three years in prison. The action in *Tragic Magic* begins when Melvin is released and returns home from prison, after which he sets out on an identity quest in a postwar society from which he feels alienated. The "jazzerly" text of this novel grounds it squarely in the Black vernacular tradition. Finally, in *De Mojo Blues* by Flowers (1985), the protagonist Tucept High John, along with two other Black soldiers, returns to San Francisco in the last load of returnees from Vietnam in handcuffs and chains. They have been court-martialed and dishonorably discharged as a result of being accused of a "fragging" incident (which they did not commit) in Vietnam, resulting in the death of a White officer.[27] Feeling that he has lost control over his life, Tucept adapts the persona of High John the Conqueror from Black vernacular tradition and empowers himself through the "Black Book of Power." In all the novels under review, the Black hero is able to survive by reconnecting with Black vernacular culture.

To appreciate novels about the Vietnam War by African American authors, it is necessary to understand the history of the Black hero relative to his interdependent relationship with the Black community and his constant struggle against racism in American society. By the application of vernacular theory, as opposed to postmodernism or other Eurocentric theories, one can place his heroic exploits within the context of African values and cultural world view. Therefore, my study locates each novel within a specific manifestation of Black vernacular culture that advances the hero on his quest for wholeness and harmony with the community: *Captain Blackman* and the African trickster myth of Ananse the Spider; *De Mojo Blues* and the African American hero High John de Conquer; *Tragic Magic* and the improvisation exemplified in jazz; and *Coming Home* where "the club" figures as a "site of memory" as aid in (re)connecting with Black vernacular culture, thereby enabling the hero to survive.

CHAPTER 2

Untangling a Paradoxical Web for the Black Warrior

The Anansean Motif in *Captain Blackman*

Mu kala kintawadi ye tuku i mu zinga (To be in touch with one's origins is to live).

—Ancient Bakonga proverb

We are vessels of speech . . . we are the memory of mankind.

—Mamadou Kouyate, griot

God gave Ananse the meaning of order. . . . This is symbolized by his web.

—John Biggers, *Ananse: The Web of Life in America*

We have unself-consciously used our creativity (Kuumba) to express the African spirit. . . . The story of our sojourn in the Diaspora has been a spiderweb consistently blown apart by the wind only to be respun again and again.

—Dona Marimba Richards, "The African Aesthetic and National Consciousness"

I n African culture, griots are memory personified. As repositories of historical and cultural knowledge dating back to ancient African kingdoms, they are "walking libraries" (Mugambi 29) whose knowledge spans the centuries to translate the wisdom of the elders and the rich heritage of the African past to present and future generations. Like Mamadou Kouyate on the African continent, John A. Williams serves as modern-day griot for Africans in America to correct the historical record of Black involvement in all of America's wars. As a "vessel of speech," he bequeaths the gift of cultural memory to put African American soldiers in touch with their origins in his novel *Captain Blackman*. He creates the hero, Capt. Abraham Blackman, who takes the reader on an odyssey through African American military involvement in all of America's wars, like the archetypal African trickster Ananse the Spider weaving his wily web throughout Black history. Filling in the gaps left in the historical record, this narrative is testament to the heroism and survival of Black fighting men despite discrimination and sometimes purposeful elimination of their heroic exploits from the history books.

This chapter explores the nature of heroism for the Black soldier in *Captain Blackman* through the application of Black vernacular theory expressed in the adaptation of the Ananse the Spider myth. Ananse's ability to bring together seemingly disparate realities lends itself well to the African American writer's attempt to make sense of the paradoxical nature of the Black man's role as a soldier in America's wars, particularly the Vietnam War that was fought against another people of color. "Literary sense-making" is what Phillip Beidler calls the task of Black and White writers alike who attempt to portray the outrageousness of the "real experience" in Vietnam that seemed more fictive than the fictions fashioned to explain the war. Consequently, he observes, "what sense was to be made of it at all would lie in the self-conscious exploration of relationships between experiential and aesthetic . . . possibilities of truth-telling, in the realization that far from being incompatible or opposite, they would often imply and even entail each other" (33).

Williams blends Black historical experience with the aesthetic possibilities of African myth to make sense not only of the Vietnam War but also all the wars in which Blacks have fought historically for America, even when they had to fight for the right to fight in those wars. The flexibility and adaptability of Ananse, a heroic character from Black cultural memory whose myth originated on the African continent and survived the horrors of the Middle Passage and enslavement in America, metaphorically speaks to the ability of the Black soldier to survive the vicissitudes of racial discrimination and emasculation in the military during war as well as in American society after his return home. The protagonist in *Captain Blackman* discovers the study of Black history as the key to his survival when he returns to the World following his first tour of duty in Country. Then he reenlists and becomes a personification of Black cultural memory metaphorically through the persona of Ananse the Spider, thereby serving as spiritual guide to other Black soldiers in Vietnam to aid in their survival.

Ananse as Trickster: Hero and Culture Bearer

The definition of a hero is derived from the normative values of a society. Because of the dehumanizing institution of American slavery a Black man was considered property, hence less than human (later modified to "three-fifths" for political purposes). Additionally, his attributes were omitted from America's definition of a hero. Undaunted, however, and always ingenious, the enslaved devised their own heroic models from African oral tradition, of which the trickster is a signal example.[1] Because the trickster is often viewed as rebellious, and somewhat outlandish, he is not included in the pantheon of mainstream American heroes, which includes Daniel Boone and Davy Crockett among others. Rather, to understand the trickster tale as a "normative model of heroic action," I agree with John W. Roberts that recognizing the "African roots of the tradition from the vantage of African culture" is essential because the trickster tradition has been, and continues to be, a source of "Black identity and heroic values" ("Strategy" 101). In other words, an appreciation of this character can be gained only through an assessment within his own cultural milieu rather than in the context of a Western cultural world view.

However I take issue with Roberts's assertion that "the trickster tale is curiously fatal," exhibiting "that callousness to cruelty found in expressions of a fatalistic worldview" (105). To the contrary, the oxymoronic trickster who balances wit and cunning with guile exhibits a duplicitous nature enabling him to control his destiny through that balancing act for which he is admired across the African Diaspora. Therefore, I agree with Ousseynou Traore in his introduction to *The Literary Griot* that Ananse, "a world traveler, master trickster, and a wordsmith" is a representation of global linkages among peoples of African descent from Africa, to the Caribbean, to African America. Consequently, the trickster tale is life affirming rather than "fatalistic" and is based on African norms (iii).[2] John Biggers, a visual artist, provides the basis for this important link between African and African American trickster tales and the cultural values upon which they are based.

Contrary to Hynes and Doty who assert that "Ananse is not a culture-hero" (117), Biggers points to the cultural significance of Ananse as a concept that helped him appreciate and have a fuller understanding of Akan society during his sojourn in Ghana.[3] In a splendidly illustrated book titled *Ananse: The Web of Life in Africa*, he reveals the trickster spider to be a composite of "spiritual and aesthetic values" for the Akan; moreover, he is a heroic character to whom "God gave the meaning of order, teaching him the structure of life and society that is symbolized by his web, which stands also for the sun and its rays, and the sun personifies God" (29). Ubiquitous and protean, Ananse is a shapeshifter, both a man and a spider. When things go well he is a man; but when in danger, he spins his web and perches on the ceiling out of harm's way, a prominent characteristic in Ghanaian and Jamaican tales where he assumes the name "Ceiling Thomas" or "Annancy," as S. L. Ansah points out (47).

As a holistic conceptualization of experience, Ananse is also dual-gendered. He appears in some tales as either female or male, assuming the name "Aunt Nancy" or, interchangeably, "Brer Fox" in some African American tales (46–47). This dual gendering reflects matrilinearity in Ashanti culture, which is one of its most "striking features" (Pelton 63). Matrilinearity figures prominently in Ghanaian culture because of their creation myth, which Biggers outlines as follows: "The Akan people of Ghana—the Fanti and the Ashanti—believe in male and female entities of God—Nyame. The female entity is personified in Ohemmaa—the female king or the queen mother—who created the universe by giving birth to the sun." She is regarded as "the creator and owner of the state and the mother of everyone in it, including the king" (28).

I agree with Ansah that whatever his name, wherever he is found throughout the African Diaspora, Ananse is a paradoxical character who displays any number of the following contradictory characteristics: "a family man" and a lecher, "a quick-witted thinker, a conniving and cunning deceiver, and, above all, a very wise fellow" (48). Furthermore, this master of doubleness is simultaneously "creator of order and lawless fool" (37), as Robert Pelton observes in his extensive treatment of the West African trickster.

A multifaceted character, Ananse has one long leg (on earth) and one short leg (in the heavens), symbolizing his role as a mediator between man and the gods. Houston Baker Jr. compares his liminality to that of the blues, "breaking down resistance . . .—one foot among the gods, the other planted squarely in the world of men" (*Blues* 65). Ananse's one short and one long leg signify not only the connection between spiritual and material existence but also the concept of time as a continuum rather than separate phases of past, present, and future—both characteristics of the African world view.[4] In *Talkin' and Testifyin': The Language of Black America*, Geneva Smitherman perhaps best sums up this phenomenon of simultaneous existence when she says that "progression" in the rhythmic, cyclical African universe, "occurs only into the past world of the spirit" and that "the 'future' is the past" (75).

It is important to note that the trickster myth has been adapted over time, from its origins on the African continent to use across the Diaspora in the Caribbean and America. Knowing the origin of the trickster provides a clue to its appropriateness for Williams's use as a metaphor to represent the Black war experience. Before European conquest the role of trickster among West Africans was related to the desire of the human psyche for "freedom from fixed ways of seeing, feeling, thinking, acting; a revolt against a whole complex of 'givens' coded into a society," according to Ivan Van Sertima in "Trickster, the Revolutionary Hero" (103). The symbolism of the trickster operates on several levels simultaneously. In addition to tricking the lords of the jungle—tiger, elephant, lion—which symbolize the ruling class or the most powerful in society, Ananse also plays tricks on "the rulers of Heaven itself, stealing fire or food for his fellows under the noses of the gods" (104). Trickster's multilevel revolt is also against the codes of conduct of his own group, as he commits acts that are taboo and outrageous, which absolve him of the guilt that his peers feel when they trespass societal mores. At times his behavior is, by acceptable human codes of behavior, perverse or degenerate, a tendency that is revealed in the dualistic character of Capt. Blackman.

For African Americans the trickster has always been viewed as a revolutionary. In fact, the slave trickster, according to Lawrence Levine, "figured prominently in the tradition of resistance to slavery" (*Black Culture* 389). This revolutionary behavior in *Captain Blackman* is played out on various levels. For instance, as an officer in the army, Capt. Abraham Blackman changes the way the military trains soldiers. His classes in Black military history are offered over the objections of his commanding officer, Maj. Ishmael Whittman (a symbol of White military leadership), who often puts obstacles in Blackman's path. Not to be deterred, however, Blackman changes the thinking of young Black recruits concerning the historical role of the Black soldier as well as his current mistreatment by the White military establishment;

hence these history lessons aid in their survival. Then, at the end of the novel, Capt. Blackman foments a literal revolution to subvert the evil designs of Maj. Whittman and his cronies who plan a futuristic nuclear war to annihilate the African continent.

Trickster as underdog, representing the oppressed in terms of racial class and group, appears to be the major role transplanted from Africa to America. He is often portrayed in African American folklore as a rabbit, tortoise, or spider. Though small, these animals use their wit to outsmart the larger animals such as bear. In modern society, according to Van Sertima, Ananse as trickster is an overarching presence, the personification of "power," a "center of Consciousness" that demonstrates the "capacity of the human spirit to recreate itself" (109). In Williams's novel, the African American soldier is likewise in a constant state of re-creation, throughout time, to meet the demands of a military establishment that often treats him as less than a man but nevertheless exacts of him near superhuman effort in carrying out his duties on behalf of America.

Mythic Time: Organizing Principle in *Captain Blackman*

The mythic structure of *Captain Blackman* depicts the protagonist, Capt. Abraham Blackman, "in time" as a ubiquitous Black Everyman soldier (Peavy 249) who, like Ananse, is both teller of and participant in the tale. Also like Ananse, he is constantly at war with his nemesis and archrival, Maj. Ishmael Whittman, fictional corollary to the Sky God in Anansean myth. Symbolically this attribution is appropriate, considering the fact that the American military viewed itself as god of the skies with its use of the helicopter that afforded air superiority over the Vietcong during the Vietnam War. Although an omniscient narrator is apparent throughout the book, the voice is that of Capt. Blackman. Weaving a web through time from one historical incident to the next, he takes the reader with him on an epic odyssey through all the battles in which Blacks have fought for America.

Part 1 finds Blackman serving in the militias during the American Revolution and the War of 1812. During the Civil War he is a soldier with the Union Army. In Part 2 he fights in the Plains Wars as a member of the legendary Buffalo Soldiers of the Ninth and Tenth U.S. Cavalries. He later becomes a soldier in the Spanish-American War, and this section ends with the Brownsville, Texas, insurrection of 1906. World War I is the focus of Part 3, and the Spanish Civil War is the subject of Part 4. In Part 5 Blackman gets promoted to second lieutenant during World War II. Finally, in

Part 6 he not only becomes a soldier during the Korean War but also is promoted to captain during the Vietnam War. Later he thwarts attempts by White supremacists to annihilate the continent of Africa in a proposed futuristic race war. Ending back in Vietnam, where Abraham awakes from his reverie, the action of the novel comes full circle. In each of these wars several characters, in addition to Maj. Whittman, appear and reappear: Blackman's confidante and romantic interest, Mimosa, as well as soldiers under his command—Griot, Antoine, Woodcock, Doctorow, and Harrison. Their love for one another and their camaraderie enable them to survive—physically and emotionally—through all of America's wars in which they have fought with Capt. Blackman.

Rather than proceeding linearly through each of these time periods, however, through "multiple time shifts" (B. Bell 254) the action weaves in and out of time—from present to past to future to past again—in a cyclical fashion. Though each part depicts Blackman in a different war, action within the chapters flashes either forward or backward to the Vietnam War. This structure is significant because it emphasizes the "changing same" situation of the Black soldier in all of America's wars: that is, though the time and place might change, the discriminatory treatment is the same. It also underscores the Afrocentric world view that is cyclical. Williams's narrative technique, according to Gilbert Muller, reveals "there is a continuity to history: the present can be explained by the past . . . and the present can also predict the future" (105).

Beginning in present time during the Vietnam War, *Captain Blackman* opens with the protagonist being wounded and pinned down by machine-gunfire during a Vietcong ambush (13–15).[5] Blackman advances into enemy territory several paces ahead of his men, and realizing that they have been ambushed, he heroically jumps up to draw enemy fire. Putting himself in harm's way while firing his M-16, Blackman provides time for his men—Griot, Antoine, Harrison, Doctorow—and others to escape. Blackman's camaraderie with and protection of his men in Vietnam is a defining feature of his leadership style in all the wars that they have fought. His resulting injuries from the ambush include a very badly damaged leg, resulting in amputation. He also sustains a wound to the scrotum.

Blackman lies wavering between consciousness and unconsciousness (first in the Vietnam jungle and later in postsurgery convalescence), and Williams uses his "unconscious reveries" (Munro 92) to let him "relive in dream and hallucination" (Barthold 73) the role of the Black soldier in all of America's wars. Having done one stint in the army prior to the Vietnam War, Abraham has seen how Black soldiers have been deluded into believing that the military would give them a chance to demonstrate heroism and thereby win the respect of their officers and American people in general. Therefore, when he reenlists for another stint during the Vietnam War, he decides to teach a seminar on Black military history so that he can inform these modern Black soldiers, "with their . . . Afros and off-duty dashikis that they were not the first black soldiers to do what they were doing. He'd gone back to the American Revolution to Prince Estabrook, Peter Salem . . . and all the unnamed rest—all the wars" (14). In all of these wars, throughout the novel, Capt. Blackman is morale officer, charged with maintaining the "equilibrium" of the men in his all-Black regiment. As a confidence booster he assumes the role of mediator, like Ananse who mediates antinomies, between the Black soldier and the White military establishment.

Appropriately, and in accordance with the myth of Ananse, Williams casts Blackman in a dreamlike semiconscious reverie, a sort of shadow play, as though he were an actual participant in all of America's wars. Similarly, animal representations of human traits in African myth appear as a "shadow play." As such, according to Ivan Van Sertima, through these "dream figures" various "personality traits, values, or power relations of groups—commoner and king, slave and master, the weak and the strong, the powerful and the suppressed—may be reflected in a dreaming drama of the social world" (106). When this "dream figure (animal archetype)" subverts and overpowers societal oppression, then he acquires "a heroic cast and revolutionary function." In this respect, Abraham Blackman is not only a cultural hero but also a revolutionary.

Task of the Time Traveler: Setting the Record Straight

In his semiconscious state, Abraham Blackman hovers experientially throughout time like the trickster spider on the ceiling, watching events unfold and commenting on, while simultaneously participating in, all of America's wars in which Blacks have fought but have been denied equal treatment with their White counterparts. Like Ananse, with his short leg in the future and his long leg treading the path of the present and past, Capt. Blackman—who now has "one short leg" after his injury and subsequent amputation—provides a firsthand history lesson to reconstruct and thereby "correct the historical record" (Munro 93). He accomplishes this task by conflating events with abrupt time shifts.

During World War I, for instance, Capt. Blackman and his men are stationed in France. The French greatly admire Black fighting men, one of whom is Paul Belmont, a fighter pilot. Watching a "dogfight" between two "looping and spinning" planes, one French and one German, during World War II, Blackman wonders if the French plane is piloted by Belmont, a legendary Black flier. The scene abruptly switches to a young man named Belmont, who is a soldier during the Vietnam War, reading a newspaper clipping with the following headline: "PAUL BELMONT, EX-PILOT, DEAD; AMERICAN FLEW FOR FRENCH IN '18" (167). Sixty-seven years old at his death, the elder Belmont, grandfather of this Vietnam-era soldier, had been a distinguished member of the French Flying Corps in World War I, a spy for the French Army in World War II, and a bandleader and nightclub owner in Montmartre. His military honors were legion: Croix de Guerre, Médaille Interalliée, Croix de La France Libre, and Chevalier of the French Legion of Honor, to name a few. After several paragraphs listing the elder Belmont's accomplishments, the newspaper article ends on a note of irony: "More recently he operated an elevator in the RCA building here" (168). Consequently, the lot of Black war heroes is to come back to America to menial jobs and to die in obscurity. Shortly after reading this article to Capt. Blackman and taking pride in the fact that his grandfather was a man first and a heroic soldier second, young Belmont is killed in Vietnam by incoming rounds of mortar fire.

Many such incidents of unfair treatment as well as atrocities committed against Black soldiers in America's wars are often omitted from the historical record (as in the case of Dorie Miller mentioned above). In *Captain Blackman*, Williams includes many such instances, albeit in a fictive way. As a soldier with Peter Salem and Crispus Attucks in the Revolutionary War, Blackman notices that he (from the future) is the only Black soldier with a gun because during that time Blacks (slave and free) were issued only stakes, clubs, and spears (despite being put on the front line of battle), while White soldiers were armed with muskets. Angrily, the White soldiers set upon Blackman and beat him because he has a gun, but other Black soldiers come to his aid. Prior to this incident, Blackman, speaking in present-day vernacular, tells Peter Salem and Prince Estabrook (two Black Revolutionary soldiers who fell at the Battle of Lexington) about Paul Revere's ride and about their losing the Battle of Lexington: "them redcoats are gonna lay some shit on you dudes in a couple a days. That's what all the books say" (19). Salem and Estabrook think he is a "voodoo priest" because of his knowledge of future events.

The atrocities committed against Black soldiers are legion. During the Civil

War, Gen. Nathan Bedford Forrest ordered the slaughter of three hundred Black troops, dismembering their bodies, after they had surrendered at Fort Pillow (67). Additionally, after declaring there was "no such thing as a black prisoner of war," the Rebels decapitated, castrated, and shredded with bayonets captured Black soldiers (65). Other atrocities include the massacre at Tombolo during World War II in which two hundred Black soldiers, fed up with harsh treatment from White officers, deserted the army with their Italian girlfriends and took refuge in the swamps. Under pretext of fighting the Germans, the general ordered a battle against the Germans "near enough to Tombolo for Tombolo to be the objective" (267).

After the massacre, an ambulance detail removed only White bodies for four days. Noticing no Black bodies in the ambulances, Blackman discovers that "they were left where they fell" (267). Whittman then tells him derisively that these Black soldiers will be listed as "killed in action" and that their surviving families will receive "ten thousand bucks." Blackman, outraged at the army's callousness, threateningly jabs his finger in Whittman's face, swearing: "I don't know when [or] . . . how, but Whittman, I swear before God . . . you . . . [will] pay for this" (268). Prior to this incident, these same soldiers had been beaten and harassed by White officers because they were dating Italian women. An ensuing riot precipitated the Tombolo incident (260–70). Whether the incident at Tombolo actually happened is a matter of speculation, as Dan Georgakas discovered in an interview with Williams who said that "the black grapevine said it happened," and that based on the "bits and pieces of information" available, he constructed the story (56). Williams goes on to say that all the other historical incidents in the novel were well researched and are true, a fact to which C. Lynn Munro attests in vouching for Williams's accuracy concerning these historical events, fictive embellishments notwithstanding (92).

Williams further sets the historical record straight by focusing on broken promises made to Black soldiers as an incentive to fight. For example, enslaved men who fought during the American Revolution were promised their freedom (34) and compensation (48–49) provided they fought on the side of the American colonists against the British; similarly, years later during the Civil War they would be promised freedom again. However, in both cases neither freedom nor pay eventuated (37). During the War of 1812, a group of Black soldiers whom the Whites called "Freejacks"—a "tough," "proud" clan—had fought valiantly and were promised a place in the army for doing so. However, in February 1820, the offices of the adjutant and inspector general issued the following statement: "No Negro or Mulatto will be received as a recruit of the Army" (56–57). Then in 1944, Gen. Dwight D. Eisenhower issued an order granting all soldiers, "without regard to color or race," the opportunity to fight with veteran soldiers to deliver the "knockout blow" to the Germans (273). However, this order was rescinded when Lt. Gen. Walter B. Smith revealed to Eisenhower the implications of putting Blacks "shoulder to shoulder" with White soldiers on the front lines of battle (274–75). The overriding concern was that Black troops, if deployed for combat on the front lines in Europe, would be "left over there to get *French, German, Dutch, English, Belgian, Luxembourger women*" (277). As critic Houston Baker Jr. points out, this preoccupation with Black men having sex with White women results from White male ambivalence about the "black phallus" (*Blues* 181).[6]

Partially because of the extensive historical detail interspersed with fictive elements in *Captain Blackman*, Dan Georgakas has described Williams's style as "melodramatic" (56). To the contrary, I agree with Muller that the effectiveness of Williams's technique in the novel resides in "narrative fiction and narrative fact . . . fus[ing], becoming mutually sustaining elements" (104). This innovative technique is especially well suited to Williams's purposes. Because of the novel way that Williams employs documentary fiction, Barbara Foley refers to *Captain Blackman* as a "metahistorical novel" (256). For example, he devises the "Drumtaps" and "Cadences" sections, which cite actual incidents interspersed with fictional events and historical documents, for dramatic impact. Additionally, he fictionalizes accounts of real incidents, such as the massacres at Fort Pillow and at Tombolo. These incidents lend credence to the futuristic genocidal war that Whittman, in collusion with other European military powers, concocts. It is quite conceivable, then, that the same "powers that be" who authorized these incidents in past wars, in which Blacks were killed en masse, could set in motion events leading to the nefarious scheme of a futuristic war that Maj. Whittman plots and that Capt. Blackman thwarts. Williams's extensive documentation, according to Foley, "invests his metahistorical prophecy with . . . historicity" (257). In other words, Williams makes the point that the same kind of discriminatory treatment Blacks experienced during the Vietnam War has been the lot of Black soldiers throughout American history and will continue as long as racism exists in American society.

Marching to the Beat of Black Cultural Memory: "Cadences" and "Drumtaps"

Williams uses the "Drumtaps" and "Cadences" sections, interspersed throughout each of the historical periods in the novel, not only to juxtapose historical military events as they were reported but also to reveal the underhanded plans or the perverse motivations behind them. "Cadences," signifying the unimprovised, measured beat(s) of Eurocentric culture, detail the racist and/or imperialistic motives behind the actions of White characters (Harris, *Connecting Times* 30). Italicized at the beginning of several chapters, these sections present what Muller refers to as "parables" about the "hidden governments, composed of the military, economic, social, and political elite who conspire to rule the world and subjugate various peoples and races" (108). In that respect they serve as foreshadowing devices of the schemes that are devised by the protagonist's archrival, Maj. Whittman, to prevent Capt. Blackman and other Black soldiers from receiving the honors they deserve for acts of bravery.

Whereas "Cadences" signify the lockstep regimentation of the Eurocentric military establishment, the "Drumtaps" sections connote an Afrocentric world view wherein Williams uses improvisation to link certain incidents to African American cultural memory. In early African societies, the drum was very important as a means not only of communication but also of "historical preservation" (Asante, *Afrocentric Idea* 71). On a deeper level, Jahnheinz Jahn views the drums as tapping out a privileged "language" called "Nommo: the word of the ancestors" who "speak through the drums" (qtd. in Floyd, "Toward A Theory" 53). Williams uses the "Drumtaps" interludes between chapters to present heroic feats of Black soldiers during a particular war, as the ancestors speak to them throughout time. These segments include statements from military officers, presidents, and congressmen attesting not only to acts of bravery that contribute to the African American soldier's wholeness and self-identity but also miscarriages of justice by the military establishment that have the opposite effect.

Much more than an omniscient narrator, Capt. Blackman (in the guise of Ananse) is a "presence" throughout all the ages. Equipped with a sixth sense, an advantage of double consciousness, he observes and comments on all the behind-the-scenes maneuvers used to keep Black soldiers subjugated, demoralized, and emasculated and to deny them their rightful place in the annals of American history. For instance, in the "Cadences" section that precedes a chapter devoted to the Ninth and Tenth U.S. Cavalries who became known as the Buffalo Soldiers, a group of White army officers points to a U.S. map while speaking of western expansion and "Oriental" trade. The officers express the need to lay railroad tracks to "establish Anglo-Saxon civilization" across land that was occupied by Native Americans when they arrived and increasingly is being occupied by Whites known as "Squatters." To deal with this "problem," a general in the room suggests that the Ninth and Tenth Cavalries be brought in. Some of those present ask: "*Are those the niggers?*" Their overall irrational concern is the possibility of Blacks cohabiting with some of the White female settlers among the Squatters. The general then quips: "*Yes, sir . . . we're merely employing one group of natives, the niggers, to fight another group of natives, the Indians. The strategy has met with marked success in the British dominions; we would be seriously amiss if we failed to use the same method*" (96).

The Buffalo Soldiers played a contradictory role in the Plains Wars, the irony of which is not lost in Williams's novel. In an article about an American history tribute at the Buffalo Soldiers Museum in Tacoma, Washington, Sgt. Daniel Schroeder relates the history of these cavalry and infantry regiments that were formed less than seven months after the Emancipation Proclamation. They were comprised of Black enlisted men, many of whom were veterans of the Civil War, and staffed with White officers. Additionally they fought in the Spanish American War, Philippine American Insurrection, the Mexican War, San Juan Hill, World Wars I and II, and the Korean War. The museum event was held not only to pay tribute to the Buffalo Soldiers but also to honor Danny Glover, who coproduced and starred in the made-for-television movie *Buffalo Soldiers*. In his remarks he expresses their dilemma thusly:

"As I learned more about the soldiers, I felt they had to prove themselves as Americans post slavery," Glover said. "The Buffalo Soldiers were caught up in the dilemma of racism and trying to find a way to be respected and honored as citizens. The soldiers were used in various ways, sometimes not in favorable roles."[7]

Despite the paradoxical situation in which they were placed, the Buffalo Soldiers proved themselves worthy warriors and were greatly admired because of their bravery by the Native Americans against whom they were ordered to fight; however, they received little recognition from the U.S. military for their efforts. Responsible for the Roughriders' victory at San Juan Hill during the Spanish-American War, they received no acknowledgment in the history books, a fact that the "Drumtaps" section reveals. Despite Theodore Roosevelt's racist remarks that "Negro soldiers were peculiarly dependent on their white officers," Senator Nathan B. Scott presents a different view. He reports that "if it had not been for the gallant and courageous action of the Tenth Regiment of Cavalry at the battle of San Juan we might not have the privilege of having in the White House that . . . 'square deal' and patriotic President [Theodore Roosevelt] of ours" (131).

Time Travelers: Soldiers in Arms on the Heroic Quest

Throughout *Captain Blackman* Williams uses as a unifying device the appearance and reappearance of certain characters. Some of these are men in Blackman's military company or platoon who appear and reappear fighting alongside him in various wars, from the Revolution to the Vietnam conflict. These include Griot, Antoine, Harrison, Doctorow, and Woodcock. One of the major characters, however, is a woman named Mimosa, Abraham Blackman's love interest.

Interestingly, the narrator describes Mimosa as "kind of Amazonian" and speculates that this attribute brought her and Blackman together: "a big man, a big woman" (285). She is, literally and figuratively, a larger-than-life character whose role is nurturer and sustainer of the larger-than-life hero.

In present time, Mimosa works for the U.S. embassy in Vietnam (316). As a librarian, she supplies Abraham with books to teach Black history classes to the young Black recruits. As his soul mate, she anticipates his needs and is constantly by his side, comforting him during his hospital stay after he is wounded in Vietnam. During the Civil War she is an enslaved woman whom Blackman defends against Whittman, a Southern White soldier, who attempts to rape her (73–74). Being wounded in the process, Blackman is thrust back into the present time and is angry beyond belief when he regains consciousness. As a college student at Drake University in 1917, Mimosa Rogers works with a civilian committee during World War I to "deal with the officers" against whom Black servicemen have leveled complaints. During World War II, 'Osa (as she is called in this chapter) is a woman whom Blackman meets at a United Service Organization show (235–38).

Mimosa as Tree of Life

Each time Blackman regains consciousness in present time, Mimosa is by his side offering words of comfort and whispering sweet nothings in his ear. Despite the injury to Blackman's scrotum, she constantly reassures him of his masculinity. As his sexual partner in the past, present, and future, she is a constant reminder of his manhood. The supplier of books for his Black military history courses, she provides an important connection with the African and African American past. Mimosa also becomes an important link with the future when Blackman enlists her help researching information about the African continent so that he can devise a strategy for short-circuiting the futuristic war against Africans that Whittman and his cronies have planned. Williams's choice of this larger-than-life woman as companion for Capt. Blackman enhances the overall mythic structure of the novel.

Mimosa helps Capt. Blackman regroup, or pull himself together, after his literal and figurative fragmentation from gunfire during the ambush in Vietnam. Representing the African "Tree of Life,"[8] she stands by Blackman, giving him psychological support. Symbolically Blackman's scrotum injury is a commentary on the genocidal tactics of the American military, who place Black soldiers in large numbers on the front lines of battle. Abraham, for example, later discovers that Ishmael Whittman set him up by knowingly sending him into a hot landing zone, placing him in the line of enemy fire and making him a sitting duck for ambush. Consequently, Blackman symbolizes Black soldiers, in wars prior to and including Vietnam, who incurred dismemberments and casualties disproportionate to those of their White counterparts.

In African myth, the Tree of Life is represented by a baobab tree, which is used to symbolize strength and cultural connectedness. However, since the baobab, more than a thousand years old, is not indigenous to the West and does not thrive on American soil, Williams adapts for his use the mimosa tree. Even though alien to America (having been transplanted from the Eastern Hemisphere many years ago), it thrives in American soil. With lush, expansive foliage and graceful, spreading armlike limbs, it has beautiful, pink, delicately fragrant blossoms. The mimosa grows mainly in the warm, almost tropical regions of the southern United States where transplanted African cultural values are firmly rooted. Here the Black vernacular tradition thrives. Abraham Blackman's love interest Mimosa, whose ancestry is in Africa, like the mimosa tree is alien to America yet thrives on American soil. As Blackman's Tree of Life, she represents the nurturing influence of a time in Africa when heroic traditions from vernacular culture were intact and uninfluenced by Western conquest, dispersion, and colonization. Her healing presence, as a nurse in one of the wars, is a balm to soothe the sting of racial oppression and emasculation for Abraham. Mimosa therefore literally and figuratively grounds him in African and African American culture.

Capt. Blackman as Epic Hero

The main larger-than-life character in the novel is, of course, the protagonist Capt. Blackman. An epic hero of a very imposing stature, he is referred to throughout the novel as "big, tall, and muscular." Griot, a Creole fighter during the War of 1812, says he wants to fight "beside the big man, Blackman" (50) for protection. During World War I while in training to be a medic, Blackman has been labeled "a troublemaker" for trying to institute changes to make life better for Black soldiers. While walking one day, preoccupied with his thoughts, he accidentally bumps into a White lieutenant named Gahagan, and his "two hundred pounds" knock the lieutenant down and send him skidding down the street (149). Also during World War I in France, Gen. Le Gallais, while watching (at that time) Sgt. Maj. Blackman put several squads through drill, quips: "What a huge man he is." Moreover, the French general is amazed at the accomplishments of the "colored" troops in spite of the American military's refusal to issue them guns (163).

Later, in a battle with the Germans, Blackman with a lead squad is shooting from a foxhole. After heavy shelling, "Blackman's position was a gaping hole of fresh-black earth" (185). Seeing pieces of human bodies strewn everywhere, Lt. Woodcock suspects the worst has happened to Capt. Blackman: "First they uncovered Blackman's head, sure it was all they'd find because of the angle at which it was stuck in the ground. But the neck came after, then the shoulders . . . then the torso, the arms intact, the pelvis and legs attached" (186). All the men in front of and behind Blackman have been blown to bits; however, his body is miraculously reassembled, a feat befitting an epic hero. Later, following the mortar attack in Vietnam, his physical strength is evident when, during the Medal of Honor awarding ceremony in the hospital, the general shakes his hand. Blackman's grip is so strong, despite his weakened condition, however, that it causes the general to grimace. He emits a sigh of relief when Blackman releases his hand (318). After being blown to bits in World War I, weakened by battle fatigue and injuries in other wars, and gravely wounded in Vietnam, Abraham Blackman is still strong and virile, as opposed to his wimpy nemesis, Maj. Ishmael Whittman.

Maj. Whittman as Archenemy

Ishmael Whittman, a mean, mindless megalomaniac, is the White Everyman officer who is foil to Capt. Abraham Blackman. Though his characterization may be somewhat oversimplified (his name being a play on the words "White man"), he wanders through time with Capt. Blackman as his epic enemy, and their classic battle is replayed over and over throughout the novel in various wars. For instance, during the American Revolution, it is Bn. Cmdr. Whittman who takes away foot soldier Blackman's gun and beats him because only white soldiers have permission to carry guns (22–23). During the Vietnam War, when Whittman hears that Blackman has been injured in the mortar attack, he hopes Blackman has been killed. One reason (among many) is his anger about Blackman's teaching the Black military history seminar, which the general approved over his objections (40–42). During World War II Whittman is furious when the general permits Blackman to remain in the room while white officers discuss the Tombolo massacre (268). Having met during the Korean War as buck privates, Blackman and Whittman are constantly engaged in contentious struggles. For instance, Blackman scored Grade I on the Army General Classification Test (AGCT), while Whittman scored Grade III (297–98); however, Whittman is later promoted to captain while Blackman only attains the rank of lieutenant. According to Blackman, this promotion, as well as Whittman's promotions over the years, has been based on "his skin and not his skill" (116).

Whittman's insecurity about being promoted over Blackman simply because of his race rather than his ability causes constant friction. An incident during the Korean War demonstrates their enmity: Blackman clubs Whittman to the ground because the latter cannot read a map but refuses to admit it, thereby causing potential harm to two squads of Black soldiers. This situation is not the only one in which Whittman has endangered Black soldiers, as later he reveals (in an aside) that he was responsible for the attack on the all-Black regiment in which Blackman was injured in Vietnam: "I sent him in when Intelligence, as usual, didn't know shit from shinola about what was out there" (301). Whittman's statement, "Die, you Black sonofabitch, this is the white man's army" (116), aptly sums up their adversarial relationship.

This battle between Whittman and Blackman is similar to that between the allegorical Ananse and the Sky God in many West African tales. According to Roberts, through sheer cunning and wit, the spider trickster, sometimes conceptualized as a demigod, manages to obtain from the all-powerful Sky God his food, thoughts, and stories. In these tales, the trickster's actions not only win the Sky God's respect but also benefit the community ("African American Animal Trickster" 106–7). Similar to Ananse who receives tangibles from the Sky God, Capt. Blackman receives from Whittman (symbolic of the U.S. military) the Purple Heart during World War I and the Medal of Honor in Vietnam for heroism, having been wounded in the line of duty while protecting his men under attack (317–19). Also during the Korean War he receives a medal. In terms of rank, over the years he has been promoted from buck private to sergeant major to captain. Blackman (despite his lower rank) also demands respect from Whittman, and he gets it, albeit in a most contentious way.

However, the most significant rewards are the honor and respect he receives from fellow Black soldiers and from the Black community in all the wars he has fought, from the Revolutionary War to Vietnam. For instance, the Black soldiers under his command in Vietnam readily acknowledge how they have benefited from the Black military history seminars by raising their fists in the Black power salute and giving the "handshake [the dap] . . . the same one being used all over the Army these days, wherever there were Brothers" (15). During World War I, Mimosa's parents (as symbolic representatives of the Black community) give Abraham a high approval rating when he takes her on a date during leave. Her mother keeps repeating what a handsome couple they make, while her father quips, "this *here feller* look to me like he can take care hisself with them Huns, Mamie" (152). While visiting Blackman in the hospital following the rocket attack, Woodcock, a Black medic, expresses the admiration of his fellow Black soldiers for the captain, telling Mimosa that he really "turned our company around. . . . A lot of the Brothers, they come over here and think they're the first . . . to ever get into the sh- stuff. . . . But the Captain, like, he brought everything down front for us. . . . Like, you know, Chuck's been f—. . . . tellin us how great it is to die for him."(286)

It is through Abraham's Black history lessons that these Black soldiers have been able to see through the illusion that America will deal fairly with them if they fight its wars. Asante's assertion that the "function of Afro-American myth in discourse is the demonstration of control over circumstances" (*Afrocentric Idea*

100) certainly applies in this instance. For Williams has shown, through the Ananse myth as embodied in Capt. Blackman, how knowledge of their history has enabled these Black soldiers to survive, cr in the vernacular to "get ovah."

The Signifying Monkey and Shine and the Titanic: Assertiveness and Survival

In addition to knowledge of Black history, yet another strategy of survival in African American culture is signifying,[9] and no one is better at this hallmark of Black vernacular cultural expression than the trickster. In addition to his adaptation of the Anansean trickster myth to fiction, Williams uses for narrative purposes another trickster figure—the Signifying Monkey—from the African American oral tradition called the "toast." An example of what Geneva Smitherman refers to as "lightweight" signifying (*Talkin' and Testifyin'* 120), the Signifying Monkey provides a rhetorical technique for Williams to handle the dynamics of character. Such balancing and counterbalancing of "techniques from oral tradition with those indispensable to writing" makes "morality work in written literature," according to Gayl Jones (13). The character Williams uses to introduce the Signifying Monkey is Linkey, an allegorical figure in *Captain Blackman* serving as a "link" with African American cultural memory by performing this "toast."[10]

The trickster, as embodied in Ananse and the Signifying Monkey, is a topos in Africa, the Caribbean, South America, and African America, according to Henry Louis Gates Jr., who also states that this toast "functions as a sign of the disrupted wholeness of an African system of meaning and belief that Black slaves created from memory, preserved *by oral narration* . . . and willed to their own and subsequent generations" (*Signifying Monkey* 5; emphasis added). The veracity of Gates's statement goes without saying because most African Americans who know the tale of the Signifying Monkey learned it from hearing someone else recite it orally rather than reading it. Linkey has learned this toast from other Black men, and during his incomparable delivery, he succeeds in lifting the spirits of the other men in his platoon as well as his own (243–45).

Despite a variety of versions (each taleteller developing his own style), the substance of the tales is the same now as it was before and during slavery, and Gates summarizes it thusly:

The Signifying Monkey invariably repeats to his friend, the Lion, some insult purportedly generated by their mutual friend, the Elephant. The Monkey, however, speaks figuratively. The Lion, indignant and outraged, demands an apology of the Elephant, who refuses and then trounces the Lion. The Lion, realizing that his mistake was to take the Monkey literally, returns to trounce the Monkey. (*Signifying Monkey* 55)

Guile and wit, characteristics that the monkey exemplifies in this toast, remained "necessary and ubiquitous tools with which to confront the dominant culture during and after slavery," observes Levine (*Black Culture* 380), and Williams uses it the same way in this modern context. The soldiers in *Captain Blackman*, many of whom are "grunts," or low-ranking soldiers, know that they do not have the rank necessary to confront their commanding officers directly. However, in this homogeneously Black communal setting they can vicariously participate in the psychologically satisfying pastime of "signifying" on their superior by listening to the performance of "The Signifying Monkey" in the same way that their predecessors in all the previous wars have done. In this respect, the trickster serves as a link among past, present, and future generations of African American soldiers.

In *Captain Blackman*, Linkey performs "The Signifying Monkey" during a time of Black resistance to the military. As a conduit for the transmission of folk cultural values, he is the allegorical "link" between the unbearable present for the Black soldier and his past oral tradition that helps him to survive. Linkey enters Blackman's life during a particularly depressing time when the captain discovers, despite having made the highest grade on the AGCT of all men (Black and white) in the company and having finished at the top of his class, that he will not be permitted to enter Officer Candidate School as the white recruits will. Instead, he and the other Black soldiers are assigned to a "Services of Supply unit" (241–42). During this time "Linkey was his [Blackman's] only consolation, he being even more glum than Blackman" (242).

Linkey's "glumness" results from his being fed up with the unfair treatment of Black soldiers (threatened with court-martial resulting from a riot started by whites) and his desire to go home to his wife whom he misses dearly. So he confides in Blackman about his plan to get a medical discharge, which involves having Blackman burst his eardrum. Blackman resists, of course, but Linkey makes him promise to do it anyway. After Abraham fails to accomplish the desired result by boxing his ears and firing a gun at close range, Linkey gives Abraham a hypodermic needle and asks him to puncture the eardrum. With great reluctance, Abraham complies, and Linkey receives a medical discharge. This incident is one of the many illustrating the desperation of Black soldiers, fed up with discriminatory treatment, who go to extreme lengths to be discharged from the military.

Just prior to his discharge, Linkey finishes his nightly letter to his wife. He then enters the barracks where the men are so enthusiastic about his performance they are willing to pay for him to "do the Signifying Monkey" and "Shine" (242). They love to hear him recite these toasts because "Linkey had a big, basso profundo voice, and he could recite with all the nuances; it was easy to laugh night after night" (242). They always get a good laugh because his presentation is as much performance as it is recitation. This kind of comic relief enables the men to "make the best of a bad situation," as Bobby Blue Bland croons in his blues song "I've Got to Use My Imagination," and survive to fight the next battle, on and off the battlefield.[11]

But the trickster tales, including "The Signifying Monkey" and toasts such as "Shine and the Titanic" (often shortened to "Shine"), offer more than comic relief. The performer of these oral folk tributes also demonstrates self-assertiveness, a trait that would be viewed as insubordination in another setting among military superiors. Earlier in the novel during World War I, a character named Richard Boston performs "Shine." Assigned to Sgt. Maj. Abraham Blackman's 369th Regiment, Boston is one of the "colored" troops who serve as "Infantry pioneers" in Gen. John J. Pershing's army in France. Described as "the company's raconteur, a bright-eyed slender ex-dining car waiter," Boston's "life until the Army" has been "measured by the three-foot aisle between tables and flashes" of innumerable towns "on the New York–Chicago run" (164). This "life" had offered little except taking orders interminably from whites and one-night stands. Here in Company C, however, while performing "Shine," he "basked in the attention of his comrades, . . . a life perhaps fuller than ever" (164–65).

Purported to have originated from the refusal of the captain of the Titanic to permit the legendary Black prizefighter Jack Johnson to book passage on its maiden voyage (Smitherman, *Talkin' and Testifyin'* 158), the legend of "Shine and the Titanic" (165–66) was born. According to the legend in this toast, a Black man named Shine is assigned one of the lowest jobs on the ship as stoker in the boiler room below deck. All the passengers, crewmen, and captain are, of course, white. Even though time and time again Shine warns the captain that the ship has sprung a leak and is sinking, the captain ignores him. When Shine persists, the captain tells him that the pumps will get out the water. However, the water level in the ship becomes dangerously high; so Shine, who is a good swimmer, jumps overboard and swims for shore. Despite appeals for help from a millionaire (offering the stock market), the millionaire's daughter (offering him sex), and the captain (offering him money), Shine swims on to safety. However, all the other passengers on the ship (all white) drown. With a name that has pejorative connotations, Shine reverses the negativity that his name connotes and becomes, instead, as Levine observes, "a culture hero whose exploits are performed in the name of the entire race. He breaks all precedents and stereotypes; he defies white society and its technology; and he triumphs" by asserting himself when it matters most (*Black Culture* 429). As a result, he survives.

Similar to Shine who defies the stereotype of the dumb darkey, the "colored" troops assigned to Sgt. Maj. Blackman disprove the stereotypical image painted by Gen. Pershing in particular and America in general (161–62). The French simply marvel at their exploits and show their appreciation by supplying the men with rifles (164), a privilege denied the Black soldiers by their own American military. Consequently, the men are given a tremendous morale boost from "nothing up to excellent" (162). Also similar to Shine, a lowly ship stoker on the Titanic, Boston who performs the toast is in a subservient position as dining-car waiter. Asserting himself among the dominant society on the train would have dire repercussions, but signifying here among the "brothers," he can shine doing "Shine." Note that the other men tell the performers of the toasts—both Boston and Linkey—to "do" rather than "say" the toasts ("Signifying Monkey" and "Shine"), emphasizing performance rather than mere recitation. Their performance of the toast is illustrative of the holistic aspect of Black vernacular culture that some refer to as "'dancin' the talk," wherein the speaker "dramatizes himself" and his presentation in "physical ways" (Caponi 28; Abrahams 135).

Signifying as Revenge: Blackman's Baser Side

This performance aspect underscores the "functionality" of signifying. Similar to the verbal dueling that the antagonists undergo prior to battle in the African *Epic of Sundiata*, "a dude can be properly put to rest" with signification (Smitherman, *Talkin' and Testifyin'* 82). Throughout the novel, Abraham Blackman signifies on his foil, Ishmael Whittman, by posturing in this manner. Williams's intent in the narrative is to dismantle all of Whittman's defenses, to chip away at his illusion (or rather "delusion") of power, while at the same time empowering Blackman. For instance, in response to Whittman's feigned gesture of "bury[ing] the hatchet" at the Medal of Honor ceremony, Blackman retorts, "Listen Ish. Don't pull that rank shit on me. I'll climb over there and beat your ass again. . . . And another thing: in Saigon they tell me this battalion believes in using black men on point for patrol units, squads and platoons. You still don't like niggers do you?" (315). Such encounters bring out the "baser" side of Capt. Blackman's character.

Like the duplicitous Ananse, Capt. Blackman exhibits paradoxical traits. In addition to being kindhearted and trustworthy, he can be bad-tempered and brash; and, at times, he engages in behavior that could be labeled degenerate through his defiance of society's acceptable codes of decent behavior. However, Ananse's appeal in Diasporan cultures is in his ability to balance these opposite traits. Williams uses Blackman's character in a similar way, for Ananse is, as Pelton characterizes him, also "'a schemer' . . . yet, he is, prototypically, 'wonderful'" (28). Considered by some as an iconoclast himself, Williams was criticized by many in society at large as well as the Black community for his views on Dr. Martin Luther King Jr. in his book *The King God Didn't Save.* In 1970 a reviewer at *Kirkus Reviews* reflected on what Williams viewed as King's key weaknesses: his religious naivete and idealism; his middle-class orientation that prevented his ability to relate to the underclass; his susceptibility to popularity and prestige; and "his tendency to step down from crucial confrontations and accept compromises."[12] His book having been published in 1970, Williams was castigated for such strong criticisms of the leader, especially so soon after his assassination. Controversial himself, it is little wonder, then, that Williams could also portray Blackman engaged in an iconoclastic act in the novel. In a display of what Smitherman would call "heavyweight" signifying (*Talkin' and Testifyin'* 120), Blackman exhibits lechery and cruelty when, in his semiconscious reverie from the bombing in Vietnam, he becomes a soldier during the Civil War.

As a vengeful act toward the South for all the horror that slavery has wreaked upon his people, as well as for all the Black soldiers who have lost their lives fighting to end it, Blackman conjures up a scheme to exercise his masculine sexual prowess on a white southern belle. This act will also be in retribution for that perpetrated by Whittman when he took advantage of Mimosa sexually on a nearby deserted plantation during the Civil War. Of course no society would consider such a reprehensible act to be acceptable according to civilized codes of behavior; hence the "taboo conduct" for which the trickster is known, according to Van Sertima (104). Jeanne Rosier Smith, in her discussion of tricksters in Toni Morrison's novels, points out that Sula, as trickster, "does not embody pure evil in the traditional religious sense, but rather she exists outside of a dichotomized good and evil. She is not immoral but amoral." Williams's adaptation of the trickster myth functions in a similar way; consequently, the trickster's amorality "sharpens the community's sense of a moral code" (117). Moreover, Trudier Harris notes the controversy among scholars about the "clash between amorality and the presumed morality practiced by people who ostensibly embraced Christianity."[13] Time and again in the "Cadences" and "Drumtaps" sections of *Captain Blackman*, Williams shows how numerous officers, professing Christian values, in the white military establishment have trounced upon and outrightly disregarded moral codes in their maltreatment of African American soldiers with castrations and other atrocities.

Nor should it be assumed that Williams condones sexual exploitation; rather, he depicts Blackman in a "shadow play" during his semiconscious reverie. Musing about his nefarious plan, he *imagines* "the sheer audacious horror of it, a black man barreling through centuries of monumental and ritualized taboo to revenge himself" (87). In this section of the novel, Williams exploits the most sensational of America's sexual taboos, a Black man copulating with a white woman, using it as a foreshadowing device for the dramatic conclusion of the novel, in which a mulatto (the result of miscegenation) strike force foils Whittman's plans to annihilate the Black race.

Finding an antebellum mansion, deserted of all its occupants except a "Rebel soldier and his woman" asleep, Blackman hovers over them (like the trickster spider), gun in hand, "enjoying the *prevision* of the shock the officer would have when he woke and found himself in the middle of the white man's nightmare" (88; emphasis added). Knocking the officer unconscious with the barrel of his revolver, Blackman gags him and then ties him to a chair with the woman's undergarments. Awaking, the woman faints when she sees Blackman. During this reversal of miscegenation in a *ritualized sexual encounter* with Capt. Blackman, she awakens again, "moving with him, her arms reaching up to encircle his back" (89). Symbolically, Williams expresses in this scene the revulsion-attraction, love-hate relationship of white America toward Blacks, a theme of ambivalence that is exploited in numerous other fictional works such as Richard Wright's *Native Son* and Ralph Ellison's *Invisible Man* wherein "the black phallus" is an "implicit major symbol" (Baker, *Blues* 181).[14] The same holds true for *Captain Blackman* in which the Black phallus symbolizes an "unconstrained force that white men contradictorily envy and seek to destroy" (182).

After Blackman completes his symbolic conquest, the woman faints again. By this time the officer is conscious, watching the encounter but unable to do anything about it: "his thin blue eyes made Blackman feel that he was looking through windows out into a universe empty of life" (90). Through the trope of "repetition and revision" (Gates, *Signifying Monkey* xxv), this ritualized sexual encounter is yet another example of Blackman's signifying on white society, whose greatest fear is of Blacks avenging the wrongs committed against them by whites during slavery. By taking the white woman and exerting complete control over her, he is symbolically overpowering American society, stripping it of all its pretensions to power and control. At the same time he is seeking retribution for all the wrong that whites have perpetrated on Blacks in the past. This act of sexual retribution is accounted for in the Anansean myth, which portrays the trickster spider as "loved and lovable," according to Van Sertima, yet iconoclastic "because his evil liberates rather than oppresses. He assumes aspects of evil in order to elude and conquer a condition of evil" (108). Also, Baker, in his treatment of the duplicitous trickster, observes that he participates in "radically antinomian activities—[such as] murder. . . . Paradoxically [he is] both anticonventional and culturally benevolent" (*Blues* 184).[15] Blackman's shadow play of "symbolic rape" of the southern belle during the Civil War era is done in the interest of critiquing America's actual rape of African women during enslavement.

On an extratextual level for the reading audience Williams as trickster and a writer who does not shy away from controversy, signifies upon, by calling out, European imperialists who forcibly took millions of Africans over a period of four hundred years during the *maafa raping the entire African continent.* In addition to the brutality of beatings and dismemberment, displacement and dislocation, and even death, across the African Diaspora, the Middle Passage caused further fragmentation of soul, spirit, and body. Similar to the Confederate soldier whom Abraham bound and gagged and who was helpless to come to the aid of the antebellum woman, this scene is symbolic (in reverse) of the situation in which male Africans, fettered and manacled below deck in the holds of the slave ships, were unable to protect the African woman.

Rather than making the Atlantic crossing alongside their men below deck, enslaved African women and children were placed on the "quarter and half decks," nearer white slaveholders so they could have easy access, according to Deborah Gray White in *Ar'n't I a Woman? Female Slaves in the Plantation South* (23). Baker points out how such "access," led to "willful rape—a violent, terrorizing abuse of African women sanctioned by ownership and enslavement" (*Workings* 124). Moreover, Angela Davis illustrates how the insidiousness of the act went beyond being an "expression of white men's sexual urges" stifled by the so-called chastity of white womanhood, and that rape of African women on the slave ships and on plantations was a "weapon of domination" (qtd. in Baker, *Workings* 125). She states further that it was a weapon of "repression," the "covert goal" of which was "to extinguish the slave women's will to resist, and in the process, *to demoralize their men*" who were listening below decks to their women and children being violated (125; emphasis added). Consequently, Williams's use of the paradoxical trickster's baser side is to bring awareness to and sharpen the reading audience's sense of the transgression of a moral code by white American society generally, and the military establishment specifically, as far as treatment of African Americans is concerned.

Tactical Maneuvers: Tricksterism and Signification as Subversion

To thwart demoralization and emasculation of the hero throughout *Captain Blackman*, Mimosa continually nurtures Abraham, assuring him of his masculinity even though his wounds and his amputated leg have temporarily incapacitated him. His role as her lover and protector of his men has not been affected by his wounds, including those to his scrotum. Demoralization of Whittman, on the other hand, is the aim of Blackman as he reverses the victim/perpetrator role. And "because history influences so much of the present and the future" (Munro 93), Blackman devises a scheme whereby the sins of the fathers will be visited upon future generations when the progeny of white slave owners' debauchery of enslaved women, a cadre of mulatto soldiers, declares war on Whittman. The scheming that whites have used in all of America's past wars to exert control over Blacks and maintain positions of power suddenly changes at the end of the novel in a quick reversal of fate. Of all the skirmishes in which the two archenemies, Blackman and Whittman, clash this is the most significant.

Signification and tricksterism converge with the coup de grâce Blackman delivers after devising a clever scheme to shut down America's war machine controlled by Whittman, thereby averting the annihilation of African people on the continent and across the Diaspora. As the scene of sexual conquest is symbolic of America's reaping what it has sowed, so is the final futuristic war scene in *Captain Blackman*. The final "Cadences" section occurs thirty years into the future. A top-level, highly classified meeting, consisting only of the highest ranking white military men from western European nations, is in progress (excluding even bartenders for fear of infiltration by Blacks). Conspicuously missing from this meeting, or so they think, are Black men. Topics under discussion include "getting back to a white Army" (325) and eliminating Blacks from the nuclear strike force so that nuclear war can be declared on Africa. During the discussion an unidentified aide (actually Woodcock) is helping to assemble charts and diagrams for the discussion, and since no one recognizes him, they continue with matters at hand. He is actually Black, but because of his pale skin and Caucasian features, the whites in the room think he is one of them. In effect, according to Blackman, because white America has been unable to notice anything beyond color, this racism will be the cause of its undoing, leading to its defeat in what it had planned as the ultimate war, the aim of which would be to establish global white supremacy.

While this meeting is in progress, Blackman lies in his hospital bed reflecting on the way in which Black soldiers have traditionally been deluded to believe their "enemy" (America) would reward their "service with equality" (326) only to have their hopes dashed in each war in which they have fought. He therefore devises a plan in which a group of Blacks light enough to pass for white will compose a strike force to become an American "Trojan horse." Such a tactic will be successful because mulatto soldiers will not arouse suspicion as to their subversive goals since they will be viewed as just another group of whites. To bring white society to its knees, Blackman must also neutralize western Europe. He reasons that it will take approximately thirty years to strategically station his mulatto strike force at the North American Air Defense Command, in Skylab probes, at the Pentagon, in ICBM silos, in nuclear armed tactical aircraft, and in the ground crews of tactical nuclear weapons systems in Europe. As the novel ends, it is thirty years into the future, and by this time, Whittman has risen to the rank of general.

Along with other high-ranking military men, Whittman boards a plane loaded with state-of-the-art sophisticated weaponry, and they set out on a mission to strategically bomb countries on the African continent to annihilate the Black population. Little do they know that Blackman's strike force of mulattoes has overtaken and dismantled all the strategic systems, causing Whittman's plan to fail. They discover that the unidentified aide attending the high-level meeting of top brass was Woodcock, one of Capt. Blackman's men who has been passing for white. Upon this discovery, Whittman, now on the verge of a breakdown when he discovers that Blackman and the mulatto strike force have outwitted him, says: "We don't have any nuclear attack system, that's all. It's been captured, and for all I know completely dismantled.... We're defenseless. You've been in a war for hundreds of years and you've just lost it.... You've just lost the war to the niggers" (335).

He then goes crazy. As the novel ends, Williams signifies upon the plantation tradition that stereotypically depicts Blacks as dimwitted coons. Blaring over the aircraft's loudspeakers is "Way Down Upon de Swanee Ribber," sung in Black vernacular. Rather than the stereotypical "darkey" depicted in this antebellum ditty, however, a cadre of futuristic Black soldiers, knowledgeable of the military's most sophisticated weapon systems, has effectively dismantled a global war machine bent on Black genocide. White America, which perpetuates such stereotypes, has underestimated the cultural binding force of these Afrocentric soldiers. Figuratively, these mulattoes are the progeny of white America's illicit relationship with Africans in America. When the lines of demarcation between Black and white are no longer distinct and Blacks have access to technology befitting their expertise, the playing field levels. Whites no longer have the advantage. The mulatto strike force that Capt. Blackman assembles at the end of the novel is a case of the chickens coming home to roost: Whittman (white society) has engendered, literally and figuratively, the object of his (its) own destruction. The action of the novel has therefore come full circle. Whittman's (white America's) destructive past (slavery and miscegenation) has caused its future destruction.

Balancing the Contradictions: Black History as Corrective

Williams takes the position that throughout America's history, Blacks as a racially identifiable group have been targets of exploitation and discrimination. The institution of slavery has produced African Americans who, by virtue of their mixed heritage, are plagued with "double-consciousness." The visionary W. E. B. Du Bois expresses this peculiar situation best in his turn-of-the-twentieth-century work *The Souls of Black Folk*, when he says that the African American is "gifted with second sight in this American world.... It is a peculiar sensation, this double consciousness. ... One ever feels his twoness,—an American, a Negro; two souls, two thoughts, two unreconciled strivings" (45).

In *Captain Blackman*, Williams shows how this condition causes the Black soldier to have mixed allegiances: he is torn between fighting America's wars for freedom and democracy against other nations, while at the same time agonizing over the fact that he is not receiving the dignity and respect he deserves from America, the country in which he was born but which has never extended to him all the rights and privileges of his white counterpart. In addition to incorporating a blues paradigm through the use of the Black vernacular in *Captain Blackman*, Williams also skillfully adapts the myth of folk trickster hero Ananse the Spider, the duplicitous mediator between material and spiritual existence, to balance these inner "unreconciled strivings" as well as the external antithetical forces in society arrayed against the Black soldier. By pitting Blackman against Whittman in this manner, Williams has effectively exploited the conventions surrounding the Anansean myth to portray the Black soldier's dilemma in all of America's wars, prior to and including the Vietnam War, because as S. L. Ansah points out, the Ananse narratives "not only reflect but also seek to provide *resolutions* to underlying eternal conflicts in human societies between good and evil, right and wrong, life and death, love and hate, wisdom and folly" (51; emphasis added).

The resolution Williams provides in *Captain Blackman* is knowledge of Black history. During his first stint in the army, Blackman has only a limited perspective from which to view his role as a Black soldier fighting for America's (Whittman's) military. At the end of his first tour of duty he returns to America and enrolls in college. After finishing college and returning to the military as morale officer to teach Black military history, however, he provides for the other Black soldiers a vantage point from which to view their situation. A global war machine of mind control deludes the Black soldier into thinking that he will receive respect for acts of valor on the battlefield as well as dignity and honor when he returns home. By learning and then teaching Black history, Capt. Abraham Blackman effectively dismantles this machinery of mind control to bring about a realization that the Black man generally, and the Black soldier particularly, can control his own destiny through the knowledge of his heritage—a knowledge rooted in African American folk tradition—providing insight into the nature of heroism for the Black soldier and, above all, arming him with the skills needed to survive.

Capt. Blackman goes back to college and learns Black military history to then teach it to young Black recruits. Though many incidents of Black heroism went unrecorded, these valiant soldiers in the past persevered and passed their legacy on to future generations. Knowledge of their exploits enables present-day soldiers to survive. Similar to Capt. Blackman, the protagonist of *De Mojo Blues*, Tucept Highjohn, goes back to school after returning home from the war, but not in the traditional sense. After meeting a conjure man in Vietnam who helps him to get out of the war alive, Tucept goes to the school of life where he learns the ancient African spiritualistic practice of Vodoun (voodoo). Having learned that the rituals associated with Vodoun constituted indigenous spiritual practices of Black folk and that they were revolutionary, Tucept becomes empowered after being dishonorably discharged from the army for a crime he did not commit. The object of his heroic quest goes beyond self-empowerment, however. His journey is not complete until he empowers the Black race—past, present, and future. And the delicate balancing act of Black survival in America continues, even as Ananse continually spins his web.

CHAPTER 3

Reading the Signs

Re-Membering the Legacy of Voodoo as Path to Empowerment in *De Mojo Blues*

That which we call close "reading," the Yoruba call *Odafa* ("reading the signs") . . . *tufunaalo* ("bringing out the interstices of the middle").
>—Henry Louis Gates Jr., "The Blackness of Blackness"

Even today, much of the ongoing malaise, psychic and mental confusion, and spiritual pathology that many in the diaspora are experiencing, may be directly related to their dis-connectedness from the very gods and ancestors who are inextricably connected to their soul and psyche.
>—Mamaissii Vivian Dansi Hounon, "Vodoun"

People who understand power always understand the power of ideas and symbols.
>—Erskine Peters, *African Openings to the Tree of Life*

Characteristic of many novels about the Black experience in Vietnam, *De Mojo Blues* by A. R. Flowers opens with the Black soldier returning home from war. In this instance, the protagonist, Tucept Highjohn, and his two army buddies, Mike Daniels and W. E. B. Du Bois Brown (aka Willie D.), arrive in

California in 1970, a part of the contingent of President Richard M. Nixon's troop withdrawals on the heels of Vietnamization.[1] They are the three surviving Black members of their platoon. In addition to a court-martial, they have been stripped of their rank and all their medals, and they have been dishonorably discharged. The three returning soldiers project the classic image of Black male powerlessness as they emerge from the plane in handcuffs and shackles, victims of a false murder charge resulting from a fragging in Vietnam.[2] Sounds of clinking chains conjure up images of slavery, emasculation, and disempowerment. This sense of being helplessly manipulated by powers beyond their control recurs several times during Tucept's post–traumatic stress disorder (PTSD) nightmares when he returns to America. Despite being manacled and enchained, however, the men walk upright, their heads held high, displaying solidarity with the other brothers lined up along the ramp, who give them "power salutes" as they deplane at Oakland's army base. With "double beat to the chest and upraised fist, chains jingling faintly as if they were bells" (7),[3] the three file in for final processing. This "power salute" from Black expressive culture, as well as other Black male bonding rituals such as the "dap," enable them to cope with the racism they experience in Vietnam and in America. These rituals signify not only unity among the men but also a defiance of racist attempts to control their minds.

The Hero in Search of Power: Divergent Paths on the Heroic Quest

The action that causes Tucept, Mike, and Willie D. to return to America enchained is predicated on a racist assumption dating back as far as American slavery: that Black males seen in the vicinity of a murdered White man are responsible for his death. The victim is 2nd Lt. Andrew Kicks, the young White commanding officer of Tucept's platoon who has acquired quite a reputation for his harsh treatment of Black recruits. He usually gives them the most distasteful assignments such as "shit detail," that is, pouring on oil and burning refuse in the latrines. The odor emanating from this conflagration often penetrates the clothes and skin. The stench, which remains long after the detail has ended, penetrates the skin like the stigma of being Black in a White man's army and suffering the consequences thereof.

Blacks are most often given the dangerous assignments as well, such as the ordeal of pulling point. There are numerous instances of Black soldiers being placed on the front lines of battle, usually in the point-man position as well as the backup man directly behind him. This placement, of course, makes them more vulnerable to gunfire than those farther back in the column.[4] Kicks usually put Jethro Tree, a young Black recruit fresh out of Mississippi, on point with Tucept as backup. While they are out on a search-and-destroy mission,[5] Kicks attempts to call in an air strike while another Black recruit, Prester John, is still in a tunnel searching for Vietcong. To prevent the possibility of the tunnel rat's death while he is still trapped underground, Jethro blasts the radio to bits with his M-16 so that Prester John will have time to emerge from the tunnel. Obvious to the Black soldiers is that Kicks could care less if Prester John were killed while still underground, and this instance is only one of many in which Black solidarity ends with lives saved. However, in spite of Jethro's valiant action to save another soldier's life, Kicks punishes him severely.

A few days later the fragging of Kicks occurs, and Sgt. Gill, another White officer, sees "one of the colored soldiers" run by his tent shortly after the explosion. Because Kicks has the reputation of being a "nigger hater," often exhibiting dislike for any signs of Black solidarity, it is assumed that the three surviving Blacks in his squad—Tucept, Mike, and Willie D.—are responsible for his death (170). Consequently, based solely on the testimony of Sgt. Gill, who cannot positively identify the assailant(s), the army sends the three Black soldiers back to the United States in chains, stripped of their dignity for a crime they did not commit despite having put their lives on the line for their country.

Flowers's characters metonymically portray various approaches of the African American community's response to racism in American society. Willie D. symbolizes those who choose to defy the system, setting up nonprofits and working with the dispossessed who have been marginalized and lost hope of becoming a part of the economic and social mainstream. Mike, on the other hand, represents that segment of the Black community seeking upward mobility on the ladder of success by accumulating wealth and becoming a part of the military-industrial complex. This group aspires to assimilate and become a part of middle- and upper-class mainstream America. Tucept metaphorically occupies the middle ground between the two extremes as an arbiter of opposing points of view to search for the optimal means of survival in a racist society. As hero of *De Mojo Blues*, he then symbolizes a balanced approach by bringing together the disparate segments of the Black community toward a realization that their survival in a hostile society is taking the best of each of these paths to empowerment and working interdependently to achieve success for the whole. He empowers with knowledge of African American history and with the freedom that comes with recognizing one's own individual worth.

Willie D: Revolutionary

When they arrive back in the World, Tucept's two buddies attempt to put their lives back together by seeking avenues to self-empowerment while pursuing divergent career paths to accomplish their goals. Willie D., who grew up in Fort Bragg, North Carolina, volunteered for the army, desiring to be a lifer; however, the court-martial has cut his career short. Upon his return, he settles in Harlem and becomes actively involved in the gentrification battles that are raging in urban America during the late sixties and early seventies. A dreadlocked activist for the rights of the inner-city dispossessed, he, along with his female companion and a small cadre of like-minded individuals, wages war against the unseen but ever-present slum landlords reaping benefits from the evictions of poor tenants who can ill-afford exorbitant rents designed to force them to vacate property so that the landlord can restore it and then rent it to White suburbanites at prices too high for the displaced residents to afford.

Determined to put an end to such exploitation and reclaim the land, Willie D. occupies an apartment in one of these dilapidated buildings, gradually refurbishing it and daring the powers that be to evict him. Attempting to ambush his efforts, the absentee landlords employ arsonists to torch the buildings (one such incident having resulted in the death of an elderly Black woman) and thereby drive him out along with the other so-called squatters. Interestingly, torching homes parallels the actions of American soldiers in Vietnam. They often used flamethrowers as one of the methods to destroy Vietnamese villages during search-and-destroy missions. Similar to African American urban dwellers, these Vietnamese villagers were also attempting to reclaim their land from the imperialistic powers who had sought to colonize them and exploit their resources. Consequently, for Willie D. the war has been literally brought home. He also organizes co-ops to help low-income residents become self-sufficient so that they can survive without the assistance of the exploitative system that keeps them subjugated. Working with grassroots organizations outside the system is Willie D.'s vision of empowerment for Blacks in America.

Mike: Lawgiver

Tucept's other surviving army buddy, Mike, on the other hand, has a different vision for empowerment based on individual success within the system. While in Vietnam he constantly talks about the acquisition of money as being the path to power. Drafted into the army following his attorney father's unsuccessful attempt to get him a deferment, Mike follows in his father's footsteps by attending law school when he returns home from Vietnam. During his matriculation at Georgetown University School of Law, he aligns himself with Acme, a powerful company symbolic of the military-industrial complex with ties to the political power brokers in Washington, DC.

Having worked part-time for Acme while in school to make the right connections, he later hopes to acquire a judgeship now that he has become an attorney. For Mike, individual initiative, drive, and determination to change the power structure from within the system are the keys to effecting real change for Blacks in America. Doggedly, and sometimes ruthlessly, he forges ahead to achieve his goal. Divorced and sporting all the accoutrements of an upper-middle-class lifestyle, Mike has sacrificed along the way to make his individualistic bid for fortune and fame in the World a reality. The attempts of Tucept's buddies to find self-empowerment—one outside and the other within the system—prefigure Tucept's heroic inward journey toward self-awareness and his outward journey to empower the Black community.

Tucept: Healer

Occupying the interstices, or the middle ground, between these ostensibly opposite positions is Tucept, who has grown up in a middle-class environment in Memphis, Tennessee, his father a physician and his mother an artistic scholar who practices the African ancestral healing and spiritual system of Vodoun (voodoo). Meandering through life, unsure of his destination or how he will get there, Tucept had been a "practicing college militant" (23) before the war. When he returns home from Vietnam initially, he goes back to college where he becomes a "professional junior" at historically Black Fisk University. As a veteran, he encounters resistance and hostility from politically aware students who view his service in Vietnam as traitorous to the Black community resulting from his service overseas as a part of an occupying army fighting another people of color. They also view the Vietnamese struggle for self-determination similar to that of Blacks in America in the midst of the civil rights and Black power movements.

Expressive of her allegiance to the revolutionary thinking that grew out of these movements, Tucept's girlfriend, Ruby, now sports a halo of an Afro to symbolize her newfound Black pride. Their relationship having become a "casualty of war," she responds to him with nonchalance and indifference at the prospect of taking up their romance where they left off when he went overseas. Adding to Tucept's dubious welcome back home, his girlfriend's acquaintances who belong to a popular fraternity treat him with derision not only for his service in Vietnam but also for his decision to "volunteer" for the army,[6] calling him "a nigger fighting gooks for crackers" (26). These young men sit around and "philosophize" with Ruby about the war,[7] while Tucept and his fellow soldiers have actually experienced it. In response to the problem of his lukewarm reception by friends and associates back home, Tucept, the warrior-hero, drops out of college and decides to go to the "school of life" so that he can devote his time to the study and practice of voodoo to regain his manhood and reconnect with the Black community.

Through a series of flashes backward and forward in *De Mojo Blues*, Flowers juxtaposes the experiences of Tucept in Vietnam with those of his preenlistment family life (past), his post-Vietnam attempts to readjust to American society (present), and his panoramic vision (future) of a world that places all of his individual experiences in a wider, communal context of the Black experience from pre-European conquest of Africa, to colonization and enslavement in America, to the present-day diasporic consequences thereof. Flowers's novelistic technique corresponds with that of the heroic journey in many African myths, in which, according to Clyde Ford, "human life corresponds to [an] endless round of nature, measuring life not linearly from birth to death but cyclically from the world of the living [present], to the world of the ancestors [past], to the world of the not yet born [future], to the world of the living again" (36).

Employing this Afrocentric world view, Flowers conveys the notion of reconnecting, or re-membering, the psyche of the Black soldier, as well as that of the Black community that has been dismembered by racism. Inherent within this world view is the paradoxical nature of human existence in African culture (Sims-Holt 159) that resides in various ritualistic spiritual practices. One of many African ancestral spiritual systems is Vodoun, also known as voodoo,[8] which provides an apt metaphor for the harmonizing of ostensibly different qualities within Tucept's character and the seemingly divergent paths to empowerment sought by the Black community as symbolized by the careers of Willie D. and Mike. The character Jethro and his spiritual counterpart, Spijoko, are pivotal to Tucept's recognition of life's paradoxical nature.

Vodoun/Voodoo: Subjective Correlative to the Heroic Quest

It is fitting that Tucept, the protagonist/hero-warrior of *De Mojo Blues*, be a student because the educational system in America teaches mainly Eurocentric mythology wherein Greek and Roman heroes serve as literary models. Stories about war enhance these models. Tucept cannot immerse himself in his college studies when he returns home from Vietnam because these models do not provide a formula for dealing with the contradictions inherent in his role as a young Black man fighting for a country that devalues his worth on the battlefield and at home. Where can he find heroic models within a culture like his to enable him to get his life back together? Moreover, where does the Black novelist look to find a literary corollary to portray the duality of the Black soldier's desire to perform heroically for a racist military while dealing with his own struggle for self-empowerment and the struggle of the Black community? Flowers looks to African American expressive culture. He metaphorically applies the spiritualistic practice of Vodoun, which Gale Jackson calls an "empowering force" (313), that the hero, Tucept, must use on his journey toward discovering his own identity and rebuilding the collective psyche of the Black community.

Vodoun, an ancestral spiritual system that is indigenous to West Africa, was transplanted onto American shores, and across the Diaspora, during the slave trade. Ritual is important in the practice of Vodoun, and during their worship ceremonies, many enslaved Africans "performed secret rituals to their divinities of war," according to Mamaisii Vivian Dansi Hounon (3). She goes on to say that "it was this . . . ritual . . . that incited the most fear and hatred in the hearts and minds of the slave owners, and American White citizenry . . . [who] learned only too well of the efficacy of its power" (3). The philosophical structure of Vodoun, as well as its "ritual and cultural" practices, places emphasis on the "warrior gods," Shango and Obatala, who enabled the Africans to survive during several hundred years of struggle toward freedom. These gods are allegorically represented as concepts, or two paradoxical manifestations, of Tucept's ("two concepts") persona.

Because of defiant adherence to their ancestral religious practices during which the warrior gods were invoked to aid in carrying out insurrections, Vodoun practitioners posed a threat to the institution of slavery. Also, efforts by slave owners to convert many practitioners to Christianity failed initially. Consequently, Whites instituted draconian methods to deal with the situation, which included an aggressive campaign to eliminate traditional African religions by levying heavy fines as well as brutally beating and sometimes killing adherents. It is this revolutionary aspect of the spiritualistic practice that lends itself to use as a subjective correlative to Tucept's effort to transform himself after returning home from Vietnam, for voodoo has been referred to as a "powerfully transforming spiritual system" (Hounon 7). To be a priest or priestess in the practice of voodoo, as in most African/African American religions, one must first answer a call to lead others in the faith.[9]

Accepting the Call: Tucept as Moses of His People

Flowers, therefore, depicts Tucept as the unwitting Moses of his people, who receives the call and becomes their leader on a quest for healing and wholeness, replete with a Jethro as his guide and advisor. This depiction signifies upon Zora Neale Hurston's use of the Moses myth in *Moses, Man of the Mountain*.[10] In her fictionalized account, Moses has the distinction of being not only the "leader of the Jews" but also "the supreme magician of the universe" and the "most powerful hoodoo doctor of antiquity" (Hemenway 263). Hurston's account coincides with a pre-Christian "Talmudic ritual knowledge and practice" of many West Africans long before they were forcibly brought to the Americas. According to Hounon, these Vodoun practitioners were not familiar with him as "the Christianized Moses who led the Jews to the promised land, but rather as the 'great conjurer,' in which he was revered and celebrated for centuries as the 'bringer of the law,'" or Damballa of the Vodoun religion in Dahomey (2). Tucept learns about this heroic past as he prepares for his destiny to become Moses of his people in "dreamstate" (meditation), ultimately combining the characteristics of lawgiver, healer, and revolutionary during his heroic journey.

Flowers divides *De Mojo Blues* into three parts: "De Call," "De Quest," and "De Power." This tripartite structure coincides with the heroic quest in most cultures, which according to Clyde Ford, in *The Hero with an African Face*, can be summed up as "departure, fulfillment, and return": "A hero is called to venture forth from familiar lands into territory previously unknown; there the hero encounters marvelous forces and with magical assistance wins a decisive victory over the hindering powers of the unknown; then, with boon in hand, the hero returns to his land of origin" (18). During the course of his quest, the hero must delve deeply into his psyche to find strength and courage to survive while overcoming weakness and fear. According to the generic mythic paradigm, a hero's journey to self-actualization and fulfillment can begin with a chance encounter, a call or lure that appears to take him on a trail that sometimes leads to the underworld, symbolic of the unconscious or the subconscious. After returning home from the war, Tucept retreats to the forest where he takes up residence in a stilt house, symbolizing, in this case, his subconscious.

Tucept's call results from a chance encounter with Jethro, whom he meets in basic training camp in 1969 at Fort Campbell, Kentucky. Having volunteered for the army, Tucept must "venture forth" from his "familiar" surroundings at home and go to "previously unknown" territory in Vietnam. Though he does not know it at the time, his serendipitous meeting with Jethro sets the stage for his heroic journey in Country and later in the World. Jethro provides the "magical assistance" that the hero needs when he gives Tucept the High John the Conqueror (hereafter, the vernacular High John de Conquer) root and the mojo bag shortly before enemy fire reduces his own body to fragments—pieces of bone and blood and guts. From Jethro's fragments, symbolic of the dismembered bodies and minds of Africans who lost their lives during the Middle Passage and slavery as well as African Americans who have lost their lives in America's wars, Tucept finds new life and becomes committed to unraveling the mystery of the mojo, the "Black Book of Power."

Returning to his "land of origin" (America), Tucept, now armed with the High John de Conquer root and the mojo bag, sets out to discover the real root of power. Since the father often represents the "totality of the unknown" in mythic symbology (Ford 81), Tucept must experience a "father quest," during which he, the hero-warrior, must decide whether to choose his father's life path or to strike out into untested waters on his own. In the process, he must become reconciled with his father, from whom he has become estranged, because the father quest is also a quest to discover the hero's "own character and career" (89). After reconciliation with his father, a medical doctor, Tucept becomes a "rootdoctor"—Highjohn de Conquer, Hoodooman[11]—to cure what ails the spirit rather than the body. By doing so he conquers his lackadaisical attitude toward his goals in life and begins to heal his psyche that was wounded in Vietnam. The hero is now self-empowered, but his journey to fulfillment is incomplete until he heals the entire community, which also suffers the sting of racism and estrangement from its own heroes. By doing so, he fulfills another unique aspect of the quest for the "hero with an African face" and that is to find the point of balance, or harmony, between the individual quester and the community, "emphasizing neither to the exclusion of the other" (Ford 90).

Though man's struggle for wholeness knows no racial or ethnic bounds, the journey acquires a different hue when this cultural component of interdependence between the hero and the community is added to the quest. He has the responsibility of saving not only himself but also the whole community. Interdependence is the aspect that sets apart the African heroic tradition from that of Western or Occidental cultures (Ford 90). The communal nature of the heroic struggle that is illuminated in African epics in existence today, such as that of the hero *Sundiata*, were transcribed from African griots who performed them live before the whole village. In Igbo tradition, for instance, the protagonist in oral narrative performance is "portrayed as having to balance his personality and activities with that [*sic*] of the community" (Kalu, "Achebe and Duality" 22). This relationship can be summed up in the African proverb: "Because I am you are; because you are I am."

Tucept exemplifies the interdependent nature of African culture when he performs the final task of the African hero by consulting African elders while in a hypnagogic voodoo trance during one of his many meditative sessions in his stilt house in the woods. Re-membering the African past enables him to rely on ancient wisdom to solve his present dilemma; consequently, he is able to conjure up a myth for future generations of African Americans with their own heroes so they will not have to suffer broken minds and spirits for lack of knowledge of themselves and their culture. Instead, this myth will empower them to learn from past generations how to survive, individually and collectively, with dignity. The "mojo is knowledge," and, as Tucept discovers, "knowledge is power." Grace Sims-Holt's observation that "power is the ability to redefine" (151) appropriately sums up Flowers's conclusion in *De Mojo Blues* because by redefining the nature of the hero for the Black soldier, the protagonist has empowered himself and the Black community.

Jethro not only helps Tucept re-member by connecting him with his ancestral heritage but also aids in his survival on the battlefield in Country by helping him avoid dismemberment. Jethro Tree, "spontaneity incarnate" (44), is the opposite of Tucept Highjohn, who is laid-back and easy going. A native of Taproot, Mississippi, Jethro is "the company badman". Falling into formation incorrectly results in a punishment of ten pushups, after which he calls the drill instructor's (DI's) mother "a asshole" resulting in additional punishment on KP duty; and this is only his first day in basic training (45). Then he walks out on the training field in a bright red nylon T-shirt during the third week of basic training with full knowledge that such action will bring deleterious consequences. Jethro's body language and his rap are further cause for consternation on the part of his superior officers, as well as his insistence on wearing a loud green towel around his neck. These colors are significant relative to Jethro's symbolic persona. His commanding officer, 2nd Lt.

Kicks, invariably assigns him to KP duty or levies some other punishment because he is constantly breaking the rules. Suppression of Jethro's defiance of military dress and decorum becomes a priority for the lieutenant, who is nevertheless intrigued by Tree's indefatigability. A larger-than-life character, literally and figuratively, he becomes the crucial link in the chain connecting Tucept to a knowledge of voodoo and its psychological value.

Attempts by military officials to suppress vestiges of Black expressive culture in Jethro, such as playing the dozens, wearing bright colors, and rapping, are similar to those by Western society to suppress the practice of voodoo since the time of Black enslavement in America and across the Diaspora. Such attempts account, in part, for the element of magic becoming associated with voodoo. Because slave masters and other authorities prevented its practice as a religion, practitioners used "divination, manipulation, and herbalism" as elements to make it appear "magical" rather than religious (Mulira 36). Despite efforts to curtail its use among practitioners, however, voodoo remained a "complex and *functional* religion" with "duties, symbols, and rituals" (34; emphasis added). As Tucept later discovers, Jethro is a voodoo sorcerer who serves as an important link to his African cultural memory.

Voodoo Adaptations: Appropriating Catholicism

Tucept learns voodoo to use as a corrective for healing the fragmented spirits of Black folk resulting from the original forcible capture from their homeland and enslavement on foreign soil as well as the resultant systemic racism that continues to affect their daily lives. Fragmentation also results from the often involuntary servitude in the oppressor's military services. Flowers uses voodoo figuratively as a coping strategy to deal with the disease of racial injustice and maltreatment. Moreover, remembering this ancient ritual and applying its tenets enables Tucept and his buddies to re-member their fragmented psyches as African American soldiers so that they can survive not only the horrors of war in Vietnam but also the racism they will experience upon their return to American society.

Because restrictive laws and harsh punishment prevented enslaved Africans from outwardly practicing their indigenous religions, they had to do so stealthily or adapt to meet the situation. Adept at improvisation, enslaved Africans, like the legendary trickster figures from their cultural heritage, appropriated Western Catholic saints and cunningly worshiped voodoo deities through them (Mulira 36).

Consider, for example, the following adaptations: Obatala as Our Lady of Mercy and Our Lady of Mount Carmel; Eshu Elegbara as Saint Simon and Saint Anthony of Padua; and Shango as Saint Barbara and Saint Jerome, to name a few (Ford 154). In a similar way, African American soldiers have appropriated involvement in the military to earn prestige and status that are often denied them in civilian society. It has been said colloquially that the military is the only place where Black men, without advanced degrees, can be "boss" over Whites while acquiring recognition and awards through acts of valor on the battlefield, feats that they could not accomplish in civilian life ("Lead Story," BET).

Voodoo, similar to other indigenous African religions, is not a liturgical ritual restricted to observance on Sundays or Wednesday nights, as in many Western Protestant religions. Rather, as a "functional" spiritual system, it is interwoven into everyday cultural practices. It is a way of life. Though the perspective is debatable, Jessie Mulira argues that of all the African mores and folkways that survived the Middle Passage, including dances, folktales, music and rhythm, foods, mannerisms, extended family concepts, and respect for elders, voodoo was the most dominant and intact of all African survivals (36). Additionally, it played a role in slave insurrections; hence its association with revolutionary protest, adherents often using it as an "organized force against a common enemy" (37). Documentary evidence reveals that at least two of the many slave revolts were led by conjure men: one in New York in 1712 and the other in North Carolina in 1822, the famous "Gullah Jack" rebellion. Slave rebellion leaders often wore around their necks bags with "bits of paper, bones, or potions to provide protection and good luck by warding off bullets" (37). Significantly, Jethro wears around his neck in Vietnam a leather "mojo bag" containing bones, and shortly before being killed he gives the bag to Tucept for protection. This revolutionary component and the psychological efficacy of voodoo provide the basis of Flowers's choice of a voodoo sorcerer for the hero in *De Mojo Blues*.

Vodoun/Voodoo Functionality: Orishas as Manifestations of the Psyche

Such functional use of voodoo, the main value of which is "psychological" (Mulira 37), distinguishes it from religions such as Protestantism and Catholicism, mainly because the concepts of "deity" and "divinity" are viewed differently in African and Western religions. Ford makes the distinctions thusly: "In the West we regard deities as facts of life from which attributes proceed, rather than personifications of attributes found in nature and in ourselves" (144). Viewing a deity as a "fact" causes one to consider it as an entity "outside oneself"—in heaven above or hell below. However, as "symbols representing the source energies of life, deities are experienced as part of oneself. . . . The forces that motivate us are themselves the gods and goddesses within us" (144).

Flowers employs, structurally and thematically, this African concept of deity in his narrative adaptation of voodoo to illuminate the character of Tucept and his buddies in *De Mojo Blues* and to explore the healing process necessary to re-member the Black man's fragmented psyche, which has been torn asunder by racist forces in American society generally and by the experience of the Vietnam War specifically. Personifications of these deities, or forces in nature that reside in the unconscious mind, are called "orishas." Through meditation (dreamstate) or other types of ritual one can engage the archetypes residing in the psyche to achieve "original wholeness" (Ford 147). The origin of orishas, from West African creation myths, explains the quest of the hero for wholeness.

According to Vodoun creation myth, in the beginning, when everything was without form or substance, one godhead, known as Orisa-nla, was in existence. His slave, Atunda, one day rebelled, causing a huge boulder to roll down an embankment and smash Orisa-nla into hundreds of (by some accounts more than a thousand) fragments. The goal of the orishas, according to Ford, is "returning to that wholeness from which they were dashed" (147). The hero then pursues his quest for wholeness by engaging the orisha archetypes in his subconscious mind through various forms of ritual and meditation. As a hoodoo apprentice, Tucept engages the orishas through meditation. One archetypal manifestation of these deities, that Flowers uses symbolically in *De Mojo Blues* is Eshu, embodied in two forms: Jethro as an impetuous young man and Spijoko as an older, wiser man. The voodoo deities Shango and Obatala find expression in the dualistic, paradoxical character of Tucept.

Eshu: Cunning Trickster as Jethro

Eshu, archetypically, is the guiding force within us that leads us to "life-changing and life-maintaining insights" (Ford 159), especially when we have reached a crossroads in life and are seeking direction to make a change. There are two manifestations of

Eshu in *De Mojo Blues*—first as Jethro and later as Spijoko—both of whom serve as guides for Tucept on his journey to self-awareness and cultural definition. Exhibiting vitality, virility, and defiance, Eshu as a young man is a trickster. His characteristics are inherent in Jethro, the outlandish recruit who serves as a guide for Tucept until Jethro's death in 1971 in a hot landing zone (LZ). Prior to his untimely demise, Jethro takes Tucept through his rite of passage to Black awareness.

In the African pantheon, orishas "descend to earth from heaven seeking out humanity," whereas the reverse is true in Christendom (Ford 148). Hence, when they first meet, Jethro (Eshu disguised) says he is "assigned" to Tucept, and as a result of his clairvoyance, he already knows they are going to "hook up" in the army. Befitting any deity, Jethro is also imbued with oracular powers. His booming laughter "carries out into the jungle." The heavens even reflect his earthly presence, as "moonlight glinted off" the triangular "pale squares" that were his fingernails (62). Voodoo sorcerers are noted for filing their nails into triangular or "delta-cut" shape. Significantly, Spijoko, the voodoo sorcerer who is the spiritual counterpart of Jethro serving as Tucept's guide in the World, also has delta-cut nails.

As a "trickster," Eshu is the proverbial "bad boy" of the psyche (Ford 159). His mischievousness appears in Jethro, who has been labeled "company badman" (45). Also, similar to Eshu, Jethro's sexual exploits are legend. When the DI takes him to task for outlandish behavior, such as wearing the red nylon undershirt, he pulls down his pants to reveal the red boxer shorts that match. Disgusted, of course, the DI takes him to task, ordering fifty pushups. Jethro, whose finely toned body bristles with muscles, accomplishes this maneuver easily, after which he goes AWOL for five days, returning with "red soda." Tucept is aghast that Jethro would defy military protocol merely to get strawberry soda but learns later that he has been out on the town cavorting with the women. In fact, Jethro tells the DI that he wears red nylon underwear so that his women will not have on "better looking drawers" than his (45–46). But Jethro's penchant for bright colors is not limited to his underwear. He invariably wears a bright green towel around his neck that he uses to wipe sweat. And the Black leather mojo bag that he wears for good luck is fringed in red flannel.

Ritual Colors: Cosmic Order and Liberation

It is no coincidence that Jethro is enamored of red and green, for these two colors, along with black and white/yellow, are prominent in the trickster hat that the orisha Eshu wears. Each color represents one of the cardinal directions: north, red; east, green; south, white/yellow; and west, black (Ford 168). Furthermore,

Flowers represents the four directions through cultural mapping with the three major characters: Tucept, Mike, and Willie D. When they return from Vietnam, their plane lands in the west: San Francisco, California. Tucept then goes back home to the south: Memphis, Tennessee. Willie D. becomes a community organizer and activist in the north: Harlem, New York. And Mike becomes an attorney in the east: Washington, DC. These correspondences coincide with the mythic cosmic order from which the orishas—Eshu, Obatala, and Shango—emanate.

Symbolically, the trickster's hat is a holistic representation, according to Ford, the "key to a comprehensive mythic order that at once reclaims and rejoins the mysteries of the cosmos, the earth, and the social order with the mysteries of a divine self" (169). The colors that Jethro wears connect him with his divine purpose as an orisha sent to aid Tucept in his quest for self-identity through Mike and Willie D. They are his two buddies who hold the key to balance in his life and who apprise him of his mission to heal and deliver his people. To aid in the healing process, Tucept must first become a doctor—not the kind who is steeped in the practices of Western medicine like his father, but one who is grounded in the ritualistic traditions of his African forebears: a rootdoctor like his mother. In this regard, red, black, and green are significant not only for their association with African myth but also for their contemporary significance relative to Black pride and solidarity. From as early as Marcus Garvey's Back to Africa Movement in the 1920s to the Black liberation struggle of the 1960s and beyond, the red, black, and green flag has been a symbol of allegiance to Africa. These colors (sometimes with the addition of yellow) are adapted from those emblazoned on most flags flown on the African continent. Noteworthy is that militant GIs in various branches of the service adopted the Black liberation flag as a sign of racial solidarity.

Whereas the Black liberation flag in civilian life is unostentatious, bearing only three horizontal stripes (red, black, and green), this military adaptation has more intricate designs. According to Norman Harris, Black marines in Danang designed a red, black, and green flag that is described as follows: the red background symbolizing "blood shed by blacks in the war and race conflict in America"; a black foreground representing "the face of black culture"; and a green wreath symbolizing "peace if possible." But at the heart of this flag was a shield with crossed spears signifying "violence if necessary" ("Blacks in Vietnam" 130). The defiant tone in this pronouncement is echoed in the following legend: "My fear is for you" (Hofu yangu ni kwa ajili yenu), which was written in Swahili across the flag (Westheider, "My Fear Is for You" 170).

Ritual of Solidarity and Survival: The "Dap"

The solidarity and defiance signified by the Black military flag finds expression also in the Black cultural ritual known as the "dap," a symbol of Black male bonding in civilian and military life. Providing a sense of togetherness, or what the military would call "unit cohesion,"[12] it enables the participants to survive humiliating assaults on the psyche. Adept at transforming terminology to meet their own needs, however, African American soldiers adapted and demonstrated an intercultural kind of cohesion through the dap ritual. When Welch, the twenty-two-year-old Black New Yorker on his second tour of duty in Country, teaches Tucept and Jethro the Nam-wide dap, he tells them it means "never let a brother go down" (110). It is a sign of defiance and Black pride also, as boldly illustrated when Tucept, Mike, and Willie D. get off the plane in manacles and chains in San Francisco. In addition to raising "the fist" (of Black power), they dap brothers lined up along the area where they exit the plane. In *De Mojo Blues* this show of togetherness often intimidates White soldiers who are uneasy when they see Blacks going down the dapline in enlisted men's (EM) clubs frequented by Black soldiers, such as "the Ghetto" at Firebase Sin Loi and "Soul Alley" in Saigon.[13]

James Westheider provides extraordinary insight into discrimination against African Americans in the military; he errs, however, when he attributes the derivation of "dap" to "dep," from a Vietnamese word meaning "beautiful" ("My Fear Is for You" 171). To the contrary, the dap was a manifestation of Black expressive culture long before the Vietnam War. A Black vernacular ritual, "this physical thing," as Julie Dash refers to it, denotes a type of "male bonding" among Black men, a tradition that goes all the way back to Africa (54).[14] Such an intrinsic role does it play in everyday Black male experience that social scientists have studied the significance of this elaborate hand ritual. Benjamin Cooke, for instance, points out its importance in a variety of disciplines, including psychology. He classifies and illustrates pictorially the functionality and meaning of various movements associated with the Black power handshake, of which the Nam-wide dap is a variation:

> 1) mutual encircling of the thumbs . . . *togetherness*; 2) grasping each other's hands with ended fingers . . . *strength*; 3) mutual grasping of wrists and hands . . . *solidarity*; 4) placing hands on shoulders with a slight amount of pressure . . . *comradeship*; 5) raising the arms, flexing the biceps, and making a fist . . . incorporates the meaning of the first four, symbolizing [them] all: *black pride, solidarity and power*. (61)

Referring to this elaborate handshaking ritual as a kinesic form of expressivity, Cooke concludes that the ritual expresses conscious control of Blacks over their lives and destinies in a manner similar to hairstyles such as the afro (64). Westheider explains the Nam-wide dap in a similar fashion but adds a final defiant gesture: "One common addition to the handshake was a gesture across the throat which symbolized cutting the throats of the MPs" ("Fighting on Two Fronts" 172).

In *De Mojo Blues* when Black soldiers enter the EM club, it is customary to "go down the dapline," the brothers giving each other "power" as they go. As Jethro, Mike, Willie D., Welch, and Prester John enter the EM club at Firebase Sin Loi, a long line of "bloods" stands along the wall. They begin "with the first man on the line and [dap] their way down, fists slapping the intricate Firebase Sin Loi version of the dap—two fist slaps, the backhand slap, the grasp, the thumb hook, handshake, wrist grip, and the handshake grasp" (108). On duty in the guard tower, the brothers "returned power" to each other—"the fist, two pumps" (59). As they go through this ritual, some wear thick Montagnard bracelets that click as they go through their routine.[15] Significantly these bracelets not only express camaraderie among the Black soldiers but also reveal their identification with the Montagnards, or Mountain People, a dark-skinned ethnic group among the South Vietnamese who resided in the Central Highlands. Blacks empathized with them because they were discriminated against by White Americans as well as the South Vietnamese.

Tucept and Jethro, both from the rural South, know nothing about dapping when they arrive in Vietnam, but they meet the streetwise New Yorker Welch on their first day in Country, and he teaches them. Welch adapts to the Nam as quickly as he has to the streets of New York where he had to be slick to survive. Skilled in the rituals of Black Vietnam—on his second tour of duty at the "ripe ol' age" of twenty-two—Welch "initiates" Jethro and Tucept into "the Ghetto," explaining to them the significance of the intricate Sin Loi dap and the Nam-wide short dap: "When you see a brother at a distance you give him *power*, pumping the fist twice in the air like so . . . or twice in the chest like so" (110; emphasis added). The point Welch makes to these young bloods is that you cannot do any individualistic grandstanding and survive, neither in Country nor in the World. To be able to make it through Nam and make it back home alive, bloods must stick together and have each others' backs.

On his first encounter with the dapline, Tucept considers all this gesticulating and posturing to be nonsense. But watching thirty or forty bloods lined up along the wall going through this ritual causes him to feel a surge of "fraternal affection."

As a doctor's son, he thought, prior to Nam, that most Blacks enjoyed a similar, upper-middle-class upbringing. But in the army, his "whole world had opened up." He discovers not only different lands and different kinds of White folk but also "different kinds of black folk" (111). Essentially, the Vietnam experience is a rite of passage for Tucept, who enters the service naive about Black male bonding rituals but returns home master of them all.

Providing clarity for the questing hero on his journey to discovery, Eshu is often called "the opener of the way," a function that Jethro serves as point man in Vietnam. Like Eshu, he provides clarity for Tucept when he explains the cultural/historical significance of his last name, Highjohn. Young Eshu, as Jethro, is a guide in Vietnam for Tucept, and this is the same function the older Eshu, Spijoko, serves for him in America after the war. Significantly, Eshu provides the questing hero with not only the wisdom and insight to surmount the obstacles of racism and emasculation but also the self-confidence to reach his goal.

Similar to the proverbial Jethro in the Old Testament, who gave counsel to Moses as he led the children of Israel from captivity in Egypt through the wilderness in search of the Promised Land, Jethro Tree provides words of wisdom to Tucept as he goes through the wilderness of military protocol. Flowers creates the character of Jethro not only to serve as a guide for Tucept but also to apprise him of his mission in life—to heal the fragmented psyches of his people and lead them to the discovery that true power lies within rather than outside themselves. But first, Jethro must direct Tucept to discover his inner self, as a hoodoo apprentice, so that he can realize his own potential in order to become a full-fledged healer, or hoodoo rootdoctor for his people.

It is no coincidence that Jethro's surname is "Tree." Tall and "heavyset," he is a giant of a man. A person's last name links him with his ancestry, and Jethro's "taproot" grows out of African soil, up through Mississippi delta land, which, along with other parts of the "Old South," is noted for its African cultural retentions (B. Bell 17). Significantly, the "river soaked" chair that Tucept retrieves from the Mississippi River becomes his throne, the seat of Rootdoctor High John de Conquer, in his stilt house in the woods. On this chair he hangs the Black mojo bag that Jethro gave him on the battlefield shortly before he was killed in Vietnam.

Flowers could also be using Jethro's last name to signify the "World Tree," or "Tree of Life," from African mythology. Similar to the web of Ananse the Spider, mythologically the World Tree is the connecting link, or the "crossroads," between earth and heaven, "the conveyance by which humanity ascends to divinity and divinity [orishas] descends to humanity," according to Ford (64). When one considers that Eshu resides at the crossroads, it is highly possible that Jethro's name symbolizes the World Tree. This taproot symbolism works on yet another level as a phallic symbol. In Vietnam Jethro is noted for his sexual prowess, often sneaking off base to see women and risking punishment for doing so. Similarly, Eshu is often presented as the "lifeforce" (Ford 154), a priapic trickster. Whether phallic god or World Tree, Eshu is manifest in Jethro who roots Tucept in the traditions of his African forebears when he explains the significance of his surname, Highjohn.

Highjohn de Conquer: Legendary Healer

Jethro carries in his fatigue jacket pocket the High John de Conquer root. Having full knowledge of the root's significance and well aware of Tucept's lack of knowledge concerning its cultural history, he questions Tucept about the significance of his surname, Highjohn. Telling Tucept, "It's yours anyway," Jethro gives him the "blackbrown" root. Quizzically observing it, Tucept says, derisively, the tale of High John de Conquer is only a "slavery myth." But Jethro corrects him: "Slavery was the last time black folks needed him, but his *spirit* is in the root" (61; emphasis added). Symbolically Flowers is saying that the spirit of present-day Blacks is to be found in their roots, or African ancestry. The time is ripe now for Highjohn to return because Blacks are "backed up against the wall" and they "can't lose when the spirit of Highjohn is walking with them" (61).

High John de Conquer is a legendary hero in the African American oral tradition, and sometimes he is referred to as simply "John" or "High John," according to Julius Lester, who says that he has been found "wherever things were rough" (18).[16] Elderly Blacks attest to his presence as far back as slavery, attributing their survival of the harsh realities of that "peculiar institution" to High John. One enslaved person put it this way: "Us didn't have no power of protection, and God knowed it," so he put them under "watch care" with High John de Conquer (18), whose dictum was that you should never tell anyone all that you know. That is why White folks did not know he was around during slavery.

High John de Conquer, in Julius Lester's account, was the "first slave brought to America and he's been here ever since" (19). His "Massa" often bragged that he was the "strongest nigger" in the county. Most significantly, High John symbolizes *survival.* The "old folks" who were enslaved say they "wouldn't have made it through all the trials and tribulations which were put on them if not for High John. . . . John de Conquer means power" (18). Though big and strong, however, High John disliked fighting. His role, instead, was protector and healer. To take on the mantle of healer of the race like his legendary counterpart, Tucept Highjohn, as hero-warrior, must find the "Black Book of Power," which Jethro says has its origin in "the Big Muddy," the Mississippi River. Symbolically, the Mississippi River serves as a connecting link between Africa and America.[17] The blood of the enslaved mingles with its murky waters as they were literally sold down the river to experience the most horrendous form of institutionalized slavery in the modern world. What is the "Black Book of Power" (75) that Tucept must discover? Jethro tells him to "go back to where the blues was born" (61). Though he does not understand it at the time, Tucept later learns that he is talking about the home of the blues in Memphis where he will meet the older manifestation of Eshu named Spijoko. But before Tucept can carry out his mission of empowering the Black community, he must truly know himself. To gain self-knowledge in the African mythic paradigm, the questing hero must first reconcile with his father.

Why is Tucept Highjohn the logical choice for hero? First, heroism and survival are in his bloodlines. The High John de Conquer root and its significance culturally and historically have already been established. Jethro is the crucial link to this forgotten family past that holds significance for Tucept individually. But, in a larger sense, High John de Conquer is the connecting link to the past for the entire Black community, whose oral tradition and material culture have been, and continue to be, the vehicle for transmission of cultural values. By connecting with it, Tucept is able to re-member the fragments of the tale of the legendary High John that were handed down orally by his "greatgrans . . . after the Civil War" (60). Knowing the significance of this tale from his ancestral past helps him to chart his future.

By clarifying for Tucept the significance of his family name, Jethro provides what Toni Morrison calls "rememory"—a "memory loaded with the past" (qtd. in Samuels and Hudson-Weems 90). He fills in the missing pieces of Tucept's history with the legend of the larger-than-life Highjohn de Conquer. As a result, Jethro assumes the stature of the proverbial griot who had several roles in traditional African society, one of which was "maintaining a cultural and historical past with that of the present," according to D'Jimo Kouyate, a modern-day griot (179). Knowledge of one's past then enables him to be equipped psychologically and spiritually for the present and the future. At the outset Tucept is not imbued with such knowledge, but during his heroic quest he learns of High John de Conquer's role as a healer.

Tucept is also a logical choice for hero-quester because he is the progeny of two parents who, literally and figuratively, are practitioners of healing arts. A medical doctor, his father heals the body. A student of psychology and a practitioner of voodoo, his mother heals the mind and spirit. From them he has inherited a perspective from which to view the fragmentation of the Black psyche and to find ways to ameliorate the situation for survival of the race. Tucept's mother, Della Highjohn, is very high-spirited. Described as "grit tucked under a mask of sophistication" (21), she has an outward appearance that conceals the earthiness that lies beneath her middle-class polish. She is a weaver who often hums the blues while toiling over her loom. Significantly, she weaves emerald cloth with a Black web. Consequently, she is symbolically connected to African myth as represented by the dual-gendered trickster spider Ananse whose matrilineal connections to power are legendary.[18]

Not only do the colors, green and Black, link Della with the trickster orisha Eshu but so does the web, which is suggestive of Ananse's web that symbolizes the connection between spiritual and material reality. This characteristic adds a mystical dimension to Mrs. Highjohn's character. She is steeped in folk culture because her family practiced hoodoo. She used her knowledge of it while a student at Fisk University to write two papers, "Power and the Negro Worldview" and "The Blues and Hoodoo as Negro Psychology and Treatment," which Tucept discovers as he is rummaging through the attic. A strong, no-nonsense woman, she is "built solid from the spirit up" (16). Mrs. Highjohn's spiritual nature as a practitioner of folk cultural arts expresses itself in Tucept's quest for spiritual fulfillment through the study of hoodoo and in his sensitivity to the needs of others. His father's scientific bent in the practice of Western medicine, on the other hand, leads to his desire to be a doctor, albeit one dedicated to the study of folk medicine rather than traditional Western medicine.

The Father Quest: Revelation of Character

James Henry Highjohn, Tucept's father, is somewhat insular and withdrawn, characteristics that some who do not know him well view as arrogance. Rather rigid, he wears a "well-orchestrated front," a quality that Tucept inherits from him. Though not totally unemotional, he is reluctant to reveal to others his emotional side. Underlying this stern exterior, or "mask of cool" as Tucept describes it, is a compassionate person who has spent many years of his life attending to the needs of the less fortunate by delivering health care services to the rural poor even though they often had nothing more than a chicken or some vegetables with which to pay him. In other words, Dr. Highjohn has a heart, but his poker-faced exterior, or "manmask" (198), hides it well, an aspect of his character that Tucept's father must reveal to him before reconciliation can occur.

For years the two Highjohn men have been distant because the father rarely, if ever, spent time with his son during his formative years. But after Tucept comes back from Vietnam, his father doffs his "manmask" and goes to see Tucept in his stilt house in the forest. Dr. Highjohn then apologizes for humiliating his son when he was a little boy by making him wear a dress. Following this act of contrition, Tucept sees his father cry for the first time. This act is significant because during his childhood Tucept would cry with the least provocation, a habit that irked his father to no end, mainly because he felt that a male's crying was indicative of weakness. When Tucept was nine years old, his father told him that if he were so intent on acting like a girl by crying so easily, then he should wear a dress. Tucept never forgot the humiliating incident. As a result, for years Tucept has thought they have nothing in common; however, listening to his father stumble through his apology he realizes how much he is like his father, how much he owed him for what he was, "even the mask of cool he now clutched so determinedly to his face" (150). As a result of this reconciliation, Tucept advances on his quest toward self-knowledge and fulfillment.

Tucept—Harmonizing Duality: Obatala and Shango

This profile of Tucept's parents reveals both sides of Tucept's own dualistic personality, for he is the embodiment of two, seemingly contradictory qualities or orishas, hence the name Tucept (two orisha concepts). His quest for self-empowerment combines the compassion of Obatala with the tenacious, strong will of Shango, both from the Yoruba pantheon. Furthermore, he personifies W. E. B. Du Bois's notion of "double-consciousness" in that he combines the Eurocentric approach to medicine inherited from his father and the Afrocentric healing practices of voodoo from his mother.

In West African mythology Obatala is a creator orisha (Biggers 29). The Yoruba view him as a compassionate, protective Great Father. But the mythology also portrays his "being drunk at the crowning moment of his glory," as Ford points out (152). Oral tradition declares that in the beginning of time Obatala found himself on earth with only a Black cat as a companion. Desiring others like himself for company, he took clay in his hands and made humans. However, in the midst of his creation he drank some palm wine. In a drunken stupor, he continued to create humanity. He then fell into a deep sleep, and upon awaking he discovered that he had created misfits—creatures with various deformities. Out of remorse and compassion for these malformed beings, he vowed to always protect those created with imperfections and deformities (151). Ford points out that Obatala can be either male or female and that as a male deity he exhibits aspects of the male psyche that are often "undervalued in modern society: caring, nurturing, feeling, self-sacrificing" (154).

Like Obatala, Tucept has a Black cat (132) as a constant companion when he becomes a hoodoo apprentice. Also their personality traits are similar, prompting Tucept to refer to himself as an emotional punk. He constantly empathizes with his only sibling, Caldonia, a strong-willed young woman who takes revenge on her baby's daddy (who has left her stranded out of wedlock) by torching his car. Tucept invariably listens to her problems, sometimes offering to babysit her child. He also gives her money, which she reluctantly takes because she is trying to be an independent woman (140–43). This compassionate trait leads him to constantly meet women who take him for a ride and then drop him, cold. Such is the case with Ruby (22–29), his ex-girlfriend at Fisk. After their breakup, he becomes involved with other such women in two subsequent relationships—Marva, who attempts to stab him in a fit of anger because he pays more attention to his river-soaked chair than he does to her (36–39), and Lynn, a wannabe starlet who cares more about herself than him and his discussions of hoodoo (96–100)—both of whom dump him. Tucept also empathizes with the Vietnamese. Making eye contact with an elderly Vietnamese man whose village the Americans have bombed, killing many of the old man's relatives, Tucept is so remorseful and disgusted at his own participation in this merciless carnage that he slaps a water buffalo.

After his encounter with Jethro and his transformation to a hoodoo apprentice, Tucept acquires the characteristics of Shango, one of the most revered and feared orishas in the Yoruba pantheon. He represents "tenacity" in the personality—will, determination, commitment (Biggers 29). Referred to as "the Thunder Hurler," Shango takes as a symbol the Oshe-Shango, or double-headed axe, which looks like a thunderbolt attached to the head. Its significance is that the thunderbolt symbolizes "spiritual consciousness, entering the body through the portal of illumination," according to Ford (163). Shango's "sound" is that of the "storm." Because of his belligerence and impetuousness, he represents a "'take no prisoners' attitude to life, often reacting before thinking things through" (162).

Tucept begins his journey toward spiritual consciousness through meditative introspection after he takes up residence in the stilt house that he discovers in the wooded area of a park in Memphis. He goes to this place of refuge to meditate as well as to study and practice his voodoo technique. Literally and figuratively, Tucept has brought the war home. His postwar stilt house resembles the guard house in Vietnam, and Flowers skillfully makes a narrative shift in a flashback from the jungle in Vietnam to the forest in Memphis. While Tucept was meditating, "a vision slid into his mind" (63) during a thunder and lightning storm.

For three years now he has had Jethro's mojo bag hanging on his "river soaked" chair without opening it to see what is inside. Finally opening the black bag, he discovers pieces of bone, which the cacophonous thunder and lightning knock from his hand. The fragments spill onto the floor in a pattern that forms a circled cross, which is a Vodoun symbol. This cross within a circle also coincides with the symbol of a shield with crossed spears abstractly depicted on the Black liberation military flag, and Flowers uses it effectively to wed form and content in *De Mojo Blues*. Prior to Tucept's meeting Jethro, Flowers does not use section dividers within the three chapters. However, after their first encounter, the voodoo symbol, signifying Jethro's role as voodoo guide for the hero, appears between all the sections from that point to the end of the novel. This symbol converges with the depiction of the trickster's cap, which is circular with a cross in the center, representing the four cardinal directions.

Eshu: Wise Guide as Spijoko

Momentarily, Tucept has a vision in which processions of people are moving in an "elegant, graceful dance of survival," and for a quick moment, he had "known power" (65). His vision of the survivors leads him to Beale Street, the blues capital, where Jethro has told him to go for "sign" of the mojo—the Black Book of Power. It is here he encounters Spijoko, a cunningly wise old man whose nails are filed in the same triangular "delta" shape as Jethro's, an indication that he is a voodoo sorcerer. As an older manifestation of Eshu, Spijoko becomes Tucept's guide on his spiritual quest in America. Not unlike the wizened old man in Nathaniel Hawthorne's "Young Goodman Brown," Spijoko is more an apparition than a person. He is "conjured up" when Tucept thinks about him and suddenly "appears" beside him on the bench in Handy Park, conversing with him familiarly as though they have met before. Spijoko confers on Tucept the name "Spiritwork Apprentice Highjohn" and informs him that since "power" is in "the will," he must use his will to "tap the mojo" (87).

The significance of the mojo lies in its relation to the will to survive. Spijoko tells Tucept its origin. The story goes that before humankind existed, a monkey named "Moj" had a "vision," telling his clan: "If we are to survive we must be more than monkey." Being the first monkey to "stand," he defied the "gods" who said "monkeys must walk on all fours" (160). Seeing the strength of Moj, other monkeys stood also, spreading across the earth while conquering others. Therefore, one who possesses the mojo has the will and the power to defy authority and be in control of his own destiny, a symbolic message to the Black community.

So determined is Tucept to empower and bring psychic health to the Black community that he begins "probing the mind" of a man on the sidewalk with his "spirit vision" and using what he calls his "feed tech" to reach out to the man's will, "planting a consciousness of self and determination" (113). His "tech" improving with time, Tucept "does a reading" of a line of young Blacks "with lackluster and ailing spirits" at a downtown theater. Having tapped into the minds of so many with his spirit vision, Tucept concludes, "We are a broken people" and weeps (114–15). His spirit vision convinces him that the Black mind, traumatized by racism, has been fragmented and therefore is in need of healing.

Alone in his tower, the stilt house in the woods, Tucept develops his meditative powers (dreamstate) to the point that he now has out-of-body experiences—a type of double-consciousness. In dreamstate he is able to "see with his mind"; that is, his extrasensory perception is being developed and fine-tuned. He intuitively "knows" when his Black cat walks into the room behind him (86) though he cannot see it. Spijoko wants Tucept to develop his meditative and extrasensory perception abilities so that he can "tap into the mojo" or, as he calls it, "the power boy, the lifeforce of all things" (88). If Tucept successfully masters these exercises, then he will become clairvoyant and earn the title of full-fledged Hoodooman, that is, if he can wait that long.

Unfortunately Tucept, like Shango, whose determined will at times leads to "excess" and sometimes "acting before thinking things through" (Ford 162), becomes impatient with being an apprentice, desiring to become a full-fledged Hoodooman sooner than the three months it takes to do so. Therefore, Spijoko chides him, informing him that discipline and patience are paramount for a sorcerer in training.

As a consequence, Spijoko extends Tucept's training period to four months because of his impetuousness.

As hoodoo apprentice, Tucept continues to advance on his quest toward spiritual enlightenment and fulfillment. While in a meditative state, he conjures up "the Board of Destiny" (158), drawing power from thunder and lightning (Shango). In his highbacked river-soaked chair he is surrounded by spirits of Black heroes from the past: Nat Turner, Gullah Jack—both of whom led slave revolts—and others. Remembering these warriors from Black history, some of whom allegedly carried the mojo, "empowers" Tucept with "futuresight." Like having a religious experience, he is "born again (186)." He also learns how to "seed myths" from Spijoko who tells him, that as a bona fide Hoodooman he is responsible for the "survival and destiny of the tribe." Tucept has now placed a sign on his stilt house that reads: "Rootdoctor T. Highjohn, Rootwork and Conjury, Hoodoo my Specialty, Sliding Fees" (178). During a storm Tucept "feels the blues walking" as he conjures up "the Board of Destiny" (158).

Flowers adeptly juxtaposes this present event with that of the military tribunal in Vietnam during which Sgt. Gill, a White officer, determines the destiny of Tucept and his two comrades by testifying that he saw a "colored" guy near the tent where Kicks was fragged (170). The Board of Destiny, which will determine the destiny of Blacks as a race, is similarly situated to the military tribunal that determined the fate of Tucept, Mike, and Willie D. The major difference lies in their verdicts: the Board will ensure continuation and survival of the tribe; whereas the military tribunal attempts to cut off opportunity for survival of these Black soldiers by dishonorably discharging them.

Visionary Mythmaker Transformation: Hoodooman

Flowers then fast-forwards to the future where Tucept uses his "futuresight" to "trace the path of power" (177). With the thunderstorm still raging, which he now refers to as "my lightning" and "my thunder," he is so immersed in the elements that he weaves an "inexorable will to power" in Blacks and declares that they will never be reenslaved. Conjuring up the Board of Destiny again, he "seeds a myth" of the "Saga" of Blacks: first, conquest and dispersion, which he calls the "Lean Years" of survival; and then struggle and mastery, or "the Longmarches" (192). His aim is to program into the tribe arrogance and pride, and into the heart of the myth he places his "survivor's visions." He howls, "I am Highjohn, and this I swear, the Blacks will never again be enslaved." Within this vision is "gut acceptance of life as unceasing challenge" with "ironic amusement": "The ability to laugh in fate's face, to demand of life its pleasures and to enjoy its struggles . . . rough or smooth." (193). His vision is indeed a definition of "the blues"—"de mojo blues." This definition coincides with Spijoko's earlier observation that the "blues . . . adjusts to circumstance. As we have done and continue to do. Taking the hump with style is the genius of our survival" (156).

Having attained the status of mythmaker, Highjohn now *becomes* the storm" (174), the thunder being his "wardrum," as he declares: "There will be no ambushes while I am point" (195). In this state of ecstasy Tucept declares: "I am High John the Conquerer. Hoodooman. I walk in storm" (193). His zealousness again gets out of hand, causing Spijoko to caution him that "power without compassion is a sin" (195). Shango without Obatala can lead to destruction. According to West African myth, each of us has within our psyche characteristics of each of the orishas—the compassionate Obatala, the destructive Shango, and the trickster Eshu. But we must have a "center of control" to keep these tendencies in proper alignment (Ford 167). Therefore, these contending forces in Tucept must be balanced. How does he achieve this balance? Spijoko tells him that the answer lies with his two army buddies, Mike and Willie D.

A. R. Flowers chooses the age-old conflict in the Black community—the choice between working within the system or challenging the system by working outside it to develop a self-sufficient approach to achieve power—as one aspect of intracultural struggle that must be ameliorated to achieve clarity of vision that will aid in the survival of the race. Seemingly diametrically opposed, these two approaches toward Black empowerment have a common goal but employ different means to accomplish it. The apparent polar opposites coalesce in two major characters—Willie D., the socialistic Black activist, and Mike, the capitalistic bourgeois attorney—who return with Tucept from Nam and gravitate toward opposite ends of the economic spectrum. The reason Spijoko tells Tucept that he will find the Black Book of Power when he finds Mike and Willie D. is that bringing together their ostensibly different approaches to acquiring power will enable him to complete the final leg of his quest.

Feeling the Power: Mediating Antinomies

On the road to empowerment, Tucept becomes an unwitting and reluctant mediator between two seemingly opposite paths to power for himself and for the Black community symbolized by the actions and careers of his two surviving army buddies. After Mike and Willie D. leave Washington, DC, and New York, symbolically representing power and wealth, respectively, they come to Memphis where Tucept has invited them to join him at his stilt house in the woods where the power of hoodoo is on. Having rejoined them, Tucept, with "spiritvision," "opens their minds and plants his myths," from the distant past to the far future (210–11). Mike and Willie D., though at odds earlier, each feeling that he has the answer to solving the Black community's problem, now feel a camaraderie not felt since "foxhole Nam and Firebase Sin Loi." Tucept then confers on them the power of conviction and "armors them in a sense of destiny." While still in "trancestate," he gathers all Blacks into his myth, telling them of "heroes and sheroes," filling them with "visions of [Blacks] as powerful, respected people . . . Survivors" (213). This is the holy war that Tucept, from his stilt house in the clearing of the woods, has brought home.

As far as bringing the war home is concerned, Tucept's occupation of the stilt house in the woods amounts to a transplantation of Vietnam in America, for it mirrors the guard tower on stilts in the jungles of Vietnam. He also finds himself, or discovers his identity, in Vietnam (through a rite of passage effected by Jethro) and in America in the stilt house where he practices voodoo. As an extension of the Vietnam experience, this refuge among the treetops enables Tucept to become one with nature, thereby discovering his own nature, or his identity as a Hoodoo man. In a meditative state, he has several out-of-body experiences.

In Country external realities/forces contributed to Tucept's self-actualization, as when he met and befriended Jethro and eventually joined the dapline. On the other hand, in the World connection with his inner self through voodoo ritual and meditation characterize his identity quest. Tucept's membership in "the Ghetto," the all-Black EM club at Firebase Sin Loi, helped him to embrace the real meaning of camaraderie and trust. When he first arrives in Vietnam and enters the EM club, Tucept observes all the brothers going down the dapline but does not join in himself, feeling that it is a superficial sign of togetherness among the Black recruits. It is not until he experiences several losses in Vietnam that Tucept joins the dapping ritual to become a part of the group.

First his friend Welch goes AWOL after fragging Kicks, the White officer who discriminated against Blacks (186). Then Prester John and Jethro are killed in a hot LZ. Considering the way they met their deaths, it is little wonder that Tucept realizes finally the significance of Black brotherhood. In a friendly fire incident, the army's own strafing jets fire and drop napalm on his platoon, wreaking havoc and leaving dismembered bodies and death in their wake. When Welch taught Jethro and Tucept how to dap, they said, "Never let a brother go down" (110). With only Willie D. and Mike, along with himself, remaining from the original Ghetto 6, Tucept now joins them going down the dapline (184). By doing the dap, brothers give each other power. In his stilt house in woods near the Mississippi River in Memphis, Tucept feels this power, signaling his psychical transformation, when the lightning strikes and the thunder roars.

Discovering the Point of Balance: The Mojo

Spijoko, the wily old man who becomes Tucept's spiritual guide to inner awareness and community clarity, is an extension of the Jethro character (as the aged manifestation of Eshu). Just as Jethro helped Tucept to survive physically in Vietnam and to value camaraderie among fellow Black soldiers, Spijoko helps him to survive psychologically the aftereffects of the war by leading him into an awareness of his own identity and showing him that he and the community are interdependent. The significance of Spijoko's role becomes clear in Anthonia Kalu's observations about Igbo culture where group solidarity is implicitly maintained with the help of elders who "check and balance" the individual's participation within the group and his alliance to it ("Achebe and Duality" 24–26). The importance of this interdependent relationship lies in the fact that a person's well-being in the spirit world after death depended on his harmonious relationship with the community while he was alive. The Board of Destiny confers this knowledge on Tucept during his consultation with them in meditative trancestate.

Several aspects of Tucept's character prevented the type of introspection necessary for spiritual growth prior to meeting Spijoko. He had been a Professional student disillusioned by the war and its effects on himself and society. This disillusionment led him to become a philanderer with women like Marva, who becomes so enraged at his inattention to her that she attempts to stab him, and Lynn, the blasé would-be starlet whose life of misuse and abuse has left her so emotionally and spiritually starved that she finds it difficult to maintain an emotionally stable relationship, dumping Tucept with the same abandon that allowed her to let him pick her up on the city bus. Though Tucept's inertia is in some respects the result of a character flaw, it also stems from the psychological toll that the war has taken. He constantly has flashbacks to the war that are triggered by events in present time.

One such event occurs when he goes to Ruby's apartment while he is still a student at Fisk University. After watching television, they go to bed. Later that night he attempts, unsuccessfully, to have sex with her (28). Disillusionment, embarrassment, and anger all surface simultaneously. His mind is too preoccupied with the war as he falls asleep and dreams about the choppers spitting "buffalo soldiers into a muddy gold ricepaddy . . . puppets on a string, buckdancing minstrels dodging slow motion bullets to the tune of Yankee Doodle Dandy" (29). His inability to perform sexually conjures up images of lynching and symbolizes the emasculation of the Black soldier by feelings of powerlessness while being used as cannon fodder by the military-industrial complex. Added to his PTSD is the fact that Ruby had attached a certain glamor and romance to the notion that her man was fighting in the Vietnam War when he was away. However, she is now revulsed not only because of the loss of her freedom as he makes demands on her time but also her newfound anti–Vietnam War sentiments. Also, having loved others while Tucept was away, she no longer has the same old feelings for him; and his psychological trauma she now witnesses puts even more strain on the relationship.

This feeling of helplessness, powerlessness, and manipulation at the whim of forces beyond the control of Blacks dangling like puppets on a string is Tucept's recurring dream: "you dance on gossamer strings sometimes seen sometimes not" (29). One of the hindrances to the survival of Black folk mentally, physically, and emotionally is the lack of power, as he sees it. So the cumulative effect of these flashbacks with images of minstrels and puppets is to create within Tucept not only a sense of outrage and disgust—"We just a punk people. We weak"—but also a desire to do something about it. This insight leads to his decision to become a Voodooman in order to have "sayso," or power (30). He therefore declares war on Blackfolks' thinking and on Whites who are determined to keep Blacks psychologically subjugated.

The wise Spijoko warns him, however, that "to conquer a beast you must become a better beast." In other words, as High John de Conquer he should not use the same tactics to conquer a foe that were used to subjugate him, or he will become as despicable as those whom he despises. Surviving the onslaught of the oppressor requires adaptation, or in Spijoko's words: "Taking the hump with style is the genius of our survival. Not only do we adapt, we finesse." This adaptation occurs when one centers himself on the "balance point of reality and illusion, de mojo" (158).

This "balance point" is the recognition that true power resides within oneself and not in the forces outside. Though certainly the outside forces play a role, one must realize that his own will to survive is more important than someone else's desire to see him fail. The power of the will resides in the knowledge of life's inherently contradictory nature. Such knowledge comes from an awareness of Black cultural history, which emanates from a world view in which paradoxical complementarity is the foundational belief system. Several generations removed from indigenous African cultures where this belief system is practiced every day, African Americans indirectly receive its tenets through expressive cultural practices handed down orally from one generation to the next. Myths, heroic folk tales, religion, and even ritualistic kinesic practices such as "dapping" are in this category. That is why Tucept must first become a part of the dapline before realizing the significance of his quest to heal the fragmentation within his own psyche as well as that of the Black community. On the universal human stage he must not see himself as an individual player but rather as a part of an ensemble cast that functions interdependently with all others, summed up in this African proverb: "One hand washes the other."

On unnumbered pages, Flowers strategically places excerpts from the toast "Shine and the Titanic," at the beginning ("And the Shark said: Shine, Shine, you doing fine, but if you miss one stroke your ass is mine") and at the end ("And Shine said: There's fish in the ocean and there's fish in the sea but ain't none of these fish gon outswim me") of De Mojo Blues. The "shark" therein is symbolic of racial oppression in the military and in civilian life, like an ever-present ogre waiting to swallow the Black man who lacks self-knowledge and direction. Like Shine, the Black soldier must devise stratagems to survive—physically, mentally, emotionally, and spiritually. By the end of the novel Tucept Highjohn the hero-warrior discovers, by connecting with his African cultural memory, that the key to survival lies within his own will. He also discovers that such empowerment comes in conjunction with rather than at the expense of the community. Having tapped ancestral resources residing in the wisdom of voodoo, he, like Shine, is able to swim on because survival is as much psychological as it is physical.

Until Tucept meets Jethro in Country during the Vietnam War, he attempts to make it in life alone. In the army he purposely separates himself from the other Black men in his company. Jethro reveals to him, however, the necessity of interdependence rather than independence as an aid to survival, not only in Vietnam but also on the home front. He therefore encourages Tucept's relationship with the other "brothermes" and gives him a talisman, the mojo that is symbolic of self-empowerment, to enable his survival when he returns to the World.

In a similar manner, the protagonist in Wesley Brown's *Tragic Magic* attempts to go through life solo. However, he experiences a different kind of battlefield from that of the Vietnam War during his stint in prison as a conscientious objector. There he is aided in his quest for self-awareness and survival by a fellow inmate. While he is having this vicarious war experience, his childhood friend, Otis, is fighting in the war in Vietnam. Having volunteered for service, Otis is gung-ho about his role as a military hero. When he returns to the World, however, he self-destructs after failing to make the connection between interdependence and Black survival.

CHAPTER 4

Playin' It by Ear

The Jazzerly Sound of Survival in *Tragic Magic*

The sound of the novel, sometimes cacophonous, sometimes harmonious, must be an inner ear sound just beyond hearing, infusing the text with a musical emphasis that words can do sometimes even better than music can.

—Toni Morrison, "Unspeakable Things Unspoken"

I see speech as rhythm, I mean that's what Black speech is all about . . . and that's what I want to capture in my music.

—T. J. Anderson, composer of the Vietnam War opera, *Soldier Boy, Soldier*

Improvisation is the ultimate human (i.e., heroic) endowment . . . flexibility or the ability to swing (or to perform with grace under pressure) is the key to that unique competence which generates the self-reliance and thus the charisma of the hero.

—Albert Murray, "Jazz Is a Dance: Jazz Art in Motion"

An important characteristic of "Signifyin(g)," a complex phenomenon in Black expressive and discursive culture, is "repetition and revision," according to Henry Louis Gates Jr., who considers it the "most striking aspect" of the African American literary tradition (*Signifying Monkey* 124).[1] Textually, signification occurs when a novelist repeats a theme developed by earlier writers. One such prevailing theme in the Black novel is a young man's search for identity that, more often than not, is complicated by racism, a signal example of which is Ralph Ellison's *Invisible Man*. Signifyin(g) upon Ellison's novel, Wesley Brown's *Tragic Magic*[2] repeats, revises, and extends this theme of self-discovery by invoking *Invisible Man* not only through the protagonist's picaresque experiences but also through what I call the "jazzerly" text. In so doing, he is able to articulate and continue for our contemporary generation the bildungsroman in the African American literary tradition. James Coleman's contention that *Tragic Magic* is too heavily influenced by *Invisible Man* in theme and structure, which he calls "dull and repetitive" (48), overlooks Brown's extraordinary adaptation of the invisibility metaphor. To the contrary, Brown's novel revises and extends the theme of the Black male search for identity in a hostile environment by placing it in the context of the Vietnam War. Gates's definition of a "revising text," as one that is written in "the language of the tradition, employing its tropes, its rhetorical strategies" (*Signifying Monkey* 124), certainly applies to *Tragic Magic*, and in that respect, it signals a continuation of the Black vernacular tradition in fiction.

Signification is also a "black mode of discourse" in African American vernacular culture, and it is expressed through certain "verbal strategies, rhetorical devices and folk expressive rituals" that Geneva Smitherman calls the "Forms of Things Unknown" (*Talkin' and Testifyin'* 103). Through the musicality of the Black vernacular embodied in signifyin(g) and the jazz/blues aesthetic, *Tragic Magic* employs various aspects of signification to explore dissonance and harmony in the coming-of-age relationship between the protagonist, Melvin Ellington, and his friend since boyhood, Otis, as the two men take divergent paths when confronted with the military draft and service in Vietnam. Coping with the phenomenon of growing up Black and male in a racist society, Melvin declares conscientious objection and is sentenced to three years in prison, while Otis goes off to fight in the war. The heroic models they choose in each of these situations determine their fates. After high school, Otis, brawny and heartless, goes to the marines, while Melvin, brainy and compassionate, goes to college. These divergent paths in life cause a gap in their friendship that widens after Melvin gets out of prison and Otis comes back home from Vietnam.

In prison society, a simulated war zone with a subculture and its own rules, Melvin re-members by recalling events from home and by tapping into the cultural resource of a jazz heritage, characterized by his "solo and ensemble" interaction with people in his past, to negotiate his environment and to survive. In the process he begins to discover his identity. Otis, on the other hand, having survived long enough in Country to discover that his conception of heroism from John Wayne movies and the streets is only an illusion, devises a scheme to get sent back home to the World, where his inability to cope with postwar frustration leads to self-destruction. Events in *Tragic Magic* occur in one week. Similar to many other novels about the Black experience in Vietnam that begin with the soldier's return from the war, action in *Tragic Magic* begins on the day that Melvin gets paroled from prison for having protested the draft. It ends seven days later when Otis, suffering from post–traumatic stress disorder (PTSD), ironically meets an untimely demise soon after returning home from the war.

Psychogenesis of the Novel: Rite-of-Passage Story

The psychogenesis of *Tragic Magic* is similar to that of *Invisible Man* but in reverse. Interestingly enough, what started out as a war novel for Ellison ended up being a bildungsroman.[3] John Wright tells how Ellison was sent home from the army overseas during the winter of 1944 to "recuperate from wartime stress" (157). During this period, he began what he thought would be a war novel with the conviction that, artistically rendered, it could reveal more about the experience of Black men in war than the surface violence. Ellison was distraught about the age-old dilemma Black soldiers faced when going off to some foreign land to fight for the freedom of others only to return home to endure the shackles of racism. But his "inner voice" convinced him to abandon this kernel of an idea for a novel in favor of one focusing on the problem of Black identity and the crisis of Black leadership in America. The result was *Invisible Man*, which was undergirded with the nuances of jazz because Ellison, an accomplished jazz musician, believed that the art of music offered some "possibility for self-definition" (*Shadow and Act* xii).

On the other hand, what began as a rite-of-passage novel for Brown resulted in a war novel. Similar to his literary predecessor Ellison, Brown also uses jazz to "tell the story" (O'Meally 389) of a sensitive young Black man trying to find himself. Charles Lynch asked Brown during an interview in 1977 what inspired him to write *Tragic Magic*, his first novel. Brown's response was both interesting and unexpected. He told Lynch that around November or December of 1971 he decided to write a fictional account of a young man going through important transitions in life and to associate that process with popular music that was current during the period of his own adolescence and young adulthood. But an event occurred—spanning the period from January 27, 1972, to June 27, 1973—that would change his life forever and the focus of the novel as well. That event was his own incarceration in Lewisburg Federal Penitentiary for protesting the military draft by declaring conscientious objection.[4] The story explores some of the inherited notions about manhood that cause some Black men to end up in prison, as well as the effects of military service on the psyche of those who go to war. However, to allay any suspicion that the text is simply autobiographical rather than fictional, Brown is quick to point out that "the experiences [in *Tragic Magic*] weren't necessarily my own, but they came out of an environment that I was a part of, one that could have destroyed me" (qtd. in Lynch 48). Instead of succumbing to the destructive influences of incarceration, Brown transformed his angst into creativity, and the wonderfully crafted novel *Tragic Magic* resulted.

Jazz: Interrogating Complexities of Masculinity

What Robert O'Meally, in *The Jazz Cadence of American Culture*, means by "telling the story" in jazz is finding "an artistic voice and language of one's own" not only to tell one's personal history but also to chronicle that of one's community (389).[5] Brown's *Tragic Magic* interrogates the complexities of heroism not only for the Black male as an individual but also for the larger community that influences his self-concept. How have images of the hero in Euro-American culture influenced perceptions in the Black community? Are those images in opposition to or consonant with the depiction of the Black hero? Brown's novel, and especially the characterization of Otis, shows how heroic images such as that of the John Wayne "ideal soldier" (Herzog, "John Wayne" 16) can be life-threatening to the psyche of the Black male, especially when such images are combined with distorted notions of Black manhood from a segment of the Black community known in the Black vernacular as the "street committee" or the "Street Institution" (Cose 47). The influence of the

"John Wayne syndrome" on the Vietnam War generation notwithstanding, Brown, as novelist and Black culture-bearer, explores African American cultural memory for heroic models using a jazz motif.

Mainstream binary representations of the Black male, whether skewed to emasculated or gangsterfied stereotypes, do not capture the complexity of "ways of seeing and imagining black masculinity and black collective identity," argues Herman Gray in "Black Masculinity and Visual Culture" (404). This observation is particularly true of Vietnam War narratives. The jazz aesthetic, however, offers a multidimensional view of the Black male that defies these stereotypes. Gray also points out that

> for many of us, jazz men articulated a different way of knowing ourselves and seeing the world through the very "structures of feeling" . . . from the *defiantly cool pose* and fine vines of Miles to the . . . ceaseless spiritual and musical quest of Coltrane. . . . [They] not only challenged whiteness but exiled it to the cultural margins of blackness—i.e., *in their hands blackness was a powerful symbol of the masculine.* (401)

In his opinion Black jazz artists of the 1950s and 1960s, such as Duke Ellington and Charlie Parker, were particularly representative of "the complex social relations (race, class, sexual) and cultural politics surrounding the self-construction and representation of the black masculine in the public sphere" (401). Theirs was an "assertive, heterosexual black masculinity" that challenged assumptions by the dominant culture. Lawrence Levine supports this view in his observation that jazz "provided a sense of *power* and *control*" for Black musicians ("Jazz and American Culture" 440). James Baldwin once remarked that Black musicians often "speak for the black community" and that some writers viewed jazz musicians as "cultural leaders" (qtd. in Hollingsworth and Leake 47).

During the 1950s postwar era, White avant-garde writers and artists—the Beat generation—viewed Black jazz musicians as symbols of masculinity because of the "alternative" masculine model they offered in the age of "the gray flannel suit, suburbia, and other emasculating forces," observes Robin G. Kelley (139). They were particularly attracted to Thelonious Monk whose towering six-foot, three-inch frame was imposing. The Beats ambivalently considered his masculinity as threating and attractive, which continues to characterize America's love–hate relationship with Black males. They also considered his mannerism of dancing around the bandstand to his own music as a unique way of putting his masculinity on display. Additionally, Monk's appeal resided in his music, considered "masculine" as a result of the "dissonant harmonies, startling rhythmic displacements and swinging tempos" (139), prompting jazz critic Steve Lacy to characterize his music as having a "balanced virility" (qtd. in Kelley 140).

These jazz styles have been instrumental in the development of a "jazz aesthetic." Rhetorical strategies from the jazz/blues aesthetic that Brown employs in *Tragic Magic* are similar to those of other jazzy prose writers. Alan J. Rice summarizes these strategies as "antiphony," alternating responses; "riffing," involving improvisation in music and speech; and "signifying," a verbal strategy in black colloquial speech" (106). Using these jazzerly approaches through an exploration of the different jazz styles of Ellington and Parker, Brown explores in *Tragic Magic* the dialogical tension between Melvin and Otis and their two different approaches to the Vietnam War as the protagonist sets out on the heroic quest.

It might appear that memory of African culture for African Americans suffered a tragic death following the devastating effects of the Black Holocaust, also known as the Middle Passage, and American slavery. To the contrary, argues Eleanor Traylor, cultural memory was retained in "the individual soul" that became a "self-created carrier" of what was remembered (286). For our generation, Brown is a culture bearer. He creates Melvin in *Tragic Magic* to be the carrier of the jazz/blues aesthetic from Black cultural memory in his identity quest for self-determination against the backdrop of the Vietnam War. As first-person narrator Melvin tells the story while struggling to "free himself of notions of himself which are not his own creation," according to Brown (qtd. in Lynch 48).

Implicit in the title *Tragic Magic* is the inability of the protagonist to see beyond the "surface embroidery of things," according to Brown. He is "narcotized" by the "appearances" of people, that is, the way they present themselves as opposed to who they really are, which is portrayed in the novel as "style versus character." As a result Mel often finds himself, like the "'mel'ody" in a jazz composition, in a point-counterpoint situation with others. His greatest challenge is to make his own judgments and to trust his own instincts regardless of the perceptions of family or friends. He calls this interaction with others "a type of ensemble playing," which "rises from the streets of my life like a herd of elephants running off at the mouth. A space opens up where I can take my solo" (6). Adept at improvisation, Mel considers the prospect of freedom by comparing his life to that of a fish as he spots a "fish 'n chips joint across the street" when he gets off the bus after arriving home from prison:

> Now some folks hold to the notion that fish were made for the dish and let the chips fall where they may. But just maybe, as a side-order argument, fish were made to swim free and let the chips fall where they can best get a play. . . . Like all the rest before me I seem to be doomed to dissonance and thoughts like highwater pants that are too far from where they're supposed to be. (6)

This jazzerly, metaphorical language sets the stage for Melvin's improvisational approach to life. Rather than following his own dictates, or charting his course in life, he often improvises and adapts to what others want him to be.

Identity Search: Improvisation as Aid

In the prologue titled "A Few Words Before the Get Go," Brown presents the protagonist as a self-described "intern in the reed section of sound" that is a part of the jam session of life. Mel says he is adept at playing one of the classics: "To Get Along, You Go Along." However, in spite of his best efforts to agree with others just to get in their good graces, he often "undermine[s]" this popular rendition by "not playing it as it was written" and instead "flirt[s] with the tragic magic in *If, Maybe, Suppose*, and *Perhaps*" (3). Whenever he is confronted with the dilemma of his survival as a Black male, Melvin re-members by "recall[ing]" the advice that his namesake Duke Ellington received from his mentor, Dad Cook: "Learn the rules, then forget them and do it your own way." This advice parallels the immortal words of the grandfather to the unnamed protagonist in Ellison's *Invisible Man* in that it encodes a message of Black male survival in a hostile, racist environment.[6] In other words, implicit in improvisation, according to Albert Murray, is a coping mechanism: "flexibility or the ability to swing (or to perform with grace under pressure), [which] . . . generates the self-reliance and the charisma of the hero" (qtd. in O'Meally 277).

"More than once," Melvin muses, "this advice has subverted my best intentions to go along with the program" (6). Therefore in his interactions with the greater society, which he calls "auditions to enter the fold," he says he "get[s] the urge to play against the melody, behind and ahead of the beat, to bend, diminish and flatten notes, and slip in and out of any exact notation of what and how I should play" (6). This statement of his modus operandi signifies, in a jazzerly fashion, upon the experience of the protagonist in *Invisible Man*. In his performance on the stage of life Melvin constantly allies himself with people whose personalities are the opposite of his, in what I view as a call-and-response relationship; and as James Coleman, in "Language, Reality, and Self in Wesley Brown's Tragic Magic," observes, he pays "obeisance to people he feels can accomplish things at which he is a failure" (49). This proclivity does not change even during college, where Melvin joins various organizations in an attempt to discover his niche in life. In his creation of this character, Brown improvises, similar to Ellison, who relies on "improvisation to reinforce the theme of identity" in *Invisible Man* (Callahan 153). As a "solo performer" Melvin intermittently interacts with the Black community—his family, his boyhood friends, his former schoolmates, his activist college friends, and the prison inmates—in much the same way that the jazz artist steps out front to play a solo and then steps back to play with the ensemble.

Brown represents the multidimensionality of Black manhood by integrating the arts. According to Rex Nettleford, proponent of integrative arts inquiry, the quest for identity and self-definition among Black artists often resides in methodologies that integrate several artistic modes of expression (30).[7] Duke Ellington, through his integration of the arts, became the litmus test by which other jazz musicians were measured. Nat Hentoff observes that Ellington "worked in a multitude of forms—stretching them, transmuting them, interrelating them all in a spectrum of expression with its own logic of evolution, expansion, continual generation" (qtd. in Nettleford 31). He often blended visual, musical, and literary art for a holistic rendering of Black experience. For example, Mark Tucker calls Ellington's "Afro-Eurasian Eclipse" a kind of "painting with tones" (142). At times he "conjured up" visual images, creating a narrative element in his work, such as that of a man going home after a hard day's work in "East St. Louis Toodle-oo." Often his music imitates the sound and movement of trains, a reference to the major mode of transportation for Blacks during the Great Migration from the South to the North and the place where Duke composed many of his tunes while traveling to and from engagements in the Jim Crow car. Like Duke Ellington, the consummate jazz artist who worked in a multitude of forms, Brown combines artistic modes as well. Not coincidentally, then, Brown prototypically fashions his protagonist, Melvin Ellington, in the cool, sophisticated style of Duke Ellington.

Signifyin(g): "Musivocal"/Speakerly Text

In his exploration of the Black man's journey from innocence to experience against the backdrop of the Vietnam War, Brown combines the arts using a methodology that integrates aural and pictorial attributes of musical (jazz and blues) and spoken (the rich tones and flavors of the Black vernacular) cultural artistic modes, to produce what I call "musivocal sounds." Jazz appeals to Brown because of its "reliance on improvisation" (qtd. in Lynch 49). Black vernacular discourse also relies on improvisation and is characterized by what Gates calls "the speakerly text" (*Signifying Monkey* 181), which Carol D. Lee says "elevate[s] Black English to an art" (15). Brown's improvisatory stance in *Tragic Magic* is informed by the lyrical quality of Black speech, which he refers to as "language play embodied in . . . the dozens and signifying"; and by "language" he means "idiomatic expression as opposed to dialect or accent" because idioms are suggestive of "worldview, an approach to life or a way of dealing with chaos" (qtd. in Lynch 48). This view also coincides with that of Geneva Smitherman, who defines the "Black Idiom" as that which "has allowed blacks to create a *culture of survival* in an alien land" (*Talkin' and Testifyin'* 2; emphasis added). The Black idiom is only one aspect of the complex vernacular term known as "signifyin(g)," which serves a variety of purposes in discursive and expressive contexts.

I agree with Carol D. Lee who views two purposes of signifyin(g) as "empowerment and cultural self-definition" (16). As an outgrowth of Black cultural history and one of the expressive modes of Black semantic discourse, signifyin(g) means "to speak with innuendo, to play rhetorically upon the meaning and sounds of words, and to be often quick and witty in one's response" (12). Smitherman further identifies signification as "a witty one-liner, a series of loosely related statements, or a cohesive discourse on one point" having any number of the following characteristics, including "indirection," language that is "imagistic" and/or "metaphorical." Signifyin(g) can also employ double entendre and is often humorous and/or ironic (*Talkin' and Testifyin'* 121).[8]

Tragic Magic incorporates several of the above characteristics of signification, which Brown refers to simply as "black talk" that he uses for its inventiveness "in the arrangement and choice of words" and insightfulness in "its interpretation of the human predicament" (qtd. in Lynch 49). For instance, several of these characteristics are evident in the following encounters between Melvin and other inmates at the federal penitentiary. Shortly after entering prison he takes a shower with other inmates in a long open stall without partitions. Melvin notices that the man next to him is well built, "firm and fully-packed"; however, he catches himself staring and quickly looks away for fear of someone spotting him and labeling him homosexual. He says that if they catch him they will probably take it one of two ways: "I'm either an asshole bandit or looking to be held up by one" (20). Brown says the "rigidity" of standards in American society for what constitutes manhood caused him to purposely inject such humor in the novel ("You Talk Like" 20). His adeptness at accomplishing that feat is also evident in the following episode where Black and White inmates signify on one another in the shower. The inmate at whom Melvin has been staring quips:

> "Hey, blood," he says, "why you jerking your head like that for? I know you ain't no Elgin Baylor." We both have a good laugh.... Nobody is paying me any mind. They're too busy indulging in a favorite shower-room pastime: comparing the size of each other's Swanson Johnson. According to penis mythology, black dudes are supposed to have long banana-clip johnsons, while white dudes sport drawed-up pee shooters.
>
> "Don't worry about it," a black counters. "Time has just about run out on you whiteys. When Martin Luther King said, 'How long, not long,' he wasn't just talking about your futures!" (20)

This prison shower room call-and-response conversation also illustrates a type of signification called "cappin'," or what is better known as "lightweight" signify-in(g) that involves playfully calling someone out of his name to evoke laughter (Smitherman, *Talkin' and Testifyin'* 120). In addition to exemplifying several characteristics of signification, this colorful interchange foreshadows certain stereotypical conceptions about Black and White masculinity that are interrogated in *Tragic Magic*.

This lighthearted banter soon changes to more serious matters, however, when Melvin meets Chilly, a hot-headed rabble-rouser who strikes fear in the hearts of most inmates. He is all style and no character. He tells Melvin that "most of the cats in here is hard" and that they are going to resent him for being a conscientious objector:

> They figure they got more of a beef with society than you do. So you not going along with whitey's program don't cut no slack with them. Cats in here been messed over. And here you come, not a mark on you, lookin just as tender as you wanna

be, talkin bout you don't wanna fight in no war. . . . To them you no different than a white boy. (25)

He then offers Melvin "protection" from these toughs. Though Mel does not realize it at the time, Chilly's taking him into his confidence and offering him protection is only pretext to manipulation. That opportunity presents itself shortly thereafter when Mel is accosted by Showboat who kisses him on the cheek, a setup by Chilly to see if Mel will fight back. Mel fails to do so. When the word gets out, he becomes the object of piercing stares—"the heavy wattage being laid on me from the headlamps of dudes in the chow hall"—because he failed to "kick ass and take names" (29), which, according to the prevailing myths of manhood, he would have done if he were a "real man."

The opposite of Chilly is Hardknocks, who says he will be Mel's "road dog" to offer him protection from "cats" like Chilly who only want to use him. Hardknocks's name signifies upon the lessons he has learned from the vicissitudes of life, or in the vernacular, "from the school of Hard Knocks," which can teach a person more about life than he will learn in an institution of higher learning like the college Melvin attended. Hardknocks knows the streets, which he has survived without letting the experience rob him of his character. Melvin admits that he does not know who to trust in this "war zone" called prison, but he sees in Hardknocks's eyes a certain honesty: "They were a tired wise, smacked with a quiet strength [that] played no games." Admiring Melvin for "the way he held his head up" when he walked through the chow hall, Hardknocks tells him not to worry about sometimes showing signs of weakness. Having checked Melvin's file, Hardknocks tells him, "I know what you in here for and I think you for real" (29), that is, for having declared conscientious objection to the Vietnam War. He cautions Mel, however, to watch the company he keeps, mainly Chilly, and to keep to himself. So Mel decides to become a loner.

Later, another inmate invites Melvin to go to the gym to play ball. Remembering Hardknocks's advice, he refuses the invitation. The other man is so upset his jaws "loaded up with rocks until his face was only a stone's throw from Mount Rushmore" (34). Melvin is confused at his reaction, especially since he thought Hardknocks rather than Chilly had given him the right advice: "It was as though I was back at day one, trying to figure out the basic prescription for survival. Before I wasn't enough. Now I was too much" (27). Later Melvin sees two inmates fighting, the smaller of the two "selling wolf tickets," or bragging about what he will do to the other. Yet another inmate Mel encounters in "the joint," full of braggadocio and style, is Cadillac, who got his name because

> everything was a big thing with him "He had a well-stocked torso with arms and legs for days. When he walked he was a V.I.P. brougham limousine Bogarting its way into two lanes. When negotiating a corner he would slink into a Cleveland lowride . . . while grinning like the grill on a Fleetwood. (35)

This kind of metaphorical-imagistic language that is rooted in everyday experiences Brown uses throughout *Tragic Magic*, as well as another aspect of signifyin(g) called pastiche.

Signifyin(g): Parody/Pastiche

Gates's research on the Black vernacular discursively signifies upon that of Smitherman through repetition and revision by his addition to her list of characteristics the following two aspects of signifyin(g): "parody," or an "exaggerated imitation of a work of art that interprets a work from within rather than without"; and "pastiche," a type of literary parody that "caricatures the manner of an original without adherence to its actual words" (*Signifying Monkey* 107).[9] An example of such signifyin(g) in *Tragic Magic* is Brown's use of a common saying in the Black vernacular, "Quiet as it's kept" (13), to parody or call out Whites who move out of neighborhoods when Blacks move in, better known as "white flight." The parody then critiques Blacks who follow Whites to their neighborhoods. When he was a boy, Melvin was puzzled by Whites vacating his neighborhood when other Blacks moved in. This practice continued until only one White family was left. When he grew up, he learned that some Blacks were migrating to the neighborhoods where Whites had moved to get away from other Blacks.

Melvin says this paradoxical situation enabled him to get "a more sophisticated understanding of the pronouns *we, us, they* and *them*" (12). He learned that Whites view Blacks as "them" rather than "we" or "us"; consequently, based on that premise they justify White flight. This situation causes him to speculate that "the way they hated us, you'd have thought we were the second coming of the Moors. . . . It could be the restless spirit of Columbus, in order to redeem his pitiful sense of direction, was urging whites to complete his journey to the East in search of spices and fabric."

Humorously, then, he concludes: "Quiet as it's kept, that could be the reason why so many blacks follow whites whenever they move. It's a well-known fact that we have a heavy jones for highly seasoned food and fine threads" (13). Signifyin(g) on Blacks and Whites, Melvin playfully puns on the concept of people as "pronouns":

> It's too bad about them [i.e., Whites], if that's why they moved. And shame on black folks, too, if all the migrating we've done in this world was just to break into the ranks of somebody else's parade. If this is true, we have all become words used in place of ourselves. But I keep forgetting. If in each other's eyes we are simply pronouns, it's nothing personal, since *we* can never know *them*. (13)

Intraculturally, "Quiet as it's kept" is one of those expressions that people use in conversations where only the conversants are privy to its broader implications or share a common cultural background that places the experience in perspective. Toni Morrison, in "Unspeakable Things Unspoken," says she uses "Quiet as it's kept" in the opening sentence of *The Bluest Eye* for purposes similar to those above and "for how speakerly it is, how it speaks and bespeaks a particular world and its ambience" (21). The words in this phrase are "conspiratorial," emblematic of a secret that is not to be revealed, the "conspiracy" paradoxically being "both held and withheld, exposed and sustained," or the "public exposure of a private confidence" (20). Implicit in this phrase also is a certain intimacy between the reader and the page that the writer establishes, by setting up a jazzerly call-and-response situation where a secret in the text is being shared. In this instance, Melvin shares with the audience the desire of some Blacks who secretly wish to be with Whites even though they do not acknowledge it and of some Whites who have an ambivalent desire to experience Black culture ("highly spiced foods and fine threads") even as they attempt to flee from it—Sh-h-h-h, "Quiet as quiet as it's kept."

Swinging with the Jazzerly Text: Black Talk and Music

Signifyin(g) as used in the preceding contexts is both "metaphoric and ironic" (C. Lee 12). In *Tragic Magic* Brown also focuses extensively on another element of "Black Semantic" expression—"music and cool talk" (Smitherman, *Talkin' and Testifyin'* 50)—to convey the jazz/blues paradigm. Whereas the "speakerly" text privileges the human voice, what I call the "jazzerly" text privileges the jazz/blues aesthetic that Gloria T. Randle characterizes as "music as text" (131). Similar to Toni Morrison's *Jazz*, in which vernacular language and music are inseparable (Griffin 192), *Tragic Magic* embodies a feeling and tone with the jazz/blues impulse woven throughout the vernacular like a thread in fine tapestry. For instance, when Melvin is in a quandary about who he should trust in the penitentiary he starts avoiding Chilly. They had not spoken since the "kissing" incident with Showboat. Like a predator on the prowl, however, Chilly has been seeking out Melvin to whom he issues a threat of injury: "You may think its over but it ain't . . . [i.e., submitting to his offer of protection from people like Showboat]. You may not have submitted to the draft but you'll submit to a skin graft from a shank" (38).

Confused about who he should trust, Melvin runs into Hardknocks again, who tells him there is nothing wrong with wanting protection, but he just needs to find his own way of surviving: "Some cats join the Muslims. Others lift weights. But most find a road dog they can talk and walk with" (40). Furthermore, he assures Melvin that he is not the only man in prison who is afraid: "Every man in here got some cauliflower in their heart. And don't let nobody fool you. The cats that got the most are those that claim to be something more than a man," to which Melvin responds:

> There was no way I could follow that. And I didn't even want to. It was the kind of solo work that reminded me of Gene Ammons playing "Willow Weep for Me," without ever making it sound like he's copping a plea.
>
> Being around Hardknocks was like listening to the Count Basie Band doing "April in Paris." No matter how many times you heard the tune, you just had to hear them do it "one more time." (40)

Shortly thereafter, Melvin goes before the parole board and uses the advice that Hardknocks has given him on "the varieties of truth that will and won't set you free" (41), by telling the board that his views about the war have changed since his imprisonment. Improvising as usual, Melvin manages to get paroled after serving only a year and a half of his three-year sentence.

The influence of the jazz/blues aesthetic along with the oral tradition, especially signifyin(g), to portray the search for Black identity and heroism works well stylistically because these two modes of Black expressive culture have the following common characteristics: "restatement of traditional forms, followed by their revision or reinterpretation" (A. Murray, *Stomping* 6, 126; see also R. Ellison,

Shadow and Act 234; Gates, *Signifying Monkey* xxiv; Hollingsworth and Leake 50; Smitherman, "Talkin' That Talk" 199). Their commonality resides in the process of making that which has come before a part of the present, then elaborating on or modifying the inheritance to make it unique yet reflective of the inherited traits. As such, these forms reflect what Amiri Baraka calls the "changing same" (qtd. in Werner xxvi) of Black experience.

Furthermore, the jazz/blues aesthetic captures, in "form, style, tone, and language," the "intimacy and the reciprocity between artist [writer] and listener [reader] that are so crucial to the vital, dynamic format of musical production and performance" (Randle 132). Through cultural memory, then, Melvin engages this changing same aspect of Black expressive culture—the individual working within his own tradition as a coping mechanism to deal with the changing same situation of America's drafting of young Black men to fight its wars despite discriminatory treatment. In this respect, Brown accomplishes in discourse what jazzmen adeptly accomplish with their instruments—"playing the changes." In jazz playing the changes occurs when a musician changes the melodic line to coincide with chord changes, often by yet another musician. Such musical ingenuity made bebop a unique jazz expression.[10]

The beboppers, who were quite adept at playing the changes, would take a composition, such as "What Is This Thing Called Love?," make a different melody (a bebop line) of it, and change a few chords in the structure of the tune. For example, in 1945 the White jazz saxophonist Charlie Barnett popularized "Cherokee." However, when Charlie "Bird" Parker played the tune, his version ignored melody entirely. Referred to as "an assault on musical convention" by mainstream music critics, Parker's bebop adaptation is called "Koko," one of the most "outstanding tributes" to the bebop canon, according to Ted Ross, narrator of the video "Celebrating Bird: The Triumph of Charlie Parker." Similarly, Bird's "Ornithology" (referred to as the National Anthem of Bop) is an appropriation and reconfiguration of "How High the Moon" (Lott 465). This type of creativity, that is, playing the changes, finds expression in *Tragic Magic* by the way in which Melvin improvises on the old theme of Black men being drafted into a racist military. Some, like Otis, respond to the draft by going into battle, whether as a volunteer or a draftee. Others, like Melvin, play the changes by taking a different route from that traditionally taken by Black men when he becomes a conscientious objector.

Flashbacks: Call-and-Response

The text of *Tragic Magic* is so rhythmical that one could refer to it as a musical score, a characteristic that has also been applied to some of Toni Morrison's novels, such as *The Bluest Eye*, *Beloved*, and *Jazz*. In much the same way that *The Bluest Eye* captures the "sounds and flavors" of Black folk during World War II (Randle 133), *Tragic Magic* moves to the jazzerly beat of the Black community during the Vietnam War era. For instance, when the gate opens to let Melvin out of prison, he says: "I took that long walk out the front gate. My heart played Miles Davis doing 'Walkin' with all his quick note shifts, double-clutching slurs, and staccato skips" (9). Brown makes the reader not only see the protagonist walking with a swag while skipping and dapping along but also hear the music, with its smooth horn tempos and skipping staccato percussion beats simulating the joy the protagonist feels as he leaves the place that has held him in bondage for the past year and a half and enters society again. Brown's use of alliteration, punctuated with both cacophony and assonance underscores the action in this textual/musical phrase.

After Melvin gets back to the neighborhood, he and Otis go to a club with their friends, Pauline and Alice, and as they enter they hear a Gloria Lynne recording titled "Trouble Is a Man." The song sounds so good to one listener that she shouts "You chewin' my cabbage now girl" and "Go on, Gloria! Sing the shoulda, woulda, coulda blues, girl!" (124). Then a man "staggers" in wearing platform shoes "elevating his heels like staircases were about to cause him to make a crash landing." He says:

> "I don't know what you women talkin bout. . . . I'm Sir Rap A Lot and it's time for me to get a shot at the limelight. I was born in the Dixie Peach but raised in the Big Apple. I'm still fruit but on a different tree. But now nobody can take a bite out a me, you dig. If looks could kill, I'd be murder one!"
>
> "Somebody should," a woman said. (124–25)

Melvin, fed up with this interlocutor in his conversation with the women, expresses his exasperation. And in his usual mode of evasion, he tells the women to exclude him from this dude's braggadocious boast about a man being "trouble." But one of the women won't rest until she gets his opinion. So continuing the organic metaphor established above and well aware that he just got out of prison, she tells Melvin, "But you've already been picked." So siggin' on him, she continues: "And there's always a chance that if you chew your cabbage slick enough, one of us might be willing to relieve you of some of that sweet batter we know you got backed up in you" (125). Such antiphonal responses characterize much of the jazzerly call-and-response dialogue in *Tragic Magic*.

Similar to the text of Toni Morrison's *Jazz*, which Farah Jasmine Griffin says "is like an arrangement for a jazz orchestra" (196), there are neither chapter divisions nor headings in *Tragic Magic*; rather, incidents flash back to the protagonist's early life and then forward to the present, and then back again, simulating the way in which a jazz composition goes back to a refrain after the main melody. These flashbacks function as a type of (re)call and response apparent in Melvin's present-time response to past events—childhood, college, and prison—providing the reader a vantage point from which to evaluate his actions as he progresses through various phases of awareness during his coming-of-age, or rite-of-passage, experience. For example, the first person in the neighborhood he sees when he is released from prison is Mrs. Cotton, an elderly neighbor with whom his parents have left the key to their house since they are at work and unsure of the time he will arrive. Seeing her causes him to flashback to the time when, as a little boy, he defiled her garden by trampling the vegetables on a dare from Otis and some of his other mischievous friends. The dignity and self-control that Mrs. Cotton exhibited upon discovery of the prank, however, causes Melvin to say the "guilt whipped me into a fare-the-well" (15). He knew he had one of two choices: to save face with his friends by acting on what he knew was wrong or doing it anyway and risking the loss of respect that his neighbor had for him. Consequently he voluntarily "made restitution"; and at the risk of being called a sissy by the boys, he helped Mrs. Cotton restore the garden. This incident marks one of several early tests of his masculinity by the "street committee" that Melvin fails because he feels remorseful for his mischievous actions.

Such incidents reveal Melvin's compassion, which was developed at an early stage in his life, as evidenced by his call-and-response relationship with his father and mother, Walter and Rachel Ellington. When Melvin arrives at his parents' empty house following his prison release, he sees the crumpled covers on his father's empty bed reminding him of his father's snoring and his constant complaint: "Damn whiteys, buildin a kingdom off a my back!" (22). As a young boy Mel had not the slightest idea what his father meant. He only knew how comfortable it felt when he crawled in the bed with his father and "snuggled his nose" smelling his father's breath, "letting it mingle with mine." Then, Mel says, "from the pull and smell of his rest, Pops spoke to me, exhaling the whys and wherefores of his life. . . . His snoring was filled with the lingo that a father must pass on to his son if the son is to pass on the family tongue, get a grip on his own voice, and not lose himself in babbling" (22). The rhythmical essence of his father's breath bequeaths a legacy not unlike that which Duke Ellington's mentor bequeathed to him. Such memories played a role in Mel's survival while in prison, as he observes: "Recollections such as these are part of the valuables I buried deep within me while I was away" (15).

Finding his voice, therefore, begins early for Melvin and does not reach completion until he has served time in prison for refusing to go to Vietnam. As coparticipant in this continuum, the reader can grow in awareness along with the protagonist in his quest toward self-understanding. This organizational principle in *Tragic Magic* parallels the design of call-and-response generally in African American vernacular culture. Politically, the implications are that this cultural form "enables both the individual and the community [within and outside the text] to define themselves, to validate their experiences in opposition to dominant social forces," as Werner points out in *Playing the Changes* (xviii).

Speaking of voice, jazz is so integrally related to Black idiomatic expression and so potent that in *Tragic Magic* it spawns its own language. While Melvin is still in the shower room in prison, and the masculinity debate is still in full swing, he observes: "Steam rages in the shower room, and the talk is of the final comedown in the test of manhood between black and white being determined by the one who can get his rizz-od as hizz-ard as a rizz-ock at a mizz-oments nizz-otice" (20). This type of signifyin(g) called "buzz talk" was a private language that Blacks developed during the era of bebop. Melvin says once he went to a "chili house" in Harlem where it is rumored that "ideas going through boot camp in Charlie Parker's head resulted in his finding a metaphor inside old chord changes that no one had heard before," prompting the creation of this language. He reports that the people who were in attendance said:

Bird's playing started everyone in the joint to jumping giddy and yapping in a strange tongue that emphasized the buzzing sound of the letter Z. It started when someone said—

"Kiss my ass!" And the comeback was—

"That don't make me no nevermind cause eee-it-tiz neee-iz-zot the beee-iz-uuuteee, eee-it-tiz the bee-iz-zoooteee!"

Bird wailed on at the top of the chords, and the Z string rap spread its healing and hurting potential all over Seventh Avenue. Over the years this so-called "buzz talk" became the most popular lingo and the most difficult for outsiders to decipher. (4–5)

As in this instance, Blacks often use the vernacular as a private language with which to communicate while excluding Whites from its private intracultural rituals. By the time Whites catch on, Blacks have created a different lingo.

Tragic Magic is not *about* jazz; rather, Brown uses its style as a form of Black expressive culture to organize imaginative concepts in his narrative (Early 742). Just what, then, is the jazz/blues aesthetic and how does it serve as an apt metaphor for Melvin's quest? The answer lies in four concepts: struggle, improvisation, identity, and survival. Thematically, *Tragic Magic* epitomizes the jazz impulse as defined by Ellison, who theorizes the relationship between literature and jazz as a "way of *defining/creating the self* in relation to community and tradition" (*Shadow and Act* xxi; emphasis added). The "tradition" of which Ellison speaks originated in Africa, home of call-and-response and the "AAB structure of the classic blues" that, according to cultural theorist Amiri Baraka, are "sacred forms which encode West African understandings of self, community, and spiritual energy" (qtd. in Werner xxii). *Tragic Magic* is rife with the tone and mood of the blues, which includes jazz, because "jazz is the fully orchestrated blues statement such as you would find in a Duke Ellington sonata," observes Murray ("Function of the Heroic Image" 573). Survival is the "central metaphor" of the blues (574). It is a matter of "affirming life in the face of adversity," which constitutes "heroic action" (575). To survive requires that a person be resilient. In other words, he must be able to rebound from defeat. Whether a person has a success story is not as important as his ability to come back after life has pushed him down. A person must "improvise" to be resilient (577). The jazz impulse, according to Werner, provides a way of exploring implications of realizing "the relational possibilities of the (blues) self, and of expanding the consciousness of self and community through a process of continual improvisation" (xxi).

As a solo performer on the stage of life, Melvin has a call-and-response relationship with those close to him and with the rest of society. His decision not to enter the military, the defiant act upon which the whole novel pivots, is viewed with suspicion by family and friends alike. Even he is unsure himself at first why he dared defy authority in this manner, indicating it was done more or less by default. But by asserting his individuality, he later arrives at self-knowledge through this improvisational relationship with the larger Black community. He goes through this process in much the same way that the jazz artist develops his oeuvre: "assimilation, counterstatement, and elaboration" (A. Murray, *Stomping* 121). When he was a little boy, Melvin assimilated the notion of heroism that most American boys inherit: "I wanted to hang tight with my cap pistols and the vacant lot revivals of John Wayne and Randolph Scott Westerns" (17). But as he grows older, the lessons he learns from the experiences of his father, whose constant refrain is "Damn whiteys, buildin a kingdom off a my back" (21), and other Black men in society prove to him that the heroic models in those Westerns do not apply to Black men. So he decides to make a "counterstatement" when drafted and becomes a conscientious objector. For his stance he serves time in prison where he undergoes a rite of passage.

Melvin experiences an identity crisis because he has permitted himself to be defined by others most of his life, often without question. Sometimes deluded by what others appear to be, he becomes subject to what Brown constructs as the major "tension" in *Tragic Magic*: "Melvin's attempt to come into command of himself, to really gain an intuitive grasp of his life and the world" (qtd. in Lynch 48). During his boyhood and adolescent years Melvin has been spectatorial, living vicariously through his friend Otis, who approaches life more aggressively. Similar to his namesake, Duke Ellington, however, Melvin Ellington deals with life through a "strategy of evasion" (Lock 125), albeit for different reasons.

The inimitable Duke defied categorization (Hasse 29), which is precisely what accounted for his evasion. The critics could not label his music as simply swing or jazz. Music critics, for example, labeled one of Ellington's compositions "a tone poem," an additional example of his integration of the arts. Titled *Black, Brown and Beige*, this orchestral piece was his contribution to the war effort. It relates the saga of Boola, an ageless African, who is brought to America and enslaved. He tries, unsuccessfully, to enlist on the American side in the Revolutionary War. Later, he joins the Union Army in the Civil War. Jumping for joy at the issuance of the Emancipation Proclamation, he becomes the hero at San Juan Hill. Played at Carnegie Hall in 1943, this orchestral piece marked Ellington's debut concert performance in America (Hasse 39), setting the tone for Black male involvement in America's wars in which the Black soldier had to fight for the right to fight. So adept is he at painting musical pictures while also telling a story, Ellington begins with a grand flourish with horns and strings followed by a long interlude of solemn music reminiscent of the Black sacred sphere. Then the orchestral piece is punctuated throughout with drumming evocative of Boola's African cultural background as well as the measured cadence of military marching in his adopted (without choice) American home.

To many, Ellington's views about his craft seemed "contradictory" and "ambiguous"; however, his main concern was probably less to present a carefully argued definition of his music than to resist all attempts at pigeonholing and leave to himself as much creative space as possible (Hasse 125). In *Tragic Magic* Melvin's evasion, on the other hand, grows out of his inexperience in the game of life that will not fall into place for him until he spends time in prison, ironically. In other words, he had not yet understood the relationship between himself and society that would be necessary to shape his ideas about manhood. Brown uses the jazz/blues impulse to clarify this relationship for Melvin in *Tragic Magic*.

I take issue with jazz poet Hayden Carruth's assertion that "of all sounds that destroy music, the human speaking voice is worst" (26). Apparently he is not taking into account "scatting," which is the human voice transformed into a musical instrument, or words become music. In the prologue to *Tragic Magic*, Melvin tells how jazz artist Ella Fitzgerald, performing in a concert overseas, forgot the lyrics to "Mack the Knife." So she improvised by scatting, which began a jazz style that she and Louis Armstrong brought into international prominence. The importance of the speaking voice relative to music is hailed by another jazz artist and critic, Nancy Wilson, who says that for her as a singer "the spoken is more important than the music" ("Jazz Profiles"). When the spoken word captures rhythm in the same way as a song, it can be categorized as what August Wilson, in an interview with Gwen Ifill on PBS *Newshour* calls the "musicality of language" Consider for example this "dissin'" (C. Lee 11) episode between two prisoners, Hardknocks and Cadillac: "You may've been named for them Hard Knocks you've taken but that don't call for no celebration. They ain't even givin up watches for that shit no more. But I'm a put in a good word for you, cause with all the time you got in they ought a give you Big Ben" (36).

Indeed, for Brown, the Black spoken word (vernacular) has power, or *Nommo*, that he captures with the cadences and inflections of Black speech in *Tragic Magic*. In an interview he said that listening to Mrs. Fannie Lou Hamer address the National Democratic Party Convention in 1964, with her dialect ringing through mainstream American culture, convinced him of the "power" inherent in Black vernacular speech ("You Talk Like" 20). She implored: "I question America. Is this ... the land of the free and the home of the brave?"[11] The content of her speech as well as her impassioned delivery in the Southern vernacular were so powerful and convincing that the major networks took the convention off air until she was done. Her words were not some empty, abstract treatise on justice and freedom; rather, they were buffeted by experiential toil as a sharecropper and suffering at the hands of sadistic police who imprisoned and beat her unmercifully for simply seeking the right to vote, a privilege granted only to Whites in the state where she lived at the time. The cadence of her speech evoked pathos and power simultaneously, with unrehearsed vigor. In a similar manner when the vernacular "flows freely" in the text, it gives a "rhythm and lyricism to the prose" (Randle 135). Such linguistic attributes are applicable to *Tragic Magic*. Melvin, for instance, riffs on the standard literary meaning of "scatology" and expands it in the vernacular to define the practice of "scatting" in jazz.

As a jazz/blues "philosopher" Melvin defines scatting as "a renegade form of scatology developed by people who were fed up with do-do dialogues and created a kind of vocal doodling that suggested other possibilities within the human voice" (5). As one of the leading scatting "practitioners," Ella used "the air as her scratchpad" and "scribbled much syllabic salad into song." After her performance in Berlin, where she "bullskated her way through with some bodacious makeshift palaver," she was declared unanimously the "official voice of the Land of Ooh Blah Deee, traveling air mail special and postmarked 'from now on'" (5).

Brown expresses a "fascination" with "language play . . . in the dozens and signifying" (qtd. in Lynch 48). Listening intently as he frequented barbershops and churches enabled him to hear everyday conversation raised to "a high art" (Brown, "You Talk Like" 19). The "talk" of Black folk impresses him not only because of its inventiveness and insightfulness but also through its sound. Not unlike legendary jazz saxophonist Gene "Jug" Ammons, who, Nancy Wilson says, "put his voice through his horn" ("Jazz Profiles"), Wesley Brown put his voice through the text of *Tragic Magic*. He readily acknowledges the influence of the Black vernacular on his writing style in an article aptly titled "You Talk Like You Got Books in Your Jaws" (20), which, in the vernacular, is another way of telling a person that he has become so educated that he can no longer communicate in the language of common, everyday people. The language in this title lends credence to what Zora Neale Hurston says in *Dust Tracks on a Road*, namely, that Blacks think in "hieroglyphics" or "word pictures" (qtd. in Gates, *Signifying Monkey* 199). For instance, on one particular occasion during Melvin's stint in prison, Hardknocks and Cadillac are arguing about how he should act. Cadillac says, "You know what the trouble with most niggers is? They wanna own a Cadillac instead a bein one! But I want what the Caddy stands for. That's why I'm in the joint now" (36). Obviously oblivious to his twisted logic, he then tells Melvin that there are only two kinds of people in the world and he must make up his mind which he will be: "If you don't speed on people, you the one gonna end up getting peed on." Hardknocks, extending and revising Cadillac's automotive metaphor, then takes Cadillac to task: "You run a Coupe de Ville game, Cadillac, but your mind is strictly Pinto material," which prompts Melvin to say: "My nerves had gotten raggedy at the root from listening to them run off at the mouth" (36).

The Jam Session of Life: Bebop vs. Cool Jazz

The sound and rhythm of language in the Black vernacular find parallels in jazz and the blues. Brown, as did his predecessor, Ellison, acknowledges the influence of jazz and blues on his writing, characterizing the dialogues in *Tragic Magic* as functioning like "an improvised jam session" (qtd. in Lynch 49). Most often informal, the musical contest known as the jam session, as Murray points out, is based on "improvisation rather than musical scores and has no set program or repertoire" (*Stomping* 245). It does require, however, "technical mastery" of one's instrument. Some music critics call the jam session a "battle" (Traylor 287). Also known as a "cutting session," it is a contest of improvisational skill and physical endurance among two or more musicians wherein the jazzman "learns the traditions, group techniques, and style," according to Ellison ("The Golden Age" 208). After learning the basics of playing his instrument, as well as the jazz tradition, he must then "find himself . . . his own unique ideas and his own unique voice . . . his self-determined identity and recognition of his manhood" (209). To prove oneself competent in a jam session, the "blues (jazz) musician must not only be a virtuoso performer but also be able to create in a split second . . . Elegance under pressure or bust" (245). Melvin discovers his manhood in the jam session of life with Otis.

A prelude to Melvin's and Otis' "performance" on life's stage is the verbal slugfest Melvin describes between his aunt and uncle in the prologue to *Tragic Magic*. As in the jam session, her intent is not to hurt or destroy her nemesis but rather to best him verbally by signifyin(g) on him. According to Melvin, their "battles" remind him of the jazz contests in the early days of the New Orleans jazz scene. To illustrate, he says one time they were "on the outs," and his uncle refused to engage his aunt in "any verbal slugging." She was so angered by her unanswered challenges that she began badmouthing him in some strange talk she called "Tut." Not knowing what she was saying about him roused Melvin's uncle back into combat, and "their jam sessions were restored in the best New Orleans tradition" (5, 6).

This scene foreshadows the jam session in which Melvin and Otis are involved during their youth and that continues after Otis comes home from Vietnam and Melvin gets released from prison. Throughout childhood and young adulthood they have competed with each other, whether in matters of the heart or head, despite being best friends. Otis has usually taken the lead with Melvin in his shadow. Postwar and postprison, however, their relationship becomes strained, and they find themselves at odds more than in accord. The strain on their friendship reaches a crescendo when Otis freaks out and is later killed. Like Miles Davis's "So What," theirs is a call-and-response relationship. Melvin calls Davis's trumpet solo in "So What" a "wolf ticket signifying behind the dozens" because the musical instruments are "talking at" rather than communicating with each other (163), similar to Melvin and Otis during their verbal jousts.

Cool jazz and swing reigned supreme from the 1920s through the following decade. By the 1940s, however, bebop, a new jazz style, issued onto the scene. Interestingly, the Second World War, in large part, fomented this new genre. Black soldiers coming home from war often saluted each other with upraised fingers forming two Vs. The sign of "Double-V" meant "Victory Abroad and Victory at Home" for Blacks who fought in America's segregated armed forces in Europe during World War II. Owing in part to the soldiers' defiant return home to America and their unwillingness to be subjected to prewar racism, riots broke out in Los Angeles, Detroit, New York, and other urban centers. In this postwar milieu, bebop "exploded" on the scene, a revolutionary music for revolutionary times. The competition between Otis and Melvin is like a jam session consisting of these two music styles, bebop and cool jazz, respectively. Otis exhibits the "raucous," "frantic" pace of beboppers like Charlie "Bird" Parker with his out-of-control temper and spastic behavior. Mel, on the other hand, epitomizes the "cool, laid back" jazz style of Duke Ellington resulting from his serenely cautious approach to life (Lott 458).

Having mastered the jazz tradition as it existed prior to his solo career, Bird, the consummate bebopper, introduced new techniques. He focused on "higher intervals of chords" than jazz men who preceded him and who, in general, ignored "ninths, elevenths, and thirteenths" in jazz improvisations, according to Gary Giddins ("Charlie Parker" 55). These higher intervals were viewed as "dissonant and obscure," but Bird mastered them. Additionally, the pace of his music, especially the composition "Koko," was frenzied and described by some critics as "brutally fast." Such brutality was emblematic of Parker's personal war. He struggled not only with his own personal demons, such as drugs and alcohol, but also was overcome by the "horror" of racism. He seemed "at war" with life until he succumbed to his addictions, according to Hollingsworth and Leake, finding he could no longer "overcome that world with the weapons of purely lyrical art" (46). Like "Bird," Otis is possessed with personal demons, which ultimately leads to his untimely demise.

In the early days, demons that haunted Black men were mainly external—"paterollers," Ku Klux Klansmen, and such who threatened and lynched with abandon. In modern times, despite the continuation of external threats from overzealous, racist law enforcement officers whose racial profiling cause many to end up being victimized by the legal system, according to Black journalist Ellis Cose, "many of our demons . . . reside deep within us, invisible yet powerful, eating away at our confidence and sense of worth" (5). Sometimes they even cause Black men to destroy their brothers, or themselves. Otis's demons cause him to eventually destroy himself.

The code of bebop's hipster music, in speech and dress, gave a surface appearance of defiance. The music was fast and furious. In response to the experiences of Midwestern and Southern Black immigrants to the Northern cities, bebop evolved as an "esthetic of speed and displacement," a type of music that Lott describes as "jagged chords and horn-like linear solos" (461). Some even called Parker's style of bebop an "assault on musical convention" (Giddins, "Celebrating Bird").[12] Even the language of the beboppers was "rapid-fire, scattershot talk" with a pace similar to that of the music (Lott 459). Additionally, this zoot-suit-wearing clan challenged America's dress code, causing one city council (in Los Angeles) to consider passing an ordinance to make the wearing of this style illegal (Lott 460). Without a doubt, bebop was "the war come home," but the open defiance of this music masked an underlying insecurity.

Otis: Blindsided by His Own Bebop Beat

Obviously all the beboppers were not wildly out of control and insecure, which was the public perception; however, like some of them (particularly Bird), Otis is outwardly defiant but inwardly insecure. His boast is louder than his bop. Shortly after Melvin is released from prison, he and Otis go out for a night on the town at the Club Magnifique. On the dance floor, Otis becomes embroiled in an altercation after stepping on the shoes of a nearby dancer. Beginning with verbal insults, the fracas escalates into a potential full-blown brawl. Otis, posturing, threatens the man to stop, or he is " gonna end up with some extra lip" (115). The other man responds in kind. Then Otis contorts his face into a mean, menacing expression and uses gesticulating movements similar to those in Tai Chi, while swinging his arms into "arcs" and swerving left to right. Someone summons the police, and the so-called fight breaks up, after which Otis, Melvin, and their friends, Alice and Pauline, catch a taxicab uptown to a house party. Obviously having failed to carry through on his threats despite all his posturing, Otis, breathing heavily, tells his friends in the taxicab: "Yeah, I know what you thinkin. . . . That dude came at me in-between moves. I didn't have a chance to get my breathin together." Signifyin(g) on Otis, Pauline replies to his lame excuse: "Nigger, . . . if you was as bad as your breath, you would a been able to deal no matter how he came at you. . . . You the one grandstandin . . . " (116).

The prototypical bebop musician is, according to Gerald Early, "brooding, self-destructive . . . [and] dedicated only to the sounds he hears in his head" (734), and so is Otis. Because he hears only his own "sounds," Otis is unable to place his angst in a larger framework and thereby find a solution to his dilemma of having been a Black soldier in a White military establishment. His inability to do so becomes apparent when he convinces Melvin to go with him to a television station that is "wired for sound" where all-night movies are played. As a disc jockey for the radio station, WHIP, Otis has access to several television stations whose film libraries house thousands of silver discs with footage of old John Wayne war movies.

Trippin' Out on Machismo: the John Wayne Syndrome

Whereas Melvin outgrows the John Wayne and Randolph Scott cowboy games he and Otis played as boys, Otis takes them seriously, and his love for John Wayne movies has a great deal to do with his joining the marines, the branch of service noted for machismo. Heroes associated with the Old West, such as John Wayne, often contributed to the idealism of many soldiers who anxiously joined the marines and other branches of service and went to Vietnam. Many Vietnam generation youth, White and Black, had constantly watched John Wayne movies such as *The Alamo*, which affirmed, according to Tobey Herzog, "the indomitable American spirit" and promoted, ironically, the same principles of "nation building and adventure underlying Kennedy's New Frontier" ("John Wayne" 18). John Wayne had produced and/or starred in many of the Westerns and World War II movies to which these young men had been exposed. Therefore, he exerted tremendous influence on these young soldiers' perceptions of war.

As an American "cultural icon," according to Herzog, Wayne symbolizes so-called traditional American values of "patriotism, courage, confidence, leadership and manliness," and he, as well as the characters he portrays in the movies, has become a "mythical figure . . . the American warrior-gentleman," indeed, the representative of "manhood" ("John Wayne" 18). In these Westerns and war movies Wayne appears in a variety of roles, from cavalry officer to soldier and sailor to cowboy. In 1960 he played the role of the western hero Davy Crockett, the "king of the wild frontier." He also played the roles of pilot and Seabee. In other words, he was no respecter of military branches of service. The "combat version" of the obsession with John Wayne during the Vietnam War is what Robert Lifton calls the John Wayne "thing," or syndrome, which meant "military pride, lust for battle, fearless exposure to danger, and prowess in killing" (qtd. in Herzog, "John Wayne" 19).

It is this John Wayne syndrome that infects Otis and sends him over the edge mentally. After Melvin says that he refused to go to Vietnam because he had "no stake in what the Army was doing," Otis gets upset, accusing Melvin of calling him "stupid" and "crazy" for joining the marines and fighting in the war (96). Expressing disillusionment and anger, he then tells Melvin that he used to believe "all that war crap" in the movies. He even commits to memory the "Marine Prayer": "Yea though I walk through the Valley of the Shadow of death I will fear no evil cause I'm the biggest, baddest muthafucka in the valley. . . . [But] that prayer didn't work in 'Nam because the Vietnamese don't believe in all that 'come-out-and-fight-like-a-man shit'" (96). He then explains how the Vietcong would sneak up on American soldiers and knife them to death and how ambush was their modus operandi rather than the macho stance of American soldiers.

Otis gives up his macho stance in the face of the guerilla warfare tactics of the Vietcong. Therefore, when he and several other soldiers find out that getting "three hits" earns you a "purple heart and a one-way ticket home," he "holds up his hand" during a mortar raid and gets it shot off, saying, "I figured it was better to bleed for a little while than be dead for good" (97). Otis obviously has lost his hand in Vietnam by acting like a coward rather than a hero, as he has portrayed himself to friends and family when he returns home from Vietnam. Symbolically, Otis's holding up his hands is an indication that he has surrendered to the disillusionment of the false ideals of manhood and patriotism engendered by the John Wayne syndrome. Ultimately, he surrenders to death because of false heroism.

Holding the nub of his arm in Melvin's face, Otis then tells him about a recurring John Wayne dream he has had since the injury. In the dream "the Duke" (Wayne) is sentenced to the Pacific Ocean by Iron Eyes Cody, a Native American. While Wayne is treading water, "Woody Strode, the black cat in *Sergeant Rutledge*, paddles by in a canoe singing a blues. . . . It's all in the blues line. Once you know the reason shit happens, you shouldn't have to ask the question anymore" (98). Therefore, in retribution for having lost his hand in the war, Otis feels compelled to destroy all the John Wayne movies at a local television station that shows all-night movies. He convinces Melvin to go with him.

But first they go out to a house party. While there, Otis begins to freak out, telling Melvin that the only thing that can help him get himself together, paradoxically, is watching those John Wayne movies that he wants to destroy. However, since it is after hours, they must break into the television studio. Reflecting on Audie Murphy, who slept with a German Luger under his pillow after fighting in World War II, where he won several medals, Otis says he understands why: "[Murphy] was caught up because he had been to hell and back. . . . And he found out that a hero ain't nothing but a sandwich. That's why he started making movies. That was probably the only thing he felt safe doin'. Well, I been hellified too" (130). Otis, being disillusioned about Murphy's brand of heroism, constantly watches these movies (some of which portray Murphy as a lead character) in an attempt to "get himself together," as he tells Melvin: "What you don't understand is that when losing my hand starts to get to me sometimes, it's because I'm pissed off that the war wasn't like the movies. But once I watch a few John Wayne pictures I'm all right" (130).

Brown's fictional presentation of this obsession with Audie Murphy and John Wayne mirrors the actual experiences of many White and Black soldiers who fought in the Vietnam War. William D. Ehrhart writes in his memoir about the influence not only of John Wayne but also Audie Murphy on his "unrealistic perception of what it meant to be in the service and fight a war" (qtd. in Herzog, "John Wayne" 19). Similarly, many of the respondents whom Wallace Terry interviewed for his collection of oral narratives, *Bloods*, express a desire to be like John Wayne. One said that he was "brought up on . . . Robin Hood . . . and John Wayne [who] came to save people," while another said as soon as many recruits would arrive in Vietnam they would want to emulate heroes of Western films by asking for "a .45, hand grenades, and a bandolier" so they could "fight like John Wayne" (qtd. in Herzog, "John Wayne" 19).

At the television station where the John Wayne movies are housed, Otis summarizes for Melvin several of the movies, talking at breakneck speed (as though he were high on speed). Brown has a way of injecting humor in this desperate scene during Otis's obvious meltdown where the pace of his speech is fast and furious, similar to that of Bird Parker playing "Koko," and he disallows Mel to get a word in edgewise:

> "Here's the John Wayne section," Otis said when we reached the last level. "They got everything the Duke has done since 1939 when he made *Stagecoach*. That's when he really started to work his show with that yippy-yi-yay shit. Look, here's *They Were Expendable*, *The Fighting Seabees*, *Back to Bataan*, and *Sands of Iwo Jima*. . . ."
>
> "I run this scene over and over because this dude, the one pointing up at the plane and saying, 'Look.' See how he got it in the mouth? Right in the middle of a word. That's the way it was in the Nam. The VC didn't wait around for you to finish a sentence before they interrupted your train of thought with a mortar." (138)

Totally self-absorbed and on the edge mentally, Otis continues giving a play-by-play description of scenes in numerous John Wayne movies. At times he forgets that Melvin is there with him because he is so caught up in the moment. Trying to get his attention and bring him back to reality, Melvin constantly calls out his name:

> "Otis!"
>
> "This is where John Wayne gets it. . . . Check the Jap playin possum! You gotta give it to the Duke, though. He . . . blew that sucker away! . . . Watch John Agar empty a whole clip in that Jap. . . . He definitely gave him a Japanese rupture—One Ball Hung Lo!"
>
> "Otis!"
>
> "This is the part I like, when John Agar raps. I know it by heart. 'Aw right, you Marines, let's saddle up and get back in the war!' That reminds me of the scene in. . . ."
>
> "Otis, the film snapped!" (139)

Like the film, Otis's mind has "snapped" during this racist tirade about Japanese fighters. In his frenzy, he tells Melvin a story about a Vietnamese village called Ben Suc, in which military intelligence suspected Vietcong activity. Though they could not prove the village was sympathetic to Vietcong, they bulldozed it anyway, without "leaving a trace that it ever existed" (138). Otis then reveals: "These flicks did to my mind what them bulldozers did to Ben Suc. The funny thing is, I can't stop watching them. There's something in me that still wants to believe that the Nam was like what we used to see in the movies" (138).

Even though the film snaps (because the reel is spinning too fast) Otis is oblivious to it. Next he accuses Melvin of thinking he has "flipped out" when the lights are turned on. Feeling guilt, shame, and any number of conflicting emotions related to his decision to join the military and go to Vietnam rather than refusing as did Melvin, Otis screams: "I ain't stupid. Just 'cause you didn't go into the service you think you better than me" (139). He jumps on Melvin, pushing him against the wall, setting off the alarm. Running out of the television station, alarms blaring, they encounter two policemen. To divert the officers' attention, Melvin plays the trickster, and just like a jazz artist in a jam session, he improvises a story on the spot. Being ordered to halt about a block away, he must come up with a plausible reason for running. Melvin relates to them a humorous, entertaining story chock-full of stereotypical images of Blacks. Signifyin(g), Melvin concocts the story that is actually "double speak" for the express purpose of providing a means of escape and a cover-up for the breaking-and-entering violation Melvin and Otis have just committed when they go into the TV station after closing hours to view John Wayne movies. Just like Ella Fitzgerald (whom Melvin praises in the prologue for her ability to perform the art of scatting, which he calls "scatology" or "talkin' shit"), Melvin improvises by signifyin(g) for the policeman who laughs so hard at the story that he lets them go, thereby enabling them to survive this brush with the law and escape being jailed (142).[13]

After the incident at the television studio, Otis's mental and emotional insta-bility further deteriorates, as Brown adroitly paints a picture of PTSD through this character. Still upset, Otis goes to Wells's Restaurant with Melvin to meet with their friends Pauline and Alice. But they have left. Since Melvin will not engage him in a fight, he picks a fight with an anonymous, mean-looking, "scarred-face dude" in a red suit with rings on every finger. Resisting all of Melvin's attempts to dissuade him, Otis calls the man "a punk" and then asks him: "Do you believe style is character?" (144). The man, who obviously does not want to be bothered, slaps Otis down and leaves the restaurant.

Livin' by the Code of the Streets: Style vs. Character

In addition to being indoctrinated with the John Wayne syndrome, Otis like the "scarred-face dude" has also grown up in the streets. During adolescence, Otis appointed himself to instruct Melvin in the fine art of "getting his mack on" with the girls. A macho type, he lives by the code "love 'em and leave 'em." Or, as Mel so aptly describes his technique: Otis could "find them, fool them, feel them, fuck them, and then forget them with exceptional agility" (23). I agree with Ellis Cose, author of *The Envy of the World: On Being a Black Man in America*, that such a lack of respect for women often comes from the "code of the streets" (11) where Black boys learn biology from others having sex "in dirty alleys" (47). Those who ascribe to this code value style over character.

A "dude" gets his "rep" on the street, according to John Horton, depending on his "style" (29). The meaning of style can range from carrying oneself well to dressing well to showing "class." The person with style usually *demands* (as opposed to *commands*) "respect . . . in such a way that he is able to look tough and inviolate, fearless, secure" (29). But appearances can be deceiving. This dialectic of appearance versus reality in *Tragic Magic* has a metaphorical correlative in the "style versus character" debate regarding heroism that is ongoing between Melvin and Otis. Otis's style contributes to his self-destructive demise because he has been unduly influenced by claims to manhood deduced from John Wayne movies and the hard bad man image of the streets. On the other hand, Melvin's character equips him with the knowledge not only to survive the harsh reality of prison life but also to return from prison to society with a renewed desire to work toward heroic efforts that warrant a claim to manhood based on introspective reassessment and service to the community. Consequently, Melvin completes the journey toward self-discovery that was begun in prison when he heroically intervenes to thwart a senseless act of violence between two neighborhood boys who are victims of the street image of manhood that contributes to Otis's death.

The paradoxical nature of exuding style as a Black male in America, according to Cose, is that as

> self-destructive as the macho street attitude can be in the long term, in the short term it can be life-preserving, which is to say that the very attitude that sends so many of us to the morgue sometimes can seem our only hope for survival . . . in both a physical and a psychological sense. (56)

This phenomenon explains Otis's hair-trigger temperament and his rough edge. Style is everything in the streets, and Otis is constantly stylin' and profilin' to project a rough and tough image as a sort of protective shield. The other reason is to establish his "rep." For instance, while they are at Club Magnifique with Pauline and Alice, Otis and Melvin go to the men's room. As they talk, Otis constantly "checks himself out" in the mirror. "Tighten[ing] up his image," he "carefully" adjusts his shirt collar and goes through "a series of leaning, ducking, and feinting maneuvers" (111). After he goes back into the club he becomes involved in a fight on the dance floor, which is expected, according to the code of the streets, as Cose points out, because a man has to always show his "tough side" and be willing to use "violence," or at least "threaten" to use it, to "face people down" (56). Cose's rejoinder to James Baldwin's assertion in *The Fire Next Time* that the White man has become entrapped in his history of violence is that "we [as Black men] are trapped right there with him," accepting the notion that Black men are brutes according to prevailing stereotypical images (13). Nowhere is this concept more apparent than in Otis's actions. He confronts the brutish in himself that he has covered up with style. Ironically, the violent tendency in Otis that keeps him alive also causes his self-destruction.

Brown paints a dramatic image of how style versus character can lead to no good end. Living up to his John Wayne macho image and trying to be streetwise (though obviously shaking in his boots) because he is being ignored, Otis leaves the restaurant in pursuit of the anonymous scarred face dude wearing a red suit into the alley. The man stands at the corner waiting for Otis to catch up "with his coattail flung back, his right arm cocked on his hip." Then,

> propelling himself toward the other man, . . Otis slammed into him and they stuck together. Then the dude stepped away and disappeared around the corner. Otis tottered and fell backward in a heap on the pavement. The flash of something metallic protruded from his stomach like a grave marker.

Just like Chilly in prison who gets shanked for styling and running off at the mouth, Otis pays the price for his style. Ironically, Otis's worst fear while in Vietnam was being ambushed and "shanked" by the Vietnamese who he thought was his enemy. He survives to come back home from the war only to be shanked by a street thug, metaphorically the enemy within himself. The symbolic significance of Otis's meeting his untimely demise at the hands of this anonymous "presence" lies in his harboring a death wish, as he throws himself onto the man who obviously has a knife. Therefore, in effect, he commits "homicide" on himself, taking suicide to "another level" in true bebop fashion, like the beboppers who took music to "higher intervals of chords" than their predecessors (Giddins, "Charlie Parker" 75).

Melvin: Cool as Survival Strategy

Melvin, on the other hand, epitomizes the "cool jazz" sound heard in the music of such jazz masters as Duke Ellington and Lester Young. Historically, according to Majors et al., in "Cool Pose: A Symbolic Mechanism for Masculine Role Enactment and Coping by Black Males," "coolness" was a trait evidenced in the African oral tradition, having to do with "character building, artwork, language, dance, initiation rituals, warrior cults, and rituals for acquiring a mate" in several African civilizations dating back as far as 2000 to 3000 B.C. (247). In modern society, coolness, or cool pose, is mainly a "coping mechanism." Joel Dinerstein lists the following four "core African American cool concepts" that issued in the era of cool jazz and that continue to influence contemporary jazz: "to control your emotions and wear a mask in the face of hostile, provocative outside forces; . . . to maintain a relaxed attitude in performance of any kind; . . . to develop a unique, individual style that communicates something of your inner spirit; . . . to be emotionally expressive within an artistic frame of restraint" (241).

These characteristics of the smooth jazz men, which Geneva Smitherman discusses in "Word from the Hood: The Lexicon of African-American Vernacular English," describe Melvin, who develops cool as a "survival strategy" (206). As a young Black man growing up in the urban environment of New York, he has not yet discovered his true identity. Unskilled in the ways of manhood, he plays life "by ear" like a musician with improvisational skill. Observant and contemplative, he is slow to act, a practice that characterizes Melvin's life from childhood to adolescence. For instance, at parties he will extend his hand several times to girls to see if they want to dance. If no one takes his offer, he eases his hand into his pocket and quietly walks away from the scene. During adolescence he sits on the sidelines wondering if he should "get it on" with a girl only to be dared into and instructed about the finer points of "mackin" by Otis. Nervously fumbling to steal a kiss while being egged on by his peers, Melvin overshoots his target, ramming his and the girl's teeth, and earning for himself the not so complimentary nickname "Mouth," a source of much derision and a name that sticks with him. Symbolically, this name fits Melvin because he has a way with words that has enabled him to deal with many situations, including the fabricated story that allows him and Otis to be released from the police following Otis's escapade at the television station.

The Heroic Quest: Separation, Instruction, and Aggregation

Melvin's father advises him to take an approach to life that embodies the ideal state of balance, or coolness, that Duke Ellington personifies. Joel Dinerstein, in "Lester Young and the Birth of Cool," defines "balance" as an "ideal state" of "cool" that is characterized by "an engaged state of mind between the emotional poles of 'hot' (aggressive, intense, hostile) and 'cold' (unfeeling, efficient, mechanistic)" (241). Mel's father, an accomplished pianist whose aspirations are cut short by a hand injury at work, is such an ardent admirer of Ellington that he has collected nearly all of his records and practically raised Melvin on his music (79). One particular Ellington composition, titled "Diminuendo and Crescendo in Blue," is the embodiment of what Mel's father considers the balance he must maintain to survive (80). As Melvin grows older, his father continues to emphasize staying this "middle ground," between the lows and highs of life, because life is a struggle, like a continuous jam session. He must keep his head and maintain a sense of balancing the extremes in life because "freedom is staying loose when time is tight" (80). So Melvin adopts an attitude of mellowness.

As a young man, Melvin followed his father's advice. But as he gets older, he struggles to discern the characteristics of being his "own man" and to deal with issues of trust. This theme of finding oneself at the nadir of existence is not new to literature; however, Brown puts a slightly different spin on it. He uses a tripartite structure to develop Melvin's journey to self-knowledge that is similar to the design developed by anthropologist Arnold Van Gennep to describe rites-of-passage ceremonies in most cultures and adapted by Baker for use in a Black context to construct what he calls *rites of the Black (w)hole*:

> The first . . . involves the black person's separation from a dominant, white society. . . . The black initiand in the second or liminal phase enters a period of instruction that is "betwixt and between" anything approximating fixed social status. . . . The third, and final, phase is aggregation [during which] the marginal initiand is reintegrated, with a new status, into the society from which he has separated. (*Blues* 154)

Separation: Beginning of Journey to Self

Melvin becomes involved in the civil rights movement at City College in New York, where he meets Theo, a fellow student and Black activist who promulgates a philosophy of racial relations that is not only controversial but also contradictory. Theo organizes "freedom high" parties ostensibly to raise money for the civil rights movement, though whether he actually contributes the funds is doubtful. At these parties, he encourages Black and White students to hurl epithets at each other to supposedly "get racism out of their systems" and clear their minds for really dealing with the struggle (58). In preparation for this verbal slug fest, Theo requires the students to read Allen Ginsburg's *100 Years of Lynching*.[14] He even goes so far as to encourage sexual liaisons between Blacks and Whites so they can "rid themselves" of the desire or lust for someone of the opposite race. Theo's plan backfires, however, when his own girlfriend, Geneva, not only sleeps with but also leaves him for a fellow White student, Keith, with whom he has forced her to get "freedom high." As far as she is concerned, these sexual exchanges are merely a ruse for Theo to sleep with White girls anyway. Theo then abandons his plan to work together with Whites in the struggle for Black equality and replaces it with a Black separatist philosophy.

The assassination of Malcolm X coupled with Geneva's decision to leave prompts Theo to retaliate by forming a Black nationalist organization. Afterward, he convinces Melvin to join his new group, called "The Blue Monks," who wear hooded black sweatsuits. Their mantra is quoting the titles of Thelonious Monk tunes such as "'Little Rootie Tootie,' 'Straight, No Chaser,' 'Epistrophy,' or 'Round Midnight'" whenever a White person attempts conversation with them. Similar to "buzz" talk, jazz provides the "code" to their secret language.[15] As the Vietnam War gains momentum, Theo, always in the forefront of rallying around a cause, forms the "No Vietnamese Ever called Me a Nigger Caucus."[16] And, true to form, Melvin joins. Again using his contradictory logic, Theo convinces the members in his newest organization to resist the draft by going to the registrar's office and giving up their student deferments. Then they must write a letter to the local board indicating what they have done so that when drafted they can protest by claiming conscientious objection and thereby refuse to go to war. But it turns out that the army refuses to recognize "Blue Monks" as a bona fide religion; therefore, when their demand for conscientious objection status is denied, Melvin and Theo are stuck with one of three choices when drafted: going to Vietnam, skipping town, or going to prison.

In the midst of their dilemma, Keith (Theo's White friend) commits an act of self-immolation in protest of the war (similar to the Vietnamese Buddhist Monks),[17] proving himself to be more committed to the struggle than Theo himself who constantly tells the other students they must be willing to give their lives for the cause. Theo's own cowardice (couched in pseudo-revolutionary rhetoric) and despair over Keith's death leads to his skipping town like other draft dodgers. Melvin, on the other hand, standing up for his convictions and upholding the principles that Theo propounded but failed to follow, keeps his appointed day in court for refusing to go to war and is sentenced to three years in prison for draft evasion.

It seems there is no end to the people who want to use Melvin to advance their own agenda. For example, the "out-to-lunch" attorney whom Melvin consults to represent him at his conscientious objection hearing has a hidden agenda. Instead of pleading his client's case, this attorney is more interested in proving some outlandish legal thesis he has concocted, which involves maximum sentencing and his client being bound and gagged, like the Black Panthers, to draw public attention to their cause (132–35). Melvin's subsequent imprisonment, resulting from his actions and his decision not to serve in Vietnam, causes him to become separated from the dominant society, thereby setting in motion an odyssey characterized by a search for his identity.

Therefore, Melvin, the Black quester, must separate himself from White society to "find" himself through an immersion in Black culture (during which he is marginalized from the dominant culture). The Black (w)hole is the mythological "descent into the underworld" that the heroic quester must take into his own subconscious, "an inner realm" within which he will gain some insight or revelation to help him deal with some "personal" and/or "social" crisis (Ford 20). For Melvin, the Black (w)hole is prison.

Instruction: Rite of Passage into the Black (W)hole

For Melvin, the fragmentation caused by lack of self-knowledge must be re-membered through immersion in Black cultural values. As did his literary predecessor, Richard Wright,[18] Houston Baker Jr. feels that in a society where Blacks are dominated by Whites "a 'life crisis' of Black identity" is inevitable. Using the trope of the "Black (w)hole," Baker says to deal with this identity crisis the Black man must go through a rite of passage to gain (w)holeness of self. He must have an "underground experience, i.e., . . . go through the black (w)*hole*, where the trickster has his ludic, deconstructive being . . . the domain of *wholeness*, and achieved relationality of black community in which desire recollects [re-members] experience and sends it forth as blues" (*Blues* 151). Melvin's penchant for experiencing contradictions follows him to prison, which ironically affords him the opportunity to discover his identity.

Melvin is separated from the rest of society when he is sentenced to three years (half of which he serves) in the federal penitentiary for refusing to be inducted into the army. Ironically, his incarceration provides his place of instruction in a makeshift (improvisational) Black male community where Melvin encounters a variety of ideas about Black masculinity to help him sort through his own dilemma of survival. His guide on the journey to self-discovery is Hardknocks. In the final phase of his rite of passage, Melvin is reintegrated into the community of relatives and friends with a new status as a free, mature man. As an ex-prisoner he is physically free; however, having become aware of the true meaning of "manhood," and in the process discovering his own identity, he is also emotionally and psychologically free. As illustrated in the section of *Tragic Magic* titled "Separation," Melvin has been at the mercy of others because he lacks self-knowledge. Having separated himself from society, he must now enter a liminal existence on the journey toward self-knowledge.

Similar to the hero in classical fiction, the hero of *Tragic Magic* goes into a symbolic underground inside prison, an inward journey to awareness and wholeness. Metaphorically Mel becomes Legba, the prototypical liminal trickster who resides at the crossroads of life between extremes of manliness and cowardice, between boyhood and manhood, between civilian life and service in Vietnam. As the spectatorial thinker, he goes through life on the outside looking in. This type of existence befits his liminal status.

Prison Experience as War Experience

During this liminal existence in prison Melvin vicariously experiences the Vietnam War. Certain aspects of prison life simulate those of soldiers during wartime: entrance preparation (i.e., induction/processing and orifice inspection); dependence on the buddy system for survival and issues of trust; interaction between short-timers and lifers; and avoidance of getting to know people well for fear of never seeing them again—either because they will be transferred, get out, or be killed. Lawson refers to the new recruits as having a "dislocating experience" ("Old Kids" 30) when they went to Vietnam. The same is true for Melvin whose entrance into prison is similar to induction in the military. After stripping, he and the other new inmates give "the hacks a peep show up our asses and change into prison-issue clothing" (24), which is similar to basic training where the recruits are examined (after being told to drop their pants) and issued military uniforms. There is animated banter between White and Black prisoners, and they engage in a variety of male-bonding rituals, such as signifying on each other about the sizes of their sexual organs (19). Similar to the situation in a military barracks, their accommodations are crowded, as Melvin says, "about sixty of us . . . jammed into a dormitory for new arrivals" (24).

Melvin and the other new prisoners are sized up by the old-timers similar to the way that enlisted men in Country who were nearing the end of their one-year tour of duty viewed the new wet-behind-the-ears recruits when the latter were brought in by helicopter and deposited in the Mekong Delta, the Central Highlands, or some other remote region of Vietnam. Although these old-timers in Country were only in their late teens or early twenties, many of them had aged prematurely because, according to one psychologist, compared to the older recruits of previous wars, they were "less mentally prepared for the carnage and terror that marked the Vietnam experience" (qtd. in Lawson, "Old Kids" 27). When Mel enters prison, some of the inmates "make catcalls and whistle"; however, this noise does not bother him as much as the "howling silence from stares . . . the hard, gritting faces . . . and the eyes that never ignore you" (24). A similar specter greeted newly arrived soldiers in Vietnam who spoke of the blank, empty stares of the men, "the 'old kids,' those seasoned veterans whose glassy eyes and filthy, tattered uniforms gave the lie" to the John Wayne syndrome (Lawson, "Old Kids" 31).

In each situation, prison and war, a person loses the idea of self. Prison-issue clothes are distributed on the first day during processing similar to military uniforms that are handed out to new recruits in basic training. Also, prisoners receive a uniform with an identification number, while recruits get a chain and a dog tag. Such uniformity and anonymity can result in erasing the individual's identity. In war, this erasure of identity makes the recruit more malleable and susceptible to the will of his commanding officer by destroying the person to make a soldier. In prison society the destruction of a person's identity or individuality enables others to manipulate him, as Chilly attempts to do to Melvin.

Then there are the stories that the old-timers tell the new prisoners/recruits, in some instances to see what they are made of and in other instances to take these innocents into their confidence. Chilly acts from both motives. He convinces Melvin that the other inmates will resent him when they find out that he is not only college educated but also a draft dodger. They will take him for a "chump" for being unable to figure out a way to avoid prison since he was "smart enough" to avoid Vietnam; but since he was not, says Chilly, "all that education you got ain't worth a damn" (26). This approach is only a tactical maneuver to scare Melvin into seeking protection from Chilly when the word gets out about his reason for being incarcerated. Chilly's warnings about watching how he walks and sits, avoiding being seen half-nude, and so on, make Melvin nervous and suspicious that everyone can be a potential assailant. A similar situation existed for the soldiers in Vietnam. Because the enemy (the Vietcong) and the ally (the South Vietnamese) looked the same, soldiers had always to be on guard to determine the real enemy because a favorite tactical maneuver of the Vietcong was the ambush. Consequently, soldiers were always on edge wondering if they would step on a land mine or be shanked in their sleep by the Vietcong.

In prison or in war there is a certain tension that comes with the territory. But despite the tenseness of the situation and the possibility of violence or death lurking around every corner, Brown finds a way to interject humor. As Melvin moves about "self-consciously" watching his every move, a "cagey black dude" startles him by asking if this is his first time in prison, why he landed there, and how much time he will have to serve. To Melvin's response, Chilly, the menacing interlocutor, questions why he did not want to go to the army:

> "Oh, you one a them draft dodgers. How much time did you get?"
>
> "Three years."
>
> "Well, that ain't much time. Why didn't you want to go to the army? You a pacifist?"
>
> "No. I'm just not about what the army stands for, that's all."
>
> "Are you about what this place stands for?" (25)

This is the first time Melvin sees Chilly, but it certainly will not be the last.

The betwixt and between nature of Melvin's liminal status becomes apparent when he meets Chilly and Hardknocks, both of whom present themselves initially as buddies but only one of whom has Melvin's best interests at heart. Hardknocks, for instance, advises Melvin not to be ashamed for having resisted the draft because, contrary to what Chilly has told him, the men in prison admire him for his stance. He gives Melvin advice similar to that of his father: "Be what you are. That's what it's all about" (30). Hardknocks then advises him to travel alone and keep to himself, since one is judged by "the company he keeps" (the reference here being made to Chilly). As the time approaches for his release from prison on parole, Melvin promises to write Hardknocks when he gets on the outside. However, Hardknocks advises him against it. Furthermore, he will disassociate himself from Mel the closer he gets to his release date because their closeness will only serve to make him think more about the outside. So he tells Melvin, "with all the time I got [six more years] I don't need to be hangin around nobody that's gettin short" (42). Soldiers also refer to the approaching end of their military service as "getting short in the Man's army."

Addicted to Jazz for Survival

Another person Melvin meets in prison who advances him on his quest for wholeness is Shoo Bee Doo Bee. His name is not only rhythmical but also is the title of a bebop tune, "Ooh, Shoo Bee Doo Bee," by Charlie Parker and Dizzy Gillespie. Literally and figuratively "high" on jazz, Shoob speaks in a jazzy, rhythmical tone. He epitomizes the word *jasi*, which means "to act out of the ordinary" in the Mandingo vocabulary (Randle 141) and is purportedly the word from which "jazz" originated. Melvin describes him as a "cat with a heavy jazz jones who supported his habit by shaking his head, tapping his feet, and tampering with the origins of famous jazz standards" (37). Similar to soldiers in Vietnam who got so spaced out from battle fatigue and witnessing untold carnage that they would sometimes cut off ears and other body parts of Vietnamese and string them around their necks, Shoo Bee Doo Bee wears "a string of reed mouthpieces around his neck and a drumstick strapped to his waist" (37). He is so deep into his "jazz jones" that it has literally become a part of him. When the projection room is not being used to show movies, Shoo Bee Doo Bee broadcasts music to all the prison "dormitories" and cell blocks. Therefore, the prisoners are fed a "steady diet" of jazz. The music room becomes a place of refuge not only for Shoob but also for Mel when his nerves have gotten bad from the noise of the other inmates trying to tell him what is best for him (36).

In Shoob's philosophy, a jazz high is "cathartic" and has the potential for delivering you from a drug high. To illustrate, he relates to Mel a story about a conversation between Miles Davis and John Coltrane when Miles asked why he played so long: "And Trane said, 'it took that long for me to get it all out.' I used to keep it all in and wound up knockneed in a jive humble. . . . Thanks to jazz my toes don't knock no more. I cold-turkeyed to Bird doin 'Now's the Time'; and hucklebucked out a the spell of heroin" (37). In the same way, jazz has been a sobering and liberating influence on the protagonist and the other inmates. It not only releases them from the memory of why they were incarcerated in the first place but also enables them to survive while they are in prison. Shoob is so immersed in jazz that he even speaks in scat. When Mel asks him if he plays an instrument, he replies: "What. . . you think I was just doin'! Bwah bwahdee dah, bwah bwah dee dah, bwah, bwah" (38).

Aggregation: Reconnection with Community

Melvin's release from prison for refusing the draft and declaring conscientious objection prompts jazzerly thoughts as he walks through the prison gates: "My heart played Miles Davis doing 'Walkin' with all his quick note shifts. . . . But my head slowed the tempo of my heart, cautioning it to treat freedom as if it had a very short fuse that could blow up . . . any moment" (9). While in prison he tries not to let his emotions get the best of him and spends his time "sandbagging myself emotionally against feeling anything" (9). Therefore the elation of being free enables him once again not only to experience emotions (albeit somewhat ambiguously) but also to express them metaphorically through the upbeat tempo of Davis's composition. Melvin's walking free is not without some trepidation because he cannot be too sure what fate awaits when he reenters society as a conscientious objector, as well as an ex-prisoner, and is consigned to the scrutiny of the general public, some of whom will not hold him in high regard.

Melvin intuitively feels the disdain of society when he arrives back in the World. After his release from prison in Philadelphia, he catches the bus to New York. Upon his arrival he personifies the city as an enemy, complaining that "New York began pushing me around" (10). The first indignity issues from a newsstand owner who, suspicious that Melvin will try to steal something, asks in an accusatory manner, "Can I help you?" When Melvin answers "No," he experiences the classic stereotypical response to a young Black man in the vicinity of goods for sale when the vendor retorts: "Well, if I can't help you, just make sure you don't try to help yourself." Although no longer in prison, he nevertheless is made to feel like a criminal. On the E-train to Queens he is self-conscious among the other passengers, who make him feel as though he is still "doing time," their "tight drawn faces" reminiscent of those of the prisoners he has just left. Always upbeat, however, Melvin is undaunted. Refusing to let those around him "rain" on his "parade," he improvises by personifying the city again, but this time signifying upon it in a jazzerly tone: "'What's happening, home?' I said, waiting for New York to give me five. But the Big Apple rounded on me and didn't give up any skin. 'Well, later for you, too, then, chump-ass city,' I said to myself" (10).[19]

Melvin's prison experience has taught him that improvisation is the key to survival, and when he returns to the World, he performs his most significant improvisatory act, which thrusts him into the role of a hero. The opportunity presents itself shortly after Otis is knifed by the scar-faced assailant in the alleyway. Two boys, who are among the crowd gathered in the street to witness the incident, begin arguing. One calls Otis a coward and says he would never have let another man stab him but that he would kick him to death first, while the other vehemently disagrees by calling him a "punk." Their fight mirrors the one that they have just witnessed between Otis and his anonymous assailant. One boy goes into a martial arts squat like Otis, flailing his arms and gesticulating in a menacing way. The other picks up an empty wine bottle off the street, breaks it, and rushes toward his assailant. Melvin, noticing the impending fight, responds without thinking: "Suddenly, involuntary muscles activating me thrust me between the two boys" (147).

Jumping between the two boys arguing about Otis's scuffle and eventual death, Melvin gets cut on the hand and in the side, this bloodletting a symbol of his willingness to put himself in harm's way for a just cause to benefit others. Significantly, Mel has served a stint in prison for refusing to fight what he feels is an unjust cause, the Vietnam War. Though he could very well have been killed in this street fight, however, he chooses to act based on his conscious will to do so. His action is significant because he is not following the advice of Otis, or Theo, or Hardknocks; rather, it is what *he* wants to do. Moreover, his most significant act is improvisatory. It goes counter to most of his responses to situations in the past that often found him thinking things over before acting, that is, if he acted at all. His Black (w)hole experience, or rite of passage, in prison, has produced a change in him for the better.

Like the soldier in Vietnam in the heat of battle who sees the enemy encroaching on his territory and then reacts immediately to save his regiment, Melvin intervenes on impulse to break up the fight. Unlike the soldier, however, whose concern is only for his comrade and not the perpetrator of the assault, Melvin shows compassion toward both boys—the assailant and the victim. He does not want the rite of passage for either of these young Black men to be characterized by violence, as it has been for Otis who has been feigning bravado to cover up his insecurities—all style and no character. This type of attitude has warped his notion of masculinity and heroism. Melvin's intervention to break up the fight between these two young men, on the other hand, exemplifies heroism not only as improvisatory but also as an act of compassion rather than bravado.

Dreamin' the Blues/Jazz Coda: The Tragic Magic

Bleeding profusely, Mel ends up in the hospital's emergency room where he is attended by the ER physician Dr. Blue as he loses consciousness and begins to dream. Brown devotes ten pages to Melvin's dream (148–58), in which his whole life flashes before him, albeit in a surrealistic way. At his improvisational best as a writer, Brown weaves a metaphysically symbolic tapestry of Melvin's rite of passage from boyhood to manhood. During an out-of-body experience, Mel says: "A boy resembling me ran into a building. I followed him and knocked on a door to one of the rooms" (148). Each time he enters another room he engages another stage in his life, though the people and the situations are contorted in his dream.

First a childhood friend calls him a "mama's boy," prompting him to ask his mother why he cannot be in the room with her when she is dressing. The scene then shifts, like a movie camera, to Mrs. Cotton, whose garden he trampled on a dare from Otis when they were kids. Next he appears with a group of older boys, all of whom are dressed like cowboys, replete with cap pistols. Melvin coughs in one boy's face because he ran out of caps for his pistol, which goes against the "Western code." Therefore, for his "crime" (of coughing in someone's face), he has to appear in court before a judge, who says: "Your behavior makes it clear to the court that you are in need of corrective detention. Your coughing and spitting are clear signs of your inability to make the appropriate responses during the rites of manhood" (151). Consequently, he sentences Mel to "three years of hard labor at the state camp for fucking and fighting" (151). These scenes interrogate definitions of manhood received from the streets weighed against Melvin's attempts to discover the true meaning of manhood.

In the next scene during his dream, Mel sees a door labeled "wolf tickets and ass kicking." In an atmosphere reminiscent of that in the "Battle Royal" scene of Ellison's *Invisible Man*, Mel finds himself in an arena with hundreds of other "heartless dudes," his heart having been snatched out of his chest by Chilly. Managing to escape the melee by running, Mel is told: "it will go down on your record that you were released because of your skill in evasive action" (154). Leaving this building of rooms, he goes out into the courtyard and hears a homeless man playing the guitar while singing a blues song: "I'm a MAN! / M, man / A, a child, / N, non-spoiled! / I'm a MANN!" When he asks the man to explain the song's meaning the following conversation ensues: "I can't tell you Nothin' bout it"; Melvin says, "But maybe if you could—"; and the man responds, "I can't do Nothin with your maybes, ifs, and supposes. You got to pay your own fare when you in the tragic magic" (157). In other words, knowing what it takes to be a man comes only from the experience of going through the rite of passage from boyhood to manhood; consequently, this marginalized man cannot simply *tell* Melvin what his song means. The meaning is experiential. With a "gift for gab," Melvin has gone through life using words to deal with situations; however, now he is confronted with a situation where words are inadequate.

As Melvin slowly comes out of his state of delirium, he hears the following blues song: "some people long ago were searching for a different tune.... They only had to find the rhythm.... That is how the blues really began" (157). Dr. Blue questions Melvin about his refusal to go to Vietnam, to which he responds: "I guess I didn't understand how the Army had a right to decide when I should put my life on the line.... When it comes to my life, I figure I should have the final say on what I will or won't do" (161). Dr. Blue responds to this bit of wisdom by saying that nothing really matters and that one's general response to life's dilemmas should be "So What," which is so audaciously stated in Miles Davis's jazz song of the same title. He then goes through a lengthy discussion of the narrative call-and-response in the composition "So What" (163).

Dr. Blue then calls Melvin a fool for putting his life on the line to break up the fight between the two boys. But Melvin defends his decision to intervene in the fracas during which he is badly cut: "I didn't do what I did for those kids. I did it for myself. And you know that was the first time I can remember doing something where I wasn't trying to prove something to somebody else?" (164). The atmosphere created in this dream sequence is reminiscent of a composition by Duke Ellington called "Blutopia" that he performed at Carnegie Hall in 1944 (Lock 2). Of all the cardinal colors, blue was Ellington's favorite. Viewing the title of this composition as signifying more than Ellington's predilection for the color, however, Lock feels that it signals a "utopia tinged with the blues, an African American visionary future stained with memories" (3). In the atmosphere of this dream sequence in which the blues is woven like a thread through the tapestry of life, Brown creates a past for Melvin that is laden with such blues-stained memories.

Recounting the details of Melvin's dream, my aim is not so much to explain it as to show how Brown uses it stylistically. Rather than mere summary of his life, the dream serves as a coda, as in a jazz composition, to Melvin's heroic search. Moreover, it signifies upon the story by serving as a repetition of the events of Melvin's life, albeit in an improvised, surrealistic fashion. In this respect, the dream sequence symbolically reinforces the theme that life itself is the "tragic magic."

By taking action on an impulse when he lays his life on the line to part the boys, Melvin makes the most important decision in his life, a choice that is his rather than one made by someone else for him. Having taken this decisive step into manhood, Melvin finally has the courage to approach Alicia, whom he has been admiring from a distance since he was a boy but has never had the courage to ask out on a date because she seems unapproachable. On the day of Otis's funeral, Mel visits her. Despite guilt for desiring her in the midst of grieving for Otis, he successfully consummates his relationship with her. It is as though Melvin's alter ego, Otis—this looming presence of pseudo-manhood—has to die (literally and figuratively) for Melvin to achieve real manhood. This prelude to possible procreation symbolizes a sign of hope for Melvin's jazzerly, improvisational, balanced approach to life based on character, which enables him to survive, as opposed to Otis's out-of-control approach based on style, which causes him to self-destruct.

Otis's defiant attitude is all a facade, masking insecurity. In an attempt to destroy the illusion, he destroys himself. He is unable to deal with the dichotomy between what America professes and what it actually accomplishes in Vietnam to the detriment of the Vietnamese. He becomes mesmerized by the illusion put forth by Hollywood's depiction of heroism—wherein the good guy wears the White hat and the bad guy wears the Black hat, as in the John Wayne movies. But in real life everything is not all Black and White. On a deeper level, or jazzerly speaking, on a "lower frequency" is a middle ground—the "betwixt and between"—where the liminal trickster resides and where dichotomies are harmonized. To survive in this place of balance, one must improvise, as Melvin discovers in prison. This discovery accounts for his ability to adapt to life on the outside, exemplifying grace under pressure, while Otis, when he returns to the World, is destroyed. Melvin's pseudo-war experience in prison teaches him true heroism, whereas Otis's real war experience in Vietnam teaches him pseudo-heroism.

Whereas the price for heroism in *Tragic Magic* is the loss of freedom through imprisonment for refusing service in the military, loss of self could result from heroic action in the Vietnam War. Taking the opposite approach to that of the conscientious objector, Ben Williams, the protagonist of George Davis's *Coming Home*, joins the air force and becomes a pilot after finishing college. He believes that individual effort in academia and the military will enable him to acquire the honor and recognition he deserves. Though to some degree he accomplishes his mission by graduating from Harvard and becoming an officer in the air force, he soon realizes the inadequacy of these accolades to bring him self-fulfillment as a Black man in America.

CHAPTER 5

Transcending Abstractions by Re-Membering Self in *Coming Home*

The air war in Southeast Asia must be the great metaphor for depersonalized evil of our age. It dehumanizes the killers.

—Peter Rand, *New York Times*

The essential tragedy of being Black and male is our inability, as men and as people of African descent, to define ourselves without the stereotypes the larger society imposes upon us.

—Manning Marable, "The Black Male: Searching beyond Stereotypes"

We can only know ourselves through our histories, but once we've discovered that history-defined self, we must transcend it.

—Charles C. Verharen, "African-Centeredness and the New Black Millennium"

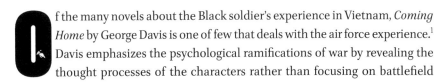f the many novels about the Black soldier's experience in Vietnam, *Coming Home* by George Davis is one of few that deals with the air force experience.[1] Davis emphasizes the psychological ramifications of war by revealing the thought processes of the characters rather than focusing on battlefield

carnage, a strategy that results, perhaps, from the air war being viewed from a different perspective than the ground war and therefore lending itself to a different kind of treatment. Because pilots were removed from the results of the damage they caused in the wake of bombing missions, they often dealt with their destructiveness in an abstract way.

Focusing on the tremendous, seemingly insurmountable, odds the Black pilot faces because of institutionalized racism, *Coming Home* has been described as the first "naturalistic" Black novel about the Vietnam War (Watkins xii). Mel Watkins, who edited the 1974 edition of the novel, lists several reviews in the appendix, one of which is by Jerry H. Bryant, a reviewer for *The Nation*, who claims that it is "neorealistic" and "breaks no new ground" (qtd. in Watkins 214). To the contrary, *Coming Home* explores the depths of the Black hero's angst as he fights against the enemy of racism in the upper ranks of the military while empathizing with the ostensible enemy he bombs in Vietnam. As one of the few novels that probes the psychological victimization of Black fighter pilots, it depicts more the cerebral rather than the visceral aspects of battle. Unlike many mainstream authors who depict the battlefield carnage of the ground war through the eyes of infantrymen and artillerymen, Davis gives readers a bird's-eye view from the perspective of the fighter pilot.

War on Two Fronts: In Country and in the World

Davis focuses on the mindset of the characters, through first-person narration, as a way of making the psychological and emotional impact of the war immediate and compelling. All the characters spend an inordinate amount of time thinking—about why they are in Vietnam, about their tenuous relationships, about the larger implications of the war, about the consequences of their actions.[2] They spend very little time interacting with each other. Not unlike the Black deserter Terry Whitmore, who says in his dramatic autobiographical account *Memphis-Nam-Sweden* that "the Nam really forced me to think" (33), Davis portrays the thought processes of a Black air force officer who is plagued by his complicity in the oppression of other peoples of color and by the loss of his identity as he ascends the ladder of success in academia and the military.

Instead of the war being foregrounded, however, it serves as a backdrop to the main action at an air force base in Thailand from which the pilots fly bombing missions over North Vietnam. Perhaps Davis uses this literal distancing from the war as a basis for his metaphorical treatment of the distanced, rationalistic approach that was responsible not only for America's engagement in the Vietnam War but also for its continued assault, even after all signs pointed to its inability to win, as Philippa Schuyler demonstrates in *Good Men Die* (1969) and as the 2017 film *The Post* so vividly illustrates.[3] Whatever the reason for his focus, Davis gives a poignant and memorable portrait of the psychological implications inherent in killing an unseen enemy by a Black fighter pilot whose alienation, from himself and others, hinders his ability initially to take decisive action. Only after he realizes the extent of his complicity in the oppression of the Vietnamese is he led to an awareness of his own oppression as a Black man in America. This awareness leads to his decision to become a deserter from the Vietnam War as he attempts to find wholeness of self and freedom from the binary thinking that has held him in psychological bondage.

In his portrayal of the protagonist, Davis captures the psychic transformation from what Linda James Myers refers to as a Eurocentric (suboptimal) to an Afrocentric (optimal) world view that Ben undergoes on his heroic quest. After traveling the journey to self-awareness, Ben adopts an epistemological framework that "contains and transcends all opposites" (Myers 34) and that enables him to discover that he cannot know himself without an awareness of his being a part of a larger communal experience encompassing his ancestral past. Davis employs the stream-of-consciousness technique in *Coming Home*, which is one of the earliest fictional representations of the Black experience in Vietnam.

Interior and Exterior Battles: The Plight of the Black officer

Coming Home is the story of a Black fighter pilot's search for self during wartime, the quest having been precipitated by events during his service in Vietnam. The protagonist, Lt. Benjamin Williams, is an air force officer stationed in Thailand. His hootchmates are two other officers, Lt. Childress, also Black, and Lt. Stacy, who is White. Childress is a militant, flamboyant ladies' man. Ben, on the other hand, is more reticent, somewhat reclusive, and more prone to acceding to the status quo. Stacy prefers the company of Ben because he is more "acceptable" according to the standards of White middle-class society. Though Ben is married to Rose back home in Washington, DC, he and Childress, who is single, are consorting with the same Thai woman, Damg Tasuri, while on assignment in Thailand. Also single,

Stacy attempts to be liberal in his views; however, his uneasiness around Blacks is often reflected in racist remarks. He is also insecure and ambivalent about his own masculinity.

Childress, who is flying his final mission over Vietnam and anxiously awaiting his return to the World, regrets leaving Damg in Thailand to become Ben's companion exclusively. Therefore, devising a scheme to break up Ben's and Damg's relationship, he places Communist documents in her bungalow. He then alerts the authorities in hopes that their discovery of the documents will result in declaring her off-limits to any American serviceman, but especially Ben. Before his plan can have its desired effect, however, Childress, having completed his tour of duty, goes back to America where he accidentally kills a White policeman and is imprisoned. Though he does not realize it, Childress already exists in his own "psychic prison" (Rand) because of binary thinking and his inability to connect with Black cultural memory prior to his literal imprisonment in America.

Ben, on the other hand, never experiences fallout from the nefarious so-called prank that Childress concocts. Having become disheartened about his contributing role in the slaughter of the Vietnamese to advance what he calls the "capitalistic," "imperialistic" motives of the American government, he decides to stop flying bombing missions over North Vietnam. Then he goes on R&R in Bangkok where he meets a Black enlisted infantryman from the army who gives him a view of the horror of the war from the ground. Following this consciousness-raising experience, Ben is brought face-to-face with the devastation and destruction of war from which he has been distanced as a pilot. The GI, having decided himself to desert the military, informs Ben of the Japanese "underground railroad" to Sweden for deserters. Ben follows suit. Consequently, unlike Childress, he is able to break away from "psychic imprisonment" to freedom and self-fulfillment. Stacy—whose conflicted notions about his own sexuality, ambivalence about Blacks, and paranoid thoughts of being cuckolded by Childress push him to the brink—commits suicide. Consequently, exile, imprisonment, and death result from the experiences of these three air force officers who are victimized by their complicity in the misguided goals of America in the Vietnam War. Only Ben, the hero, is able to survive and to find himself before it is too late. His survival is inextricably tied to his connection with African American cultural memory.

Mainstream Vietnam War novels often depict Black officers as noncritical of America's role in Vietnam, or at least less critical than Black soldiers of lower rank, such as enlisted men and grunts. The implication is that Black soldiers who have been college educated, and/or have matriculated at Officer Candidate School (OCS), are less likely to criticize America's involvement in the war. Ostensibly their acculturation into American society leads them to uphold and carry out, often without question, the imperialistic ideals that the American military fosters. Such is the case with the portrayal of David Walsh, a Black captain, in *Masque of Honor* by Edward Lim and Jack Pearl. John M. Del Vecchio's *The 13th Valley*, which depicts a Black lieutenant named Rufus Brooks, provides another example from a White novel about the Black experience in Vietnam (Bates 68). Both of these characters follow the dictates of the American military establishment without question.

Presumably only the less-educated, lower-ranked Black soldiers, many of whom had come from poverty-stricken areas in the rural South or crime-ridden areas in the urban North, would take issue with being used as cannon fodder themselves while also oppressing another minority group. This myth Davis explodes with his depiction of Ben, whose conscience will not permit him to continue the annihilation of the Vietnamese after his rite-of-passage experience. He not only is dissatisfied with the military system but also intent on subverting it (Bates 68) or at least making a conscious decision to no longer be complicit in it.

While climbing the ladder of success, Ben is unaware, initially, of the existential ramifications—the isolation and loneliness—of his stellar achievements in academia and the military, a fact that becomes patently clear after he is assigned to duty in Thailand to fly bombing missions over North Vietnam. As the only Black officers in their squadron, Ben and Childress are plagued with what Ronald Billingsley calls the major "burden" of the hero in Black fiction. Like the tortured hero in Wright's naturalistic novels, Ben must strive to find meaning in his absurd existence and then "actively forge an identity out of the agony it brings" (39). He accomplishes this task initially by ritualistically abiding by Eurocentric precepts for upward mobility in the military and in civilian life. In other words, he does what is expected of him rather than follow the dictates of his own mind.

Childress, on the other hand, uses his status as an officer to attempt to chart his own course individually. To his chagrin, however, he discovers that White society punishes Black men who do not follow its prescribed program of thinking and acting according to Eurocentric dictates. For instance, standing while Black he does not "move fast enough" for the White policeman who kicks him in his rear end upon his return to the World. Childress's explanation of the incident speaks volumes about the refusal of Black soldiers returning to America from the war to endure racial harassment, especially after putting their lives on the line:

> I was walking down the street in Baltimore in the middle of the day and this young black dude was handing out leaflets on the corner. So I took one and started to read it. Then this big ugly white cop come up and told me to get moving, like that. So I told him to wait a minute.... And he said, "Get your black ass moving. *Now*." I said, "Man I got a Constitutional right to be here just like everybody else." And the sucker draws his pistol and tells me, "This is all the Constitution you need." So I go to get in my car, and when I started to get in, the cracker kicked me dead in the ass. So, I picked up a jack handle and knocked the gun out of his hand and knocked him down.... All I was trying to teach him was not to kick anybody any more. (185–86)[4]

Unexpectedly, Childress comes up fighting when he is knocked down, and as a result the police officer is killed. Childress's hair-trigger response, however, is what the White world expects so that it can render swift retribution. The fate of countless Black men who stand up to the "system," imprisonment is Childress's sentence despite his actions being in self-defense and despite having put his life in jeopardy for America as a fighter pilot in Vietnam. In other words, to stand up and be a man if you are Black is to be kicked down by White society.

Symbolically, Childress's imprisonment represents his inability to perceive the trap that awaits the Black soldier who buys into the mistaken assumption that his accomplishments on the battlefield will earn him respect and admiration among White society when he returns to America. Rather than accolades, his military honors kindle racial antipathy and disfavor because he has the audacity to think that he can be on par with his White male counterpart who comes home as a decorated hero. And so Childress continues to fly, with relish, his bombing missions over Vietnam, distancing himself from the horror he creates below and naively seeking plaudits in the World for his bravery.

As his name suggests, Childress is also representative of childish, adolescent behavior: rebelliously resisting authority, engaging wantonly and irresponsibly in sexual escapades (among these the wife of his hootchmate), and bragging incessantly about his ability to drop bombs and kill Vietnamese, whom he refers to stereotypically as "gooks" (14). Through his outlandish behavior he becomes the "Signifying Monkey" when he plays what he considers to be a harmless prank on Ben, unaware of, or oblivious to, the dire consequences of his own actions.

In Black folklore the Signifying Monkey stirs up a commotion through "indirection" (Gates, "The Blackness of Blackness" 689), when he tells the lion that the elephant has "bad-mouthed" him. The lion searches out the elephant to make him apologize for the ostensible indiscretion. Totally unaware of the accusation the monkey has made against him and consequently outraged at the lion's demands for an apology, the elephant becomes upset at the lion and beats him. When the lion discovers he has been duped, he goes back disheveled and beaten to the monkey perched in a tree to seek retribution, only to discover the monkey laughing uncontrollably at the way he has misled the lion. What the monkey does not bargain for, however, is falling from the tree to the ground. Now the lion has his turn to beat the monkey, which he does with relish. In other words, the monkey gets his just deserts, as the signifier gets signified upon.

Like the Signifying Monkey, Childress signifies upon Ben when he plants Communist documents in Damg's bungalow hoping that the authorities will discover them and declare her off-limits to Ben. The Office of Special Investigations (OSI) later discovers, as a result of Stacy's testimony, that Childress devised and carried out the scheme of planting the Communist leaflets. Interestingly these leaflets are "directed at colored troops exclusively, describing the American effort in Southeast Asia as a racist, imperialist war" (163), information the OSI considers seditious. Stacy attempts to convince the authorities that this is just a joke that one friend (Childress) plays on another (Ben). To the OSI, however, the so-called prank is no laughing matter, and Childress himself becomes a suspect, in addition to Ben, as a Communist sympathizer. Like the Signifying Monkey who falls out of the tree after tricking the lion only to be trounced by him later, Childress is caught in the trap he set for Ben.

"Indirection" is only one of the many meanings of the multifaceted term "signifyin(g)." Davis also uses the term rhetorically as "hyperbole" through Childress's braggadocious interior monologue. A show-off, Childress seeks an audience for his last bombing raid in Country before going back to the World, as he tells Stacy, "I'd like one of you to see-me-do-it this one last time" (4). Ensconced in his cockpit as he flies in formation with the squadron, he thinks: "For a moment I almost wish I'd see a Mig today so I could get me one before I go home. Win another medal. Take it back to Baltimore and wave it in the Man's face. When he says: 'Boy . . .' I'll say, 'Boy, my ass, and slap him across his motherfuckin' nose with one of my medals'" (13). However, despite his boasting about how he will "flash his medals [earned in Vietnam]" in "the Man's face" when he returns to the United States, Childress gets kicked in the rear end by "the Man" and thrown in prison for defying his command to "move along." Therefore, he becomes the butt of his own signifying.

Influenced by binary thinking, which privileges the individual over the group, Childress believes that he can be successful with only individual effort and that the rewards that effort brings—his war medals—will earn him the respect he deserves when he returns to the World. Because he does not connect with Black cultural memory as does Ben, he either is unaware of or oblivious to the fact that generations of Black men before him have come back from every war in which they have fought for America—from the American Revolution to the Indian Wars to Vietnam—hoping for recognition and honor only to be ignored, or kicked down, through unemployment or imprisonment for crimes real or imagined. The kick that he gets from the cop symbolizes not only the historical response of White authority to Black civilian men who stand up but also militant Black Vietnam veterans who came back to America after their tour of duty with the attitude that they were not going to stand for the treatment they had received prior to the war.

I agree with Norman Harris that Childress serves as a metaphor for numerous Black veterans whose inability to "generalize their war experience" caused them to end up in prison, or to become drug addicts or be killed in disputes with civilians after they returned to the World (like Otis in Brown's *Tragic Magic*). Childress fails to realize that the double-consciousness dilemma cannot be effectively resolved by applying a "static, or onetime resolution" (*Connecting Times* 45). Instead, it must be viewed as an ongoing part of life that must be dealt with every day. As a Black man facing problems resulting from racist treatment within and outside the military, Childress leads a bitter and confused life. Ben, on the other hand, survives not only because he re-members, or connects with racial memory, but also because he transcends the double-consciousness conundrum.

Memory and Black Consciousness: Comparative World Views

Davis's narrative focus in *Coming Home* is similar to that of Toni Morrison in *Beloved*. Relative to the slave narratives, Morrison chronicles not what was recorded but "what was missed," according to Samuels and Hudson-Weems (96). Similarly, Davis records what the Vietnam War oral narratives "missed." In what I call a "fictional oral narrative," *Coming Home* captures the psychological tension, or the interiority, of those affected by the Vietnam War: the soldiers in Country as well as their families and friends back home in the World. By entering the consciousness of his characters, Davis performs what Morrison calls an act of "rememory," which she explains "as a journey to a site [of memory] to see what remains have been left behind and to reconstruct the world that these remains imply" (qtd. in Samuels and Hudson-Weems 97). Furthermore, it implies delving into and then "ripping the veil" off the psyche so that a character's motivations can be revealed (139).

Davis delves into the "the deepest recesses of consciousness" of each character's interior life to reveal how the devastating effects of racism on the Black male psyche, during and after the war, engendered anomie, self-doubt, self-abnegation, and identity crises. Consequently, similar to Charles Johnson's *Middle Passage* and Morrison's *Sula*, Davis's *Coming Home* offers a critique of binary thinking and its role in creating these psychological conditions.[5] Using a tripartite structure in the novel, he traces the quest of the hero for self-knowledge through the following phases: ascendance, immersion, and transcendence. Since binary thinking delays the hero on his quest for wholeness, a discussion of it and its oppositional complement, diunital thinking, is in order.

Binary Thinking: Eurocentric World View

The way a person thinks and the way he views himself in relation to others emanates from his world view (Richards, "The Ideology" 244), and Linda James Myers examines how it determines his ability to "survive." Ben finds hindrances to his quest for self-fulfillment and freedom because he becomes distanced from his own world view. Having originated in Western culture, binary thinking is characteristic of a Eurocentric, or a "sub-optimal," world view, according to Myers. Its primary mode of reasoning is "dichotomous, yielding either/or conclusions," often resulting in we/they configurations inherent in such terms as "racism, sexism, and imperialism which breed fear, anxiety, insecurity and alienation" (9). Additionally, the "epistemological perspective" of binary opposition "assumes external knowledge [or that which we can perceive with the five senses rather than intuition] to be the basis of all knowledge" (11). A resulting byproduct is a mechanistic, fragmented approach to life, which breeds alienation from the self and others.

This dichotomized view of reality, which bases reason on "rational" logic, is characterized by "dualities," among which are either/or bifurcations: of mind/body, theory/practice, and art/science, to name a few (13). During his undergraduate years at Harvard, Ben has been influenced by binary thinking that, according to Marimba Ani, is based on the philosophies of Plato and Descartes that form the basis of Eurocentric culture and thought. As Ani discloses, Plato propounded the "invention of an abstract language of descriptive science to replace a concrete language or oral memory" (31). Ben has unfortunately become distanced from the orality of his cultural upbringing while becoming influenced by abstractionism, which is diametrically opposed to orality. Owing to binary opposition, this situation leads to Ben's self-alienation.

Furthermore, binary thinking posits a dichotomy between the mind and the body, which established, according to Descartes, "the superiority of the intellect over the emotional self" as "spirit is separated from matter" (qtd. in Ani 32). This philosophy of the "divided self" has been pervasive throughout western European history and continues today. Such dichotomization has the effect of sacrificing the "wholeness of personhood" (32). Ben feels this self-alienation as he wonders about the destruction he and Childress have caused in Vietnam:

> Eighty more missions for me. Twenty gone. I wonder how many people I have killed. I never think about killing unless I consciously decide to think about it. Childress must never think about it. I must be more lost than he is, more self-divided, or maybe he's more self-divided than me. (6).

His discourse is fragmentary and disjunctive, indicative of the influence of binary thinking and of his attempt to sort out his paradoxical situation as a Black soldier fighting against an ostensible enemy in the service of his own oppressor.

This Eurocentric world view also values materialism based on competition, aggression, and individualism (Ani 97), all of which have prevented Ben from realizing the benefits that aggregation and communality within his own vernacular culture afford. The nature of binary thinking is that one term is always privileged over the other. Rational thought, or reason, which encompasses abstract language, is considered to be a "higher function," while emotion is considered "lower or base" (Bergenholtz 91). In other words, rationality is more highly valued in Western culture than intuition, which is dominant in many nonwhite cultures, particularly in the vernacular culture of the American South where Ben grows up and in Thailand where he is stationed during the Vietnam War.

Diunital Thinking: Afrocentric World View

Conversely, originating in Africa, the Afrocentric, or "optimal," world view is so named according to Myers because it assumes the "interrelatedness and interdependence of all things"; therefore it is "holistic" (4) rather than fragmented. African philosophy (forming the basis of African American culture) consequently holds that the mind and the spirit, or emotions, are not antagonistic; neither is one valued more highly than the other. Rather, these so-called opposites—intellect and emotion—are viewed as "complementary and necessary parts of a whole" (33). The aim in Afrocentric thought is to achieve "balance of complementary," seemingly "antagonistic," forces in humans (35), which African philosopher John S. Mbiti refers to as "paradoxical complementarity" (32).

The ultimate aim of the African world view is harmony between the individual and the collective will, by placing emphasis on communal rather than individual pursuits. Time, therefore, is conceived as a continuum of existence in which the spiritual and the material are viewed as two expressions of the same reality. The epistemological foundation of the African-centered world view resides in "self-knowledge" being "the basis of all knowledge," which is acquired through "symbolic imagery," according to Myers who says: "One can primarily get access to such knowledge through consciousness, that permeating essence or pervasive energy, or spirit" (34). Characteristic of this system of knowledge is "diunital logic, or the union of opposites," which encompasses "both/and" (13) rather than "either/ or" conclusions. Consequently, it emphasizes an expressive mode that is "dialogic," such as call-and-response (Caponi 10), rather than dialectic discourse, which is emblematic of the Eurocentric world view.

Dialectic versus Dialogic Thinking: Internal Call-and-Response

Dialectic, a type of "authoritative discourse," according to Mikhail Bahktin (qtd. in A. Coleman 42), is associated with binary thinking. Peter Elbow supports this notion of dialectic discourse being characterized by rhetorical language, not addressed to anyone in particular, in which "meanings, concepts and words interact with each other," the goal of which is to get language to "make meaning rather than display that meaning toward an effect" (72). Consequently, it is often laden with abstractions (74). How does this discussion of dialogic versus dialectic discourse relate to the protagonist in *Coming Home*? During his tenure at Harvard, Ben has been unduly influenced by binary thinking that affects his self-image and causes him to take himself to task for periodic Eurocentric lapses as the reader learns during his interior monologues. As he fleshes out Ben's character, Davis counterpoises dialectic with dialogic expression. Emanating from Black expressive culture, dialogic expression is characterized by what Gates calls the "speakerly text" that privileges the vernacular, or "the black speaking voice" ("Blackness of Blackness" 698). Its communicative modality is call-and-response that emphasizes synthesis of dualities.

Davis, therefore, uses a dialectic/dialogic juxtaposition in Ben's interior monologues; or, stated another way, Ben has a call-and-response dialogue with himself. In one instance he ponders the deleterious effects of Eurocentric thinking on his psyche when he says, "I've gotten into a habit of hiding myself. I don't trust friendliness. Harvard started me to believing that a smile covers malevolence as often as it does . . . malevolence, damn. Ben, you're a pitiful poor nigger" (86).

This internal conversation reveals Ben's struggle to think in the vernacular from which he has become distanced. On more than one occasion he wrangles with the internal war between the expressive (Afrocentric/dialogic) and the discursive (Eurocentric/dialectic) modalities. For instance, one particularly hot day in Thailand, Ben does not feel like taking a shower. His self-consciousness concerning his personal hygiene becomes apparent as he muses: I have sweated in bed. . . . I feel the sweat—perspiration, a Harvard man would say—along the side of my body . . . so that my arms stick to my body when I press them against me. I feel myself funky. I feel like I am funky. As if funky" (7).

Ben's conscious thoughts are deteriorating under the strain of the two clashing world views. The sentences above—disjunctive, abbreviated, and fragmentary— convey the true nature of dialectic discourse, or "language as play." So entrenched is his psyche in Eurocentric culture at this early stage of the heroic quest that Ben's words are attempting to "interact with each other" (Elbow 72) rather than to convey a unified thought or idea. Characterized by abstractions, his thoughts are rambling, indicative of the warring tendencies of double-consciousness associated with his early attempts to divest himself of dichotomous binary thinking and invest himself with the vernacular as he attempts to re-member his fragmented psyche. These internal conversations, counterpoising two different yet complementary world views—Eurocentric and Afrocentric—exemplify diunital thinking, in which, as Ani points out, "things can be apart and united at the same time" (68). This externalization of Ben's subconscious thoughts epitomizes what W. E. B. Du

Bois calls the "peculiar sensation" of "double-consciousness," "this sense of always looking at oneself through the eyes of others. . . . One ever feels his twoness,—an American, a Negro; two souls, *two thoughts*, two *unreconciled* strivings, two warring ideals in one dark body" (*Souls of Black Folk* 215; emphasis added).

Ben is at war not only with the Vietnamese and with his fellow White officers but also with himself, and his dilemma as a Black soldier in the Vietnam War is only half the battle. The war he still must wage is rediscovering his identity, or finding the self that his wife, Rose, says he lost after he went to college. In fact, she says he married her "because he had to learn what it means again to be black after four years at Harvard" (36), which, in *Coming Home*, symbolizes the Eurocentric world view that subsumes binary thinking. During the ascendant stage of his heroic quest, when he is climbing the ladder of success according to ideals of American society, Ben is unable to balance his Eurocentric education with his vernacular upbringing but later finds the means to do so.

Davis externalizes Ben's interior dialogue by setting up parallel universes structurally in the text with a call-and-response virtual dialogue between characters in Country (Thailand) and those in the World (America) who speak to each other across space and time by having a topic discussed in Southeast Asia that reflects or responds to a conversation or an interior monologue by a girlfriend, wife, or friend back home. This style is a further example of the bifurcated, fragmented view of binary opposition.

Most of the action in *Coming Home* occurs on the periphery of Vietnam in Thailand that supported the U.S. mission in Vietnam. The air force bases there served as points of departure for flying missions over Vietnam to cut off supply routes for Vietcong from the North to the South (Wakin 180).[6] Distancing, "spare style and oblique viewpoint" contribute to a view of war by most people back home in America who failed to experience what the war was like unless a close relative were killed (Watkins xiv). This marginal view of the war metaphorically underscores the theme of Ben's marginality as a Black male in the officers' corps.

Space/Place Continuum: Metaphorical Middle Passage

Distance, as it relates to the space/place continuum, lends structure to *Coming Home*. I refer to Houston Baker Jr.'s use of the conceptual framework for "space" and "place" in his study of Black expressive culture titled *Workings of the Spirit*. Neither of these entities can exist alone, one requiring the other for definition. Consequently, from the "security and stability of place we are aware of the openness, *freedom* and threat of space.... [If] we think of space as that which allows movement, then place is pause" (71–72). In *Coming Home* the "space" between earth and sky is a paradoxical "middle passage" (a place of confinement similar to that of Africans on slave ships) for Ben. "Place," on the other hand, particularly as it relates to Thailand, becomes a compass point on the hero's cultural map.

Using "space" and "place" as organizing principles, Davis spans what Robert Stepto refers to as the "symbolic geography" (67) of the hero's cultural map on his journey to self-awareness. "In the quest for identity" according to Geneviève Fabre and Robert O'Meally, places, or "sites," are "anchors and frames." Geographical places and place-names map out bearings in space and time. Memory, consequently, is viewed as a "metaphor" for confronting a "troublesome past and the uncertain present" (10). Therefore, rather than chapter numbers or titles, Davis divides the novel into major parts headed with names of places, or geographical locations—in Country, that is, "THAILAND"; and in the World, "WASHINGTON, DC," and "SCHENECT-ADY FALLS, NY." These parts are in all capital letters throughout, whereas the sections are in initial capitals. Structurally, *Coming Home* approximates a flight pattern map. In his attempt to re-member, or connect with Black cultural memory, Ben, like Okonkwo in Chinua Achebe's heroic masterpiece *Things Fall Apart*, constructs "a cultural map" as he strives to harmonize his opposing selves."[7]

Within each of the parts of *Coming Home* are sections, headed with the names of characters, associated with Ben's memory of the Vietnam War, who are in Thailand: "Ben," "Childress," "Stacy," "LTC Milligan," "Captain Fitzhugh," "Bordreau," and "Damg." Dovetailing with the thoughts of the soldiers in Thailand are those of their counterparts in America: "Rose," "Calvin," "Edward," "Roxanne," and "Lionel." By using names as section headings, Davis focuses on the characters and their conscious thoughts rather than on their actions per se.

Instead of proceeding in a linear progression of time that is characteristic of a Eurocentric world view, the action proceeds instead in a cyclical fashion, as in African cosmology, with a confluence of past, present, and future as a continuum that depicts simultaneity of existence. Action begins in Thailand and then goes back and forth from Washington, DC, back to Thailand, to Schenectady, New York, then back to Thailand, cyclically repeating itself and ending in Washington, DC. In some instances action flashes back in time, while in other instances it flashes forward, though being presented simultaneously. This conceptualization of time is akin to that in Afrocentric cultures in which "metaphysically, *being* was equivalent to *duration*: each moment embodied a recurrence of a past moment, and implied was a potential future recurrence," as Bonnie Barthold observes in *Black Time: Fiction of Africa, the Caribbean, and the United States* (10). Stylistically, *Coming Home* is "cinematic," which, in addition to the time reference, enables Davis to achieve a certain "immediacy" (Rand) that places the reader in the action. Consequently, like a movie camera, each part, or section cuts from one geographical location and from one person to the other.

For instance, the action begins in Thailand where Childress is flying his final mission before going back to America. He is excited about leaving the war but regretful that he will leave Damg to be Ben's woman. Davis puts the reader in the middle of the action as Childress flies bombing raids over a North Vietnamese encampment, interspersing his interior monologue with crude ruminations about Ben and Damg:

> Red Dog 1 and I come in first. Number 1 lays his bomb close to the road. . . . My stomach is knotted, tensed for the first burst of machine gun fire. . . . Three more bombs to go. Gooks in trucks pulled off the road . . . , For a moment I feel giddy . . . my hands sweating on the stick. . . . I think about Ben and my moon-faced yellow whore. . . . I come across upside down, screaming, . . . then let my bomb fly into the orange smoke. (14–15)

After exulting in his expertise at bombing the Vietnamese whom he derogatorily calls "gooks," Childress tells Stacy about his plan to frame Ben by "planting" Communist leaflets in Damg's bungalow. Influenced by binary thinking, he has little compunction about and even less compassion for the Vietnamese as his racist remarks reveal. Since Childress's tour of duty in Vietnam is nearing an end, he does not want to leave his former girlfriend as free game for Ben. Besides, quips Childress with a mocking laugh, "Ben doesn't need her anyway. He has a wife at home—named Rose. . . . Pretty little sister too" (31), a backhanded reference to his affair with her.

The action then cuts to Washington, DC, where Rose, a keypunch operator in the military-industrial complex, laments her dead-end job. Through her interior monologue the reader learns that, in her loneliness since Ben left, she not only is on the verge of giving in to the advances of her coworker Calvin, but also that she has had an affair with Childress before he was shipped out to Vietnam. She also flirts with Edward, an errand boy like Calvin. Both men slavishly push and pull a cart while picking up used keypunch cards that Rose and other female employees place on their desks in long rows of cubicles equipped with IBM machines. Symbolic of the military-industrial complex, the setting is in an office building where they all work at their humdrum jobs. The work is tedious, repetitive, and uncreative, lending itself to the kind of fantasizing to which Rose, Calvin, and Edward succumb.

In her reverie, Rose reminisces about the commander's New Year's Eve ball, at which she and Ben were the only Blacks and for which she convinced Ben to bring her long white gloves from Spain and a wig from Formosa so that she could be "like them," that is, the wives of the White officers. She even admits that she married an officer rather than an enlisted man so that she could be "put on a pedestal" and mimic the "white people on television" (36). Self-divided and confused about her racial consciousness, Rose says:

> I wanted to be the little woman, the modern American housewife . . . with the French Provincial furniture. . . . Ben wouldn't cooperate so when he wanted me to be the first officer's wife in the Air Force to get an Afro I went to the beauty parlor and got it straightened slick . . . and dyed it red, like a fool. . . . I feel like spitting in my own face. (37)

Her thoughts reveal her double-consciousness dilemma. How can she help Ben recapture his Black identity when she is confused about her own? After this daydreaming episode, she accedes to Calvin's advances and is unfaithful to Ben.

The action then cuts back to the next part, "THAILAND," where Stacy wonders if Roxanne, his girlfriend, is being unfaithful to him back home. A virgin, he is saving himself for her. He thinks about his vicarious love affair with her as he watched her going to and from classes on the college campus they both attended before he was sent to Vietnam. Sometimes he would enlist the aid of his friend, Lionel Mitchell, who would follow her around with him, as they commented on how beautiful she was.

The following part, titled "SCHENECTADY FALLS, NY," reveals Roxanne attending a New Conservative Coalition Young Republicans forum with Lionel. This group, an example of extremist binary thinking, upholds the "us/them" dichotomy that undergirds White supremacy. Supporting America's intervention in the Vietnamese conflict, their position states: "the burden is on us to safeguard civilization from the Mongolian hordes. . . . If the proud white race falls, . . . there is no way to purify the blood once it has been tainted either with alien ideology or defeat" (99). As they sit in the audience listening to the speaker, Roxanne is spellbound while Lionel thinks about just how shallow and self-centered she is and that she is not really in love with Stacy. Listening intently to the speaker, Roxanne obviously agrees with the coalition's suboptimal view that Whites should be "conquerors" and "world saviors" (Ani 251) so that "America will remain the hope of the Free World" (*Coming Home* 100).

Meanwhile, the action cuts to "THAILAND," where an organization espousing similar principles to those of the coalition is in the process of investigating Ben. The OSI, Lt. Col. Milligan, and other authorities interrogate Stacy concerning the source of Communist leaflets in Damg's quarters. Since he is the hootchmate of Childress and Ben, who have been implicated in the crime by virtue of their association with Damg, the OSI figures that he is a good source of information. Also, since they cannot locate Ben (who, unbeknownst to them, has by now deserted to Sweden) and Childress is in prison, Stacy is their only hope for a lead. Despite Stacy's attempts to convince them that it was all a joke that Childress played on Ben when he planted the documents, the authorities view it as no laughing matter; consequently, they accuse not only Ben but also Childress of being a Communist coconspirator and "a black militant, black racist with the avowed purpose of overthrowing the Government of the United States" (164). They then reveal to Stacy that Childress has been jailed in Baltimore for killing a policeman.

Later the action cuts back to "WASHINGTON, DC," where Roxanne has received a letter from Stacy detailing events related to his interrogation and Childress's imprisonment for murder and planting the Communist documents. Since the incident implicated Ben, Roxanne then contacts Rose and takes her to see Childress in prison so they can find out two things: why he framed Ben and where Ben has gone. Childress is despondent in prison but not remorseful for killing the policeman, who he says "killed his own damned self when he hit the concrete" (186). He then explains to Rose and Roxanne that he picked up the anti–Vietnam War literature that he stashed in Damg's bungalow (that the OSI and FBI call "communist propaganda") in Hong Kong because he was "looking for answers just like everyone else." The predicament" of which he speaks is that of his paradoxical role as "a black man fighting yellow men for white men" (185) who are the source of his own oppression. Everyone thought that Childress was so self-assured and confident about his own identity because he was always joking with the Thais and putting up a militant front with Whites.

Next the action cuts to "THAILAND" where Stacy reads a letter from Lionel stating that Roxanne has gone to Baltimore with Rose to see Childress in prison. Knowing that Childress is a ladies' man with no compunction about sleeping around with other men's women, he imagines Childress sleeping with his girlfriend (an irrational fear since Childress is incarcerated). Stacy laments his inability to stop this supposed "liaison" because he is too far away, and he gives in to insecurity and paranoia. Therefore, fearing that he has lost his woman (despite their relationship being more fantasy than reality) and unsure of the fate of his friend Ben (who he knows has defied his superiors by refusing to continue bombing the Vietnamese and now has been accused of being a Communist), Stacy goes into a nose dive on his final bombing mission and commits suicide.

Because they are alienated from others as well as from themselves, these characters suffer a myopic view of their circumstances. A review of *Coming Home* that appeared in *The Nation* refers to Davis's characters as "stereotypical" (qtd. in Watkins 214). To the contrary, they are not so much stereotypical or one-dimensional as they are trapped by limited perceptions of the world and their place in it. Influenced by binary thinking, they have a refracted, fragmented view of reality. Childress's misogynistic and racist views (for example, references to Thai women as "whores" and the Vietnamese as "gooks"); Roxanne's and Lionel's White supremacist leanings; Rose's emulation of upper-middle-class values because she considers Whiteness better than Blackness; Lt. Col. Milligan's "world savior" and "conqueror" mentality, which contributes to his bloodthirstiness; and Stacy's ambivalent and distorted views of his own and Black male sexuality—all these tendencies result from binary thinking to which Black and White characters alike succumb.

Davis emphasizes the notion of distancing by eliminating the authorial voice. All twelve of the characters speak directly for themselves. Written entirely in first-person point of view, the narrative allows the characters to give voice to their own thoughts. In that respect, neither their actions nor their thoughts are filtered or interpreted by an omniscient, controlling presence. This approach provides an immediate, first-hand account of the effects of war on military personnel and civilians alike. In so doing, Davis breaches the literal and figurative space between war and everyday experience for the reading audience—for present and future generations. Focusing on each of the characters in this manner also emphasizes community, or place, which will figure prominently in Ben's identity quest.

These call-and-response situations *are not* about the war and they *are* about the war. In other words, though the characters are not fighting in the war per se, their actions are governed by events related to the war in Vietnam. In the same way that they are separated from the war they are also separated from themselves. In societies dominated by Western cultural ideals and ways of viewing man's place in the universe, African Americans, particularly, experience a form of mind control that prevents their experiencing true self-knowledge and hence freedom, according to Myers. She suggests that the extent to which a person "consciously or unconsciously adhere[s] to the sub-optimal conceptual system, that is composed of either/or dualities," determines whether s/he can be truly liberated. On the other hand, when on a "deep level," that is, the level of world view, a person's thinking is changed to reflect a world view that is self-affirming, then s/he will indeed be free (14). This change is the type that Ben undergoes in *Coming Home*, while the other characters remain trapped in their limited visions of themselves and the world around them.

Stages of the Black Heroic Quest: Knowledge and the Application of Racial Memory

Coming Home has a tripartite structure that conforms to the framework for analysis of the heroic quest in African American narrative established by Robert Stepto and revised and revoiced by Harris. In his pioneering work titled *From behind the Veil: A Study of Afro-American Narrative*, Stepto identifies a central motif of Black narrative in "prefiguring" and "modern era" texts as a quest for "freedom" and "literacy" (ix). In his study of Black literature of the Vietnam War titled *Connecting Times: The Sixties in Afro-American Fiction*, Harris adapts Stepto's concepts of "freedom," redefining and broadening it as "knowledge of the racial memory," and "literacy" as "the application of the racial memory as dictated by the confluence between personality and situation" (29). For the Black hero in Vietnam War fiction, knowledge of the racial memory and individualized application are at the center of successfully dealing with the contradiction of double-consciousness and survival. "Revoicing" (Stepto 192) and extending these approaches, I have adapted vestiges of both Stepto's and Harris's studies to my analysis of *Coming Home*.

In his identity quest for wholeness, Ben goes through the three stages that Stepto delineates as necessary for the Black hero to experience on his journey to self-realization: "ascendance," "immersion," and "transcendence." The ascendant stage is one of isolation and indecision. The second, or immersion, stage is characterized by community and camaraderie wherein the heroic quester finds direction in "ritual grounds" within a "symbolic geography" (68). The final, or transcendent, stage consists of a metaphysical space, "outside of time," offering hope for resolution of double-consciousness, or a "harmonizing of the two selves" as Harris rightly observes (*Connecting Times* 57). In the transcendent stage race is not the primary issue. Instead, this is a symbolic space of racelessness and humanitarianism.

Ascendance: Experiencing Isolation and Anomie

In the ascendant stage, the Black hero takes a "ritualized journey to a symbolic north" (Stepto 167), which for Ben is his rise to the height of academic and military pursuits at Harvard and Air Force OCS, respectively. Armed with such stellar credentials, he is no ordinary fighter pilot. The approbation he has garnered would ordinarily result in a sense of self-worth for such accomplishments, particularly for a male of European descent in America. Being of African descent, however, Ben is fraught with anomie, ambivalence, and isolation because the same self-affirming rewards, whether in the military or another field of endeavor, available to males of the majority population in America are not forthcoming for him.

While ascending the ladder of success, Ben is unaware of the existential ramifications of his eventual achievements. Because of his alienation, from himself and others, his "ritualized" behavior on the journey breeds "feelings of futility" (C. Franklin 280). Ben experiences a sense of isolation in the ascendant stage because he lacks self-knowledge and the ability to "connect" in a meaningful way with others. James Williams perhaps expresses it best with his observation that the alienation an African American feels from the greater society does not result from any "personal defect or shortcoming" on the part of the person of color but rather from the "hypocritical nature of that society which professes to be color blind, but in practice often acts otherwise" (33). Similar to Richard Wright's protagonist in "The Man Who Killed a Shadow" Ben feels helpless, or at least powerless, in the oppressive environment of a "white world he allows to rule him" (Cauley 331). For example, he remonstrates himself for being led like a lamb to the slaughter when he goes to fight in Vietnam: "I should never have come to the war but I came like a sheep. During all my life in America I've been led to loving the wrong things and hating the wrong things (18).

Because Ben lacks self-knowledge, he is constantly deluged with conflicting thoughts. Even though he says he does not think about getting shot down, at the same time he wonders what others will think of him if he gets shot down flying over the mountains because he is "not wearing socks," revealing his concern with societal conventions rather than his safety or that of the people he is bombing (7). Ben is both attracted to and repulsed by White society. He attends Harvard because it epitomizes the best that America has to offer in knowledge and Western cultural refinement. However, he refers to his instructors there as "narrow gnomish bastards" for failing to teach him more than "abstractions," feeling that his Thai consort could teach him more about life than they could teach him "in a million years" (18). Taking himself to task for having been gullible enough to volunteer to fight in Vietnam, he says: "I keep letting myself be led the wrong way because our survival depends on our lying to ourselves" (18). As long as the Black soldier can convince himself that he is fighting for democracy in Vietnam against a Communist enemy, then he can justify bombing people of color by telling himself the country he is fighting for—the United States—is justified in its action as an aggressor/imperialist.

Ben cannot decide whether to envy or dislike Stacy for his ability to "kill without remorse three thousand miles from home" (84), which is indicative of a hidden desire to be like the very White man who he says he hates. He then questions himself about why he is helping Whites to be a part of the killing machine in Vietnam, anyway. Considering the fact that he is a Harvard man, he says he could have just as well opted not to go to the war.[8] However, to have exercised that option would have been tantamount to identifying with the favored status of those in the upper echelons of society that he detests. Consequently, he wonders: "How could I have escaped the fate of the oppressed without using the privileges of the oppressor?" (110).

Male Self-Image and Cultural Memory: Euroamerican and African American

Coming Home, therefore, "revoices and revises" the theme of double-consciousness in three other novels about the Black experience in Vietnam: *Captain Blackman, De Mojo Blues*, and *Tragic Magic*. Dual allegiances, to race and to country, characterize the Black war hero's paradoxical quest for wholeness on the journey to selfhood. His survival on this quest is inextricably tied to his ability to immerse himself in Black cultural ritual by connecting with Black cultural memory. The protagonist, who is alienated from not only himself but also the Black community and White society, can only hope for "reconciliation and self-identification" by "establishing or restoring a sense of cohesion with his own race through some symbolic folk member or custom" or experience, as Mary Ellen Doyle notes (165). Before Ben can find himself, he must rid himself of the dualistic, binary way of viewing the world. He must reconstruct his cultural outlook to try to redefine himself in terms of his own heritage because heretofore he has been laboring under a cultural world view that has been inimical to his self-concept as a Black male.

Since "self-representations of black masculinity," according to Herman Gray, "are structured by and against dominant (and dominating) discourses of masculinity and race, specifically whiteness" (401), it is necessary to determine the basis of the Euro-American male self-image. Eurocentric culture, according to Ani, places priority on "rationality," a cognitive style derived from Plato, which holds that "thought is only properly so called when isolated from feeling and when based on 'objectification'" that is, separation of the "self" from the "contemplated object" (94). And because the rational man perceives himself "in control" of his own "passions," he considers himself "in a position to manipulate and control others" (239). This kind of thinking leads to the "dichotomization of self from other," or "othering" those who are different from the European self, which places them in a "threatening" and "antagonistic" relationship, mainly because they are different (239). For instance, Stacy, on his last strafing assignment over North Vietnam before he goes into a nosedive and commits suicide, reflects: "I think civilization itself is in danger right here in the mud of Vietnam and you've got to fight even if no one else wants to help. The world is full of gooks and niggers and they'll tear down everything the White man has ever built, I say to myself as if I am talking to Roxanne" (201).

Stacy's racist ruminations are what Barbara Foley points to as a "quintessential mode of abstraction," and I agree with her that the practice of referring to anyone who is non-European as "other" is the "epitome of objectification" (236). Such racist remarks reveal how "one person's [or one group's] selfhood hinges upon the abolition of another's humanity" (237). As a Euro-American male attempting to hold his hegemonic status, Stacy finds it necessary to subordinate the self-images of those whom he calls "the other" to his own.

Another aspect of the Eurocentric male image is to dominate others while also elevating so-called scientific thought above other modes of expression, which implies "universality" and "objectivity." He also prides himself on being a "conqueror" and "world savior" (Ani 263). Consequently, he purveys a mythology as a "self-appointed leader of the world" who "conquers" others to "free" them from political/social/religious systems that are different from his own. This freedom is defined in terms of "individualism" and the license to achieve regardless of the cost to others. Once having "conquered" others, he then attempts to transform them to conform to his image (267).

Lt. Col. Milligan in *Coming Home*, who desires to develop Thailand, is a prime example of this "conqueror" mentality who attempts to effect such transformation on the indigenous people. Consequently, he ponders the "advantages" of American intervention: "Thailand has potential. . . . All they need is a little Yankee know-how. . . . We've got a long way to go over here, but if you come back in two years, you won't recognize the place . . . two-billion-dollar permanent establishment in less than two years, you watch" (130). He is trying to convince a younger officer of the need for America to place its stamp on this part of the world where he feels the inhabitants are too "backward" to "improve" it for themselves. In his arrogance he figures that when the Americans finish their "transformation,"

> it will be a symbol of the American presence in Southeast Asia. I . . . imagine how the base will look when all the canvas and wood has been replaced by steel and brick. Then all the roads will be paved. . . . I bet before the Americans came, the Thais weren't fully utilizing this piece of real estate. (131)

Milligan's interior monologue reveals the true nature of America's presence in Thailand, which is not to help either the Thais or the Vietnamese but rather to engage in imperialistic pursuits and capitalistic gain as they try to forge the people into their image. This kind of thinking breeds the Great White Father complex that Ben detests. With cynicism and outrage he expresses his disgust at White men imposing their self-image on others, as he wonders why

> there could not be some kind of divine law that says men can only come to another man's country as tourists, and not as colonizers or exploiters. But when white men came to countries where people were just sitting on natural resources . . . [they] discovered them, Christianized them, annihilated them or tried to make them into tools . . . for the great march of civilization. (199)

Conquest and capitalist exploitation are hallmarks of the Euro-American male self-image. It was this type of binary thinking that got America involved in the Vietnam War in the first place.

Because most modern studies of masculinity have focused on the hegemonic White male, according to Clyde Franklin, renowned sociologist and pioneering researcher on the Black male, Black masculinities have gone largely unexplored. During the era of slavery, for example, Black males were not even considered "men" because they (and African American women) were referred to as chattel, or property. In American society and culture since slavery, the image of the Black male has been "contradictory" ("Ain't I A Man?" 274). As a result, Black men in American society often experience social disorientation, as do Ben and Childress in *Coming Home*. Because of societal exclusion, many feel it futile to try to remedy their situations. Consequently, what Franklin calls "masculinity adaptations" result, and he divides them into five categories: conformist, ritualistic, innovative, retreatist, and rebellious. The ontological assumption governing these adaptations is that "black masculinities are socially constructed" rather than "biological," this social construction being a framework of "power relations or dynamics often dominated by powerful white males and subordinated minority males" (279).

"Conformist" masculinities accept society's "prescriptions and proscriptions" for heterosexual males relative to a work ethic that ostensibly ensures success if one works hard and is goal oriented. At the same time society downplays the possibility of failure owing to "blocked opportunities," despite the Black male's playing the game by "their rules." Those who exhibit "ritualistic" behavior play by the rules of the hegemonic male in society; however, they are only "going through the motions" (C. Franklin 281). Unlike the conformist types, they become cynical, following society's dictates regardless of consequences to themselves and those around them. "Innovative" masculinities, though not posing a threat, nevertheless exhibit "socially distasteful" behavior. They cater to the more salacious aspects of manhood that are nevertheless acceptable to the hegemonic male, such as the use of misogynistic and sexually explicit references, such as lyrics in songs. Their aim is to acquire materialistic success at any cost. Because the "retreatist" type has been denied for so long the opportunities extended to their White counterparts, these males often retreat from society, emotionally and/or physically, becoming drug addicts, alcoholics, or homeless men. The "rebellious" Black male type often rejects America's goals and the means of achieving them. Men in this group would be similar to present-day gang members, according to Franklin (281). In *Coming Home* Childress typifies "rebellious" and Ben "ritualistic" behavior; but despite their differences, they both are victimized by the same kinds of stereotypical images.

It is risky for Black men to believe in the notion of competitive individualism as the road to success in America because the same rules do not apply to them as for White males when it comes to upward mobility. Paradoxically when Blacks attempt to move up by sharing of resources and skills, they are often blamed for "not being aggressive enough" and not being "emotionally stoic enough," according to Franklin ("Men's Studies, the Men's Movement" 10). In addition to external factors such as the economic and political systems, the problematic nature of the way Black men are socialized is "conflictual, contradictory, and riddled with mixed messages" (11). The influences in his life come from three main sources: the Black community, his Black peer group, and mainstream America; and though the first two influences are the sources of some mixed messages, "mainstream society-controlled Black masculinity . . . is most contradictory and conflictual of all three," as Franklin reveals (12). It often projects negative images of Black males in general as pathological, and those who do excel are presented as anomalies or enigmas (17). Ben's self-conflict arises from this negative influence induced by the majority society, which often projects stereotypical images related to Black male sexuality. Because of the "socially constructed" definition of Black masculinity, Franklin feels that the ambiguity surrounding the Black male sex role today may result in part from the slavery legacy of "nondefinition of the black male sex role and continued reluctance to perceive the black man as a man" (" Ain't I A Man?" 276).

Several characters in *Coming Home* are influenced by sexual stereotyping of the Black male, including Roxanne, Stacy's girlfriend, who sizes up two young Black men seated two rows behind her at a New Conservative Coalition meeting. Wondering why they would be attending this right-wing gathering, she becomes curious beyond mere questioning of their presence. Her thoughts reveal a classic stereotypical myth: "The darkies make me feel nervous. I hear them whisper something and hold my breath. . . . The 'darkie' seated behind me must be undressing me with his eyes" (97). In other words, the mere sight of a White woman by a Black man is enough to evoke lust and perhaps the desire to have sex with her. This type of shallow, binary thinking led to White societal indictment of Bigger Thomas as a rapist, even before he was tried by a court of law, simply because he was in the same room with a White girl in Richard Wright's *Native Son*.[9]

Ben reflects on the way White males in Vietnam, as in previous wars, have played on such ostensible sexual fears of foreign women. Comparing Black men with animals, they attempt to frighten Thai women away from Black soldiers by spinning tales of oversized Black genitalia. He muses, "I can only hate whitey for the smaller symptoms of the disease that he is spreading around the world, like segregating . . . the bathhouses over here. . . . Like trying to get the Thai girls to hate Negroes by telling them niggers have tails and niggers have big dicks and will hurt them" (17–18). Such occurrences have the effect of a "metaphorical castration." Even though chattel slavery, with its violent aftermath during which untold numbers of Black men were literally castrated, does not exist to the same extent in modern society, I agree with Derrick Bell that institutionalized racism "continues to exert dominion over black men and their maleness in ways more subtle but hardly less castrating than during slavery" (146).

Bombing metaphorically indicates the destruction to Ben's psyche, which has been bombarded with such negative images of Black masculinity. Like the earth in Vietnam that has been fragmented by relentless bombing raids, the psyche of the Black soldier has been torn asunder with stereotypical, emasculating images. On his heroic quest Ben searches relentlessly for a way to thwart this dehumanization and negativism in an attempt to become whole again. Having been distanced from other Black men, he finds this task difficult. First he matriculates at Harvard where he learns about Eurocentric culture but is distanced from his own. Then he attends Air Force OCS where he is one of only a few Blacks among a majority of White candidates. When Ben goes overseas to military duty in Southeast Asia, as an officer he is not afforded the opportunity to interact with the majority of Black soldiers who are enlisted men in infantry and artillery. Consequently, he leads an isolated, alienated existence. Leading such a marginalized existence forces him to seek avenues for communal engagement and interaction. However, before making this connection, he must first stop flying.

Flying as Bondage: Symbolic Middle Passage

Traditionally flying has mythic implications in world cultures. Susan Blake points out in her study of Black folklore that in Greek mythology it represents "the superhuman power of the gods," in Freudian psychology, "male sexual potency," and in Black folklore, "freedom" (83). Ironically, however, for Ben in *Coming Home* flying represents bondage rather than freedom—bondage to binary thinking that is inimical to his belief in self-determination for peoples of color and to the development of a positive self-concept. Consequently, he must make a conscious decision to stop flying.

Prior to his decision to do so, Ben is suspended in the middle distance, a symbolic middle passage, as he flies his jet in the space between earth and sky. As one of the "defining moments" in African American culture and history, the

Middle Passage functions as a "space-in-between," or a "bridge" across which "memory retraces[s] the journey of Africans to the Americas," according to Carl Pedersen (43). This space was one of "transformation" and "reconfiguration" where "an African past and the American future, one in danger of fading from memory, the other imposing its hegemonic will," were constantly in conflict over contested spheres of power. In *Coming Home* the sky represents the "hegemonic will" that Ben experiences in academia (Harvard) and the military (OCS). The earth, on the other hand, represents the vernacular, or the place that will ground him in African American culture and provide a sense of identity. In this symbolic middle passage, Ben has to decide whether to continue his aspiration in Eurocentric terms or to try to reconnect with Black vernacular culture from which he has become alienated. In this respect, the middle distance becomes a space of "growing self-awareness" (48) similar to that Charles Johnson presents allegorically in his novel *Middle Passage*.[10]

If Ben chooses to follow the path that has taken him to the hallowed halls of ivy, he will continue to be distanced from himself. Furthermore, he faults his Ivy League education for having robbed him of his ability to feel empathy or remorse for the people he kills during bombing raids. The type of raids in which Ben participated was called "carpet bombing," and his experience in the novel mirrored that of actual pilots who flew bombing raids in Vietnam. The severity of the destruction and devastation was such that Senator Gaylord Nelson introduced a bill in Congress in 1972 to assess the horrific loss of human life as well as the harm done to the ecological system in Vietnam. He gave evidence of devastation to an area "the size of Rhode Island," amounting to approximately "750,000 acres," and these thousands of forested acres, on which tons of defoliants were dropped, afterward appeared like the "crater-laden, pock-marked surface of the moon, uninhabited and uninhabitable" (126). With shock and outrage, Sen. Nelson takes to task those in the military who plan such strikes and the pilots who carry out their directives: "Those grand strategists who draw the lines on the maps and order the B-52 strikes never see the face of the innocent peasant whose land has been turned into a pock-marked moon surface in 30 seconds of violence. . . . This is impersonal, automated and mechanistic warfare brought to its logical conclusion—utter, permanent, total destruction" (127). Similarly, Ben thinks about the impersonal aspect of bombing people without seeing the result of his actions and about his complicity in the destruction. He then analogizes the experience to matriculation at Harvard: "For me this war is like Harvard. . . . Everything is abstract. This is like Harvard. The killers never see the killed" (17).

What has Harvard killed in Ben? Western civilization and the educational system it perpetuates have killed Ben's connection with Black cultural memory, making him an "abstraction" (86). Similar to the fighter pilots who never see the people whom they kill on the ground, the proponents of Western civilization, who view anyone outside their realm of experience as "the other," psychically (and sometimes physically) kill those whom they marginalize. But because this liminal individual is, for all intents and purposes, an "abstraction" who is relegated to "invisibility,"[11] the oppressor never sees the killed. Ben, therefore, questions his own involvement in the war and empathizes with the Vietcong, concluding: "Maybe I really want the VC to win" (18).

Davis interrogates this middle distance, the space that Ben inhabits between cultural world views, in *Coming Home* as a liminal phase, or middle passage, serving for Ben as the beginning of a rite of passage that will not be completed until he stops flying and is grounded, literally and figuratively. Liminality, according to Berndt Ostendorf, refers to rites of passage not only from youth to manhood but also to that "imaginary or real social line which defines the self and the group against others"; consequently, hegemonic systems "protect the norm" resisting change, and, as such, are "incapable of moral and artistic renewal" (148). A view from the marginalized segments of society is necessary to question "rigid norms" and thereby to activate their renewal. Therefore, Ben questions America's role in Vietnam as "world savior" and "conqueror." Because of his double perspective on the situation, as a marginalized person of color and as an American soldier, he can see the need to stop fighting the war and causing all the carnage as a result of massive bombing raids.

Daniel M. Scott III views the "'middle' passage" as the "ontological and epistemo-logical material that gets locked out of binary oppositions and dualism—or—the matter of experience and consciousness that exists not in pure allegiance with one or another extreme, but rather . . . in between where an abstraction fades and blends into its exact opposite" (646). Suspended between opposing cultural world views, Ben, as a fighter pilot in the war, has made a conscious decision not to kill in the name of American capitalism and imperialism. At the nexus of consciousness and experience, Ben discovers who he is, an observation that Johnson makes in *Being and Race*: "the interaction of consciousness and experience is identity" (qtd. in D. Scott 645).

While flying one of his bombing missions, Ben refuses to drop bombs on what his field officers have told him is a bridge on the main trail-line from North

Vietnam to China. If they successfully destroy this bridge, then the Vietcong will be unable to get supplies and munitions from the Chinese. Since the time of Ben's refusal to fly, Lt. Col. Milligan has had him under investigation. Though Ben thinks the investigation has to do with his failure to drop the bombs, the authorities are trying to find out what his role is in the ostensible Communist plot related to the leaflets they have found in Damg's bungalow.

Ben flies back to the airbase with a full load of bombs and tells his commanding officers that he did not drop the bombs because they "wouldn't toggle and they wouldn't jettison" (88). However, Stacy learns that Ben has concocted that story to mask the real reason. Admitting to Stacy that he made a "conscious" decision not to bomb the Vietnamese, Ben says, "I did not see any troop concentration. It looked like a village to me and all I could imagine was millions of pellets of steel ricocheting through an unbunker [*sic*] village. I couldn't drop them. . . . I lied and said they wouldn't toggle" (88). Stacy warns him: "the top brass will fry your ass" when they discover the real reason he disobeyed orders.

Ben tricks his commanding officers into thinking he did not drop the load of bombs because of a malfunctioning lever. However, he has purposefully defied authority by choosing not to drop the bombs to destroy innocent peoples of color. This course of action is decidedly different from that of the old Ben, the pre-self-aware Ben. Similar to the grandfather in Ellison's *Invisible Man*, he is a "subtle deceiver" (Baker, *Blues* 187). Because of Ben's "ritualistic" behavior in the past, of course the authorities do not suspect this act of rebellion on his part.

In this middle passage Ben is the liminal trickster at the crossroads. Baker defines liminality as the "betwixt and between" phase of rites of passage when an individual has left "one fixed social status but has not yet been incorporated into another" (*Blues* 183). Between heaven and earth as he flies sorties over Vietnam, Ben has left his old status as an indecisive young man in lock-step obedience to the dictates of mainstream society by consciously deciding not to drop the bombs; however, he has not yet entered the ritual ground, where he will be assisted by a foot soldier on his quest for freedom and self-fulfillment. An attribute of the wily trickster, according to folklorist Robert Farris Thompson, is his ability to "turn himself into wind for quick travel" (qtd. in Grayson 47), a phrase that, appropriately enough in this instance, serves as a metaphor for Ben, a pilot.

Grounding as Freedom: Symbolic Cultural Connection

Ben's conscious decision not to drop the bombs reveals that he can no longer straddle the double-consciousness fence. The side of his consciousness that identifies him with mainstream America can accept the delusion that he is bombing the North Vietnamese to contain the spread of Communism among the South Vietnamese. On the other hand, the Black side of his consciousness shakes him out of this comfort zone, causing him to question his involvement and take action against continued complicity in the war. Resolved to carry out his act of defiance, he tells Stacy: "I decided what I'm going to do. When I get back from Bangkok I'm not going to fly any more. . . . I'm tired of helping white men keep their hold over the world" (88). By remaining resolute in his decision Ben not only takes a stand against killing for the White man but also consciously makes the decision to repudiate the White world and Eurocentric culture. He has discovered the connection between killing other peoples of color and destroying himself. The only way to find himself is to stop carrying out the wishes of the oppressor. At the same time this action signals his decision to embrace his own culture.

In the metaphorical middle passage, Ben re-members "walking through ghosts," an expression from Black folklore, which connects him to his ancestral past while walking through the warm night air in Thailand. Black folklore serves the same purpose for Davis in *Coming Home* as it does for Ellison in his short story "Flying Home," as a connection to Black ancestral memory that provides a source of "genuine black self-definition." Furthermore, and most importantly, the uniqueness of Black self-expression in folklore resides in the Black character's "willingness to trust his own experience, his own sensibilities as to the definition of reality, rather than to allow his masters to define these crucial matters for him," according to Susan Blake (78). Double-consciousness, as far as Ben is concerned, distinguishes between the "folk" (African) and "formal" (American) aspects of African American existence, with the folk side predominating as far as identity is concerned. Or, as Harris puts it, "the more immersed a character is in the folk culture the more likely he/she is to be able to resolve conflicts" (*Connecting Times* 5). To rekindle this nurturing sensation of Black folklore, Ben has several experiences in Thailand that remind him of the folk, or vernacular, culture from his southern roots.

Immersion: Connecting with Black Cultural Memory

The immersion stage of the Black heroic quest is characterized by community and camaraderie. Prior to his decision to stop flying, Ben feels bereft of emotion, and he has a desire for those things that make him feel connected to his Black heritage. Because of the bifurcation of his psyche (the rational versus the intuitive) that occurred during his undergraduate years at Harvard, however, he was unable to connect with that part of his past that made him feel alive and human.

Thailand, as a site of Black cultural memory, serves as a symbolic connection to Ben's Southern roots in Georgia. While walking through the streets of Bangkok with Papa San's daughter, for instance, he muses: "In some places the air is chilly, and in others we walk through warm air. Walking through ghosts we used to call it down South" (27). This immanence of the ancestors expresses the notion of harmony with nature that symbolically reveals universal truths inimical to the Eurocentric concept of nature that Ben has experienced during his tenure in academia and the military. In the Platonic world view nature is "disorderly" and "chaotic" and therefore must be "controlled" by man. Consequently, the relationship between man and nature is "hostile," leading to exploitation (Ani 84) and destruction, as in the strafing runs with napalm and carpet bombing missions by the American military that have denuded and made uninhabitable huge swaths of the Vietnamese countryside. Agent Orange and other defoliants have effectively destroyed thousands of acres of land that will never again be arable. Instead of being in harmony with nature the war is a sign of man's alienation from it.

The significance of Ben's experience of "walking through ghosts" in Thailand resides in what the French historian Pierre Nora refers to as "*lieux des mémoire*," or "sites of memory" (qtd. in Fabre and O'Meally 7). This interplay between "personal and collective" experience, a facet of the African-centered world view, can be used to represent a "place or an idea . . . available in sensuous experience." Significantly, sites of memory are "*functional*" as well as "symbolic" and can prompt the processes of both "imaginative recollection and historical consciousness" (27; emphasis added). Symbolically, therefore, "walking through ghosts" signals an early indication of Ben's attempt to recapture the racial consciousness that he has lost on his ascendancy up the ladder of success in Eurocentric culture.

During his sojourn in Thailand, Ben feels a sense of freedom from the constrictions of his academic and military experiences. The tone of his interior monologue is more mellifluous at this time than in previous instances in which his thoughts are abrupt, disjunctive, and fragmentary. The extent to which this verdant paradise represents a type of newfound freedom to him is evident when he wonders, "What would happen if I disappeared forever into the human and bamboo jungles of Asia?" (27). Strolling along the beach in Bangkok, he muses: "As I walk I feel strangely free, and I dread the thought of going back to America" (28). The America he "dreads" is that associated with the U.S. military and his Harvard education but not that associated with his familial ties in the South. Thailand evokes a certain emotional sense of belonging that he has not experienced in a long time. On Ben's cultural map, Stepto would refer to this Southeast Asian country as "symbolic geography" wherein the hero experiences "*genius loci*," or "spirit of place," a defining feature in cultural immersion rituals (70). The "spirit" of Black culture is here in Thailand.

The striking similarity between Thai people and African Americans causes Ben to feel a closeness that is like kinship. Childress comments that Thai girls look like "little yella colored girls" (23). Damg, on one occasion, compares her skin with that of Childress and tells him: "Soul brudder, soul brudder, me same same you" (15). When Ben goes to Bangkok on R&R, the water taxi driver who has been "chauffeuring" him and Damg often casts friendly smiles at Ben, prompting Damg to say: "Thai people like you. . . . He say you same same Thai people. American Negro" (150). Beautiful, enterprising, and politically aware, Damg even shares the same sentiment as Blacks for American political leaders who champion human and civil rights. Ben says: "She adored John Kennedy. . . . For more than a month after the assassination . . . she spit every time someone mentioned America" (137). Establishing such "skinship" ties not only evokes a sense of solidarity among these peoples of color but also an acknowledgment of their oppression by a common enemy.

While he is on R&R in Bangkok, Ben's ancestral consciousness is stirred in the hospitable presence of the elderly Papa San who, at the rear of his business, is preparing food for his family while at the same time inviting Ben, a perfect stranger, to partake as well. Here Ben witnesses the same kind of hospitality and warmth of a down-home Black gathering in the Deep South state of Georgia where his mother and grandmother live. Even the lines of bungalows in the Thai villages remind him of "outhouses in back of an old Southern church" (27). Thailand, as *lieux des mémoire*, rekindles the life-force in Ben that Harvard had killed.

Ben feels a oneness with nature as he walks through the warm, sentient night air with Papa San's daughter in Bangkok. The "ghosts" that they walk through are the immanent spirits of the ancestors, native to a cultural world view in which diunital logic (the spiritual and the intuitive) is as highly regarded as rational logic.

In an Afrocentric cosmological context there is no dichotomy between the material and the spiritual; rather, they are two expressions of the same reality (Mbiti 57), or "paradoxically complementary" (32). In African culture "ancestral spirits" serve as "intermediaries between the material world and the spiritual world," according to Barthold, providing the means of "protecting the present, guaranteeing the future and generally assuaging doubts and worries" (11). The spirit world is a part of the sacred cycle of existence; consequently, Ben can "feel" the nurturing "presence" of these spirits, which is the initial evidence of his effort to reconnect with Black cultural memory that will help him advance on his quest for re-membering the self.

Ben says he had this kind of connection with his ancestral past "before Harvard, before everything became literal and scientific, and then became more unreal than it ever was before, leading straight to Vietnam" (27). How could Harvard lead "straight to Vietnam"? Established upon Platonic principles, Harvard is a metaphor for Eurocentric philosophy and epistemology in *Coming Home*. It epitomizes the pinnacle of academic pursuits in America, and as Ani points out, Plato established "the Academy" (93). During his matriculation in academia, Ben has been introduced to the valorization of "abstract" or "scientific" thought, a characteristic of Platonism whereby "thought is only properly so called when isolated from feeling" (Ani 94).

This ideological basis of European culture leads to the "will to exert power and control over others" (Ani 105). In order to control there must be "dichotomization," of "self from other," reason from emotion, mind from body, and intellect from nature—all of which lead to "abstraction." This aspect of Platonic thought causes Ben to ponder: "For me this war is like Harvard. Everything is abstract. Everything is an argument or a question" (17). Platonism also fosters oppositional, confrontational, antagonistic relationships, such as "othering" those who are different from the European self, which places them in a "threatening" and "antagonistic" relationship because they are different. This practice encourages "imperialistic behavior" toward, rather than an acceptance of, other cultures (Ani 105). Therefore, exerting its imperialistic will over the "other," in this case the Vietnamese, the United States justified the war in Vietnam based on the same Eurocentric principles that established the epitome of higher education in America, Harvard.

Site of Memory: Community, Ritual Ground, and Eulogizing Space

The Black protagonist who is alienated not only from himself but also from the Black community and White society can only hope for "reconciliation and self-identification" by "establishing or restoring a sense of cohesion with his own race" through some symbolic "member or custom" or experience (Doyle 165). Similar to the way in which Ben's experience in Thailand—its lush jungles, the sentient night air, the warm people—functions as metaphysical *lieu de mémoire* by evoking for the hero a sense of "community," the "club" serves as physical *lieu de mémoire*, or "ritual ground," on the heroic quest. Ritual grounds are important in the hero's quest for self-fulfillment and wholeness because they provide a place where "race spirit or race message" can be expressed, occurring within the realm of what Victor Turner calls "communitas," which "characterize[s] relationships between those jointly undergoing ritual transition" (qtd. in Stepto 69). The other Black GIs Ben encounters in the club atmosphere share his negative attitude toward the war and a common desire to leave it as they go through male bonding rituals, such as "the dap."

Soul Alley, the place of the blues, is a marginalized space on the periphery of the officers' club and other facilities that are frequented most often by Whites. Gaston Bachelard's term "eulogized space," or space that has the "potential to liberate" (qtd. in Baker, *Workings* 72), aptly describes Soul Alley. Immersing himself in this cultural milieu gives Ben the will, the courage, and the fortitude to advance on his quest, or in the vernacular, to "keep on keepin' on." James Weldon Johnson, in *Autobiography of an Ex-Coloured Man*, uses the club symbolically as a space where "responses to oppressing social structures are made or in some measure sustained" by what Stepto calls "tribal bonds" (123). In a similar way, Davis uses the club in *Coming Home* as a eulogized space that conjures up conviviality, camaraderie, and brotherhood. Ben has missed this feeling of community in the officers' corps where he is in a small minority of Black officers and where he has to wear the mask of upper-middle-class so-called civility. In the clubs where enlisted men hang out, on the other hand, he does not have to be concerned about all the affectations of upper-middle-class society. Since the officers' club is separated from the enlisted men's clubs, Ben rarely has a chance to interact with other Black men, especially those of lower rank. But here, in the club, he is treated like another brother with the nurturance of self-affirming values from which he has been distanced.

Desiring the camaraderie of other Black men, Ben goes to the "strip" lined with clubs, and he smiles as he passes several Black marines harmonizing to soul music as they and their Thai girlfriends "bop" down the sidewalk club hopping. On one occasion Ben feels relaxed enough to "shoot the breeze" with another Black soldier, as he and Damg walk down the street and pass clubs with names such as "Sweet Dream," "the 69 Club," "the Casanova," "the Casbar," "Thai Paradise," and the "Lance-A-Lot," into which they decide to go to hear Big Buddha, a "heavy-set" Asian who sings and plays soul music belting out the Wilson Pickett tune "I Found a Love." Using similar gestures to this soul artist, Big Buddha elicits sounds of joy and approval from Ben and other Black soldiers who yell: "Go 'head Big Buddha" (136–39). This feeling is a far cry from the ennui Ben has experienced during the ascendancy phase of his quest. Listening and dancing to soul music in this atmosphere of conviviality prompts Ben to laugh, which he has not done in a while, as he sways on the dance floor with Damg.

Being on ritual ground puts Ben in his element, in a manner of speaking. He relaxes as he engages in jocular banter with a Black GI who imitates the Asian singer who is imitating the soul singer Wilson Pickett, an example of signification at its finest, under the "sign" of the blues. The Black GI bends over a cane as though it were a microphone, singing "I Found a Love." But the love Ben has found is not that of a woman. Rather, it is the love of himself and his people in the early stages of his reconnection with and acceptance of his Black cultural heritage that will reach fruition when he later goes to "the African Star Club" and has a heart-to-heart talk with an AWOL Black enlisted man who plants the idea for desertion and exile to Sweden.

While fraternizing with the other Black soldiers, Ben no longer feels self-conscious about the way he speaks, as he did earlier when he castigated himself for saying "sweat" rather than "perspiration," which a Harvard man would say. Davis produces this code switch in language because of the intrinsic interrelationship between language and culture. Linguist Francois Muyumba calls language a "coded medium" that a "community" of speakers understands and through which "culture is developed, preserved and stored" (87). He reveals current research on Ebonics or Black English, which recognizes that such "black expressive structures exhibit . . . connectedness between the African continent and the African Diaspora" (88).

Consequently, Ben and the other Black GIs converse in the vernacular, something he has not done in a long time. A sign of his self-awareness, it allows the former tension and feelings of restraint and uncertainty to dissipate. In fact, his demeanor changes during the following interchange with a fellow Black GI as they watch the Asian "soul singer" wallop out a tune:

> "Go 'head Big Buddha," I yell and laugh. "Go 'head with yo' bad self."
>> "If Big Buddha does a James Brown number, I'm gonna fall out," the GI says.
>> ". . . You? Me. They gon' have to carry me out." (139)

Ben feels a sense of community and oneness with the enlisted men and the Thais. Prior to his encounter with other Black men in the ritual grounds of Soul Alley, Ben has been a brooding, preoccupied, unhappy person.

An obvious sign of Ben's transformation to self-awareness is the breaking down of boundaries between himself and the Black enlisted men. As an officer he has been placed on a pedestal, of sorts. This status has given him privilege in the White world. However, much to his chagrin, it has also set up boundaries between himself and the majority of Black men in the military, particularly in the army where most Blacks are in infantry and artillery units fighting in the muck and mire of the ground war. When Ben enters the African Star Club (owned by three Black ex-GIs who remained in Bangkok after getting out of the army), he hears music that reminds him of the Hollywood Club that he used to frequent back in Washington, DC, when he was stationed at Andrews Air Force Base. Ben is "happy to be hearing familiar tones and familiar rhythms" (167). A young Black GI named Wilton Smith sits at his table, and they converse. As a result they learn that they are both from the East Coast. Introducing himself as "Army, Infantry," Smith exclaims, "Oh . . . a glory boy, Officer," when Ben reveals that he is an officer in the air force.

Smith tells Ben that he had wanted to be an officer but hurt his chances when he had to drop out of college. In an attempt to minimize the importance of his rank, and hence the "distance" between them, Ben tells him there is not much difference between them as far as being an air force officer and an army enlisted man are concerned. But Smith retorts: "No, man. . . . It's a whole lot different war down in the mud" (168). In his own self-effacing way, Ben attempts to put himself on the same level with Smith when he says, "I'm quitting flying anyway" (169). Smith, who has already been AWOL for twenty-one days, reveals to Ben that he cannot take the war anymore and that he is going to desert to Sweden. Aghast at the notion initially, Ben says he does not want to "run away." Smith informs him that as Black men having gone against the establishment—going AWOL and refusing to continue flying—their only choices are prison or "catching trains." Consequently, Smith says he will choose going into exile in Sweden over going to prison, which, for a Black man, means death.

Ben tells Smith that Black men have been "running" long enough, to which Smith retorts: "*You* been running. I ain't been running nowhere. I was born in the shit and I want a chance to live" (169). Then he poignantly contrasts the impersonal, distant air war with the more visceral ground war, explaining to Ben his reason for leaving not only the military but also his plans for leaving the United States—for good.[12]

I shot a kid, man. I shot a little Vietnamese kid right in the back, man. The night before I left the 'Nam. I was on patrol in a village near Thuc Yen and this little kid came up to me in an alley and asked me did I want a shoeshine. And sometimes they have bombs in those little boxes. So I told him to set his box down and back off, and he turned and ran, and I shot him right in the back.

His voice cracks and he is silent for a moment.

Then I went up and looked in this little box and do you know what I found? . . . Shoe polish, man. Not a goddam thing but shoe polish. I went back to the base and packed my shit and left. I ain't never gon' kill no more innocent people, man. And I ain't going to no jail either. I'm still young. (169)

Acting out of paranoia and fear, Smith has committed an act so inhumane and reprehensible that his conscience will not let him rest. The military has reduced him to the status of a child killer, all in the name of so-called stamping out Communism and bringing democracy to Southeast Asia. Through this soldier, Ben is brought face-to-face with the ground war in a way that he never would have otherwise. As a high-flying pilot oblivious to the carnage being caused on the ground during the war, he descends to knowledge and awareness. This awakening parallels that of the protagonist in a short story by Ralph Ellison titled "Flying Home."

"Flying Home": Comparison to Coming Home

Ben's experience of separation from and eventual reconnection with Black cultural memory through folklore "revoices" that of Todd, the protagonist in Ellison's "Flying Home," who is a pilot in the Army Air Command during World War II. In his ascendance to becoming one of the famous Tuskegee Airmen, he forgets, or ignores, where he came from. As it does for Ben, this lack of historical knowledge leads to the creation of a "false identity." In other words, he must re-member by symbolically connecting with Black vernacular culture. Whereas for Ben that symbolic folk member is Smith in the club, for Todd the symbolic person is an old illiterate Black man named Jefferson who rescues him after he flies into a buzzard and crash lands in a field. Jefferson provides the linchpin for Todd's re-membering, or his reconnection with, historical African American culture when he tells two folktales about pride, or flying too high, going before a fall.

Similar to *Coming Home*, "Flying Home" has a tripartite structure, having to do with three stages of development of Todd's awareness: the first stage involves his admiration of and desire to have a toy airplane while a child; the second has to do with his frustration at earning his wings but being prevented, because he is Black, from flying bombing missions during World War II; and the third stage deals with his "fall to maturity" (Ogunyemi 27). Interestingly, Ben and Todd reverse the direction of what Eurocentric society considers as making "progress," because rather than ascending they are brought down to earth, in the vernacular, where they descend to self-knowledge. For each of them this downward movement is a growth, or maturation, process.

During World War II Black soldiers such as Todd were denied the right to fly in combat even though they had proven themselves to be some of the best prepared and trained soldiers in the Army Air Command Corps (Doyle 169). In other words, the army denied them what Ben is now permitted to do in Vietnam. Interestingly, during World War II Blacks had to fight for the right to fly. With the assistance of Eleanor Roosevelt, funds were made available to construct a flight school at Tuskegee Institute, out of which the famous Tuskegee Airmen emerged.[13] When Mrs. Roosevelt discovered the combat flight restrictions, she saw to it that such restrictions were lifted; consequently, the Tuskegee Airmen were permitted to fly missions over enemy territory in Germany. These Black pilots produced a stellar record of destroying enemy strongholds while losing very few men in the process. Todd's experience metaphorically portrays that of the Tuskegee Airmen.

When Todd's plane crash lands, he "reintegrates," or immerses, himself back into the Black world (Ogunyemi 24). In so doing he undergoes a type of metamorphosis, a death and rebirth of sorts, worked out in imagery of insects and animals in the air (locusts, wasps, buzzards) and on the ground (horses and oxen). Also, similar to Jonah's death and rebirth when he is swallowed by and emerges from the whale, Todd emerges reborn from the body of the plane in which he has crashed. I agree with Ogunyemi that the buzzard he flies into that causes his plane to crash represents "jim-crowism" in the military (25). However, Todd's descent from the airplane when he crash lands among the common folk restores a "bond" with them, and he is therefore able to find a sense of peace within himself that enables him to survive (Doyle 171).

In his ascent up the ladder of success seeking recognition and acceptance by White society, Todd has condescended to other Blacks. He is also embarrassed to be around so-called "lower-classed blacks" such as Jefferson, the illiterate old Black man who finds him in the crashed airplane. After his "fall" to awareness (Ogunyemi 27), however, Todd discovers that the expectation of self-fulfillment in White society is illusory because their cultural values are designed to keep Blacks in their place.

As Joseph Trimmer observes, rather than being a "way to fulfillment," Todd's seeking White approval for his flying is "a way to psychic suicide" (181), as it has been for Childress and Ben.

After his fall Todd not only accepts his own identity as a Black man in a White world but also recognizes that he and Jefferson are inextricably bound together as part of a communal experience. It is this encounter with vernacular experience that enables Todd to be resurrected from his old way of thinking to a new life as a Black man interdependent with the Black community. Despite his crash as Trimmer notes, he "in the process . . . has destroyed the harness of his white aspirations, the plane, and has been resurrected by a song of communal acceptance" (182). Todd re-members his Black roots to survive the psychological assault on his manhood by the White military establishment that placed boundaries on the heights he and other Black pilots could attain during World War II.

Similar to Ellison's "Flying Home," Davis's *Coming Home* reverses the ascendant mode, which is conventionally associated with freedom. However, the higher Ben ascends the ladder of success, the more he becomes bound and entrapped by stereotypical and limiting conceptions of his manhood. In this instance, the nadir of the quest is also the place where the Black hero has his epiphany and begins the process of coming home to self. Similar to Todd, who crash lands to find himself, it is not until Ben stops flying and becomes grounded that he is free to express himself and discover who he is. The Black hero reverses the quest from "upward towards the demoralizing influences of a pretentious black or white society . . . to what might rightly be called the 'bottom,'" according to Jerome Thornton (262). Ben's experience is not unlike that of Janie, Zora Neale Hurston's heroine in *Their Eyes Were Watching God*, who descends to a prototypical "bottom" when she goes "on de muck," a place of self-discovery that is both a physical and a symbolic setting where "the black hero repeatedly accomplishes the feat of self-knowledge" (Thornton 262). Downward is the place where the Black hero finds his identity.

Similar to Old Man Jefferson in "Flying Home," who provides instruction on the rite of passage for Todd, Smith plays the role of guide for Ben on his quest for self-awareness. Following his harrowing experience with the little Vietnamese boy, Smith has now been AWOL for twenty-one days. He then tells Ben about a Japanese underground network that is mainly run by Buddhists who can help him escape the country by going though Japan, up to Russia, and then over to Sweden into exile.[14] Smith's demeanor and passion are such that the horror of the ground war becomes real and tangible to Ben, and for the first time he begins to ponder the two alternatives that Black men have historically had a choice between in impossible situations: "catching trains" (i.e., hitting the road), or waiting around and being imprisoned.

Prior to his meeting with Smith in the African Star Club, Ben has been nervous, preoccupied, and anxiously anticipating what will happen the next day after his commanding officers discover that he has grounded his plane. For instance, on R&R in Bangkok, Ben rides in a taxi with Damg through the city considering his possible fate: "I look at the sky and think about prison. Being in prison must be like being dead" (109). Feeling "weak," as Damg scrutinizes him, he thinks: "She can see the tension in my face. I try to relax slowly. I unclench my teeth slowly. . . . I want to know too if there are the beginnings of tears in the corners of my eyes" (110). As he leans forward in the taxi seat his "hands begin to sweat" (111). Later he and Damg walk along the river where sampans are lined up with produce. Still nervous and fidgety, he considers: "Tomorrow I will have to go back to the base to face charges, I think . . . I can't think straight" (148). Damg is oblivious to Ben's internal anxiety because, according to him, "she cannot understand how desperate I am" (148). His uneasiness results from the stress of wondering what his fate will be as a result of his decision to disobey orders and discontinue flying.

Terry Whitmore reveals in his autobiography, *Memphis-Nam-Sweden*, that when he decided to desert the military he found himself having to make a decision: "to say *no* to Sam and *no* to America and its jails . . . [that is,] *no* to everything I know, my family, my block, everybody—have to start out all over again" (120). After Ben ponders his choices, like Whitmore, he decides to desert the military and go AWOL to Sweden. Though desertion carries an amount of uncertainty, he is willing to take that chance in the interest of finding himself and freedom (199). According to Whitmore, Sweden offered the chance to "start to live my life" (200). It represents the same for Ben. Similar to the nameless protagonist in Ellison's *Invisible Man*, Ben had to "discard his old identities and illusions" (J. Wright 158) before he could have a voice in determining his own destiny. His self-awareness could not come until then.

Transcendence: Symbolic Space of Humanitarianism and Racelessness

Before Ben can discover his identity, he must divest himself of the binary, dualistic world view that has hampered his self-awareness. He must adopt a different way of seeing the world and his place in it. Ben's predicament can be summed up in a similar way to that of Okonkwo in *Things Fall Apart*, which Ousseynou Traore assesses as follows: "When in an environment that is 'foreign' to your world view, you are not allowed to choose 'your own space'" ("Quarrel"). Having one's own space is liberatory, as it was for the enslaved Linda Brent, who "deliberately confined herself to a cramped attic space" over a period of years so that she could "achieve freedom" (M. Washington, "Meditations" 12) from enslavement. Ben, consequently, is liberated when he occupies the symbolic space that he consciously chooses in Sweden.

To discover his identity, Ben must transcend both the dichotomous, binary vision of Western civilization and the harmonizing, diunital paradoxes of African civilization by seeking a humanitarian solution that mediates between these two world views when he goes AWOL to Sweden, a "neutral" country that symbolizes "humanitarianism" (Whitmore 169). Having become fed up with all the senseless killing he has done in Vietnam, ostensibly in the name of "freedom," Ben seeks what the Swedes call "humanitarian asylum" that, according to Whitmore, means that the Swedes "will allow a person to live at peace in Sweden if his own country is forcing him to kill other human beings in a war that he believes is immoral, unjust, illegal—in other words, if there is no goddam good reason for all the killing he refuses to do" (169). After several consciousness-raising experiences, Ben decides that the war is immoral and unjust. Consequently, his refusal to drop any more bombs and his decision to discontinue flying bombing missions coincide with the aims of the Swedes.

Transcendence, the final stage of the hero's quest for wholeness and freedom, is a "metaphysical space," outside of time and place. In that respect, it is a "spiritual" goal. Because it offers hope for the resolution of double-consciousness, transcendence allows unification of the human spirit. As a modern Black male, Ben desires to live what Colin Channer calls an "authentic life," which will enable him to explore "the range of possibilities between each opposing self and to create a way of being . . . authored from a place of *self-knowledge* and truth" (114; emphasis added).

Consequently, Ben's going into exile can be viewed as a period of hibernation, similar to that of Ellison's *Invisible Man*. The expectation is that he will emerge from this self-imposed exile with a new sense of awareness of himself and of his relationship to society. Stepto refers to this phase of the Black heroic quest as the "epiloguing space," similar to the underground hole in which the Invisible Man finds himself,[15] where the hero becomes a "group-conscious" as well as a "self-conscious" person (169). Ben's experiences with the Black enlisted men in the Lance-A-Lot Club and the African Star Club enable him to embrace group consciousness, which he now realizes is a necessary complement to self-consciousness.

I agree with Anne Cauley in her observation that "self-authority is a prerequisite to freedom [that] is attained by the man who . . . shakes loose the illusion that white values serve black needs" (328). When Ben deserts the air force and goes to Sweden, his decision is "less the act of an individual motivated by anger and frustration than that of a man conscious of the ways his ancestors responded to like circumstances" by choosing the uncertainty of life up North to lynch mobs and sharecropping in the South (Harris, *Connecting Times* 55). Like his enslaved ancestors before him who fled the institution of chattel slavery, Ben becomes a fugitive from America, fleeing institutionalized racism in the military, which requires involuntary servitude and the destruction of human life in Vietnam. Prior to his decision to desert the military, Ben has not consciously made decisions guided by his own sense of reality. Instead, he has relied upon the dictates of his commanding officers, his wife, and others. Now, as a step toward self-actualization, he purposefully takes action.

The final, transcendent, stage of Ben's quest can be summed up in the words of Du Bois when he says there is a constant "longing" of the Black male to "attain self-conscious manhood, to merge his double-self into a better and truer self" (*Souls of Black Folk* 215). In this phase of the Black hero's journey, race is not the primary issue, as it has been in the ascendant and immersion phases. Rather, this is a symbolic space of racelessness where Ben seeks to transcend the boundaries that race had set for him in America and in Vietnam to be treated as a human being.[16]

Ben disappears from the action before the end of the novel, with the final voices being those of his fellow officers in Country and his wife and others in the World. His final appearance occurs in a part titled "THAILAND," where Smith reveals the plan for his desertion to Sweden. After Smith leaves the African Star Club on his way to make his connection with the Japanese "Underground Railroad," to freedom in Sweden, Ben wishes him "good luck" and then muses: "I sit down and think about all the black men who have been hitting the road, catching trains. Then I think about all the black men in prisons or on Southern prison farms. I try and weigh one group against another as I pay my check and go out the door" (170).

After this scene in the African Star that prefigures his desertion, Ben does not appear again. Three additional parts complete the novel: "WASHINGTON, DC," detailing Rose's and Roxanne's visit to Childress in prison and his explanation of how he killed the police officer in self-defense; "THAILAND," detailing a strafing run over North Vietnam by Lt. Col. Milligan's, Bordreau's, and Stacy's squadron, after which Stacy takes his nosedive to suicide; and "WASHINGTON, DC," detailing Rose's conjecture concerning Ben's whereabouts.

Ben's fate in Sweden, as it was for Whitmore when he first defected, is uncertain. Approached by the Japanese underground group, Beheiren, after recuperating from war injuries in Japan, Whitmore responded in his usual tragicomedic way when offered the opportunity to desert to Sweden: "Sweden. Where's that? I don't know. The cat says Sweden, so we go to Sweden. Where else? Sweden sure as hell must be better than the States or Nam as far as I'm concerned, so why *not* Sweden?" (200). Similar to Whitmore, for Ben things will not be the same as before his rite of passage, which began in midair and reached its denouement in the African Star. Metaphorically the African Star provides direction on Ben's journey to freedom and self-fulfillment, as did the proverbial North Star that his enslaved African ancestors followed to freedom. They did not know what fate awaited them up North, but they nevertheless trudged forward with determination because whatever awaited was certainly better than the cruelty of the "peculiar institution" of slavery they had left behind. The same is true for Ben.

Ben's external freedom scarcely compares with the internal freedom that he discovers through self-awareness. From the outset he has been troubled about his role in senseless killings and the destruction of Vietnamese villages. The reason does not occur to him until he is well on his way in his heroic quest for manhood that as a fighter pilot he has been removed from the consequences of his destructive acts. Not until he is literally and figuratively grounded does the connection between his identity as a Black man and his role as a soldier fighting a war for America become clear. He opts to be a self-conscious Black man rather than a soldier.

Ben realizes his human responsibility through fortitude and his decision to take a stand against all that the war in Vietnam represents. To be unaware of the consequences of his actions and not act is one thing, but to be aware and not act is unconscionable. Before his transformation from a doubly conscious fighter pilot to a single-minded Black man, Ben searches for his identity in all the wrong places: academia (Harvard), the military (Air Force OCS), marriage (Rose). After searching outside himself in each of these instances, he discovers that true freedom lies within.

Ben is "coming home" to himself. Similar to Janie, in *Their Eyes Were Watching God*, who "pulls in the horizon and drapes it over her shoulder," Ben is becoming aware of the "world of possibility" (Washington 48) that awaits a hero on his journey to self-discovery. By dividing the novel into parts according to geographical location,

Davis reveals that identity, or self-awareness, is a "journey" that Ben has not yet completed. Having begun, ironically, in Thailand, the journey continues during his exile in the "symbolic topography" of Sweden, away from America, which has been the source of his angst as a Black man and has contributed to his dehumanization. Consequently, he must not return to America if he desires to discover true humanism.[17] Where is home for Ben? It is the ultimate destination of the Black hero on his journey to self-knowledge, where he can re-member his divided consciousness without the burden of the confining social structures or the institutionalized racism that plagues military life in Southeast Asia and civilian life in America.

Epilogue

The shape of Africa is a heart.
— Charles Pugh, *The Griot*

"I am because we are, we are because I am." This message, widespread through African mythology and spirituality, ought to be the basis of the stories we tell the young heroes and heroines in our midst. For when I see that my existence is predicated on others' and their existence is predicated on mine, then I must see that doing violence to others is doing violence to myself.
— Clyde Ford, *The Hero with an African Face: Mythic Wisdom of Traditional Africa*

The African proverb, "I am because we are, we are because I am," reveals the interdependent relationship that exists between the self and the community, that is, an individual does not survive "alone" but rather as a consequence of the "interaction and properties of the collective," as Clyde Ford points out in *The Hero with an African Face* (21). This defining characteristic of the hero from African epic and myth also captures the essence of the heroic stance in narratives about the African American experience in Vietnam. Similar to the heroic quester in all cultures, the "hero with an African face" (Ford 1) sets out on life's journey to "find himself." Though self-awareness is necessary on his heroic journey, more important is interdependence with the community and the recognition that one's individual fate is connected to that of the whole. This relationship accounts for the remembering of African/African American cultural history that is necessary for the Black hero in Vietnam War narratives to re-member psychologically and to survive on his quest for wholeness.

Furthermore, as Ford reveals, the classic struggle of the warrior in African epics is "between his power to destroy life and his desire to renew life" (70). Consequently, to subdue the destructive and to bolster the creative urge, he must have a "spiritual life." Instead of a set of religious beliefs or dogmas, "spiritual" in this context refers to "a life in continual alignment with the source of renewal and revivification" (74). Tapping into the African ancestral past and connecting with moral values of the community provide a conduit for the transferal of attributes of the spirit enabling the hero to express compassion toward others.

This attribute of mutuality between the hero and the community on the quest for self-knowledge in African/African American culture contrasts with the tradition of the heroic quest in certain Eastern and Western traditions. For instance, many of the myths in Asian culture emphasize principally the "group" rather than the "individual" (Ford 90). On the other hand, Western mythological traditions mainly focus on the "individual to the exclusion of the group," a characteristic that Joseph Campbell's exploration of the Arthurian legends reveals. Eurocentric conceptions of the hero champion the American frontier notion of "regeneration through violence," the latter day evidence of which appears as the "John Wayne syndrome" in mainstream novels about the Vietnam War and that Wesley Brown critiques in *Tragic Magic.* Central to the folklore of White heroes, such as Paul Bunyan, Davy Crockett, and the characters portrayed by John Wayne in the movies, is a glorification of the "self." Lawrence Levine refers to such portrayals as an "inflation of the individual" (*Black Culture* 401), a view Marimba Ani purports in her assessment that Eurocentric culture defines the self in a "power" relationship to "the other" (peoples of color) who, considered as "inferior," must be conquered (297). This "conqueror" mentality is pervasive in mainstream war literature.

On the other hand, the myths embodied in many African epics, including the *Epic of Sundiata,* from the West African kingdom of Mali, and the less well-known *Mwindo Epic* from the Democratic Republic of Congo, "encode" an interdependent relationship between the individual and the group (Ford 90). Consequently, the adaptations of myths from African and African American culture in *Captain Blackman, De Mojo Blues, Tragic Magic*, and *Coming Home* reveal the necessity of the hero to (re)connect with a group identity from the past to be able to survive the horrors of the present war in Vietnam and to deal with the post-traumatic effects of war and racism upon his return to American society. In each of these novels, the conception of the hero conforms to the Afrocentric concept of the "extended self" wherein individuality is more multidimensional than in Eurocentric culture. Rather than being an entity separate and apart from others, the "self," according to Linda James Myers, "cannot and does not exist alone, but owes his/her very existence to other members of the 'tribe,'" which is "extended" to "include all of the ancestors, the yet unborn, all of nature, and the entire community" (19, 20). This view of man's relationship to society is subsumed in an Afrocentric "spiritual/ material ontology" in which one "lose[s] the sense of individualized ego/mind" and replaces it with the "harmony of the collective identity of being one with the source of all good" (12). Viewing human relationships in this manner imbues the hero with a concern for humanity that expresses itself as compassion for others.

This ontological view conforms to that in many African myths wherein the hero symbolically "dies" as a "secular warrior" following his otherworldly or underground encounter with the "gods," often a symbolic "journey" within the psyche during the rite of passage (Baker, *Blues* 153). While in this "black (w)hole" of experience, he is then "reborn," not as a world conqueror but rather as a "sacred warrior" and "world redeemer" whose enlightenment on the heroic quest causes him to have "*compassion* for humanity" (Ford 94; emphasis added). His mission, then, is to return to society to show others the path to "spiritual fulfillment and illumination." These characteristics of the hero with an African face are portrayed in the recent blockbuster film *Black Panther*. Though adapted from the Marvel Comics hero of the same name, this movie is not just another cartoon character coming to life nor coincidentally representative of African heroic myth. Rather, the film's director and co-writer of the screenplay, Ryan Coogler, an African American who researched African culture and myth to bring as much verisimilitude to the screen as possible, including female warriors, reflective of matriarchal and well as patriarchal societies in many African countries. In so doing he introduced the American public to this rich source of African history and culture for the first time. Despite the fact that it grossed over a billion dollars, Matt Goldberg, a movie reviewer for *The Collider*, says he would not be surprised if *Black Panther* were deemed one of the decade's "most influential films because "every single person in *Black Panther*, hero or villain, has agency, a purpose, and something worth saying."

This African cultural legacy is evidenced in the African American vernacular tradition that portrays the hero as strong and fearless yet compassionate. Like Joshua Jones, the hero in Rudolph Fisher's Harlem Renaissance novel *The Walls of Jericho*, whose "surface toughness reveals a compassionate heart" (B. Bell 139), the Black heroes in the Vietnam War novels under analysis are "compassionate warriors." Consequently, they are concerned not only about their own well-being but also that of the entire Black community as well as humanity in general.

It is out of compassion for his fellow Black soldiers that the protagonist in *Captain Blackman* goes back to college and studies Black history after his first tour of duty in Vietnam and then reenlists in the army so that he can teach Black military history to the idealistic new Black recruits in Country. His aim is to forestall the disappointment and cynicism that eventuates when the Black soldier realizes that America's promises of honor for battlefield bravery are not forthcoming. Consequently his lessons about the historical involvement of Blacks in all of America's wars—from the Revolutionary War to Vietnam—equip these modern day soldiers with survival strategies to cope with racism similar to their precursors who fought, against seemingly insurmountable odds, but nevertheless survived. As the modern embodiment of the African mythical hero Ananse the Spider, Abraham Blackman spins a web of historical awareness to help these Black soldiers balance both—the African and the American—sides of their double-consciousness dilemma.

Similarly, compassion leads Melvin in *Tragic Magic* to intervene in a street fight between two Black teenagers whom he encounters in an alleyway after returning to his neighborhood from a prison stint for being a conscientious objector. The youths witness an incident in which Melvin's friend, Otis, a Vietnam veteran, is knifed to death by an anonymous assailant. An argument between the two boys ensues concerning whether Otis is brave or cowardly for failing to subdue his assailant. Though they are unaware of it, they suffer from the same demons of anger and false bravado, fostered by the "code of the streets" and America's John Wayne image of heroism, that lead to Otis's untimely demise. During his rite of passage in prison for conscientious objection to the Vietnam War, Melvin learns that the definition of a true hero does not conform to these popular culture depictions; rather it involves a process of finding one's individual voice and then merging it with the ensemble—of family, friends, and community—as in a jazz composition. He therefore intervenes to break up the fight. Despite being severely wounded in the process, Melvin succeeds in preventing the deaths of a new generation of Black males from the senselessness of street violence, kindled by machismo, a fate from which, unfortunately, he is unable to save his friend Otis. Finding his identity as a Black man therefore enables Melvin to act in the interest of the community.

Moreover, it is compassion that prompts Tucept, in *De Mojo Blues*, to seek a method of empowerment for himself and the Black community when he and two friends return home from Vietnam in manacles and chains after being accused of a fragging in Vietnam, a crime that they did not commit. The progeny of a family who practices the healing arts—his father a physician who heals the body and his mother a Vodoun/voodoo practitioner who heals the spirit—Tucept is on point in a holy war to reclaim the spirits of his fellow Black soldiers. While he meditates, in dreamstate, he communes with the elders who have declared that his destiny is to restore the self-worth not only of himself and his buddies but also of the entire Black community who have been disempowered and demoralized by racism since the time of enslavement across the Diaspora. Tucept therefore delves into the study of the African ritual of Vodoun/voodoo as a subjective correlative to empowerment and healing of the Black community, in the past, present, and future.

Finally, it is compassion that leads Ben, in *Coming Home*, to park his plane when he makes a conscious decision to stop flying bombing raids over North Vietnam. Despite a stellar career in academia as a graduate of Harvard and in the air force as a graduate of Officer Candidate School, he still feels unfulfilled as a Black man. Fighting a war that he is ordered to fight against "Charlie," his alleged enemy, in Vietnam causes him to question the motives of "Mr. Charlie (the white military-industrial complex)," his true enemy, in America. Having come to grips with the imperialistic and capitalistic motives of America in Vietnam, Ben, out of compassion for the Vietnamese, decides to stop flying bombing raids over North Vietnam. This decision, as well as his discovery of brotherhood with Black enlisted men, prompts him to become a deserter from the American military and to flee to Sweden, the symbol of humanitarianism. Having discovered his own identity and realized his own human potential, Ben is able to empathize with the plight of other peoples of color in Vietnam. His desertion to Sweden consequently symbolizes "hope for humanity and the world" (B. Bell 246).

A veritable storehouse of materials awaits the curious scholar who wishes to delve into the rich variety of fictional literary expression by Black writers about the Black experience in Vietnam. Additionally, application of suitable critical methodologies, such as vernacular theory and the New Black Aesthetic, which provide clarity to the themes therein, will enable the reading public to experience another perspective of the war different from that in mainstream literature.

In addition to Williams, Flowers, Brown, and Davis, a number of other African American authors, male and female, have produced Vietnam War novels (see appendix 1), and the following synopses provide a brief overview. The earliest work of Black fiction, *Dau Tranh!*, was authored by a woman, the extraordinarily gifted and beautiful Philippa Schuyler. Her father was George S. Schuyler, noted African American journalist who was editor of the *Pittsburgh Courier* newspaper and a member of the Harlem Renaissance literati. His novel *Black No More* (1931) is a scathing satire of American race relations,[1] and his daughter Philippa appears to have inherited his critical eye and penchant for irony as expressed in her literary works. Philippa's mother was Josephine Cogdell, an artistic White heiress from Texas who was a ballet dancer, a poet, and a painter. As a writer of articles for the Black press, Josephine met and married George S. Schuyler, and they had one child, Philippa. Discovered to be a genius from the time she was a small child, Philippa, according to her biographer, Kathryn Talalay, had a "500 word reading and writing vocabulary" by the time she was three years old; and at five she had an "IQ [that] was measured at 180" (2). Significantly, both Fordham and New York Universities rate an "IQ of 140" to be that of a "genius." Additionally, before she turned five she was already performing classical music on the piano, some of which she had composed. Multitalented, Schuyler is often compared to Mozart because of her extraordinary musical ability. As an adult, she performed concerts in seventy-eight countries around the world where, according to Daniel J. Lyons who wrote the foreword for and edited her nonfictional book *Good Men Die*, she "entertained royalty, the common people, and the underprivileged." Multilingual, she spoke Vietnamese, Portuguese, Arabic, Spanish, and several African dialects. Having visited with Pope Paul, she conversed with him in English, Italian, and French (4).

Despite Schuyler's precocity, however, she experienced problems as a biracial person struggling to fit into both White and Black worlds, as Lise Funderburg reveals in her review of Kathryn Talalay's biography titled *Composition in Black and White: The Life of Philippa Schuyler.*[2] Perhaps the title of Schuyler's Vietnam War novel, *Dau Tranh!* (trans. "to struggle" or "to fight" in Vietnamese), is symbolic of that personal struggle as well as her own enigmatic personality and extraordinary talents. In *Good Men Die*, her nonfictional work, Schuyler takes pains to point out that the facile interpretation of "*dau tranh*" as merely "struggle" is an "anemic Anglo-Saxon translation." To the contrary it is much more complex, as the richness of the phrase includes the "zest, mystery, and drama, [that] is impossible to interpret in a Western language" (94). The heroine of Schuyler's Vietnam War novel *Dau Tranh!* struggles to assert herself as a light-skinned Black professional in a racist society. The omniscient narrator describes the protagonist in the following excerpt from the novel (which was never published), revealing the hypocrisy of the American government purportedly "fighting to make the world safe for democracy" in Vietnam while discriminating against Blacks in America:

> Her skin was light enough for her to be accepted as second-class white in Rhodesia, Kenya or South Africa, and its color made no difference in Europe. But to Americans it was the most important of all characteristics. It categorised one as a person to be insulted, to be treated as a pariah, to be deprived of respect in all deeper human relationships. The same white Americans who were supposed to be bringing democracy to Vietnam were incapable of practicing it themselves in any context that went deeper than superficial.[3]

This description of her novel's protagonist could just as well describe Schuyler, who despite her precocity and extraordinary talents, experienced racism while performing as a concert pianist and while serving as a foreign correspondent on several continents. Very light-skinned, she at times passed for White while performing in Europe. She also sometimes passed for Vietnamese, wearing the traditional *ao dai* Vietnamese dress and conical hat to move freely throughout the villages to avoid detection by the CIA while gathering information as a news correspondent in Southeast Asia. Living on the color line gave Schuyler a unique perspective on life, but there is speculation that her criticism of the American involvement in the Vietnam War at this early stage of the conflict in the mid-sixties probably contributed to her untimely death. Her nonfictional book *Good Men Die*, which was published posthumously in 1969, reveals her remarkable wit and her revelation of statistics about the war that would not come to light until decades later in publications such as *The Pentagon Papers*.[4] Her reportage on Vietnam where she traveled to write *Good Men Die*, and from which she did not return alive, stands as one of the earliest records of the war from a Black perspective.

Another fictional work produced early during the war years, *Vietnam: An Antiwar Comic Book*, is actually a graphic novel that Representative Julian Bond published in 1967. He wrote the narrative content, and artist T. G. Lewis drew the illustrations. At the website "The Sixties Project," Kali Tal, project coordinator, provides a copy of the book that includes black-and-white illustrations.[5] Below is a narrative excerpt from the novel with statistical data that Bond uses to support his argument against Black participation in the war and with probing questions to make Blacks think about their involvement:

> One of every ten young men in America is a Negro. But two out of every five men killed in the war in Vietnam is a Negro. When you read this book, how will you feel about your son, or husband or brother or uncle—or yourself—fighting miles away from home against a people who only want to be left alone by everyone? (5)

The narrator later poses the question: "Who is against the war?" Then for several pages he provides answers by naming and providing illustrations of Black leaders, such as Dr. Martin Luther King Jr., and organizations—including the Southern Christian Leadership Conference and the Interracial Civil Rights Group—that are against the war. The publication came out a year after Bond was expelled from his seat in the Georgia House of Representatives in 1966 for speaking out in opposition to the Vietnam War and endorsing a statement by the Student Nonviolent Coordinating Committee urging African Americans to fight injustice at home rather than fight for the American military in Vietnam; consequently, his intent is serious assessment rather than humor (as is the case with some graphic novels/comic books). Filing a lawsuit after he was ousted, Bond took his case all the way to the U.S. Supreme Court where he received a unanimous decision from the justices who ruled that the Georgia House of Representatives had violated his First Amendment rights, reinstating him to his seat in the legislature. He not only was restored to his previous position in the Georgia House but also later won two additional elections.[6]

Though not unique among early fictional representations of the war in this genre by African Americans, Bond's graphic novel is the earliest to be published. Vernon Grant wrote and illustrated his graphic novel *The Adventures of Point-Man Palmer in Vietnam* as early as 1968, though it was not published until decades later. Unlike Bond's book, *Point-Man* takes a more lighthearted approach to the war with sometimes wry, ironic humor. A Black Vietnam veteran, Grant was inspired while in service reading comics such as the "Beetle Bailey" cartoons. He began writing after he was discharged from the army and came back home. Prior to his tour of duty in Vietnam, he attended Officer Candidate School in Fort Benning, GA, where he was the illustrator for the *50th Officer Course Classbook*. As author and illustrator of *Point-Man*, he combines aspects of American comics and Japanese *manga* with a unique, somewhat quirky, sense of humor; consequently, his commentary and illustrations are not as critical of the war as those of Julian Bond. "Books in Review II" from the Vietnam Veterans of America website provides reviews of Grant's graphic novels and cartoons.[7] He passed away before many of his books reached a wide reading audience; consequently, his wife Betsy Grant compiled his writings and published them posthumously in 2014.

More recently, J. Everett Prewitt, a Vietnam War veteran, penned a novel titled *Something about Ann: Stories of Love and Brotherhood* in 2017. The book is a compilation of fourteen short stories and the titular historical fiction novella that portrays a Black veteran returning to the United States.[8] While seeking relief from the traumatizing experiences of war, the protagonist encounters a beautiful, mysterious Vietnamese woman in his hometown, Cleveland, Ohio. After spending time together and commiserating about the war and the toll it has taken on Vietnamese and Americans alike, they fall in love. However, at the outset neither realizes that they have previously met in Vietnam. The action of the novella proceeds from their fortuitous meeting in America. The short stories, on the other hand, develop individual themes on various topics related to the war. But Prewitt's foray into Vietnam fiction does not end with this short story collection.

In 2015 Prewitt published a novel titled *A Long Way Back*, one of the few African American novels to deal with the theme of soldiers missing in action (MIA). It portrays a *Washington Post* news correspondent who witnesses the reappearance in America of a group of Black soldiers, thought dead or MIA in Southeast Asia, during the late 1960s. It turns out that these soldiers, considered by the brass to be "troublemakers," were sent to Cambodia on a one-way ticket, an illegal mission from which they were not expected to return. Of the group that is sent, only seven return to the United States, and they are all given dishonorable discharges. Realizing they have been mistreated, the news reporter will not stop until he discovers the particulars of the suicide mission on which these men have been sent. In his review of the novel David Willson, editor of *Vietnam Generation*, says: "This novel takes an important place" among other African American novels of the Vietnam War.[9] An earlier novel that deals with the issue of soldiers who are MIA is *M.I.A.: Saigon* (1986), by W. J. Amos.

Similar to the theme in *Something about Ann*, empathy with those whom America has designated as the "enemy" is a defining characteristic of other Black artistic expressions about the Vietnam War as well. For example, other genres, including music, also capture this sentiment (see appendix 2). Ben Arnold lists sixty musical compositions that not only mock American troops but also portray "laments for the enemy" or that consider the "enemy's suffering equal" to that of Americans (325). One of these is an operatic composition titled *Soldier Boy, Soldier* by Black composer T. J. Anderson. The action occurring in a single day, this opera, according to Anderson, depicts the dichotomy between the idealism and the realism of war heroism for the Black soldier, as his "public and private readjustment" to civilian life that becomes problematic upon his return to America (163). Some of the narratives in the canon that explore this theme and a variety of others germane to the Black experience in Vietnam are listed in appendix 1.

Though not analyzed in this study to the extent of the four that are the focus of this analysis, several other novels deserve perfunctory treatment in the following synopses. In addition to dealing with empathy for the so-called enemy, many of these narratives explore rite-of-passage experiences for the protagonists. In Charles Pugh's novel *The Griot* (1986), for example, the protagonist Emmanuel (aka "Manny") empathizes with the villagers he is supposed to be destroying during a search-and-destroy mission in which his company torches a Vietnamese village. As he writes about the incident in a letter to his father, Emmanuel muses with regret about the defenseless old Vietnamese men and women and little children who ran in terror from the conflagration: "I knew, as they ran in fear, how our ancestors deep in the African jungles must have felt when foreigners invaded their villages and plucked them up from their way of life" (191).

Before being drafted to serve in Vietnam, Manny, an inner city teenager, encounters in his neighborhood an old man whom Manny's parents and others in the community consider a vagrant. However, it is discovered that he is not only a displaced Zulu warrior but also a griot. He gives the protagonist the African name Imani (meaning "faith" in Swahili) and teaches him African ancestral principles and methods of self-defense (including capoeira, an African martial art) that enable him to survive his tour of duty when he is sent to fight in Vietnam. Like Ben in *Coming Home*, Manny's empathy with the ostensible enemy during his tour of duty in Vietnam causes an awareness of his real enemy in America and a renunciation of the war: "I know deep down inside, I can't continue to execute innocent people in the name of freedom" (192). Having left America as a boy and experienced his rite of passage in Vietnam, Em*man*uel/*Man*ny/*Iman*i gains a newfound maturity, thereby becoming a man by the time he returns home.

Another novel, published earlier than Pugh's, that interrogates the notion of the real enemy in the Vietnam War is C. T. Morrison's *The Flame in the Icebox* (1968). It focuses on the prisoner-of-war (POW) issue, but with a different spin, that is, it presents no diatribes about maltreatment of American soldiers at the hands of sadistic Vietcong. Instead, the protagonist finds his captor, a Vietcong officer, to be a seasoned intellectual, engaging his captives in provocative and stimulating conversation. Additionally, his captor's treatment of his American prisoners is humane. The mission of the protagonist and his squad is to find a cache of arms and ammunition that the Vietcong are supposedly hiding. After decimating countless Vietnamese in a series of bloody skirmishes, the squadron fails to find any hidden weapons of mass destruction. So the American GIs head for the base, at which time the Vietcong ambush them and take them as prisoners. Incidents in the novel cause both the protagonist and his Vietcong captor to question their involvement in the war. Extending their hands toward each other in a gesture of comradeship upon the realization that they both are victims of American racism and imperialism, the two men are killed in a bombing raid by American jets at the dramatic close of the novel.

In many Vietnam War novels by African Americans the issue of the Vietcong as enemy becomes secondary because of the enmity and strife between Black soldiers and their White counterparts. *The War in I Corps* (1998) by Richard Guidry expresses this sentiment. Action in this novel occurs along the demilitarized zone, which was, ironically, the site of some of the most vicious military engagements during the war. As point man for his unit, the protagonist reveals the horror of the war from the foot soldier's perspective and juxtaposes that external war with the internal race war within his unit. Such perspectives are seldom presented in mainstream novels about the Vietnam War and are absent from most.

A variety of novels from the Black literary canon about Vietnam explore other themes not dealt with in mainstream literature. For instance, some portray collaboration between Black soldiers and the Vietcong, such as Thomas D. Williams's *Cohesion* (1982) in which the Black protagonist and a Vietcong woman work together to survive the war and then desert the American and the Vietnamese armies, respectively. Others juxtapose the civil rights movement and the Vietnam War, such as *Betrayed* (1984) by D. B. Wilson; *The One They Called Quiet* (1998) by L. J. Bolar; and *Bombingham* (2001) by Anthony Grooms. Most notable among these is Grooms's *Bombingham*, winner of the Lillian Smith Award for Fiction. The story is told from the perspective of a Black soldier fighting in the war-torn rice fields of Vietnam writing a letter to the parents of one of his fallen comrades, as he reminisces (through flashbacks) about his early boyhood in war-torn Birmingham, Alabama, when the civil rights movement was heating up with bombings and other acts of terror by Whites. Though his parents tried to shield him from Bull Conner's dogs and firehoses when he was younger, the protagonist returns to Birmingham where he joins others in the movement. Calling *Bombingham* "powerful," a reviewer for *Publishers Weekly* points out that whether "describing the daily indignities of life under Jim Crow laws or the ignorance and brutality of the men who enforce them, Grooms writes with grace and clarity, never resorting to sentimentality or gratuitous button-pushing . . . showing that hope and dignity sometimes can be reclaimed in the process."[10]

Other novels, such as *Quartermaster Rangers* (1993) by L. J. Bolar, deal with POW issues. Quartermasters are usually charged with handling supplies and equipment rather than being involved in combat. However, when some of their friends are captured and taken to a Vietcong POW camp, these soldiers combine forces with a Korean infantry unit, ambush the Vietcong guards, and, after a bloody battle, succeed in rescuing the American hostages. After the firefight, the protagonist views the carnage, which includes Vietcong fighters as young as eleven and twelve years old, wondering how he could ever consider these children as so-called enemies. Returning home to Los Angeles, the protagonist learns, ironically, that while he was fighting for America in Vietnam his father has been killed in the Watts uprising by two racist White policemen who "mistake" him for a looter.

Postwar intrigue is another theme, such as that in *The Jones Men: A Novel* (1974) by Vern Smith, exploring the issue of the drug war brought from in Country to the World. A Vietnam veteran strives to become the drug kingpin in an urban turf war that leaves carnage in its wake not unlike that he left behind on the battlefield. Blyden Jackson's *Operation Burning Candle* (1973) is a psychological thriller recounting the exploits of a small group of Black veterans, the leader of which has been declared MIA. However, the protagonist clandestinely resurfaces in the United States, and using tactics learned fighting the war in Vietnam, he and his underground cadre execute a revolutionary plan to overthrow the U.S. government. This novel is reminiscent of Sam Greenlee's *The Spook Who Sat by the Door* in which the protagonist is a Korean War veteran. Because of its controversial nature, that is, a war veteran and ex-CIA agent training gang members in guerilla warfare to foment a paramilitary revolution against America, Greenlee had to go to England to find a publisher in 1969.[11] Only later was it published in America and released as a movie in 1973.[12]

A unique contribution to this corpus of Black writing about the Vietnam War is Albert French's *Patches of Fire* (1997), a book that has been classified as straddling two genres: autobiographical fiction and fictional autobiography. It is the story of a very young man's encounter with the specter of war beyond his understanding and his struggle, as an army foot soldier in the muck and mire of battle, to make sense of it all amidst attempting to deal with his own inner demons. Another writer who engages in genre-straddling is Ruben Benjamin Whittington. His *Moonspinners: Vietnam '65–'66* (1986) also presents the plight of the Black GI but from the perspective of an air force trooper.

Some of these novels defy labels as a result of their experimental format, such as Clarence Major's *All-Night Visitors* (1969), a surrealistic foray into the mind of a man who suffers emotional and psychological degeneration under the weight of abandonment as a child and the stress of bearing witness to unspeakable atrocities in Vietnam. Using a stream-of-consciousness technique, Major juxtaposes Calibanic phallicism with Black phallic tricksterism to portray the protagonist's post-traumatic search for self through excessive drug use and sexual activity. In *Runner Mack* (1972) by Barry Beckham, surrealism and satirical allegory converge to portray the identity search of a protagonist torn between duty to self and duty to the state using a sports motif for the Black man's struggle in the game of life. The protagonist is drafted to fight in an allegorical Alaskan War where the enemy are referred to as "sloopes" and "ginks" (a play on derogatory names for Asians, "slopes" and "gooks"). This novel presents satiric commentary on America's proclivity toward devising enemies, dehumanizing them, and then concocting reasons to fight wars against them in spite of evidence to the contrary.

Juvenile literature by Black writers also offers a rich resource of Black fictional writing about the Vietnam War. Noteworthy in this category are Walter Dean Myers's *Fallen Angels* (1988) and *Patrol: An American Soldier in Vietnam* (2002). Both of these novels, the former written for teenagers and the latter for children eight to twelve years old, are told from the perspective of a recruit who enlisted to serve in the army at the tender age of seventeen. Myers, a prolific writer who has written seventy books (most of them novels) since 1978, went to Vietnam where he served for three years when he was only seventeen years old. His youth was perhaps a contributing factor in his adeptness at filtering the experience of war through a sensitive enough lens to capture the interest of young readers without jarring their sensibilities while also portraying the psychological and physical toll that the experience exacted on the participants. Some critics compare his war novels with Steven Crane's *Red*

Badge of Courage. To capture the interest of younger readers, *Patrol* is presented in a larger than usual (9x12 in.) format and richly illustrated with colorful collages detailing the lush vistas of the Vietnam countryside juxtaposed with the action of battle (though without the carnage in books for adult readers).

Besides Philippa Schuyler, at least two other African American female writers have also authored Vietnam novels, one of which is written for juvenile audiences. Candy Dawson Boyd, a prolific writer of children's literature, penned her Vietnam-themed novel *Charlie Pippin* in 1988 for children in grades 4–7. The titular character is a beautiful little Black girl in sixth grade. Quite precocious, she is concerned about the change in her father after he comes back home to California from his tour of duty in Vietnam. Her curiosity and precocity lead her to constantly question, particularly why her uncle who is also a vet responds differently from her father when she asks about the war, leading to moments of tension as well as humor that Boyd handles adroitly. Interestingly, 1988 was the same year Walter Dean Myers published *Fallen Angels*, one of his two Vietnam War novels for juvenile audiences.

In addition to Schuyler and Boyd, Marcia King-Gamble is another female writer whose novel *Jade* was published in 2002. Having authored over thirty books of fiction, King-Gamble, in this Vietnam War narrative that is intended for an adult audience, captures the angst of a young fashion designer who is an adoptee curious about her birth family. Digging into her past, the protagonist discovers that her mother was Vietnamese and her father a Black American soldier. The book covers her journey to Ho Chi Minh City to piece together the parts of her life that she never knew. All three authors—Myers, Boyd, and King-Gamble—write about the sensitive subjects of war, post–traumatic stress disorder, and adoption in an appealing manner.

The issues these novels raise are as timely today as they were during the Vietnam War era, as Black soldiers are being called to fight in other wars against another people of color, further evidence of the "changing same" situation of Black soldiers. They, too, will probably come back home to a lack of jobs and educational opportunities resulting from systemic racism that is pervasive in American culture. The more things change the more they remain the same.

In addition to narratives, fictional and nonfictional, African Americans have also produced visual and musical representations of their experiences in the Vietnam War, and they are listed in appendix 2. As this book goes to press, yet another movie about the Black experience in Vietnam is slated to be released later this year. Spike Lee currently has in production a film titled *Da 5 Bloods* starring Chadwick Boseman,

Delroy Lindo, Clarke Peters, and Paul Walter Hauser. It portrays several Vietnam veterans who return to South East Asia in an effort to try to seek healing from their traumas suffered in the war and to try to find their squad leader's remains. Although Lee has not released many details, the film is scheduled to debut on Netflix in 2020.

Among the musicians who have produced an impressive body of work is Kimo Williams whose classical composition *Symphony for the Sons of 'Nam* has been performed in over twenty venues, gaining national and international acclaim. It captures the mood of the Vietnam War era not only for the soldier in Country but also for the veteran who had to return and readjust to the World. A prolific composer, he has written and performed music in several genres, including classical, jazz, and rock. In 1986 he composed *Symphony for the Sons of 'Nam*. His second symphony, *Fanfare for Life* (1994), was commissioned by AT&T. In 1997 his symphony *Buffalo Soldiers* was commissioned by West Point Academy.[13] In addition to being a musical composer and performer, Williams is also a university professor. Through the years he has worked with various nonprofit organizations engaged in art therapy for war veterans, and he is founder of the United States Veterans Art Program that continues to provide art resources (musical instruments, photography equipment, painting, graphics, and ceramics supplies) to state and federal veterans' facilities.

I have merely scratched the surface of literary, musical, and visual artistic contributions of African Americans about the Vietnam War. By way of recapitulation, the novels selected for this study provide a panoramic view of Black representation of the Vietnam War in fiction from a variety of perspectives: the reenlisted man (*Captain Blackman*), the conscientious objector (*Tragic Magic*), the dishonorably discharged veteran (*De Mojo Blues*), and the deserter (*Coming Home*). They illustrate the unique contributions of the Black writer to the corpus of Vietnam War literature that include the role of the compassionate hero, and they interrogate the meaning of "enemy." A great deal of work remains to be done in terms of mining the rich resources that yet remain untapped by scholarly criticism. These artistic contributions provide a missing piece of the puzzle that was the American experience in Vietnam. The world will never understand the significance of the Vietnam War experience and its impact on *all* the soldiers who fought until it becomes knowledgeable of the experience of the Black soldier in the Vietnam War and its aftermath, a testament to heroism and survival.

Literary Representation of the African American Experience in Vietnam

DATE	FICTION	NONFICTION	POETRY
1967	*Dau Tranh!* Philippa Schuyler *Vietnam: An Antiwar Comic Book* Julian Bond; illus. T. G. Lewis		
1968	*The Flame in the Icebox* C. T. Morrison	*G.I. Diary* David Parks	
1969	*All-Night Visitors* Clarence Major *The Spook Who Sat by the Door* Sam Greenlee	*Good Men Die* Philippa Schuyler	
1970		*The Courageous and the Proud* Samuel Vance	
1971	*Coming Home* George Davis	*Memphis-Nam-Sweden* Terry Whitmore Just Before Dawn Fenton A. Williams	

DATE	FICTION	NONFICTION	POETRY
1972	*Captain Blackman* John A. Williams *Runner Mack* Barry Beckham	*Dellums Committee on War Crimes* Rep. Ronald V. Dellums	
1973	*Operation Burning Candle* Blyden Jackson	*Vietnam and Black America: An Anthology of Protest and Resistance* Clyde Taylor	*Debridement* Michael Harper
1975		*A Hero's Welcome: The Conscience of Sgt. James Daly vs U.S. Army* James Daly *Yet Another Voice* Norman A. McDaniel	
1977			*Between a Rock and a Hard Place* Horace Coleman
1978	*Tragic Magic* Wesley Brown		
1980		*Cannon Fodder* Phillip Coleman	
1981		*Blacks in Vietnam* Robert Mullen	
1982	*Cohesion* Thomas D. Williams	*Brothers: Black Soldiers in the Nam* Stanley Goff and Robert Sanders	
1984	*Betrayed* D. B. Wilson *Shaw's Nam* John Carn	*Bloods* Wallace Terry *Thoughts about the Vietnam War* Eddie Wright	*Crimson River Poems* Lamont B. Steptoe
1985	*Walk Me to the Distance* Percival Everett *De Mojo Blues* A. R. Flowers		
1986	*Moonspinners: Vietnam '65–'66* Ruben Benjamin Whittington *The Griot* Charles Pugh *M.I.A.: Saigon* W. J. Amos		
1987	*Charlie Pippin* Candy Dawson Boyd (JUVENILE LITERATURE)		

DATE	FICTION	NONFICTION	POETRY
1988	*Vietnam Blues* John Carn *Fallen Angels* Walter Dean Myers (JUVENILE LITERATURE)		*Dien Cai Dau* Yusef Komunyakaa
1989		*Connecting Times: The Sixties in Afro-American Fiction* Norman Harris [2007]	*Hit Parade* Jabiya Dragonsun
1992			*The Nemo Poems* Rodger Martin
1993	*Quartermaster Rangers* L. J. Bolar	*A Place Called Heartbreak: A Story of Vietnam* Walter Dean Myers	
1995	*Snitch* Jimmy Graham		*In the Garden of the Beast* Cranston Knight *In the Grass* Horace Coleman
1997	*Patches of Fire* Albert French		
1998	*The War in I Corps* Richard A. Guidry *The One They Called Quiet* L. J. Bolar *The Blood Brothers* Geno Washington	*Dixie's Dirty Secret: The True Story of How the Government, the Media and the Mob Conspired to Combat Integration and the Vietnam Antiwar Movement* James Dickerson	
2001	*Bombingham* Anthony Grooms		
2002	*Patrol: An American Soldier in Vietnam* Walter Dean Myers (JUVENILE LITERATURE) *Jade* Marcia King-Gamble		
2003	*The Silent Men* Richard Dickinson	*Soul Patrol* Ed Emanuel	*Uncle's South China Sea Blue Nightmare* Lamont B. Steptoe
2005	*A Long Way Back* J. Everett Prewitt *Lost Survivor: The Novel of a Black Soldier's Journey to Vietnam and Back, from Man into Soldier—and Soldier Back to Man* Thomas Jones		
2006	*From Williston to Vietnam and Home Again* David E. Aiken	*Soul Soldiers* Samuel W. Black	

DATE	FICTION	NONFICTION	POETRY
2013	*P. S. Be Eleven* Rita Williams-Garcia (JUVENILE LITERATURE)		
2014	*The Adventures of Point-Man Palmer in Vietnam* Vernon Grant [CARTOONS, PUB. POSTHUMOUSLY BY BETSY GRANT, WIFE)		
2015	*A Long Way Back* J. Everett Prewitt		
2016			*Rapture: Poems* Sjohnna McCray
2017	*Something about Ann: Stories of Love and Brotherhood* J. Everett Prewitt *L.B.J. [Long Bien Jail]* James Williams (PLAY)		

Visual and Musical Representation of the African American Experience in Vietnam

Music

DATE	MUSIC
1960	"I'll Be True," The Orlons "A Lonely Soldier," Jerry Butler "The Soul of a Soldier," The Chantels
1961	"Greetings (This Is Uncle Sam)"[1], The Valadiers
1962	"Soldier Boy," The Shirelles "War is Starting Again," John Lee Hopkins "Johnny's Comin' Home," The Jogettes "Bombs of Destruction," Eddie Carson "Lonely Soldier," The Illusions "When Johnny Comes Marching Home Again," The Blue Belles
1963	"Soldier Boy I'm Sorry," The Montells "Uncle Sam," The Sherwoods "Letter to a Buddie," Joe Medwick

DATE	MUSIC
1965	"My Soldier Boy," Carole Coby "Soldier Baby (of Mine)," Brenda Hall "(Mama) My Soldier Boy Is Coming Home," The Shirelles "This Land Is Nobody's Land," John Lee Hooker "The Army's Got Me Crying," Little Brenda Duff "Everybody's Crying 'bout Vietnam," J. B. Lenoir "Will You Wait for Me," Otis Brown "Vietnam Blues," Sylvia Maddox "He'll Be Back," The Players "I Believe I'm Gonna Make It," Joe Tex "Hell No, I Ain't Gonna Go," Matt Jones "Vietnam," J. B. Lenoir "Christmas in Vietnam," Johnny and Jon
1966	"A Thousand Miles Away," The Cheques "Lonely Soldier's Pledge," Gary and the Knight Lites "So Far Away from Home," Gary and the Knight Lites "Soldier in Viet Nam," The Singing Crusaders "My Ship is Coming in Tomorrow," The Pace Setters "Just Remember Me," The Creations "Tribute in Prayer," Rev. Oris Mays "Bring My Daddy Home," Chuck Corby "The Soldier from Vietnam," Dorothy Norwood "Viet Nam Blues," Sylvia Maddox "Marching Off to War," William Bell "Greetings (This Is Uncle Sam)," The Monitors
1967	"Say Welcome Home," Soul-Jers "Wish You Were Here With Me," The Fawns "When Johnny Comes Marching Home Again," Richard Barbary "I Wanna Help Hurry My Brothers Back Home," Jimmy Holiday "Don't Cry My Soldier Boy," Thelma Houston "Believe in Me Baby (Part I & Part II)," Jesse James "A Soldier's Sad Story," Tiny Watkins "Christmas in Vietnam," Soul Searchers "Lights Out," Zerben R. Hicks & the Dynamics "A Soldier's Prayer," Archie Bell & the Drells "Uncle Sam," Jimmy Hughes "Let's Face Facts," The Masqueraders "My Soldier Boy Over There," The Shelletts "Silent Night and the 11 O'clock News," The Shurfine Singers "Viet Nam," The Southern Bells "While I'm Away," Eddy Giles "Doctor Slaps, Man is Born," Jackie Ross "What A Man Will Do (When He Loves a Woman)," James Dudley "Letter from a Soldier," Bobby Joy "Welcome Me Home," Jim Jackson

DATE	MUSIC
1968	"I'll Be Back," The Opportunity Please Knock Chorus
	"I'll Be Home," Artie Golden
	"My Baby Comes Home Today," The Linneas
	"Black Skin Blue Eyed Boys," The Equals
	"Mama Hold My Hand," Troy Seals
	"Letter from My Darling," Kip Anderson
	"This Is My Country," The Impressions
	"Forget Me Not," Martha and the Vandellas
	"Am I Ever Gonna See My Baby Again?," The Sweet Inspirations
	"Please Wait for Me My Darling," Masters of Soul
	"Comfort Me," Shirley Caesar
	"Fires of Napalm," Jimmy Collier & F. D. Kirkpatrick
	"Please Settle in Vietnam," John Lee Hopkins
	"Viet Nam," Madame Nellie Robinson
	"We Gotta Have Peace," Curtis Mayfield
	"A Letter from Vietnam," Emanuel Lansky
	"Why Them, Why Me," Abdullah
1969	"It's a Time in the USA," Sister Maggie Merckson
	"Saigon Strut," The Soul Patrol
	"Promise that You'll Wait," Skip Jackson
	"Don't Forget the Soldiers (Fighting in Vietnam)," Roscoe Robinson
	"I Could Never Be President," Johnnie Taylor
	"I Stayed Away Too Long," Manuel Holcolm
	"The Knock at the Door," The Jubilators
	"Angels in the Sky," Francine "Peaches" Barker
	"Trying to Make It Home," Rudy Ludaway
	"Standing on the Corner," Watson and the Sherlocks
	"I Don't Wanna Go to Vietnam," John Lee Hooker
	"Dear John Letter," The Dixie Drifter
	"Machine Gun," Jimi Hendrix
	"Bring the Soldiers Home from Vietnam," Harps of Melody
	"The Star-Spangled Banner," Jimi Hendrix
	"Prayer From a 12-Year-Old Boy," Raymond A. Myles
	"Mail Call Time," Mel & Tim
	"When Johnny Comes Marching Home Again," Joe Tex
	"Johnny's Hill," Freddie Scott
	"A Prayer for My Soldier," Helen Curry
	"Eternally," Azie Mortimer
	"Goodbye Vietnam, Hello USA," Tommy Dorster

DATE	MUSIC
1970	"People Are Dying (And We Say We Care)," Pierson Lake
	"Let Us Be Heard (A Prayer for Peace)," Tommy Tate
	"His Homework's Done (Give Your Son a Gun)," Phil Barr
	"Fighting for My Baby," Donald Jenkins
	"From Vietnam with Love, Parts I & II," Charles E. Scott
	"Ball of Confusion," The Temptations
	"A Letter from My Son (Parts 1 & 2)," Melverine Thomas
	"Mr. President," The Pilgrim Jubilees
	"So Glad You're Home," The Devotions
	"Peace Is All I Need," Tommy Tate
	"My Baby's Gone Away," The Chymes
	"Where Did Peace Go?," Larry Sanders
	"Men are Getting Scarce," Chairmen of the Board
	"Vietnam," Jimmy Cliff
	"War," Edwin Starr
	"Why Is It?," Al Grannum
	"When I Come Home," Al Grannum
	"If There's A Hell," Curtis Mayfield
	"Save the Country," Fifth Dimension
	"Handsome Johnny," Richie Havens
	"Why (A Peace Medley)," Coast
	"Express Yourself II," Charles Wright & the Watts 103rd Street Band
	"Going on Strike," The Emotions
	"Lonely Soldier," William Bell
	"Now You are Home from Vietnam," Patricia Denson & the Soul Expressions
	"This Soldier Wants to Come Home," Earl Wright
	"(The Two Wars of) Old Black Joe," Dr. William Truly, Jr.
	"Dam Nam [Ain't Goin to Vietnam]," Leon Thomas

DATE	MUSIC
1971	"The War in Vietnam," The Five Blind Boys of Alabama "Let the Soul Roll On, Parts I & II," The Dixie Drifter "Tribute in Prayer," The Gospelettes "Victors," Tom Clay "Tell Me Mr. President," Eugene McDaniels "Something You Couldn't Write About," Gloria Edwards "Jody Got Your Girl and Gone," Johnnie Taylor "Bring the Boys Home"[2,] Freda Payne "My Brother," The Sensational Saints "Peace Is Gonna Come," The Stairsteps "Bring My Buddies Back"[3], Change of Pace "What's Goin' On?," Marvin Gaye "What's Happenin' Brother?," Marvin Gaye "Open Letter to the President," Roy C. "Peace Begins Within," Bobby Powell "You've Been Gone Too Long," Anne Sexton "Right on Jody," Bobby Patterson "Let's Make Love Not War," Charles Wright "Jody's on the Run," Sonny Green "Bury the Hatchet," Count Rockin' Sidney "What the World Needs Now / Abraham, Martin and John," Tom Clay
1972	"We've Got the Vote Now," Gary Grande "Here I Come," Beaufort Express "Starvin'," Winfield Parker "Right On Young Americans," Percy Mayfield "Our Generation," Ernie Hines "Peace," The O'Jays "The Politician," Lou Rawls "Greetings (This Is Uncle Sam)," The Isley Brothers "Vietcong Blues," Junior Wells "Heaven Help Us All," Ray Charles "That Man of Mine," Barbara Stant "Come In Out of the Rain," Parliament "See What You Done, Done," Delia Gartrell "What Color is Love?," Terry Callier "Glad to be Home," Charles Smith and Jeff Cooper "Ho Tsing Mee (A Song of the Sun)," Terry Callier "I Got So Much Trouble in My Mind," Sir Joe Quarterman

DATE	MUSIC
1973	"World War Three," Barbara Mason "P.O.W.'s of the U.S.A.," Hope Parker "Everybody Wants a Little Peace," Sonny Starns "Vietnam (You Son of a Gun)," Sammy Brown "Vietnam (INSTRUMENTAL)," The Sammy Brown Band "Welcome the Boys Back Home," Bill Moss & The Celestials "March to the Witch's Castle," Funkadelic "P. O.W.—M.I.A.," The Whispers "The Bitter and the Sweet," Floyd Johnson "End the War" (Spoken Word), The Goodtimers "P.O.W., The Bitter the Sweet "When the Brothers Come Marching Home," The Nu Page "Had Any Lately," Sylvia Robinson "Returning Home from Vietnam," The Auditions "The Back Street," Daz' Rene "Letter from My Darling," Daz' Rene
1974	"La La Peace Song," O. C. Smith "There Will Never Be Any Peace," Chi-Lites
1975	"Wake Up, Everybody," Harold Melvin & the Bluenotes "We Beg Your Pardon America," Gil Scott Heron "Where Do We Go from Here?," Joe Hinton "Our Nation, Parts I & II," Willie Dixon
1981	"The Electric Spanking of War Babies," Funkadelic
1980	"Waiting for the Axe to Fall," Gil Scott-Heron
1986	"Symphony for the Sons of 'Nam" (SOLO PIANO & SYMPHONIC), Kimo Williams
1989	"Knowledge is King" Kool Moe Dee
2013	"Into the Liquid" (STRING QUARTET) "A Veteran's Lament" (FULL ORCHESTRA, WIND ENSEMBLE, AND STRING QUARTET W/PIANO), Kimo Williams

Films

DATE	FILMS
1971	*The Bus Is Coming*, Dir. Wendell Franklin
1972	*Georgia, Georgia*, Dir. Stig Bjorkman, Writ. & Mus. Score, Maya Angelou
1973	*Gordon's War*, Dir. Ossie Davis *The Spook Who Sat by the Door*, Dirs. Sam Greenlee & Ivan Dixon
1974	*The Black Six*, Dir. Matt Cimber
1976	*Mean Johnny Barrows*, Dir. Fred Williamson

1982	*Ashes and Embers*, Dir. Haile Gerima
1986	*The Bloods of Nam* (DOCUMENTARY), Dir. Wallace Terry
1989	*Ghetto Blaster*, Dir. Alan Stewart
1994	*Jason's Lyric*, Dir. Doug McHenry *Dust of Life*, Dir. Rachid Bouchareb
1995	*The Walking Dead*, Dir. Preston Whitmore II *Dead Presidents*, Dirs. Albert & Allen Hughes
2017	*A Veterans' Lament—Live in Concert with Orchestra and Images* (VIDEO), Kimo Williams

Notes

PREFACE

1. See Lucas Carpenter, "'It Don't Mean Nothin': Vietnam War Fiction and Postmodernism," *College Literature* 30, no. 2 (2003): 30–50.

2. "Remarks by the President at the Commemoration Ceremony of the 50th Anniversary of the Vietnam War," White House, Office of the Press Secretary, May 28, 2012, https://obamawhitehouse.archives.gov/the-press-office/2012/05/28/remarks-president-commemoration-ceremony-50th-anniversary-vietnam-war.

3. See William J. Astore, "The Longest War in American History Has No End in Sight," *The Nation*, February 28, 2017.

4. See Emily Thornberry, "Fifteen Years after Iraq War Protests, Peace Is Further Away Than Ever," *The Guardian*, February 15, 2018.

5. Recordings of some of this music can be found on the YouTube playlist "Vietnam War—Soul, Gospel & Funk," https://www.youtube.com.

INTRODUCTION

1. Consider, for example, Phillip K. Jason's popular anthology *Fourteen Landing Zones* (1991), which includes writing by journalists and soldiers—from grunt to brass—as well

as women, and even Vietnamese. However, it excludes writings by and about the Black soldier in Vietnam.

2. See representative reviews of the following fiction and nonfiction: *Captain Blackman* (1972)—Fleischer (1972), *Library Journal* (1972), and *Publisher's Weekly* (1972); *Bloods* (1985)—Flowers (1985); *All-Night Visitors* (1969)—Fair (1979) and Reed (1979); and *Tragic Magic* (1978)—Watson (1978), Lynch (1979), *Choice* (1979), *New Yorker* (1978), and *New Times Book Review* (1979).

3. The "Bench by the Road Project" was established on the occasion of Toni Morrison's seventy-fifth birthday, February 18, 2006. They took the appellation "Bench by the Road" from Morrison's remarks in a 1989 interview with *World Magazine* in which she speaks of "the absences of historical markers that help remember the lives of Africans who were enslaved and of how her fifth novel, *Beloved*, served this symbolic role." Toni Morrison said: "There is no place you or I can go, to think about or not think about, to summon the presences of, or recollect the absences of slaves. . . . There is no suitable memorial, or plaque, or wreath, or wall, or park, or skyscraper lobby. There's no 300-foot tower, there's no small bench by the road. There is not even a tree scored, an initial that I can visit or you can visit in Charleston or Savannah or New York or Providence or better still on the banks of the Mississippi. And because such a place doesn't exist . . . the book [*Beloved*] had to" (*The World*, 1989). See the Toni Morrison Society website: https://www.tonimorrisonsociety.org/bench.html.

4. Deborah H. Barnes, "A Bench by the Road: In Memory of Louis Delgrès 1766–1802," https://www.tonimorrisonsociety.org/louisdelgresbio.pdf.

5. *Charter Member News*, National Museum of African American History and Culture, Smithsonian, 3, no. 1 (winter 2017): 3. Bunch adds: "While the Museum was originally authorized by an act of Congress in 1929, intense opposition blocked construction for over seven decades, until President George W. Bush signed the legislation creating the Museum in 2003." After a monumental fundraising campaign to raise $250 million in private funds to match what Congress had authorized, the NMAAHC was officially opened in 2016 when President Obama delivered the grand opening ceremony speech.

6. On March 3, 2003, Moore appeared on *The Oprah Winfrey Show* and discussed *Bowling for Columbine*, a movie he wrote, produced, and directed. The film explores the underlying causes of the mass murder by a group of young White males at Columbine High School in Denver, Colorado. In it he provides insight on America's "culture of violence" as contributory to this debacle. The significance of the title relates to the fact that the perpetrators of the carnage at Columbine went bowling just prior to carrying out their heinous crime.

7. In the online magazine *Politico*, Oprah reveals the hateful backlash she received after the show with Michael Moore. See Cristiano Lima, "Oprah on the Issues: A Guide to the TV Icon's Political Leanings," *Politico*, January 8, 2018, https://www.politico.com/story/2018/01/08/oprah-winfrey-political-issues-328242.

8. Jeff Loeb's critical analysis of nonfictional works about the Black experience in Vietnam appeared nearly ten years later as an article in the *African American Review*. I am indebted to Loeb for his analysis, although I am not in total agreement with his assessment of Harris's work.

9. Some accounts consider 1973 to be the year that the Vietnam War ended because of the signing of the Peace Agreement in Paris in January and the withdrawal of American troops in March. An article titled "The Dead Were All Around" in *Newsweek* (1999) reports the official end, however, as April 29, 1975, as U.S. forces retreated and South Vietnamese were airlifted by helicopter from the U.S. embassy in Saigon. See the chronology of war-related events in James W. Mooney and Thomas R. West's *Vietnam: A History and Anthology* (St. James, NY: Brandywine Press, 1994).

10. In her bibliographic study *Black Arts and Black Aesthetics* (Fairfield, IA: First World, 1981) Carolyn Fowler provides a comprehensive treatment of Black Aesthetic proponents, including Addison Gayle Jr., Larry Neal, Stephen Henderson, and Amiri Baraka.

11. Baker views Kuhn's "trope" of the paradigm shift as "suggestive for the sociology of Afro-American literary-theoretical practice" (*Blues* 76).

12. Michael A. Chaney, "Wesley Brown Biography," http://biography.jrank.org/pages/4187/Brown-Wesley.html. See also Margo Natalie Crawford, *Black Post-Blackness: The Black Arts Movement and Twenty-First-Century Aesthetics* (Urbana-Champaign: University of Illinois Press, 2017).

13. "Writings of Consequence: The Art of John A. Williams," John A. Williams Online Exhibit, University of Rochester, River Campus Libraries, Rare Books, Special Collections and Preservation, 1998–2018, https://rbscp.lib.rochester.edu/2972.

14. "John A Williams: Timeline," University of Rochester Special Collections, https://rbscp.lib.rochester.edu/2977.

15. "John A Williams: Timeline."

16. "John A(lfred) Williams Biography," http://biography.jrank.org/pages/4837/Williams-John-lfred.html.

17. Qtd. in "Flowers, Arthur," *Encyclopedia of African-American Literature*, 2nd ed., ed. Wilfred D. Samuels (New York: Facts on File, 2007), 187. See also the inside back dust jacket of *De Mojo Blues* (Boston: E. P. Dutton, 1985) for Wesley Brown's review.

18. See "Reviews of *De Mojo Blues*" at the website for Black Academy Press, https://www.

blackacademypress.com/2012/06/demojoblues-2/.

19. "Arthur R. Flowers," African American Literature Book Club, https://aalbc.com/authors/author.php?author_name=Arthur+R.+Flowers.

20. See his blog, *Rootwork*, http://www.rootwork.com/home.html.

21. http://rootwork.com/mojorising.htm.

22. Marissa Bell Toffoli, "Interview with Writer & Performance Poet Arthur Flowers," *Words with Writers* (blog), June 4, 2011, https://wordswithwriters.com/2011/06/04/arthur-flowers/.

23. Toffoli, "Interview."

24. https://tarabooks.com/shop/brer-rabbit-retold.

25. "Arthur Flowers Responds to Black IT Uses & Cyberspace," *ChickenBones: A Journal for Literary & Artistic African-American Themes*. The website for *Rootwork the Rootsblog* is http://rootsblog.typepad.com/rootsblog/.

26. Jerry Ward, "Wesley Brown Revisited," The Project on the History of Black Writing, February 13, 2013, http://projecthbw.blogspot.com/2013/02/wesley-brown-revisited.html.

27. Carrie Golus, "Wesley Brown 1945–," in *Contemporary Black Biography. Encyclopedia.com*, October 15, 2019, https://www.encyclopedia.com/people/literature-and-arts/english-literature-20th-cent-present-biographies/wesley-brown.

28. Colin Harrington, "Wesley Brown on His New Novel, *Dance of the Infidels*," Berkshire Edge, September 20, 2017, https://theberkshireedge.com/edgecast-video-wesley-brown-on-his-new-novel-dance-of-the-infidels/.

29. Golus, "Wesley Brown 1945–."

30. Ward, "Wesley Brown Revisited."

31. Patricia Spears Jones, "Wesley Brown's Push Comes to Shove," *Bomb*, October 1, 2009, https://bombmagazine.org/articles/wesley-browns-push-comes-to-shove/.

32. Harrington, "Wesley Brown on His New Novel."

33. Alison Carb Sussman, "George Davis 1939–," in *Contemporary Black Biography. Encyclopedia.com*, October 23, 2019, http://www.encyclopedia.com/education/news-wires-white-papers-and-books/davis-george-1939.

34. "George Davis," The History Makers, May 19, 2014, http://www.thehistorymakers.org/biography/george-davis.

35. Sussman, "George Davis 1939–."

36. Sussman, "George Davis 1939–."

37. Sussman, "George Davis 1939–."

CHAPTER 1. HISTORICAL AND LITERARY BACKGROUND

1. *One America in the 21st Century: Forging a New Future*, The Advisory Board's Report to the President, The President's Initiative on Race.

2. See Lisa Ferdinando, "Navy Celebrates Dorie Miller's Heroics During Pearl Harbor Attack," *Department of Defense News*, December 9, 2016, https://www.defense.gov/Explore/News/ Article/Article/1026118/navy-celebrates-dorie-millers-heroics-during-pearl-harbor-attack/.

3. See Gerald F. Goodwin, "VIETNAM '67: Black and White in Vietnam," *New York Times*, July 18, 2017, 33.

4. In an unpublished paper titled "'What's Goin' On?': Gauging Black Response to the Vietnam War through '60s and '70s Popular Music," I discuss the way in which the music of these two decades mirrored the attitudes toward the war in the early and later stages (presented at the American/Popular Culture Association Conference in San Diego, CA, March 1999).

5. "No Vietnamese Ever Called Me Nigger (1968) Screening 11/15 at Boxcar Books," Black Film Center/Archive Blog, November 13, 2012, https://blackfilmcenterarchive.wordpress. com/2012/11/13/no-vietnamese-ever-called-me-nigger-1968-screening-1115-at-boxcar-books/.

6. Barbara Maranzani, "Why the Battle for Hamburger Hill Was So Controversial," History Channel, May 18, 2018, https://www.history.com/news/hamburger-hill-controversy.

7. Franklin was interviewed by Zeinabu Davis, a documentary filmmaker, who collaborated with him on a biography. Zeinabu Davis and Wendell Franklin, *Wendell Franklin*, Sunset Boulevard, CA: Directors Guild of America, 1995).

8. Kevin Thomas, "'Walking Dead': Blacks in Vietnam War," *Los Angeles Times*, February 25, 1995.

9. Sergio, "Remembering Maya Angelou's Rarely Seen Film *Georgia, Georgia*," *IndieWire*, May 28, 2014.

10. Sands was an outstanding young actress whose untimely death resulting from pancreatic cancer in 1973, a year after the release of *Georgia, Georgia*, was a great loss. An actor on Broadway and in film, she had been the recipient of several awards, most notably for her role as Beneatha in Lorraine Hansberry's *A Raisin in the Sun*, on stage as well as in the film version. Only thirty-nine years old when she passed away, Sands had chosen selectively the roles she played, refusing to be typecast as stereotypical characters. Adrienne Wartts, "Diana Sands (1934–1973)," BlackPast, June 21, 2009, https://blackpast. org/african-american-history/sands-diana-1934-1973.

11. Sergio, "Remembering Maya Angelou's Rarely Seen Film *Georgia, Georgia*."

12. *Ashes and Embers*, directed by Haile Gerima (Washington, DC: Mypheduh Films, 1982), DVD.

13. Haile Gerima, "Thoughts and Concepts: The Making of *Ashes and Embers*," *Black American Literature Forum* 25.2 (Summer 1991): 335–50.

14. Carpet bombing wreaked total destruction, completely wiping out entire villages of people and turning their property into toxic wastelands. See chapter 5 for a detailed discussion and Senator Gaylord Nelson's response to the devastation.

15. Andy Stapp and Shirley Jolls, *Black Marines against the Brass: Interview with William Harvey and George Daniels* (New York: American Servicemen's Union, 1969). See GI Collection at the Wisconsin Historical Society http://content.wisconsinhistory.org/cdm/ref/collection/p15932coll8/id/56107/

16. See also the epilogue for additional information about Schuyler's extraordinary intellect and musical talent.

17. His injury caused him to be put off combat.

18. "Philippa Schuyler: Genius or Genetic Experiment?," On an Overgrown Path, August 1, 2011, https://www.overgrownpath.com/2011/08/philippa-schuyler-genius-or-genetic.html.

19. The sting of racism continued long after the war had ended, as reflected in Terry's comments regarding the 1982 dedication of the Vietnam Veterans Memorial. In an *Ebony* magazine interview he states that many Black Vietnam veterans did not attend the ceremony because they "were still carrying scars of discrimination and racism from Vietnam. For them to come and embrace their white brothers was just too much" (qtd. in Martin 123).

20. Yette, Washington correspondent for *Newsweek* magazine and past executive secretary for the Peace Corps, corroborates the notion that America had imperialistic aims in Vietnam. For instance, American soldiers defoliated rice paddies in Vietnam to increase exports of rice from America, the world's smallest producer (Taylor 119). Browne, a Black economist and foreign aid worker in Vietnam from 1955 to 1961, was fluent in the Vietnamese language. Living and conversing with the Vietnamese people, he learned that they resented America's "paternalistic approach" to helping them solve their own problems (62). He goes on to say that Blacks in America are sympathetic with this "mass of colored people" in Vietnam because of the similar fight waged against racism at home (73).

21. Representative Dellums held hearings on racial discrimination against Black servicemen (Taylor 103, 316). The Georgia legislature denied Representative Bond a seat for supporting the position of the Student Nonviolent Coordinating Committee against the

war in 1967. Not until a year later, after court intervention, was he seated (57–58). See also Zaroulis and Sullivan 69–99.

22. In the late sixties, Dr. King delivered a speech titled "Beyond Vietnam: A Time to Break Silence" at Riverside Church in New York where he condemned America's involvement in the Vietnam War. For his stance, he was castigated by White leaders as well as some who were black.

23. See also an expanded version of this speech, "Declaration of Independence from the War in Vietnam," in *Takin' It to the Streets: A Sixties Reader*, ed. Alexander Bloom and Wini Breines (New York: Pocket Books, 1986), 230–36.

24. A short-timer was a draftee or an enlisted man who was near the end of his one-year tour of duty. Officers often served much shorter terms, in many instances only six months; consequently fewer of them were killed (Creek 114).

25. See accounts of Black empathy toward the Vietnamese in the oral narrative collections *Bloods*, and *Brothers*, as well as the anthology *Vietnam and Black America*.

26. See Trudier Harris, "The Trickster in African American Literature," *Freedom's Story*, TeacherServe. National Humanities Center, http://nationalhumanitiescenter.org/tserve/freedom/1865-1917/essays/trickster.htm.

27. During the early 1970s in Vietnam real incidents of fragging were numerous as rancor between Black enlisted men and their White officers increased. Robert Edgerton reports that "fragmentation hand grenades were hurled into a disliked officer's quarters as he slept. Several hundred so-called fragging incidents were recorded with seventy-one recorded fatalities" (184), though no breakdown according to race is given.

CHAPTER 2. UNTANGLING A PARADOXICAL WEB FOR THE BLACK WARRIOR: THE ANANSEAN MOTIF IN *CAPTAIN BLACKMAN*

1. Though the trickster figures prominently in Asian, Native American, and European cultures, the focus in this study will be on the Diasporan trickster whose origin is in Africa and who traveled, by way of the Middle Passage, to the Caribbean (aka Annancy/Ananci/Ceiling Thomas) and to North America (aka Aunt Nancy/Jack or John/Brer Rabbit) through cultural memory.

2. See also Jay D. Edwards's structural analysis of the trickster myth in *The Afro-American Trickster Tale: A Structural Analysis* (Bloomington: Folklore Publications Group, Indiana University, 1978).

3. The Akan people of Ghana consist of two ethnic groups, the Ashanti and the Fanti (Biggers 28).

4. This conflation of time past, present, and future occurs throughout Black fiction, such as Toni Morrison's *Beloved*. Also, Julie Dash's book (and now a full-length movie) *Daughters of the Dust*, in which the whole story is narrated by an unborn child, offers another example of Afrocentric time. During the course of the story/film, there is constant interplay among the African ancestors in the spiritual world, the African American Gullah family in present time, and the unborn African American child of the future.

5. All references to *Captain Blackman* are from the original 1972 edition and hereafter will be followed by page numbers only.

6. Ralph Ellison also deals with the issue of White male ambivalence about the Black phallus in his short story "Battle Royal." Prominent White males arrange a "smoker" to which they invite the Black protagonist (who naively thinks he will give a speech) and other Black boys to fight a battle royal. The men then bring in a naked White female (with an American flag tattoo on her belly) to dance. In the raucous pandemonium that follows, as racial epithets are being hurled at the boys, some of the men demand that the boys (obviously afraid) look at her while others threaten they had better not look or harm will come to them.

7. Daniel Schroder, "Buffalo Soldiers Museum, Danny Glover Host American History Tribute," U.S. Army, January 29, 2015, https://www.army.mil/article/141949/buffalo_ soldiers_museum_danny_glover_host_american_history_tribute.

8. Also called the "Cosmic Tree" or the "World Tree," the "Tree of Life" is a "compact representation" in African myth of the "threefold mythic stage on which the drama of the heroic quest unfolds," according to Clyde Ford in *The Hero with an African Face*. Since the roots of the tree are deep in the earth, they coincide with "the lower kingdom of the . . . underworld, the recesses of the human unconscious; its prominent trunk represents the middle kingdom of the earth, the realm of the ordinary, wakeful awareness; and its leaves, turning toward the light, reflect the upper kingdom of the heavens, the enlightened domain of the human spirit" (42).

9. A uniquely African American mode of discourse, signification is "the verbal art of insult in which a speaker humorously puts down, talks about, needles—that is, signifies on—the listener," according to Smitherman (*Talkin' and Testifyin'* 118). She classifies signification into two categories: "light" and "heavy." In its "lightweight" forms signifying is "verbal posturing," that is, "sounding, capping, joaning, and lugging." Heavyweight signification, on the other hand, employing sarcasm, is used to "put somebody in check, that is, make them think about, and one hopes, correct their behavior" (120–21).

10. Smitherman defines the toast as "a variation on the trickster, bad nigguh theme done in poetic form" expressed in rhymed couplets. Similar to Greco-Roman "grand epics,"

toasts are "episodic, lengthy, and detailed" consisting of the exploits of a Black hero who is "fearless, defiant, openly rebellious, and full of braggadocio about his masculinity, sexuality, fighting ability and general badness" (*Talkin' and Testifyin'* 157). The "epic folk style" is a "tribute," or a "toast," to this larger-than-life, "super-bad, omnipotent" Black hero.

11. "I've Got to Use My Imagination Lyrics," Lyrics.com, https://www.lyrics.com/lyric/2989080/Bobby+%22Blue%22+Bland.

12. See Review of *The King God Didn't Save: Reflections on the Death of Martin Luther King, Jr.* in *Kirkus Reviews*, August 17, 1970, https://www.kirkusreviews.com/book-reviews/john-a-williams-2/the-king-god-didnt-save-reflections-on-the-deat/.

13. See Trudier Harris, "The Trickster in African American Literature." *Freedom's Story*, TeacherServe, National Humanities Center, http://nationalhumanitiescenter.org/tserve/freedom/1865-1917/essays/trickster.htm.

14. Born out of desire and guilt, this ambivalence is similar to that of the Puritans toward the Native Americans, as exemplified in the captivity narrative myths, which Richard Slotkin discusses in *Regeneration through Violence* (94–115).

15. See also Baker's treatment of the incestuous Trueblood episode in *Invisible Man* (184).

CHAPTER 3. READING THE SIGNS: RE-MEMBERING THE LEGACY OF VOODOO AS PATH TO EMPOWERMENT IN *DE MOJO BLUES*

1. The war strategy that became known as Vietnamization originated during President Nixon's administration. The objective of this strategy, according to Douglas Kinnard, was "to replace Americans with Vietnamese, not only in the military forces, but also in the supply and support troops" (28). Vietnamization failed miserably, however, because the South Vietnamese forces were unable to keep the Vietcong at bay without the military assistance that the United States had previously provided. It also undermined the morale of the soldiers who remained in Country awaiting their return to the World.

2. Fragging is the deliberate attempt by enlisted personnel to kill a superior officer (usually while he was asleep) using fragmentation grenades (Westheider, *Fighting on Two Fronts* 210). Additionally, the term can be applied to "manipulating the chain of command in order to have an individual, or unit, deliberately killed by placing the personnel in harm's way, with the intended result being death," as indicated in the online dictionary, *educalingo*, https://educalingo.com/en/dic-en/fragging. Though unsure how many of these incidents resulted from Black soldiers fragging White officers, Robert Edgerton reports that "several hundred so-called fragging incidents were recorded with

seventy-one recorded fatalities" (184).

3. All references to *De Mojo Blues* are from the 1985 edition and will be followed by page numbers only.

4. Unlike the fictional 2nd Lt. Kicks, some White officers were remorseful after the war ended because of their role in ordering hordes of young men, most of whom were Black, to pull point, which sometimes led to an untimely death. Such was the case of Col. David Hackworth, a Vietnam veteran. In an article titled "The Point Man," he tells how he is still haunted in the year 2000 by his complicity in such deaths: "Their faces silently come up on my mental screen as roll call sounds in my heart. I gave them the order. They died" (45). In the intervening years he has spoken out against the war, admitting that Americans were being lied to while their young men were being needlessly killed. One of his five books about his Vietnam experiences is a novel titled *The Price of Honor* (New York: Doubleday, 1999).

5. The search-and-destroy mission originated following a battle that the First Air Cavalry waged against the North Vietnamese at Ia Drang River in 1965. This victory was the first for American forces. After that defeat for the Vietcong, American forces devised what they called a "winning strategy" for an "ultimate defeat." However, a "constraints policy" had been put in place; that is, firepower could not be deployed in certain places unless there were clearances. Neither could military forces operate in North Vietnam nor—until later in the war—in Laos or Cambodia. Since he could not occupy all the enemy-controlled areas, Gen. William Westmoreland developed a strategy that became known as the "search-and-destroy mission," which involved seeking out the enemy in selected locations and attempting to annihilate him (Kinnard 22–24). SP4 Haywood T. Kirkland tells how he and other soldiers rounded up women and children and ran them out of a village. Then they threw hand grenades "inside the hootches, inside of little bunkers, down the well" (Veninga and Wilmer 38). Afterward they would burn the village, once finding only twelve suspects after destroying fifty to seventy-five villages. Sometimes the heavy damage that Americans inflicted caused civilian deaths, prompting one soldier to make the following comment about the South Vietnamese whom America was ostensibly liberating: "Their homes had been wrecked, their chickens killed, the rice confiscated—and if they weren't pro–Viet Cong before we got there, they sure as hell were by the time we left" (qtd. in Mooney and West 210).

6. Tucept is representative of those Blacks who volunteered for service in Vietnam so they could choose their assignments rather than be drafted and receive less desirable ones (Westheider, *Fighting on Two Fronts* 14).

7. Involved actively in efforts to denounce the war and anyone associated with it, these

students portray a sentiment that actually existed when many Blacks came home from Vietnam. Misunderstood by some and/or rightly rejected and ostracized by others, Black Vietnam veterans often found themselves marginalized not only by mainstream America but also by other Blacks within their own community who rejected the notion of fighting a war against another people of color overseas when a civil rights war was being waged in America.

8. "Vodoun" and "voodoo" will be used interchangeably.

9. The guide who conducts visitors on a tour of the oxymoronic Elmina "Slave Castles" in Ghana announces that Africa was "depleted" of some of its "best minds" in the persons of Vodoun "priests and priestesses" who were "raided" from their homes in remote villages and forcibly taken to America (Hounon 2).

10. Hurston's allegory links the Exodus Jews with voodoo. In her depiction "every Jew in Goshen is converted into an American Negro and every Egyptian in Old Pharaoh's Egypt into a white in America" where Blacks live, according to Blyden Jackson ("Introduction" xvi). Her literary license is not in the interest of debunking a Christian prophet as much as it is "relocat[ing] him in Afro-American tradition" as a part of the folk (Hemenway 258).

11. Hounon makes the following distinction between hoodoo and voodoo: "In America, though many of the traditional ritual and ceremonial practices of 'Voodoo' were lost, most of its healing, divinatory, and spirit manifestational elements were later forced to merge into the magico-botanical practices of what came to be known derisively as 'Hoodoo'" (6). In *De Mojo Blues*, Flowers makes the following distinction: hoodoo is the "conduit," and voodoo is "the way" to power.

12. During basic training the military emphasizes teamwork, or "unit cohesion," which Westheider defines as "the reliance on the individuals within the unit and a pride in its collective accomplishments" ("My Fear Is for You" 129). For Blacks, however, "lack of cultural recognition, coupled with both institutional and personal racism" produced Black solidarity, a different kind of "cohesion" from what the military expected (130). The novel *Cohesion* by Thomas D. Williams (1982) expresses the Black manifestation of unit cohesion in Vietnam.

13. Westheider reports that in reality dapping caused friction between Black and White enlisted men as well because Black soldiers often held up the chow line while going through the ritual. Sometimes they even caused fights. Therefore, some commanding officers "banned" dapping, as did the navy, or strongly discouraged its use, as in the marines ("My Fear Is for You" 173–74). Sometimes Blacks were even given Article 15s for dapping and displaying Black pride symbols (175). However, Whites were not punished

for flying the Confederate flag.

14. In her movie, *Daughters of the Dust* (1991), Dash portrays Black men on the Gullah Islands using hand signals, similar to dapping, to communicate. They had previously belonged to secret societies in Africa where this kinesic language was used. Dash later followed the movie with a novel of the same title in which she discusses some of the characters using "hand salutes" among the young men on Yoruba Island. *Daughters of the Dust: A Novel* (New York: Plume, 1999), 185. See also, Lizzie Francke, who discusses in an online article "a vocabulary of physical gestures—from the secret signing that the men practise together" in *"Daughters of the Dust* Review: A Transportive, Transformative Colonial Rites-of-Passage Movie," *Sight & Sound: The International Film Magazine*, September 1993, https://www.bfi.org.uk/news-opinion/sight-sound-magazine/reviews-recommendations/daughters-dust-julie-dash-transportive-colonial-rites-passage.

15. Black soldiers were often unduly punished for wearing items that demonstrated Black solidarity. For instance, one soldier received fourteen days restriction and fourteen days extra heavy duty for wearing a Montagnard, or "slave bracelet," that he made out of bootlaces (Westheider, "My Fear Is for You" 93).

16. See also Lawrence Levine's account of High John "besting" the devil by tearing off his arm and beating him to death with it then passing out ice water to all the onlookers as he left hell (*Black Culture* 403).

17. Compare the connection Langston Hughes makes between the Mississippi River and rivers in Africa (Euphrates, Nile, Congo) in his poem "The Negro Speaks of Rivers." *The Collected Poems of Langston Hughes* (New York: Doubleday, 2020), 23.

18. According to John Biggers, the "female entity [of Ananse] is personified in Ohemmaa—the female king or the queen mother—who created the universe by giving birth to the sun. She is looked upon as the creator and owner of the state and the mother of everyone in it, including the king" (28).

CHAPTER 4. PLAYIN' IT BY EAR: THE JAZZERLY SOUND OF SURVIVAL IN *TRAGIC MAGIC*

1. In *The Signifying Monkey: A Theory of Afro-American Literary Criticism* (1988) Gates distinguishes between "Signifyin(g)" and "signifying" thusly: "I have selected to write the black term with a bracketed [*sic*] final *g* ('Signifyin(g)') and the white term as 'signifying.' The bracketed *g* enables me to connote the fact that this word is, more often than not, spoken by black people without the final *g* as 'signifyin'" (46).

2. All references to *Tragic Magic* are from the 1995 edition and will be indicated in parentheses.

3. A bildungsroman is a novel focusing on the moral and psychological growth of the protagonist from youth to adulthood through a variety of experiences.

4. Whether Brown was influenced by Dr. Martin Luther King Jr.'s stance on conscientious objection to the Vietnam War is uncertain. However, one of his speeches, "Beyond Vietnam," reveals that Dr. King actively counseled draft-age Blacks to be conscientious objectors. He even urged ministers of draft age to give up their ministerial exemptions to become conscientious objectors, or, in his words, "persons of conviction" (92). One wonders if his stance could have contributed to bringing about his untimely demise.

5. This opinion also reflects that of legendary jazz soloist and music critic Nancy Wilson, who expressed during a *Jazz Profiles* episode that lyrics are more important than the music in jazz songs: "I'm telling a story . . . to take you to a place through the music. . . . A song is a miniature drama. . . . The notes may stir the soul, but it's the lyrics that pierce the heart." "Jazz in Song: The Words," NPR, January 9, 2008, https://www.npr.org/2008/01/09/17929094/jazz-in-song-the-words.

6. On his deathbed, the grandfather of the protagonist in *Invisible Man* says: "our life is a *war* and I have been a traitor all my born days, a spy in the enemy's country ever since I gave up my gun back in the Reconstruction. . . . I want you to overcome 'em with yeses, undermine 'em with grins, agree 'em to death and destruction, let 'em swoller you till they vomit or bust wide open" (13; emphasis added).

7. "Integrative arts inquiry" takes a holistic approach to the study of art. This interdisciplinary field of study delineates a "diaspora aesthetics," according to Samuel Floyd Jr., by focusing on aspects of the "black expressive arts, treating visual, verbal, and aural thinking and their unification in an integrated mode of perception and inquiry . . . as manifest in five artistic forms: poetry, prose, painting, music, and dance" (25–26). Floyd and others at Columbia College Center for Black Music Research, University of Chicago, formed *Lenox Avenue: A Journal of Interarts Inquiry*. One of their aims is to compile a lexicon of common terminology/elements that can be used across artistic genres to discuss the aesthetic qualities of various art forms (e.g., texture, narrative, space, tone/pitch, etc.).

8. See also Gates, *Signifying Monkey*.

9. Gates distinguishes between these two terms by referring to pastiche as "an act of literary 'naming.'" Parody, on the other hand, is "an act of 'calling out of one's name'" (*Signifying Monkey* 124).

10. Giddins, "Celebrating Bird."

11. Adria Battaglia, "Fannie Lou Hamer's 'I Question America' Testimony," Mississippi Encyclopedia, last updated April 14, 2018, https://mississippiencyclopedia.org/entries/

fannie-lou-hamer-i-question-america-testimony/.

12. The defiant tone of bebop is captured in a cartoon on the cover of one of Bird's albums. It depicts a White man who is "bopped" in the face with a big black boxing glove as he is reading a bebop score (Giddins, "Celebrating Bird"). Beboppers often appropriated White popular music tunes and, through chord changes, or "playing the changes," they transformed the tune into bebop. In this respect bebop signifies upon, or is a revision and elaboration of, European classical music, many beboppers having been accomplished classical musicians before changing their tune (Thomas 113). In a similar manner Otis appropriates a Eurocentric conception of heroism, the "John Wayne thing," which, however, contributes to his self-destruction rather than a mere rearrangement of style.

13. Melvin's artifice is not unlike that of Richard Wright in "The Ethics of Living Jim Crow" who, as a young boy, takes a note to the White librarian in the town's segregated library. Ostensibly written by the White man for whom he works, the note instructs the librarian to "Please let this nigger boy have the following books" (Wright 1395). Through this improvisatory act of subterfuge, Wright succeeded not only in carrying out an act of defiance against Jim Crow laws but also accomplished his goal of honing his literary skills, which enabled him to become one of America's greatest writers. Improvisation in this respect is a revolutionary act, and hence heroic.

14. Not coincidentally Brown references Ginsburg who was a jazz poet. A Beat generation writer of the 1950s, Ginsburg was pronouncedly influenced by bebop, according to Hollingsworth and Leake (46). He changed some of his poems from the conventional metrical scheme to a "jazzier downbeat rhythm" (47). So wrapped up in the jazz aesthetic was Ginsburg that Gerald Early reports he thought of himself as "blowing solos when he was reading his work, and felt he had to breathe as if he were a jazz horn player" (743).

15. Brown's choice of the enigmatic Thelonious Monk for Theo to emulate is apropos of Monk's reluctance to talk to others, causing some jazz critics, such as Ingrid Monson, to speculate that "music was his true language" (187). Monk was also actively involved in performing benefit concerts for the civil rights movement during the 1960s, one of which raised funds for the families of the four little girls who were killed in the Sixteenth Street Baptist Church bombing in Birmingham in 1963.

16. David Loeb Weiss directed a documentary in 1968 titled *No Vietnamese Ever Called Me Nigger* (see appendix 2).

17. This fictional incident simulates actual forms of protest against the war. Buddhist monks often committed acts of self-immolation during the Vietnam War era. One such incident of Buddhist monk Quang Duc burning himself on a busy Saigon street was captured in the iconic photo taken on June 11, 1963, by Malcolm W. Browne. The photo was named

the World Press Photo of the Year in 1963. See https://www.worldpressphoto.org/
collection/photo/1963/36275/1/1963-malcolm-w-browne-wy.

18. Wright deals masterfully with the distortion of Black male identity in "The Man Who
Lived Underground," which Baker uses for his "black (w)hole" model.

19. Jake, the protagonist in Claude McKay's World War I novel, *Home to Harlem*, personifies
"good old New York! The same old wench of a city" in the same jazzerly fashion when he
returns to America AWOL from his army base overseas (Rice 107).

CHAPTER 5. TRANSCENDING ABSTRACTIONS BY RE-MEMBERING SELF IN *COMING HOME*

1. In his Amazon review of *Coming Home*, Earl R. Anderson views Davis's novel as a *nostos*,
i.e., a "'narrative hypallage': a war veteran returns home with great expectations, but
finds disappointment instead." https://www.amazon.ca/Coming-Home-George-Davis/
dp/088258118X. To the contrary, the protagonist does not "return home." Instead, he
deserts the military for Sweden. Rather than returning to America, Davis's hero comes
home to himself when he discovers his identity as a Black man fighting against another
people of color on behalf of racist America.

2. Similar to the movie *Coming Home*, Davis's novel of the same title depicts soldiers
questioning "the essential rightness of what they were forced to do" (Hillstrom and
Hillstrom 73). On Amazon a reviewer of the 40th Anniversary Edition of *Coming Home*
indicates that the movie of the same title, starring Jane Fonda, was loosely based on
Davis's novel.

3. *The Post* portrays the actions of the female publisher of the *Washington Post* who
published the information contained in the Pentagon Papers by a news reporter who
leaked it to the press. The story revealed how America was losing the war nearly from its
inception; however, President Nixon and other government officials continued to send
young men into harm's way, killing thousands, a disproportionate number of whom were
African American.

4. All references are to the 1984 edition and will be indicated by parentheses in the text.

5. Daniel M. Scott III discusses Johnson's critique of binary thinking in *Middle Passage*
through his use of "Platonic parable" and "Cartesian dualism . . . [which] simultaneously
and contradictorily acknowledges its debt to preceding Western writing and defines itself
against it" (645). See also Rita A. Bergenholtz's account of Toni Morrison's interrogation
of such binary constructions as Black/White, good/evil, literal/metaphoric, etc. (91) to
shed light on Sula's identity search.

6. According to Edward Wakin, a group of fliers known as "the Wolf Pack" were a part of the Eighth Tactical Fighter Wing in Thailand. One of the commanders of this group was the legendary Black colonel Daniel "Chappie" James (promoted to general after the war) whose unit became famous for shooting down Communist MIGs.

7. See Ousseynou Traore's "Matrical Approaches to *Things Fall Apart*: A Poetics of Epic and Mythic Paradigms," for an excellent treatment of Achebe's Igbo classical epic of the African heroic quest (New York: Modern Language Association, 1991).

8. That Harvard students were, for all intents and purposes, exempt from service in Vietnam is attested by James Westheider in *Fighting on Two Fronts: African Americans and the Vietnam War*. In addition to race, he says "economic, class, and educational levels were often interrelated" as determining factors in who was or was not drafted. Harvard, Yale, and Princeton were considered "safe havens" from the draft, and it is reported that the "big three" Ivy League schools graduated only two young men "who were drafted and killed in action in Vietnam" (24).

9. Bigger, the Dalton family's driver, accidentally kills Mary Dalton when he puts a pillow over her head to muffle her voice to avoid detection in her bedroom. He has taken her there in a drunken stupor after she nearly passes out. Though he never touches her in a sexually suggestive way, the White community and the White press indict him by accusing him of having raped Mary before the trial begins. In fact, the trial centers on this supposed rape rather than Mary's death.

10. In Johnson's *Middle Passage* the African American protagonist, Rutherford Calhoun, is transformed from a philandering thief to a loving husband and family man after his encounter with his African ancestors on a slave ship.

11. Ralph Ellison's Black literary classic *Invisible Man* attests to this state of invisibility more poignantly than any other literary work.

12. A similar contrast between the air war and the ground war is portrayed in the Vietnam War movie *Bat*21*, starring Danny Glover as an air force officer who rescues his buddy after he crash lands.

13. See "Eleanor Roosevelt and the Tuskegee Airmen," Franklin D. Roosevelt Presidential Library and Museum, https://www.fdrlibrary.org/tuskegee.

14. Such an organization actually existed, according to Terry Whitmore in his autobiography, *Memphis-Nam-Sweden*, and it was instrumental in helping him to escape to Sweden. Known as Beheiren, this group consisted of "pacifists" whose avowed aim was to "try very hard to help men who do not want to kill" (133).

15. Baker refers to this space as the "black *(w)hole*," or "the domain of *Wholeness*, as achieved relationality of Black community in which desire recollects experience and sends it forth

as blues." Furthermore, adroitly signifyin(g) on its Eurocentric negative connotations Baker concludes: "To be Black and (*W*)*hole* is to escape incarcerating restraints of a white world (that is a *black hole*)" (*Blues* 151–52).

16. Black literary and musical artists such as Richard Wright, James Baldwin, and Paul Robeson left the United States for Europe where they were better received and respected as artists and as human beings.

17. I use "humanism" here, not in the manner of "classical humanism," but rather in the sense in which Phanuel A. Egejuru applies it to the character of the noted African scholar Chinua Achebe: "one who appreciates his fellow human beings and does everything possible to uphold and promote their humanity" (38).

EPILOGUE

1. *Black No More* examines the race problem in America, and this landmark comic satire ponders the question: "What would happen if all black people in America turned white?" Danzy Senna, who writes the introduction for the reprint of this classic, sums it up thusly: "A liberating and lacerating critique of American racial madness, capitalism, and white superiority. . . . In the era of Trump and Rachel Dolezal, Beyonce's 'Formation' and that radical Pepsi commercial starring Kendall Jenner, of the rise and fall of Tiger Woods' land of Cablinasia, and of Michael Jackson's 'race lift' and subsequent death, Schuyler's wild, misanthropic, take-no-prisoners satire of American life seems more relevant than ever." "Introduction," in *Black No More*, by George S. Schuyler (New York: Penguin Books, 2018), xii.

2. Lise Funderberg, "Tragic Mulatto Girl Wonder: The Paradoxical Life of Philippa Duke Schuyler," *QBR: The Black Book Review*, February/March 1996.

3. Quoted in "Philippa Schuyler: Genius or Genetic Experiment?," On an Overgrown Path, August 1, 2011, https://www.overgrownpath.com/2011/08/philippa-schuyler-genius-or-genetic.html.

4. Neil Sheehan et al., *The Pentagon Papers: The Secret History of the Vietnam War* (New York: Racehorse/Simon & Schuster, 2017).

5. This rare contribution of Bond to the anti–Vietnam War movement that vehemently argues against Black participation can be found at The Sixties Project: http://www2.iath.virginia.edu/sixties/HTML_docs/Exhibits/Bond/Bond.html.

6. See the full text of the Supreme Court Decision, October Term 1966, *Bond et al. v. Floyd et al.*, at the website African-American Involvement in the Vietnam War, http://www.aavw.org/protest/homepage_bond.html.

7. Curt Nelson, "Adventures of Point-Man Palmer in Vietnam by Betsy Grant," *Books in Review*, The VVA Veteran, November 23, 2015, https://vvabooks.wordpress. com/2015/11/23/adventures-of-point-man-palmer-in-vietnam-by-betsy-grant.

8. See Prewitt's website https://eprewitt.com/ for a listing of all his books, some of which are unrelated to the Vietnam War.

9. David Willson, "A Long Way Back by J. Everett Prewitt," *Books in Review*, The VVA Veteran, October 19, 2015, https://vvabooks.wordpress.com/2015/10/19/a-long-way-back-by-j-everett-prewitt/.

10. https://www.publishersweekly.com/978-0-7432-0558-0.

11. Sam Greenlee, *The Spook Who Sat by the Door* (London: Allison and Busby, 1969).

12. For the enduring impact of Greenlee's movie, see Matthew C. Stelly, *The Spook Who Sat by the Door Revisited: A 38-Year Retrospective on Race, Rioting, and Relevant Response* (Scotts Valley, CA: CreateSpace Independent Publishing Platform, 2017).

13. "James (Kimo) Williams," Encore.org, https://encore.org/purpose-prize/james-kimo-williams/.

APPENDIX 2. VISUAL AND MUSICAL REPRESENTATION OF THE AFRICAN AMERICAN EXPERIENCE IN VIETNAM

1. "Greetings (This Is Uncle Sam)" was recorded by three different groups in three different years: The Valadiers (1961), The Monitors (1966), and the Isley Brothers (1972).

2. Chris Taylor reports in an article titled "Old Music: Freda Payne—Bring the Boys Home," that "['Bring the Boys Home'] was banned by US armed forces radio" in south Vietnam because it was viewed as subversive to the U.S. war effort in Vietnam and aiding and abetting the enemy. Much to the chagrin of the Nixon administration, however, the song had such wide appeal that it actually went gold in the United States. *The Guardian*, December 5, 2011, https://www.theguardian.com/music/2011/dec/05/old-music-freda-payne.

3. "Bring My Buddies Back" is a plea from the perspective of a war veteran. Considered a companion piece, the music is similar to that of Freda Payne's "Bring the Boys Home" and actually references her in the first line: "Hey Freda, maybe you were right."

Bibliography

Abdul-Jabbar, Kareem, and Alan Steinberg. *Black Profiles in Courage*. New York: Morrow, 1996.

Abrahams, Roger. "Rapping and Capping: Black Talk as Art." In *Black America*, edited by John F. Szwed, 132–42. New York: Basic Books, 1970.

Acham, Christine. "Subverting the System: The Politics and Production of *The Spook Who Sat by the Door*." *Screening Noir* 1.1 (2005): 113–36.

Acham, Christine, and Cliff Ward, dirs. *Infiltrating Hollywood: The Rise and Fall of the Spook Who Sat by the Door*. Glendale, CA: ChiTrini, 2011. Film.

Adams, Val. "'C.B.S. Playhouse' Due in February." *New York Times*, November 4, 1966.

Adjaye, Joseph K. "Introduction: Popular Culture and the Black Experience." In *Language, Rhythm, & Sound: Black Popular Cultures into the Twenty-First Century*, edited by Joseph K. Adjaye and Adrianne R. Andrews, 19–22. Pittsburgh: University of Pittsburgh Press, 1997.

African-American Involvement in the Vietnam War. Kief Schladweiler, Librarian, NYC. http://www.aavw.org.

"Afrocentricity." In *The Oxford Companion to African American Literature*, edited by William L. Andrews, Frances Smith Foster, and Trudier Harris, 8–10. Oxford: Oxford University Press, 1997.

Aiken, David E. *From Williston to Vietnam and Home Again*. Chapel Hill, NC: Chapel Hill Press, 2005.

Alexander, Margaret Walker. *Jubilee*. New York: Houghton Mifflin Harcourt, 1966.

Amos, W. J. *M.I.A.: Saigon*. Los Angeles: Holloway House, 1986.

Anderson, T. J. "On *Soldier Boy, Soldier*: The Development of an Opera." *Black Music Research Bulletin* 10.1 (spring 1990): 160–66.

Ani, Marimba. *Yurugu: An African-Centered Critique of European Cultural Thought and Behavior*. 1994; Trenton, NJ: Africa World Press, 2000.

Ankeny, Jason. Review of *Does Anybody Know I'm Here? Vietnam through the Eyes of Black America 1962–1972* (Various Artists). AllMusic. https://www.allmusic.com.

Ansah, S. L. "The Ananse Archetype in Ghanaian and Jamaican Folktales." *Literary Griot* 1.2 (spring 1989): 44–53.

Armstrong, Linda. "Williams' Play Focuses on Racism between G.I.s during Vietnam War." *New York Amsterdam News*, July 1–7, 2004.

Arnold, Ben. "War Music and the American Composer during the Vietnam Era." *Musical Quarterly* 75.3 (fall 1991): 316–34.

"As Negro Veterans Come Home—Stabilizing Force?" *U.S. News and World Report*, February 5, 1968, 182–85.

Asante, Molefi. *The Afrocentric Idea*. Philadelphia: Temple University Press, 1998.

———. *Afrocentricity: A Theory of Social Change*. 1980; repr. Trenton, NJ: Africa World Press, 1988.

———. *The Painful Demise of Eurocentrism: The Afrocentric Response to Critics*. Trenton, NJ: African World Press, 1999.

Aubert, Alvin. "Yusef Komunyakaa: The Unified Vision, Canonization and Humanity." *African American Review* 27.1 (spring 1993): 119–23.

Baker, Houston A., Jr. *Blues, Ideology, and Afro-American Literature: A Vernacular Theory*. Chicago: University of Chicago Press, 1984.

———. *Workings of the Spirit: The Poetics of Afro-American Women's Writing*. Chicago: University of Chicago Press, 1991.

Bang, Billy. *Vietnam: Reflections*. Recorded May 2005. Justin Time Records, JUST 212–2.

———. *Vietnam: The Aftermath*. Recorded April 2001. Justin Time Records. JUST 165–2.

Barthold, Bonnie. *Black Time: Fiction of Africa, the Caribbean, and the United States*. New Haven: Yale University Press, 1981.

Bates, Milton. *The Wars We Took to Vietnam: Cultural Conflict and Storytelling*. Berkeley: University of California Press, 1996.

Beckham, Barry. *Runner Mack*. Washington, DC: Howard University Press, 1983.

Beidler, Philip. *American Literature and the Experience of Vietnam*. Athens: University of Georgia Press, 1982.

Bell, Bernard. *The Afro-American Novel and Its Tradition*. Amherst: University of Massachusetts Press, 1982.

Bell, Derrick. "The Sexual Diversion: The Black Man/Black Woman Debate in Context." In *Speak My Name: Black Men on Masculinity and the American Dream*, edited by Don Belton, 144–54. Boston: Beacon Press, 1995.

Ben-Jochannan, Yosef A. A. *African Origins of the Major Western Religions*. 2 vols. Baltimore: Black Classic Press, 1991.

Benshoff, Harry M., and Sean Griffin. *America on Film: Representing Race, Class, Gender and Sexuality at the Movies*. Hoboken, NJ: John Wiley and Sons, 2011.

Bergenholtz, Rita A. "Toni Morrison's *Sula*: A Satire on Binary Thinking." *African American Review* 30.1 (spring 1996): 89–98.

Biggers, John. *Ananse: The Web of Life in Africa*. Austin: University of Texas Press, 1962.

Billingsley, Ronald G. "The Burden of the Hero in Modern Afro-American Fiction." *Black World* 25.2 (December 1975): 38–45, 66–73.

Bims, Hamilton. "The Black Veteran: Battle on the Home Front." *Ebony* 27.1 (November 1971): 35.

Black, Samuel W., ed. *Soul Soldiers: African Americans and the Vietnam Era*. Pittsburgh: Historical Society of Western Pennsylvania. 2006.

Blake, Susan R. "Ritual and Rationalization: Black Folklore in the Works of Ralph Ellison." In *Modern Critical Views: Ralph Ellison*, edited by Harold Bloom, 77–99. New York: Chelsea House, 1986.

Bogle, Donald. *Toms, Coons, Mulattoes, Mammies, & Bucks: An Interpretive History of Blacks in American Films*. London: Continuum Publishing, 1973.

Bolar, L. J. *The One They Called Quiet*. New York: Vantage Press, 1998.

———. *Quartermaster Rangers*. New York: Vantage Press, 1993.

Bond, Julian. *Vietnam: An Antiwar Comic Book*. Illustrator, T. G. Lewis. 1967. Available at The Sixties Project, http://www2.iath.virginia.edu/sixties/HTML_docs/Exhibits/Bond/Bond.html.

Boulton, Mark. "How the G.I. Bill Failed African American Vietnam War Veterans." *Journal of Blacks in Higher Education* 58 (winter 2007/8): 57–60.

"Bowling for Columbine." *The Oprah Winfrey Show*. Aired March 3, 2003. WGN, Chicago.

Boyd, Candy Dawson. *Charlie Pippin*. Glenville, IL: Scott Foresman, 1988.

Braddick, Kenneth J. "U.S. Is Ruling 200 MIAs Dead." *Washington Post*, May 21, 1973. Available at African-American Involvement in the Vietnam War, http://www.aavw.org/served/pows_cominghome_abstract01.html.

"Brass Order Gestapo-Like Roundup of Black GIs and WACs." *The Bond*, New York, November

26, 1971.

Brown, Cecil. *Stagolee Shot Billy*. Cambridge, MA: Harvard University Press, 2004.

Brown, Wesley. *Tragic Magic*. 1978. Hopewell, NJ: Ecco Press, 1995.

———. "You Talk Like You Got Books in Your Jaws." In *In Praise of What Persists*, edited by Stephen Berg, 19–23. New York: Harper and Row, 1983.

Bunn, Austin. "Unarmed and Under Fire: An Oral History of Female Vietnam Vets." Salon.com. November 11, 1999. https://www.salon.com/1999/11/11/women_4/.

Burns, Ken, dir. *Jazz*. 10 Episodes. PBS. WETA, Washington, DC. January 8, 2001.

Callahan, John F. *In the African American Grain: Call-and-Response in Twentieth Century Black Fiction*. 2nd ed. Middletown, CT: Wesleyan University Press, 1988.

Calloway, Earl. "Drama 'Skipper' by Oscar Walden Is a Literary Memorial Tribute to PFC Milton Lee Olive III." *Chicago Defender*, September 15, 2001.

Canwell, Diane, and John Sutherland. *African Americans in the Vietnam War*. Milwaukee: Gareth Stevens Publishing, 2005.

Caponi, Gena Dagel. "Introduction: The Case for an African American Aesthetic." In *Signifyin(g), Sanctifyin', & Slam Dunking: A Reader in African American Expressive Culture*, edited by Gena Dagel Caponi, 1–44. Amherst: University of Massachusetts Press, 1999.

Carn, John Benjamin. *Vietnam Blues: The Story of a Black Soldier*. Los Angeles: Holloway House, 1988.

Carpenter, Lucas. "'It Don't Mean Nothin': Vietnam War Fiction and Postmodernism." *College Literature* 30.2 (spring 2003): 30–50.

Carruth, Hayden. "The Formal Idea of Jazz." In *In Praise of What Persists*, edited by Stephen Berg, 24–32. New York: Harper and Row, 1989.

Cash, Earl A. *John A. Williams: The Evolution of a Black Writer*. New York: Third Press, 1975.

Cauley, Anne O. "A Definition of Freedom in the Fiction of Richard Wright." *College Language Association Journal* 19.3 (March 1976): 327–46.

Chaney, Michael A. "Brown, Wesley." In *Contemporary Novelists*. Encyclopedia.com. September 17, 2018. http://www.encyclopedia.com.

Channer, Colin. "The Problem with Women? Men." *Essence*, May 2002, 114.

Chew, Peter T. "The Forgotten Soldiers, Black Vets Say They're Ignored." *National Observer*, March 10, 1973. Available at African-American Involvement in the Vietnam War, http://www.aavw.org/special_features/govdocs_senate_abstract20.html.

Chinweizu. *Decolonising the African Mind*. Bulgaria: Pero Publishing, 1987.

Clayton, Paul. *Carl Melcher Goes to Vietnam*. New York: Thomas Dunne Books/St. Martin's Press, 2004.

Cole, Tom. "Medal of Honor Rag." In *Coming to Terms: American Plays and the Vietnam War*, edited by James Reston, 141–78. New York: Theatre Communications Group, 1985.

Coleman, Arvis Renette. "The West African Trickster Tradition and the Fiction of Charles Waddell Chesnutt." Ph.D. diss., University of North Texas, 1996.

Coleman, Horace. "Another Brother Looks at 'Another Brother.'" *The Veteran* 29.1 (spring/summer 1999), http://www.vvaw.org/veteran/article/?id=185.

———. *Between a Rock and a Hard Place*. Kansas City, MO: BkMk Press, 1977.

———. *In the Grass*. Woodbridge, CT: Viet Nam Generation, Inc. & Burning Cities Press, 1995.

Coleman, James. "Language, Reality, and Self in Wesley Brown's *Tragic Magic*." *Black American Literature Forum* 15.2 (summer 1981): 48–50.

Collier, Geoffrey L., and James L. Collier. "Microrhythms in Jazz: A Review of Papers." In *Annual Review of Jazz Studies*, vol. 8, edited by Henry Martin. Lanham, MD: Scarecrow Press, 1997.

Congress. House Foreign Affairs Committee. *American Prisoners of War*. Washington, DC: GPO, 1973. Available at African-American Involvement in the Vietnam War, http://www.aavw.org/served/pows_cominghome_abstract01.html.

Cooke, Benjamin G. "Nonverbal Communication among African Americans: An Initial Classification." In *Rappin' and Stylin' Out: Communication in Urban Black America*, edited by Thomas Kochman, 32–64. Urbana-Champaign: University of Illinois Press, 1972.

Cose, Ellis. *The Envy of the World: On Being a Black Man in America*. New York: Washington Square Press, 2002.

Couch, William, Jr. "The Image of the Black Soldier in Selected American Novels." *CLA Journal* 20.2 (December 1976): 176–84.

Crawford, Margo Natalie. *Black Post-Blackness: The Black Arts Movement and Twenty-First Century Aesthetics*. Urbana-Champaign: University of Illinois Press, 2017.

Creek, Mardena Bridges. "Myth, Wound, Accommodation: American Literary Response to the War in Vietnam." Ph.D. diss., Ball State University, 1982.

Dalby, David. "The African Element in American English." In *Rappin' and Stylin' Out: Communication in Urban Black America*, edited by Thomas Kochman, 170–86. Urbana-Champaign: University of Illinois Press, 1972.

Dash, Julie. *Daughters of the Dust: The Making of an African American Woman's Film*. New York: New Press, 1992.

———. *Daughters of the Dust: A Novel*. New York: Plume, 1999.

Davis, George. "A Revolutionary War Soldier in Vietnam." Review of *Captain Blackman*, by John A. Williams. *New York Times Book Review*, May 21, 1972, 4.

———. *Coming Home*. 1971; Washington, DC: Howard University Press, 1984.

Davis, Ossie, dir. *Gordon's War*. Los Angeles: 20th Century Fox, 1973. Film.

Davis, Sammy, Jr. *Yes I Can*. New York: Farrar, Straus & Giroux, 1965.

Davis, Zeinabu, and Wendell Franklin. *Wendell Franklin.* Sunset Boulevard, CA: Directors Guild of America, 1995.

"The Dead Were All Around." *Newsweek* 113.10 (March 8, 1999): 58–67.

Dellums, Rep. Ron. *Dellums Committee on War Crimes in Vietnam.* New York: Random House, 1972.

DeRose, David J. "Soldados Razos: Issues of Race in Vietnam War Drama." *Vietnam Generation* 1.2 (1989): 38–55.

Dickerson, James. *Dixie's Dirty Secret: The True Story of How the Government, the Media, and the Mob Conspired to Combat Integration and the Vietnam Antiwar Movement.* Armonk, NY: M.E. Sharpe, 1998.

Dickinson, Richard H. *The Silent Men.* New York: Rugged Land, 2002.

Dinerstein, Joel. "Lester Young and the Birth of Cool." In *Signifyin(g), Sanctifyin' and Slam Dunking: A Reader in African American Expressive Culture,* edited by Gena Dagel Caponi, 239–76. Amherst: University of Massachusetts Press, 1999.

Diop, Cheikh Anta. *The African Origin of Civilization: Myth or Reality.* Edited and translated by Mercer Cook. Chicago: Lawrence Hill, 1974.

———. *The Cultural Unity of Black Africa.* Chicago: Third World Press, 1979.

Dittmar, Linda, and Jean Michaud. *From Hanoi to Hollywood: The Vietnam War in American Film.* New Brunswick, NJ: Rutgers University Press, 1990.

Dixon, Melvin. "The Black Writer's Use of Memory." In *History and Memory in African-American Culture,* edited by Geneviève Fabre and Robert O'Meally, 18–27. New York: Oxford University Press, 1994.

Dowdy, Michael C. "Working in the Space of Disaster: Yusef Komunyakaa's Dialogues with America." *Callaloo* 28.3 (2005): 812–23.

Doyle, Mary Ellen. "In Need of the Folk: The Alienated Protagonist of Ralph Ellison's Short Fiction." *CLA Journal* 19.2 (December 1975): 165–72.

Dragonsun, Jabiya. *Hit Parade: Poems.* Lexington, SC: Traditions Press, 1989.

Du Bois, W. E. B. *The Selected Works of W. E. B. Du Bois.* Edited by Walter Wilson. New York: New American Library, 1970.

———. *The Souls of Black Folk* [1903]. In *Three Negro Classics,* edited by John Hope Franklin, 207–389. New York: Avon Books, 1965.

Early, Gerald. "Jazz and American Literature." In *The Oxford Companion to Jazz,* 734–44. Oxford: Oxford University Press, 2000.

Edgerton, Robert B. *Hidden Heroism: Black Soldiers in America's Wars.* Boulder, CO: Westview Press, 2001.

Edwards, Grace F. *The Viaduct: A Harlem Thriller.* New York: Doubleday, 2004.

Edwards, J. D. *The Afro-American Trickster Tale: A Structural Analysis*. Bloomington: Folklore Publications Group, Indiana University, 1978.

Egejuru, Phanuel A. "Chinua, the Human Within the Spirit-Eyed Artist." *Literary Griot* 13.1–2 (spring/fall 2001): 35–47.

Elbow, Peter. "The Uses of Binary Thinking." *Journal of Advanced Composition* 13.1 (winter 1993): 51–77.

Ellison, Mary. "Black Music and the Vietnam War." In *Vietnam Images: War and Representation*, edited by Jeffrey Walsh and James Aulich, 57–68. New York: St. Martin's Press, 1989.

Ellison, Ralph. "Battle Royal." In *Literature: Reading, Reacting, Writing*, edited by Laurie G. Kirszner and Stephen R. Mandell, 332–42. Boston: Wadsworth Cengage Learning, 2007.

———. "Flying Home." In *Literature: Reading, Reacting, Writing*, edited by Laurie G. Kirszner and Stephen R. Mandell, 299–314. San Diego: Harcourt Brace Jovanovich College Press, 1991.

———. "The Golden Age, Time Past." In *Shadow and Act*, 199–212. New York: Random House, 1953.

———. *Invisible Man*. 1952; New York: Random House/Vintage, 1972.

———. *Shadow and Act*. New York: Random House, 1953.

Everett, Percival. *Walk Me to the Distance*. New York: Ticknor & Fields, 1985.

Eyerman, Ron. *Cultural Trauma: Slavery and the Formation of African American Identity*. Cambridge: Cambridge University Pres, 2001.

Fabre, Geneviève, and Robert O'Meally, eds. *History and Memory in African-American Culture*. Oxford: Oxford University Press, 1994.

Fair, Ronald. Review of *All-Night Visitors*, by Clarence Major. *Black American Literature Forum* 13.2 (summer 1979): 73.

Fessier, Michael, Jr. "A War Ivan Dixon Is Winning." *New York Times*, January 29, 1967.

Fleischer, Leonard. Review of *Captain Blackman*, by John A. Williams. *Saturday Review*, May 13, 1972, 25–26.

Fleming, Robert. "John A Williams." *Black Issues Book Review* 4 (July/August, 2002): 46–49.

Floyd, Samuel A., Jr. "On Integrative Inquiry," *Lenox Avenue* 1 (1995): 25–26.

———. "Toward a Theory of Diaspora Aesthetics." *Lenox Avenue: A Journal of Interarts Inquiry* 4 (1998): 25–67.

Flowers, A. R. "Blues Aesthetic and American Culture" (panel discussion). Blues Today: A Living Blues Symposium on the 20th Anniversary of *Living Blues Magazine*. Barnard Observatory, University of Mississippi, February 22, 2003.

———. *De Mojo Blues: De Quest of High John de Conqueror*. Boston: E. P. Dutton, 1985.

———. "For Blacks, Vietnam Was Different." Review of *Bloods: An Oral History of the Vietnam*

War by Black Veterans, edited by Wallace Terry. *Christianity and Crisis* 45.5 (April 1, 1985): 115–17.

Foley, Barbara. *Telling the Truth: The Theory and Practice of Documentary Fiction*. Ithaca: Cornell University Press, 1986.

Foner, Jack D. *Blacks and the Military in American History*. New York: Praeger Publishers, 1974.

Ford, Clyde W. *The Hero with an African Face: Mythic Wisdom of Traditional Africa*. New York: Bantam, 1999.

Fowler, Carolyn. *Black Arts and Black Aesthetics: A Bibliography*. Fairfield, IA: First World, 1981.

Franklin, Clyde W., II. "Ain't I a Man? The Efficacy of Black Masculinities for Men's Studies in the 1990's." In *The American Black Male: His Present Status and His Future*, edited by Richard G. Majors and Jacob U. Gordon, 271–83. Chicago: Nelson-Hall Press, 1994.

———. "Men's Studies, the Men's Movement, and the Study of Black Masculinities: Further Demystification of Masculinities in America." In *The American Black Male: His Present Status and His Future*, edited by Richard Majors and Jacob U. Gordon, 3–19 (Nelson-Hall Publishers, 1994).

Franklin, Wendell, dir. *The Bus Is Coming*. Los Angeles: K-CALB Productions, 1971. Film.

Frazier, Sandy. *I Married Vietnam: A Novel*. New York: George Braziller, 1992.

French, Albert. *Patches of Fire: A Story of War and Redemption*. New York: Anchor/Doubleday, 1997.

Funderberg, Lise. "Tragic Mulatto Girl Wonder: The Paradoxical Life of Philippa Duke Schuyler," *QBR: The Black Book Review*, February/March 1996.

Gartner, Scott Sigmund, and Gary M. Segura. "Race, Casualties, and Opinion in the Vietnam War." *Journal of Politics* 62.1 (February 2000): 115–46.

Gates, Henry Louis, Jr. "The 'Blackness of Blackness': A Critique of the Sign and the Signifying Monkey." *Critical Inquiry* 9 (June 1983): 685–723.

———. *The Signifying Monkey: A Theory of Afro-American Literary Criticism*. Oxford: Oxford University Press, 1988.

Gately, Nicole. "Malcolm X: A Search for Truth." May 19, 2005. http://www.cmgww.com/historic/malcolm/viewheadline.php?id=3133.

Gayle, Addison. *The Black Aesthetic*. New York: Doubleday, 1972.

———. *The Way of the New World: The Black Novel in America*. New York: Doubleday, 1975.

"Gene 'Jug' Ammons." Narrated by Nancy Wilson. *Jazz Profiles*. NPR. November 26, 2001.

Georgakas, Dan. "John Williams at 49: An Interview." *Minnesota Review* 7 (1976): 51–65.

George, Nelson. *Blackface: Reflections on African-Americans and the Movies*. New York: HarperCollins, 1994.

Gerima, Haile. "Thoughts and Concepts: The Making of *Ashes and Embers*." *Black American*

Literature Forum 25.2 (summer 1991): 335–50.

Giddins, Gary, dir. "Celebrating Bird: The Triumph of Charlie Parker." Season 4, episode 5 of *American Masters*. Aired August 17, 1989. WNET, New York.

———. "Charlie Parker: An Overview." In *The Bebop Revolution in Words and Music*, edited by Dave Oliphant, 53–78. Austin: Harry Ransom Humanities Research Center, University of Texas, 1994.

Gill, Gerald. "From Maternal Pacifism to Revolutionary Solidarity: African American Women's Opposition to the Vietnam War." In *Sights on the Sixties*, edited by Barbara L. Tischler. New Brunswick: Rutgers University Press, 1992.

Glassner, Barry. *The Culture of Fear: Why Americans Are Afraid of the Wrong Things*. New York: Basic Books, 1999.

Goff, Stanley, and Robert Sanders, eds. *Brothers: Black Soldiers in the Nam*. New York: Presidio Press, 1982.

Gold, Tami, dir. *Another Brother*. 1998. Distributed by Third World Newsreel Streaming. 16mm/ video. https://twn.tugg.com/titles/another-brother.

Goldberg, Matt. "'Black Panther' Spoiler Review: The Spirit of Wakanda, the Body of Marvel." *Collider*, February 16, 2018.

Goss, Linda, and Marian E. Barnes, eds. *Talk That Talk: An Anthology of African-American Storytelling*. New York: Simon and Schuster, 1989.

Gotera, Vicente F. "'Depending on the Light': Yusef Komunyakaa's *Dien Cai Dau*." In *America Rediscovered: Critical Essays on Literature and Film of the Vietnam War*, 282–300. New York: Garland, 1990.

Gould, Jack. "TV: *The Final War of Olly Winter*; Poignant Drama Opens 'C.B.S. Playhouse' Ronald Ribman's Story Is Set in Vietnam." *New York Times*, January 30, 1967.

Graham, Herman, III. *The Brothers' Vietnam War: Black Power, Manhood and the Vietnam War Experience*. Gainesville: University Press of Florida, 2003.

Grant, Betsy, ed. *The Adventures of Point-Man Palmer in Vietnam: Cartoons and Writings by Vernon Grant*. Mineral Point, WI: Little Creek Press, 2014.

Gray, Herman. "Black Masculinity and Visual Culture." *Callaloo* 18.2 (1995): 401–5.

Grayson, Sandra M. *Symbolizing the Past: Reading "Sankofa," "Daughters of the Dust," and "Eve's Bayou" as Histories*. Washington, DC: University Press of America, 2000.

Green, Jordan. "Interview with Lamont Steptoe." Tilt-A-Whirl Press. August 15, 1998. http:// mark.stosberg.com/tilt-a-whirl/tour/steptoe.html.

Greenlee, Sam. *The Spook Who Sat by the Door*. London: Allison and Busby, 1969.

———. *The Spook Who Sat by the Door*. New York: Richard W. Baron Publishing Co., 1973.

Gregory, Deborah. "Allen Payne: He's Pouring His Joy and Pain onto the Big Screen." *Essence*,

November 1994, 62.

Griffin, Farah Jasmine. *"Who Set You Flowin'?": The African-American Migration Narrative.* Oxford: Oxford University Press, 1995.

Grimes, William. "John A. Williams, 89, Dies; Underrated Novelist Wrote about Black Identity." *New York Times.* July 7, 2015.

Grooms, Anthony. *Bombingham: A Novel.* New York: The Free Press, 2001.

Guerrero, Ed. *Framing Blackness: The African American Image in Film.* Philadelphia: Temple University Press, 2012.

Guidry, Richard. *The War in I Corps.* New York: Ballantine, 1998.

Gunn, Gay G. *Everlastin' Love.* Columbus, MS: Genesis Press, 1966; Waterville, ME: Thorndike Press, 1998.

Hackworth, David. "The Point Man." *Modern Maturity* 43.3 (May–June 2000): 43–84.

———. *The Price of Honor.* New York: Doubleday, 1999.

Hall, Simon. *Peace and Freedom: The Civil Rights and Antiwar Movements of the 1960s.* Philadelphia: University of Pennsylvania Press, 2005.

Hare, Nathan. "It's Time to Turn the Guns the Other Way." In *Vietnam and Black America: An Anthology of Protest and Resistance*, edited by Clyde Taylor, 285–89. Garden City: Anchor Press, 1973.

Harper, Frances E. W. *Iola Leroy; or, Shadows Uplifted.* 1892; New York: Penguin Classics, 2010.

Harper, Michael. *Debridement.* New York: Doubleday, 1973.

Harris, Norman. "Blacks in Vietnam: A Holistic Perspective through Fiction and Journalism." *Western Journal of Black Studies* 10.3 (1986): 121–31.

———. *Connecting Times: The Sixties in Afro-American Fiction.* Jackson: University Press of Mississippi, 1988.

Hasse, John Edward. *Beyond Category: The Musical Genius of Duke Ellington.* Buddha Records, 1999.

Hemenway, Robert E. *Zora Neale Hurston: A Literary Biography.* Urbana-Champaign: University of Illinois Press, 1977.

Henderson, Stephen. *Understanding the New Black Poetry: Black Speech and Black Music as Poetic References.* New York: William Morrow, 1973.

Herbison, Chauncey C. "B(l)ack to the World: Explorations of Race, Trauma, Illness, and Healing in Selected Vietnam Films," Ph.D. diss., University of Kansas, 2006.

Herzog, Tobey C. "John Wayne in a Modern Heart of Darkness: The American Soldier in Vietnam." In *Search and Clear: Critical Responses to Selected Literature and Films of the Vietnam War*, edited by William J. Searle, 16–25. Bowling Green, OH: Bowling Green State University Popular Press, 1988.

———. *Vietnam War Stories: Innocence Lost.* Abingdon-on-Thames: Routledge, 1992.

Hillstrom, Kevin, and Laurie Collier Hillstrom, eds. *The Vietnam Experience: A Concise Encyclopedia of American Literature, Songs and Films.* Westport, CT: Greenwood Press, 1998.

Hollingsworth, Dell, and George Leake. "The Bebop Revolution in Words and Music: An Exhibition." In *The Bebop Revolution in Words and Music*, edited by Dave Oliphant, 27–51. Austin: Harry Ransom Humanities Research Center, University of Texas, 1994.

Horton, John. "Time and Cool People." In *Rappin' and Stylin' Out: Communication in Urban Black America*, edited by Thomas Kochman, 19–31. Urbana-Champaign: University of Illinois Press, 1972.

Hounon, Mamaissii Vivian Dansi. "Vodun: The Religious Practices of Southern Slaves in America." *Kalamu Magazine: The Pen of African History*, 1–8.

Hsiao, Lisa. "Project 100,000: The Great Society's Answer to Military Manpower Needs in Vietnam." *Vietnam Generation* 1.2 (1989): 14–37.

Humes, Pete. "*Home*: A Landmark Play for Its Director and for UR." *Richmond Times-Dispatch.* November 14, 2005.

Hynes, William, and William G. Doty. *Mythical Trickster Figures: Contours, Contexts, and Criticisms.* Tuscaloosa: University of Alabama Press, 1993.

Ifill, Gwen. "Interview with August Wilson." *The News Hour with Jim Lehrer.* PBS. April 4, 2001.

Jackson, Blyden. "Introduction." In Zora Neale Hurston, *Moses, Man of the Mountain*, vii–xix. Urbana-Champaign: University of Illinois Press, 1984.

———. *Operation Burning Candle.* Boynton Beach, FL: Pyramid Books, 1973.

Jackson, Gale. "The Way We Do: A Preliminary Investigation of the African Roots of African American Performance." In *African American Literary Criticism, 1773 to 2000*, edited by Hazel Arnett Ervin, 312–16. Woodbridge, CT: Twayne, 1999.

Jackson-Lowman, Huberta. "Using Afrikan Proverbs to Provide an Afrikan-Centered Narrative for Contemporary Afrikan-American Parental Values." In *Language, Rhythm, & Sound: Black Popular Cultures into the Twenty-First Century*, edited by Joseph K. Adjaye and Adrianne R. Andrews, 74–89. Pittsburgh: University of Pittsburgh Press, 1997.

Jason, Phillip K., ed. *Fourteen Landing Zones: Approaches to Vietnam War Literature.* Ames: University of Iowa Press, 1991.

———. "Sexism and Racism in Vietnam War Fiction." *Mosaic* 23 (summer 1990): 125–37.

Jay, David, and Elaine Crane, eds. *The Black Soldier: From the American Revolution to Vietnam.* New York: William Morrow, 1971.

Johnson, Charles. *Middle Passage.* Bloomington: Indiana University Press, 1988.

Johnson, Thomas A. "Negroes in 'the Nam." *Ebony* 23.10 (August 1968): 31–40.

Jones, Gayl. *Liberating Voices: Oral Tradition in African American Literature.* Cambridge, MA: Harvard University Press, 1991.

Jones, LeRoi. "The Changing Same and the New Black Music." *Black Music.* 1967. New York: First DaCapo Press, 1998.

Jones, Thomas Cadwaleder. *Stars & Stripes.* Orem, UT: Encore Performance Publishers, 1994.

Jones, Thomas R. *Lost Survivor.* Springfield, IL: J Publications, 2005.

Junne, George H., Jr. *Afroamerican History: A Chronicle of People of African Descent in the United States.* Dubuque, IA: Kendall Hunt, 1996.

Kalu, Anthonia. "Achebe and Duality in Igbo Thought." *Literary Griot* 10.2 (fall 1998): 17–33.

———. "Bill Cosby, Blues and the Reconstruction of African-American Literary Theory." *Literary Griot* 4.1–2 (spring/fall 1992): 1–15.

Karch, Beate. *No Vietnamese Ever Called Me Nigger.* Eine Analyse, 1968; Trier: Wissenschaftlicher Verlag Trier, 1994.

Keil, Charles. "Motion and Feeling Through Music." In *Rappin' and Stylin' Out: Communication in Urban Black America,* edited by Thomas Kochman, 83–100. Urbana-Champaign: University of Illinois Press, 1972.

Kelley, Robin D. G. "New Perspectives on Thelonious Monk." *Black Music Research Journal* 19.2 (autumn 1999): 135–168.

Killens, John O. *And Then We Heard the Thunder.* 1963; New York: Pocket Books, 1964.

King, Martin Luther, Jr. "Beyond Vietnam." In *Vietnam and Black America: An Anthology of Protest and Resistance,* edited by Clyde Taylor, 79–98. Garden City: Anchor Press, 1973.

———. "Declaration of Independence from the War in Vietnam." In *Takin' It to the Streets: A Sixties Reader,* edited by Alexander Bloom and Wini Breines, 230–36. New York: Pocket Books, 1986.

———. *A Testament of Hope: The Essential Writings of Martin Luther King, Jr.* Edited by James M. Washington. New York: Harper & Row, 1986.

King, William M. "'Our Men in Vietnam': Black Media as a Source of the Afro-American Experience in Southeast Asia." *Vietnam Generation* 1.2 (1989): 94–117.

King-Gamble, Marcia. *Jade.* Washington, DC: Sepia/BET Books, 2002.

Kinnard, Douglas. "The 'Strategy' of the War." In *Vietnam in Remission,* edited by James F. Veninga and Harold A. Wilmer, 19–32. College Station: Texas A&M University Press, 1985.

Kirkland, Haywood T. "Vietnam Blues." In *Talk That Talk: An Anthology of African-American Storytelling,* edited by Linda Goss and Marian E. Barnes, 167–76. New York: Simon & Schuster, 1989.

Kiss, Tony. "One Hot Week in Theater." *Citizen-Times,* October 30, 2005.

Klinkowitz, Jerome. *Rosenberg, Barthes, Hassan: The Postmodern Habit of Thought.* Athens:

University of Georgia Press, 1988.

———. "Writing Under Fire: Postmodern Fiction and the Vietnam War." In *Postmodern Fiction: A Bio-Bibliographical Guide*, edited by Larry McCaffery, 79–92. Westport, CT: Greenwood, 1986.

Knight, Cranston. *In the Garden of the Beast: Vietnam Cries of a Love Song*. Chicago: Third World Press, 2006.

Komunyakaa, Yusef. *Dien Cai Dau*. Middletown, CT: Wesleyan University Press, 1988.

Kouyate, D'Jimo. "The Role of the Griot." In *Talk That Talk: An Anthology of African-American Storytelling*, edited by Linda Goss and Marian E. Barnes, 179–81. New York: Simon and Schuster, 1989.

Kuhn, Thomas S. *The Structure of Scientific Revolutions*. Chicago: University of Chicago Press, 1970.

"Lack of Black POW's Means Barbarism." *New York Amsterdam News*, April 28, 1973.

Lawrence, Ida Mae. "Vietnam: A Poem." From Staughton Lynd, "A Radical Speaks in Defense of S.N.C.C." *New York Times*, September 10, 1967. Available at African-American Involvement in the Vietnam War, http://www.aavw.org/special_features/pofidr_poetry_lawrence.html.

Lawson, Jacqueline. "'Old Kids': The Adolescent Experience in the Nonfiction Narratives of the Vietnam War." In *Search and Clear: Critical Responses to Selected Literature of Films of the Vietnam War*, edited by William J. Searle, 26–36. Bowling Green, OH: Bowling Green State University Popular Press, 1988.

———. "She's a Pretty Woman for a Gook: The Misogyny of the Vietnam War." In *Fourteen Landing Zones: Approaches to Vietnam War Literature*, edited by Phillip K. Jason, 15–37. Ames: University of Iowa Press, 1991.

"Lead Story: A Roundtable Discussion of Current Events." BET. 1999.

Lee, Carol D. *Signifying as a Scaffold for Literary Interpretation: The Pedagogical Implications of an African American Discourse Genre*. National Council of Teachers of English Research Report No. 26. Urbana, IL: NCTE, 1993.

Lee, Don L. "Message to a Black Soldier." Available at African-American Involvement in the Vietnam War, http://www.aavw.org/special_features/pofidr_poetry_lee.html.

"The Legend of Staggerlee." Interview with Cecil Brown. *The Tavis Smiley Show*. NPR/African American Consortium. KQED San Francisco. June 19, 2003.

Lester, Julius. "High John the Conqueror." *Sing Out! The Folk Song Magazine* 15.1 (March 1965): 18–23.

Levine, Lawrence. *Black Culture and Black Consciousness: Afro-American Folk Thought from Slavery to Freedom*. Oxford: Oxford University Press, 1977.

———. "Jazz and American Culture." In *The Jazz Cadence of American Culture*, edited by

Robert G. O'Meally, 431–47. New York: Columbia University Press, 1998.

Lock, Graham. *Blutopia: Visions of the Future and Revisions of the Past in the Work of Sun Ra, Duke Ellington, and Anthony Braxton.* Durham, NC: Duke University Press, 1999.

Loeb, Jeff. "Faith's Fickle Covenant: African American Captivity Narratives from the Vietnam War. In *From the Plantation to the Prison: African American Confinement Literature,* 154–78. Macon, GA: Mercer University Press, 2008.

———. "MIA: African American Autobiography of the Vietnam War." *African American Review* 31.1 (spring 1997): 105–23.

Lomperis, Timothy J. *"Reading the Wind": The Literature of the Vietnam War.* Durham, NC: Duke University Press, 1987.

Lott, Eric. "Double V, Double-Time: Bebop Politics of Style." In *The Jazz Cadence of American Culture,* edited by Robert G. O'Meally, 457–68. New York: Columbia University Press, 1998.

Lyons, Daniel J. "Foreword." In *Good Men Die,* by Philippa Schuyler. New York: Twin Circle, 1969.

Luckett, Perry D. "The Black Soldier in Vietnam." *War, Literature, and the Arts* 1.2 (1989–90): 1–27.

Lynch, Charles. "Wesley Brown's *Tragic Magic*: An Interview." *First World* 2.2 (1979): 46–49.

Mackey, Nathaniel. "From Gassire's Lute: Robert Duncan's Vietnam War Poems." In *Reading Race in American Poetry: "An Area of Act",* 209–23. Urbana-Champaign: University of Illinois Press, 2000.

Madubuike, Ihechukwu. "Achebe's Ideas on Literature." *Black World* 24.2 (December 1974): 60–70.

Major, Clarence. *All-Night Visitors.* 1969. Unexpurgated edition, Evanston: Northwestern University Press, 1998.

Majors, Richard, Richard Tyler, Blaine Peden, and Ron Hall. "Cool Pose: A Symbolic Mechanism for Masculine Role Enactment and Coping by Black Males." In *The American Black Male: His Present Status and His Future,* edited by Richard G. Majors and Jacob U. Gordon, 245–59. Chicago: Nelson-Hall Press, 1994.

Malcolm X. *Malcolm X Talks to Young People.* New York: Pathfinder, 1991.

Mandelbaum, Michael. "Vietnam: The Television War." *Daedalus* 111.4 (fall 1982): 157–69.

Mann, Michael, dir. *Ali.* Los Angeles: Columbia/TriStar, 2001. Film.

Marable, Manning. "The Black Male: Searching beyond Stereotypes." In *The American Black Male: His Present Status and His Future,* edited by Richard G. Majors and Jacob U. Gordon, 69–77. Chicago: Nelson-Hall Press, 1994.

———. *Race, Reform, and Rebellion: The Second Reconstruction in Black America, 1945–1982.* Jackson: University Press of Mississippi, 1984.

Martin, Thad. "The Black Vietnam Vet: Still Looking for Respect." *Ebony* 41.6 (April 1986): 123–30.

Marvin, Thomas. "Komunyakaa's FACING IT." *Explicator* 61.4 (2003): 242–45.

———. "Komunyakaa's TU DO STREET." *Explicator* 64.4 (2006): 256–58.

Mbiti, John S. *African Religions and Philosophy.* Westport, CT: Praeger, 1969.

McCarthy, Gerald. "The Caged Bird and the Minotaur: Silence and Politics in the Poetry of Yusef Komunyakan and Horace Coleman." *Asheville Poetry Review* 9.1 (2002).

"Minority Veterans." In *Source Material on the Vietnam Era Veteran*, prepared by the Senate Committee on Veterans' Affairs, 173–236. Washington, DC: GPO, 1974. Available at African-American Involvement in the Vietnam War, http://www.aavw.org/special_features/reporting_terry_abstract25.html.

Mooney, James W., and Thomas R. West, eds. *Vietnam: A History and Anthology.* St. James, NY: Brandywine Press, 1994.

Moore, Michael, dir. *Bowling for Columbine.* Beverly Hills, CA: MGM, 2002. Film.

———. *Stupid White Men . . . and Other Sorry Excuses for the State of the Nation.* New York: Regan Books, 2001.

Morgan, Ken. "20th Anniversary of Vietnam War's End." *Chicago Defender*, May 23, 1995.

Morrison, C. T. *The Flame in the Icebox: An Episode of the Vietnam War.* New York: Exposition Press, 1968.

Morrison, Toni. "Unspeakable Things Unspoken: The Afro-American Presence in American Literature." *Michigan Quarterly Review* 28.1 (winter 1989): 1–34.

Mosley, Walter. "The Black Man: Hero." In *Speak My Name: Black Men on Masculinity and the American Dream*, edited by Don Belton, 234–40. Boston: Beacon Press, 1995.

Mugambi, Helen. "Africa's Walking Library." *Black Issues Book Review* 2.3 (May/June 2000): 2.

Mulira, Jessie Gaston. "The Case of Voodoo in New Orleans." In *Africanisms in American Culture*, edited by Joseph E. Holloway, 34–68. Bloomington: Indiana University Press, 1990.

Muller, Gilbert. *John A. Williams.* New York: Twayne Publishers, 1984.

Munro, C. Lynn. "Culture and Quest in the Fiction of John A. Williams." *CLA Journal* 22.2 (December 1978): 71–100.

Murray, Albert. "The Function of the Heroic Image." In *The Jazz Cadence of American Culture*, edited by Robert G. O'Meally, 569–79. New York: Columbia University Press, 1998.

———. *The Hero and the Blues.* Columbia: University of Missouri Press, 1973.

———. *Stomping the Blues.* New York: McGraw-Hill, 1976.

Murray, Pauli. *Proud Shoes.* 1956; Boston: Beacon Press, 1999.

Muyumba, Francois N. "Afrocentricity, Language and Expressive Culture." *Literary Griot* 12.2 (fall 2000): 86–99.

Myers, Linda James. *Understanding an Afrocentric World View: Introduction to an Optimal Psychology.* 2nd ed. Dubuque, IA: Kendall-Hunt Press, 1988.

Myers, Walter Dean. *Fallen Angels.* New York: Scholastic, 1988.

———. *Patrol: An American Soldier in Vietnam.* New York: HarperCollins Children's Books, 2002.

Nadel, Alan. "My Country Too: Time, Place, and Afro-American Identity in the Work of John Williams." *Obsidian II: Black Literature in Review* 2.3 (1987): 25–41.

Nelson, Gaylord. "Never Before Has the Land Been So . . . Mutilated." In *Vietnam: A History and Anthology*, edited by James W. Mooney and Thomas R. West, 125–28. St. James, NY: Brandywine Press, 1994.

Nettleford, Rex. "Black Classicism and the Eurocentric Ideal: A Case for Integrative Inquiry into Black Expressive Arts." *Lenox Avenue* 2 (1996): 27–33.

Nolan, McKinley. "Ex-G.I. Reported to Support Hanoi." *New York Times*, March 11, 1973.

"North Vietnamese Stamps, ca. 1965." From *Malcolm X: A Search for Truth*, exhibit at the Schomburg Center for Research in Black Culture, New York Public Library, May 19–December 31, 2005. Available at African-American Involvement in the Vietnam War, http://www.aavw.org/protest/malcolmx_malcolmx_abstract04.html.

Obenga, Theophile. "African Philosophy of the Pharaonic Period." In *Egypt Revisited*, edited by Ivan Van Sertima, 286–324. Piscataway, NJ: Transaction Press, 1989.

O'Brien, John. "The Art of John A. Williams." *American Scholar* 42.3 (December 1972): 489–98.

Ofole-Prince, Samantha. "Heavy D Produces *Medal of Honor Rag*." BlackFlix.com, 2005. http://www.blackflix.com.

Ogunyemi, Chikwenye Okonjo. "'The Old Order Shall Pass': The Examples of 'Flying Home' and 'Paradise.'" *Studies in Short Fiction* 20.1 (winter 1983): 23–32.

O'Meally, Robert G., ed. *The Jazz Cadence of American Culture.* New York: Columbia University Press, 1998.

Ostendorf, Berndt. "Anthropology, Modernism and Jazz." In *Modern Critical Views: Ralph Ellison*, edited by Harold Bloom, 145–72. New York: Chelsea House, 1986.

Parks, David. *G.I. Diary.* 1968. Howard University Press Library of Contemporary Literature. Washington, DC: Howard University Press, 1984.

Peavy, Charles D. *Afro-American Literature and Culture Since World War II: A Guide to Information Sources.* Edited by Donald Koster. Farmington Hills, MI: Gale Research, 1979.

Pedersen, Carl. "Sea Change: The Middle Passage and the Transatlantic Imagination." In *The Black Columbiad: Defining Moments in African American Literature and Culture*, edited by Werner Sollors and Maria Diedrich, 42–51. Cambridge, MA: Harvard University Press, 1994.

Pelecanos, George. *Hard Revolution.* New York: Little, Brown, 2004.

Pelton, Robert D. *The Trickster in West Africa: A Study of Mythic Irony and Sacred Delight.* Berkeley: University of California Press, 1980.

Peters, Erskine. *African Openings to the Tree of Life.* Berkeley: Regent Press, 1987.

Phillips, Kimberly. "And Sing No More of War: Black Women Write, Sing, and Speak about the Vietnam War." In *Soul Soldiers: African Americans and the Vietnam Era,* edited by Samuel W. Black, 66–84. Pittsburgh: Historical Society of Western Pennsylvania, 2006.

Pinson, Hermine. "Yusef Komunyakaa's New Blues." *Callaloo* 28.3 (2005): 568–71.

Pratt, John Clark. "Bibliographic Commentary: 'From the Fiction Some Truths.'" In *"Reading the Wind": The Literature of the Vietnam War,* edited by Timothy Lomperis, 115–54. Durham, NC: Duke University Press, 1987.

Prewitt, J. Everett. *A Long Way Back.* Cleveland: Northland Research, 2015.

———. *Something about Ann: Stories of Love and Brotherhood.* Cleveland: Northland Publishing Company, 2017.

Pugh, Charles. *The Griot.* Los Angeles: Holloway House, 1986.

Puhr, Kathleen. "Novelistic Responses to the Vietnam War." Ph.D. diss., St. Louis University, 1982.

Rand, Peter. Review of *Coming Home,* by George Davis. *New York Times,* January 9, 1972.

Randle, Gloria T. "Lady Sings the Blues: Toni Morrison and the Jazz/Blues Aesthetic." In *African American Jazz and Rap: Social and Philosophical Examinations of Black Expressive Behavior,* edited by James L. Conyers Jr., 131–44. Jefferson, NC: McFarland, 2001.

Rangel, Charles B. "Where Are the Black P.O.W.'S?" *Essence,* December 1973, 32–33.

Raphael-Hernandez, Heike. "'The First Animal I Ever Killed Was Gook': The Vietnam War and Its Legacy in African American and Native American Novels." In *Literature on the Move: Comparing Diasporic Ethnicities in Europe and the Americas,* edited by Dominique Marcais et al., 131–46. Heidelberg: Universitatsverlag Winter, 2002.

———. "'It Takes Some Time to Learn the Right Words': The Vietnam War in African American Novels." In *Afroasian Encounters: Culture, History, Politics,* 103–23. New York: New York University Press, 2006.

———. "The 'Non-Existent' Vietnam War in African American Novels: A Question of Shared Guilt?" In *The Sixties Revisited: Culture-Society-Politics,* 287–301. Heidelberg: Universitatsverlag Winter, 2001.

Raynor, Sharon Denise. "Shattered Silence and Restored Souls: Bearing Witness and Testifying to Trauma and Truth in Narratives of Black Vietnam Veterans." Ph.D. diss., Indiana University of Pennsylvania, 2003.

Reed, Ishmael. Review of *All-Night Visitors,* by Clarence Major. *Black American Literature Forum* 13.2 (summer 1979): 73.

Reich, Elizabeth. "A New Kind of Black Soldier: Performing Revolution in *The Spook Who Sat by the Door*." *African American Review* 45.3 (fall 2012): 325–39.

Review of *Captain Blackman*, by John A. Williams. *Library Journal*, May 1, 1972, 1942.

Review of *Captain Blackman*, by John A. Williams. *Publisher's Weekly*, February 28, 1972, 71.

Review of *Tragic Magic*, by Wesley Brown. *Choice*, February 1979, 1661.

Review of *Tragic Magic*, by Wesley Brown. *New York Times Book Review*, February 11, 1979, 14.

Review of *Tragic Magic*, by Wesley Brown. *The New Yorker*, October 23, 1978, 182.

Ribman, Ronald. *The Final War of Olly Winter*. New York: CBS Playhouse, 1967.

Rice, Alan J. "Finger-Snapping to Train-Dancing and Back Again: The Development of a Jazz Style in African American Prose." In *The Yearbook of English Studies*, edited by Andrew Gurr, 105–16. Leeds: W. S. Maney and Son, 1994.

Richards, Dona Marimba. "The African 'Aesthetic' and National Consciousness." In *The African Aesthetic: Keeper of the Traditions*, edited by Kariamu Welsh-Asante, 63–82. Westport, CT: Greenwood Press, 1993.

———. "The Ideology of European Dominance." *The Western Journal of Black Studies* 3.4 (winter 1979): 244–250.

Ringnalda, Don. *Fighting and Writing the Vietnam War*. Jackson: University Press of Mississippi, 1994.

Roberts, John W. "The African American Animal Trickster as Hero." In *Redefining American Literary History*, edited by A. LaVonne Ruoff Brown and Jerry W. Ward Jr., 97–114. New York: MLA, 1990.

———. *From Trickster to Badman: The Black Folk Hero in Slavery and Freedom*. Philadelphia: University of Pennsylvania Press, 1990.

———. "Strategy, Morality, and Worldview of the Afro-American Spirituals and Trickster Tales." *Western Journal of Black Studies* 6.2 (1982): 101–7.

Salas, Angela M. "Race, Human Empathy, and Negative Capability: The Poetry of Yusef Komunyakaa." *College Literature* 30.4 (fall 2003): 32–53.

Samuels, Wilfred D., ed. *Encyclopedia of African-American Literature*. 2nd ed. New York: Facts on File, 2007.

Samuels, Wilfred D., and Clenora Hudson-Weems. *Toni Morrison*. Boston: G. K. Hall, 1990.

Schroeder, Patricia R. "Rootwork: Arthur Flowers, Zora Neale Hurston, and the 'Literary Hoodoo' Tradition." *African American Review* 36.2 (summer 2002): 263–72.

Schulke, Flip, and Penelope Ortner McPhee. *King Remembered*. New York: W. W. Norton, 1986.

Schuyler, George S. *Black No More*. New York: Macaulay Co., 1931.

Schuyler, Philippa. *Adventures in Black and White*. New York: R. Speller, 1960.

———. *Dau Tranh!* [unpublished, ca. 1967].

———. *Good Men Die*. New York: Twin Circle, 1969.

———. *Jungle Saints: Africa's Heroic Missionaries*. Rome: Herder, 1963.

———. *Kingdom of Dreams*. New York: R. Speller and Sons, 1966.

———. *Who Killed the Congo?* New York: Devin-Adair, 1962.

Schwolsky-Fitch, Elena. "'Another Brother' Chronicles the Life of Clarence Fitch." *The Veteran* 28.1 (spring 1998), http://www.vvaw.org/veteran/article/?id=226.

Senna, Danzy. "Introduction." In *Black No More*, by George S. Schuyler. New York: Penguin Books, 2018.

Scott, Daniel M., III. "Interrogating Identity: Appropriation and Transformation in Middle Passage." *African American Review* 29.4 (winter 1995): 645–55.

Scott, Joyce Hope. "Who 'Goophered' Whom: The Afro-American Fabulist and His Tale in Charles Chesnutt's The Conjure Woman." *Bestia: Yearbook of the Beast Folklore Society* 2 (May 1990): 49–62.

Searle, William J., ed. *Search and Clear: Critical Responses to Selected Literature and Films of the Vietnam War*. Bowling Green, OH: Bowling Green State University Popular Press, 1988.

Sheehan, Neil, et al. *The Pentagon Papers: The Secret History of the Vietnam War*. New York: Racehorse/Simon & Schuster, 2017.

Sherwood, John D. *Black Sailor, White Navy: Racial Unrest in the Fleet during the Vietnam War Era*. New York: New York University Press, 2007.

Sims-Holt, Grace. "'Inversion' in Black Communication." In *Rappin' and Stylin' Out: Communication in Urban Black America*, edited by Thomas Kochmann, 152–59. Urbana-Champaign: University of Illinois Press, 1972.

Sithole, Elkin T. "Black Folk Music." In *Rappin' and Stylin' Out: Communication in Urban Black America*, edited by Thomas Kochman, 65–82. Urbana-Champaign: University of Illinois Press, 1972.

Slotkin, Richard. *Regeneration through Violence: The Mythology of the American Frontier, 1600–1800*. Middletown, CT: Wesleyan University Press, 1973.

Smith, David. "The Seven Survivors." *The Black Panther*, May 9, 1970, 7.

Smith, Jeanne Rosier. *Writing Tricksters: Mythic Gambols in American Ethnic Fiction*. Berkeley: University of California Press, 1997.

Smith, Vern. *The Jones Men: A Novel*. New York: W. W. Norton, 1998.

Smitherman, Geneva. "From 'Word from the African American Community' in *Black Talk: Words and Phrases from the Hood to the Amen Corner* (1994)." In *African American Literary Criticism, 1773 to 2000*, edited by Hazel Arnett Ervin, 200–211. Woodbridge, CT: Twayne, 1999.

———. *Talkin' and Testifyin': The Language of Black America*. Detroit: Wayne State University

Press, 1977.

———. *Talkin' That Talk: Language, Culture and Education in African America*. New York: Routledge, 1999.

———. "Word from the Hood: The Lexicon of African-American Vernacular English." In *African-American English: Structure, History and Use*, edited by Guy Bailey, John Baugh, Salikoko S. Mufwene, John R. Rickford. New York: Routledge, 1998.

Sowande, Fela. "The Quest of an African World View: The Utilization of African Discourse." In *Black Communication: Dimensions of Research and Instruction*, edited by Jack L. Daniel, 67–117. Washington, DC: National Endowment for the Humanities, 1972.

Stapp, Andy. *Black Marines against the Brass: Interview with William Harvey and George Daniels*. New York: American Serviceman's Union, 1969.

Stein, Kevin. "Vietnam and 'The Voice Within': Public and Private History in Yusef Komunyakaa's *Dien Cai Dau*." *Massachusetts Review* 36.4 (1995): 541–61.

Stelly, Matthew C. *The Spook Who Sat By the Door Revisited: A 38-Year Retrospective on Race, Rioting, and Relevant Response*. Scotts Valley, CA: CreateSpace Independent Publishing Platform, 2017.

Stepto, Robert B. *From behind the Veil: A Study of Afro-American Narrative*. Urbana-Champaign: University of Illinois Press, 1979.

Steptoe, Lamont B. *American Morning/Mourning*. Wilsonville, OR: Whirlwind Publishing, 1990.

———. *Crimson River: Poems*. Philadelphia: Slash and Burn Press, 1984.

———. *Crimson River: Poems, New and Selected Work*. Wilsonville, OR: Whirlwind Publishing, 1989.

———. "Featured Poetry by Lamont Steptoe: Paris." Louisville, KY: Tilt-A-Whirl Press. February 22, 1991.

———. *A Long Movie of Shadows*. Wilsonville, OR: Whirlwind Publishing, 1994.

———. *Mad Minute*. Wilsonville, OR: Whirlwind Publishing, 1993.

———. *Uncle's South China Sea Blue Nightmare*. Alexandria, VA: Plan B Press, 2003.

Stern, Sol. "When the Black G.I. Comes Home from Vietnam." In *The Black Soldier: From the American Revolution to Vietnam*, edited by Jay David and Elaine Crane, 215–27. New York: William Morrow, 1971.

Stur, Heather. "In Service and In Protest: Black Women and the Impact of the Vietnam War on American Society." In *Soul Soldiers: African Americans and the Vietnam Era*, edited by Samuel W. Black. Pittsburgh: Historical Society of Western Pennsylvania, 2006.

Tal, Kali. "From Panther to Monster: Representations of Resistance from the Black Power Movement of the 1960s to the Boyz in the Hood and Beyond." In *African American Rhetoric(s): Interdisciplinary Perspectives*, edited by Elaine B. Richardson and Ronald L.

Jackson II, 37–58. Carbondale: Southern Illinois University Press, 2004.

Talalay, Kathryn. *Composition in Black and White: The Life of Philippa Schuyler*. Oxford: Oxford University Press, 1997.

Taylor, Clyde, ed. *Vietnam and Black America: An Anthology of Protest and Resistance*. Garden City: Anchor Press, 1973.

Terry, Wallace, ed. *Bloods: An Oral History of the Vietnam War by Black Veterans*. New York: Random House, 1984.

———. "Bringing the War Home." *Black Scholar* 2.3 (November 1970): 6–18.

———. "Guess Who's Coming Home: Black Fighting Men Recorded Live in Vietnam." Black Forum, 1972. Available at YouTube, https://www.youtube.com.

Thomas, Lorenzo. "The Bop Aesthetic and Black Intellectual Tradition." In *The Bebop Revolution in Words and Music*, edited by Dave Oliphant, 105–18. Austin: Harry Ransom Humanities Research Center, University of Texas, 1994.

Thompson, Howard. "*Gordon's War* Views Drug Scene." *New York Times*, August 10, 1973.

Thornton, Jerome E. "'Goin' on De Muck': The Paradoxical Journey of the Black American Hero." *CLA Journal* 31.3 (March 1988): 261–80.

Tischler, Barbara L. *Muhammad Ali: A Man of Many Voices*. New York: Routledge, 2016.

Traore, Ousseynou B. "Ananse's Web: Oral and Literary Linkages." *Literary Griot* 1.2 (spring 1989): iii–v.

———. "Matrical Approaches to *Things Fall Apart*: A Poetics of Epic and Mythic Paradigms." In *Approaches to Teaching Achebe's "Things Fall Apart,"* 66–73. New York: Modern Language Association, 1991.

———. "'The Quarrel between Earth and Sky' as Thematic Paradigm in *Things Fall Apart*." Unpublished presentation. 14th Annual Pan-African Studies Conference-Global Africa: Dimensions of a Changing Society. Indiana State University, April 12, 1997.

Traylor, Eleanor. "A Blues View of Life: Literature and the Blues Vision." In *African American Literary Criticism, 1773 to 2000*, edited by Hazel Arnett Ervin, 285–88. Woodbridge, CT: Twayne, 1999.

Trimmer, Joseph F. "Ralph Ellison's 'Flying Home.'" *Studies in Short Fiction* 9.1 (winter 1972): 175–82.

Tucker, Mark. "Duke Ellington." In *The Oxford Companion to Jazz*, edited by Bill Kirchner. New York: Oxford University Press, 2000.

Turner, Daniel Cross. "'Unburying the Dead': Defining a Poetics of Trauma in Yusef Komunyakaa's *Poetry of Vietnam and the American South*." *Genre: Forms of Discourse and Culture* 39.1 (2006): 115–39.

U.S. Supreme Court. *Clay, aka Ali v. United States*. Washington, DC: GPO, 1971. Case No. 403 U.S.

698. Available at African-American Involvement in the Vietnam War, http://www.aavw. org/protest/ali_alivus_abstract08.html.

Van de Burg, William R. *Black Camelot: African American Culture Heroes in Their Times, 1960–1980*. Chicago: University of Chicago Press, 1997.

Van Gelder, Lawrence. "*Medal of Honor Rag*: The Tunnel and the Dark Didn't End in Vietnam." *New York Times*, February 1, 2001.

Van Sertima, Ivan. "Trickster, the Revolutionary Hero." In *Talk That Talk: An Anthology of African-American Storytelling*, edited by Linda Goss and Marian Barnes, 103–110. New York: Simon and Schuster Touchstone, 1989.

Velasco, Dorothy. "Tale of Women in War Powerful, Important." *The Register-Guard*, October 28, 2005.

Veninga, James F., and Harry A. Wilmer, eds. *Vietnam in Remission*. College Station: Texas A&M University Press, 1985.

Verharen, Charles C. "African-Centeredness and the New Black Millenium." *Literary Griot* 13.1–2 (spring/fall 2001): 1–12.

Washington, Geno. *The Blood Brothers*. London: The Do-Not Press, 1998.

Washington, Mary Helen. "'I Love the Way Janie Crawford Left Her Husbands': Zora Neale Hurston's Emergent Female Hero." In *Invented Lives: Narratives of Black Women, 1860–1960*, 237–93. New York: Doubleday, 1987.

———. "Meditations on History: The Slave Woman's Voice." In *Invented Lives: Narratives of Black Women, 1860–1960*, 3–70. New York: Doubleday, 1987.

Wakin, Edward T. *Black Fighting Men in U.S. History*. Boston: Lothrop, Lee and Shepard, 1971.

Watkins, Mel. "Introduction." In George Davis, *Coming Home*, ix–xxi, 1971; Washington, DC: Howard University Press, 1984.

———. "Hard Times for Black Writers." *New York Times Book Review*. February 22, 1981, sec. 7, 3.

Watson, Sandra Ruoff. Review of *Tragic Magic* by Wesley Brown. *Library Journal*, December 15, 1978, 2535.

Welsh, Anne Marie. "Politics as Usual: Vietnam-Set Play Just as True Today.". SignOnSanDiego. com, October 24, 2005. http://www.signonsandiego.com/news/features/20051024-9999-1c24heart.html (no longer available).

Werner, Craig Hansen. *Playing the Changes: From Afro-Modernism to the Jazz Impulse*. Urbana-Champaign: University of Illinois Press, 1994.

West, Cornel. "40 Years of Integration in Higher Education at the University of Mississippi." Unpublished lecture, University of Mississippi. January 31, 2003.

———. Weekly Commentary. *The Tavis Smiley Show*. NPR/African American Public Radio Consortium. Los Angeles. October 22, 2003.

Westheider, James E. *Fighting on Two Fronts: African Americans and the Vietnam War*. New York: New York University Press, 1997.

———. "My Fear Is for You: African Americans, Racism, and the Vietnam War." Ph.D. diss., University of Cincinnati, 1993.

White, Deborah Gray. *Ar'n't I a Woman? Female Slaves in the Plantation South*. New York: W. W. Norton and Company, 1985.

Whitmore, Terry. *Memphis-Nam-Sweden: The Story of a Black Deserter*. 1971; Jackson: University Press of Mississippi, 1997.

Whittington, Ruben Benjamin. *Moonspinners: Vietnam '65–'66*. New York: Vantage Press, 1986.

Wickett, Dan. "Interview with Percival Everett." Emerging Writers Forum. March 15, 2003. http://www.breaktech.net/EmergingWritersForum/View_Interview.aspx?id=29 (no longer available).

Willard, Tom. *The Stone Ponies: Book Four of the Black Sabre Chronicles*. New York: Forge, 2000.

Williams, Jamaal. *L.B.J. (Long Bien Jail)*. Scotts Valley, CA: CreateSpace Press, 2017.

Williams, James D. "The NAACP in Focus." *Crisis Magazine* 99.2 (February 1992): 33–39.

Williams, John A. *Captain Blackman*. 1972; Minneapolis: Coffee House Press, 2000.

Williams, Thomas D. *Cohesion*. New York: Vantage Press, 1982.

Wilson, D. B. *Betrayed*. Los Angeles: Holloway House, 1984.

Wilson, Nancy. *Jazz Profiles*. NPR. November 26, 2001.

Wirtz, James J. *The Tet Offensive: Intelligence Failure in War*. Ithaca: Cornell University Press, 1991.

Wright, John S. "The Conscious Hero and the Rites of Man: Ellison's War." In *New Essays on "Invisible Man*," edited by Robert O'Meally, 157–86. Cambridge: Cambridge University Press, 1988.

Wright, Kai. *Soldiers of Freedom: An Illustrated History of African Americans in the Armed Forces*. New York: Black Dog & Leventhal Publishers, 2002.

Wright, Richard. "The Ethics of Living Jim Crow." In *The Norton Anthology of African American Literature*, edited by Henry Louis Gates Jr. and Nellie Y. McKay, 1388–96. New York: Norton, 1997.

———. *Native Son*. 1940; New York: Perennial Classics, 1966.

Ya Salaam, Kalamu. "Music as Our Mother Tongue." *Black Issues Book Review* 2 (January/February 2003): 23–24.

Young, Elizabeth. "Warring Fictions: *Iola Leroy* and the Color of Gender." *American Literature* 64.2 (June 1992): 273–97.

Zaroulis, Nancy, and Gerald Sullivan. *Who Spoke Up? American Protest against the War in Vietnam, 1963–1965*. New York: Doubleday, 1984.

Index

A

ABC television, 32

acculturation, 6, 171

Achebe, Chinua, *Things Fall Apart*, 180, 207, 254 (n. 7), 255 (n. 17)

Adventures of Point-Man Palmer in Vietnam, The (Grant), 218, 219

Afghanistan, war in, 2, 45

African/African American cultural history, 54, 96; and heroic quest, 212

African American Literature Book Club, 11

African American novel, 5, 7–8, 219. *See also* Black writers

African American Review, 241 (n. 8)

"African-Centeredness and the New Black Millennium" (Verharen), 167

African Diaspora, 1, 59, 83, 193, 245 (n. 1); Bench by the Road Project

commemorates significant sites across, 4, 240 (n. 3)

African myth: and dying hero in Vietnam War novels, 213; in epics, 212; and folklore, 196, 199, 213; ritual colors in, 102–3; Tree of Life in, 73

African Openings to the Tree of Life (Peters), 89

Afro-American Novel and Its Tradition, The (Bell, Bernard), 7

"Afro-Eurasian Eclipse" (Ellington) (song), 128

Afrocentric culture, 2, 5; and cosmology, 199; dialogue in, 178; and extended self, 213; and healing, 110; time in, 65, 180–81, 246 (n. 4); "twinness" in, 56; world view, 10, 65, 70, 94, 169, 177, 178

aggregation, 154, 161, 176

Akan people, 62, 245 (n. 3)

Alexander, Margaret Walker, *Jubilee*, 21

Ali, Muhammad (Cassius Clay), 2, 43–44

allegories: of Ananse and Sky God, 76;
of *Captain Blackman*, 57, 77, 78; and
identity in *Runner Mack*, 223; of Vodoun,
95

All-Night Visitors (Major), 8, 223

American Adam, The (Lewis, W. R. B.), 45

American Book Award, 11

American Revolution, Black soldiers in, 12,
20, 64–68, 75, 174

American Scholar, The, 11

American Visions (magazine), 12

Ammons, Gene (Jug), 142; "Willow Weep for
Me," 134

Amos, W. J., *M.I.A.*, 219

Ananse (Biggers), 59, 62

Ananse the Spider, 2, 63; Baker on, 62;
Biggers on gender entity of, 59, 62, 250
(n. 18); as *Captain Blackman*'s motif,
10, 62, 87; as dual-gendered, 62, 109;
power of, 64; trickster myth of, 58, 62; in
vernacular theory, 60

And Then We Heard the Thunder (Killens),
23–24

Anderson, Earl R., 253 (n. 1)

Anderson, S. E., "Junglegrave," 19, 36

Anderson, T. J., *Soldier Boy, Soldier*, 121, 220

Angelou, Maya, *Georgia, Georgia*, 34–36, 243
(n. 10)

Ani, Marimba, 8, 56, 175, 199, 212

Another Good Loving Blues (Flowers), 13

Ansah, S. L., 62, 87

Apocalypse Now (film), 29, 45; and Conrad's
Heart of Darkness, 47

Ar'n't I a Woman? (Gray), 83

Army. *See* U.S. Army

Arnold, Ben, 220

Asante, Molefi, 54, 55, 76

Ashanti people, 62, 245 (n. 3)

Ashes and Embers (Gerima) (film), 35–37

assassinations of civil rights leaders, 26, 38,
44, 81, 155, 198

assimilation, 8, 91, 140

Association for the Study of Negro Life and
History, 51

autobiographies (Black), 13–14, 24, 31, 42,
200; on Vietnam War, 39, 206, 223, 254
(n. 14)

Autobiography of an Ex-Coloured Man, The
(Johnson, James Weldon), 200

awards: film, 17, 32, 36, 243 (n. 10); literary, 11,
43, 221; as medals in war novels, 74, 76;
military, 74, 100; recognition through, 100

B

Bachelard, Gaston, 200

Bahktin, Mikhail, 177

Baker, Houston, Jr.: on access to African slave
women, 83–84; on Ananse, 62; on Black
identity crisis, 156; and Black phallic
symbol, 69, 82; "Black (w)hole" trope
of, 156, 213, 253 (n. 18), 254–55 (n. 15);
on Blackness and artistic-ness, 9; *Blues,
Ideology, and Afro-American Literature*,
10, 69; and blues matrix, 10; on liminality,
62, 195; on *Mojo Rising*, 14; on paradigm
shift trope, 241 (n. 11); on rite-of-passage
ceremony, 154; "space/place" framework
used by, 179; trickster of, 83; *Workings of
the Spirit*, 179

Baldwin, James, 16, 125, 255 (n. 16); *The Fire Next Time*, 152

Bamboozled (Lee, Spike) (film), 16

Baraka, Amiri, 135, 139

Barnett, Charlie, "Cherokee," 135

Barthold, Bonnie, 199; *Black Time*, 181

*Bat*21* (film), 32–33, 254 (n. 12)

Bates, Milton, *The Wars We Took to Vietnam*, 25, 171

"Battle Royal" (Ellison), 163, 246 (n. 6)

bebop, 135, 138, 144–46, 153, 160, 252 (n. 12), 252 (n. 14)

Beckham, Barry, *Runner Mack*, 8, 223

Beheiren, 42, 208, 209, 254 (n. 14)

Beidler, Phillip, 46, 60

Bell, Bernard, 5, 6, 8, 22, 23; *The Afro-American Novel and Its Tradition*, 7; taproot and cultural retentions, 106; on time shifts, 65; on "toast," 54, 55

Bell, Derrick, 192

Bell, Harold, 27

Bell, William, "Marching Off to War," 25

Beloved (Morrison), 136, 174, 240 (n. 3), 246 (n. 4); imagination in, 5

Bench by the Road Project, 4, 240 (n. 3)

Berkshire Edge, The (website publication), 15

Bertrand Russell International War Crimes Tribunal, 26

Betrayed (Wilson, D. B.), 221

"Beyond Vietnam" (King Jr.), 31, 44, 245 (n. 22), 251 (n. 4)

Biggers, John: *Ananse*, 59, 62; on female entity [Ananse], 59, 250 (n. 18); and trickster tales, 61–62

Billingsley, Ronald, 171

binary opposition, 56, 175, 176, 194

binary thinking: of Black males, 125; in *Coming Home*, 169–70, 174–79, 181–84, 188–89, 191–92, 206–7; definition of, 176; and dialectic discourse, 177; Elbow on, 177–78; in *Middle Passage*, 253 (n. 5); as rhetoric, 77

Bird. *See* Parker, Charlie (Bird, Birdland)

Birth of a Nation, The (Griffith) (film), 50, 51

Bjorkman, Stig, 35

Black, Brown and Beige (Ellington) (song), 140

Black Aesthetic, 9, 241 (n. 10); and New Black Aesthetic," 10, 215

Black Arts and Black Aesthetics (Fowler), 241 (n. 10)

Black Culture and Black Consciousness (Levine), 52, 53

Black English (Ebonics), 201. *See also* Black Idiom; signifyin(g)/signifying

Black Enterprise (BE) (magazine), 18

Black female characters, 50. *See also* stereotypes

Black film (genre): definition of, 33; earliest, 33; on Vietnam War, 31–35. *See also* names of individual films

Black heroism: angst of, 168; cultural image of, 8, 124, 214; documenting, 51–53, 55, 87; and fear of Black male, 8; humaneness of, 55; and identity, 134, 185–86, 205, 210; Killens explores, 23–24; "mission" of, 55; and racism, 3, 58; and relationship with Black community, 55, 58, 212, 214; re-membering of, 2, 212; Revolutionary examples of, 20; stages of quest for, 185–87, 197, 205, 207–8; stereotypes of, 51; toast examples of, 55, 247 (n. 10); in Vietnam War novels, 2, 3, 8,

55, 58, 114, 185, 214; in war novels, 20; and
White hero models, 49; in WWII novels,
23. *See also* Du Bois, W. E. B.; Negroes;
Shine, as Black hero; toast (theme)

Black History Month, 51, 103

Black Holocaust. *See* Middle Passage

Black Idiom, 10, 129, 130; and language codes,
201; as language expressions, 138–39, 155

Black language, 10; "buzz talk" in, 138–39,
155; as "hieroglyphics," 142; vernacular as
private, 139

Black liberation flag, 15; as military flag, 104;
ritual colors of, 102–3, 112

Black Life in Corporate America (Davis and
Watson), 17, 18

Black male: "dap" bonding ritual of, 90,
104–6, 116, 119, 136, 249 (n. 13), 250 (n.
14); fear of, 8, 9, 21; and heroism, 124;
identity search of, 122, 125, 215, 253 (n.
18); and improvisation, 157; masculinity
of, 125–26, 151, 153, 157, 190–92; and
oppression and racism, 54, 175; as
powerless, 90; in rodeo circuit, 21; self
concept of, 188, 208; and stereotype,
167; and "street committee"/"Street
Institution," 124, 137

Black Male, The (Marable), 167

Black Marines against the Brass (Stapp and
Jolls), 38

"Black Masculinity and Visual Culture"
(Gray), 125, 188

Black nationalists, 26, 33, 155–56

Black No More (Schuyler, George S.), 216, 255
(n. 1)

Black Panther (Coogler) (film), 213–14

Black Panther, The (newspaper), 27

Black Panther Party, 15, 26, 27, 54, 156

"black phallus," 69, 82–83, 246 (n. 6);
mythology of, 130

Black power handshake. *See* dapping
(dapline)

Black regiments, post-Civil war: Buffalo
soldiers, 71; Ninth Cavalry, 21, 71; Tenth
Cavalry, 21, 71–72; Twenty-fifth Infantries,
21; in war novels, 64, 66, 70–71, 75, 79, 162

"Black Samson," 20

Black Semantics, 10, 53, 133

Black soldiers: atrocities against, 67–68;
dapping by, 90, 249 (n. 13); desertion,
22, 35, 42, 57, 68, 168, 206, 209, 215;
discrimination against, 23–24, 30, 38,
61, 65, 69, 79, 86, 104–5, 244 (n. 19), 244
(n. 21); "double V" symbol of, 23–24, 144;
draft rate for, 27, 43; and EM clubs, 104,
200, 207; as enlisted men, 20, 22–24,
43, 71, 140, 170–71, 202, 245 (n. 27); and
equality, 20; as fatalities, 26, 218; novels
by and about, 2–3, 7–8, 240 (n. 1); power
salute of, 90; reenlistment of, 26, 61,
66, 214, 225; regiments of, 21; and unit
disbanding, 21; valor of, 20–22, 24, 100.
See also names of individual novels

Black Time (Barthold), 181

"Black (w)hole," 156, 213, 253 (n. 18), 254–55
(n. 15)

Black women, in Black novels, 48

Black writers: awards for, 11; codify memories
of past, 5; juvenile literature by, 223;
myth, legend and ritual used by, 7;
non-fiction by, 39, 44; on opposition
to war, 44; poetry by, 44; on point-man
assignments, 39; popularity problems of,

3; are re-membering, 2, 5; reviews of, 3; toasts used by, 55; works on Vietnam War by, 7, 43–44, 48, 60, 90–97, 106, 116–20, 147, 169, 215, 221–40 (n. 1). *See also names of individual novels, poems, plays, and films*

"Black Writer's Use of Memory, The" (Dixon, Melvin), 1, 2

blackface, 51; and minstrelsy, 16, 49, 118

Blackness, 2, 9, 47, 172, 178, 184

Blake, Susan, 192, 196

Bloods (Terry), 30, 37, 43, 148

"bloods," 30, 38, 105

blues: Beale Street as birthplace of, 13, 108, 112; and Black vernacular, 87, 143; classic structure of, 139; definition of, 115, 139; Flowers's performances as, 13; and identity, 157, 165; jazz and, 122, 126, 129, 133–35, 139; and Mississippi River, 108; songs of, 79, 143, 164, 201; and Soul Alley, 200; and *Stagolee* legend, 54

Blues, Ideology, and Afro-American Literature (Baker), 10, 69

blues matrix, 10

Bluest Eye, The (Morrison), 136

Bodey, Donald, *F. N. G.*, 29

Bogle, Donald, *Toms, Coons, Mulattoes, Mammies, & Bucks*, 49–50

Bolar, L. J., *The One They Called Quiet*, 221; *Quartermaster Rangers*, 222

Bombingham (Grooms), 221, 222

Bond, Julian, 44, 244–45 (n. 21), 255 (n. 5); *Bond et al. v. Floyd et al.*, 218, 255 (n. 6); *Vietnam: An Antiwar Comic Book*, 217–18, 219

Bowling for Columbine (Moore), 8, 240 (n. 6)

Boyd, Cindy Dawson, *Charlie Pippin*, 224

Boys in Company C (film), 29

Brer Rabbit Retold (Flowers), 14

"Bring My Buddies Back" (song), 256 (n. 3)

Brodie, Bill, *Terry Whitmore, for Example*, 31, 42

"brothers," 19, 30, 38, 80, 90, 104, 105, 116–17

Brothers (Sanders), 19, 37

Brown, Caesar, 20

Brown, Cecil, 55; *Stagolee Shot Billy*, 54

Brown, Wesley: *Dance of the Infidels*, 15, 16; *Darktown Strutters*, 16; genres written by, 15–16; Ginsburg referenced by, 252 (n. 14); jazz and storytelling by, 15, 124, 129; neorealism of, 8; prison experience of, 124; *Push Comes to Shove*, 16; reviewed *De Mojo Blues*, 13, 241 (n. 17); style as theme of, 151–52; *Tragic Magic*, 3, 15, 57, 122, 124–29, 133, 136–37, 152–53, 161–62, 165; tripartite structure used by, 154; "You Talk Like You Got Books in Your Jaws," 142. See also *Tragic Magic* (Brown)

Browne, Malcolm W. (photographer), 252–53 (n. 17)

Browne, Robert, 44, 244 (n. 20)

Bryant, Jerry H., 168

Buffalo Soldiers, 21, 64, 70–71, 174

Buffalo Soldiers (Glover) (film), 71

Buffalo Soldiers (Williams, Kimo) (symphony), 225

Buffalo Soldiers Museum, 71

Bunch, Lonnie, III, 4, 240 (n. 5)

Bus Is Coming, The (Franklin) (film), 33

Bush, George W., 240 (n. 5)

"buzz talk," 138–39, 155

C

Cadence (film), 33

call-and-response, 128; in *Coming Home*, 177, 178, 179, 184; jazzerly, 133, 137, 144, 164; in *Tragic Magic*, 164, 130, 137–39

"cappin," 146, 246 (n. 9)

Captain Blackman (Williams): African Tree of Life in, 73–74; ambivalence theme in, 82; Anansean motif in, 62–66, 70, 77, 80, 83, 86–87, 214; Black Everyman in, 64, 65, 76; Black history knowledge in, 87, 214; black phallus theme in, 82–83; on Black soldiers in war, 3, 11–13, 65, 70, 78–79, 82, 86; Black vernacular in, 86, 87; Blackman as epic hero in, 74, 76, 84; Blackman's character traits, 80; blues paradigm in, 79, 87; "Cadences" in, 70–71, 82, 84; character reappearance device in, 72, 73; critical realism in, 8; cultural memory, 60, 61, 70, 77; demoralization in, 84; desperation in, 79; "Drumtaps" in, 70, 71, 82; heroism in, 57, 58, 70, 72, 76; historical events in, 70; Mimosa in, 48, 72–74, 76, 81, 84; mulatto strike force in, 82, 84–86; mythic time structure weaving in, 64–66, 72–75, 84; plantation tradition in, 86; racism in, 85; sexual exploitation in, 81–83, 84; "shadow play in," 66, 82–83; "Shine" in, 79; signification in, 80–81, 84, 86; signifying in, 78, 80–81, 83, 84; and Signifying Monkey, 77–79; signifying on coon stereotype in, 86; symbolism in, 70, 73–76, 82–84, 86; "toast" in, 77, 78, 79; trickster in, 78–79, 81–84, 86; White everyman officer in, 75, 76

Caputo, Phillip, *A Rumor of War*, 46, 47

Carruth, Hayden, 141

Carter G. Woodson Award, 11

Cash, Earl A., 12

Catch 22 (Heller), 31

Cato, Charly, 25–26

Cauley, Anne, 208

CBS television, 12, 32

Chaney, Michael, 10

Charlie Pippin (Boyd) (YA novel), 224

chattel, 21, 190, 192, 208

Chicago Defender (newspaper), 12

ChickenBones (online journal), 13

CIA, 41, 217, 222

civil rights movement, jazz concerts for, 252 (n. 15)

Civil War: African American veterans of, 4; army size reduction after, 21; atrocities against Blacks at Fort Pillow, 68, 69; Black soldiers in, 20–21, 64, 68, 81, 140; and Jim Crow, 16; novels, 20; Union Army in, 20–21, 64, 140

Clansman, The (Dixon, Thomas), 50

Clay, Cassius (Muhammad Ali), 2, 43–44

Cleveland Lee's Beale Street Band (Flowers) (YA novel), 13

Clinton, Bill, 23

Close Quarters (Heinemann), 46

Cohesion (Williams, Thomas D.), 48, 221, 249 (n. 12)

Coleman, James, 122; "Language, Reality, and Self in Wesley Brown's *Tragic Magic*," 128

Collider, The (entertainment website), 213

Coltrane, John (Trane), 15, 125, 160–61

Coming Home (Davis): 16; and African cosmology, 180, 199; African Star Club in, 201–2, 206, 208–9; Air Force bombing in, 167–72, 179, 181, 195, 202; ancestral Black folklore in, 196, 199, 213; ascendant mode in, 205; binary thinking in, 169–70, 174–79, 181–84, 188–89, 191–92, 206–7; Black characters in, 54, 57, 169–71, 178–79, 184–85, 198; Black cultural heritage and, 194, 197, 201; Black hero angst in, 168, 171; Black masculinity adaptations in, 190–91; call-and-response in, 177, 178, 179, 184; character named sections of, 180, 210; conqueror mentality in, 189; conquest and capitalism in, 188–89; and desertion to Sweden, 57, 201, 202, 205, 207–8, 225, 253 (n. 1); dialogic versus dialectic discourse in, 177–78; diunital thinking in, 178, 207; double-consciousness in, 10, 174, 178–79, 182, 187, 195–96, 198; empathy in, 220; Eurocentric world view in, 178, 179, 188, 199; as "fictional oral narrative," 174; film based on, 17; "Flying Home" compared to, 196, 203–5; flying symbology and bondage in, 192, 193, 194, 202, 215; freedom in, 198, 209–10; Harvard in, 166, 171, 175, 178–79, 186–87, 192–99, 201, 209, 215; heroic quest stages in, 185–87, 205, 209; heroism in, 57, 169, 171, 178; hyperbole in, 173; identity in, 57, 166–69, 173, 178, 180–86, 195, 201–2, 206–10, 213; immersion in, 197–99; "Introduction" by Watkins, 168; killing in, 203; liminality in, 194, 195; manhood in, 54; memory in, 174–75, 193, 200; metaphor in, 174, 195, 199; narrative focus in, 174–75, 180–85; naturalism of, 8, 168; as *nostos*, 253 (n. 1); officers clubs in, 200, 202, 206; Platonism in, 175, 176, 188, 197, 199; psychological ramifications of war in, 167–71, 174, 202; racism challenges in, 168, 172, 175, 184, 208; re-membering in, 180, 196, 203, 210; "rememory" in, 174; reviews of, 3, 17, 168, 184, 253 (nn. 1–2); sexual stereotype in, 190, 191; signification in, 201; signifyin(g) in, 173, 255 (n. 15); Signifying Monkey in, 172–73; space-place in, 179–81, 192–206; speakerly text in, 178; stream-of-consciousness in, 169; style of, 181; symbolism in, 192–94, 197, 198, 200, 206; Thailand in, 169–71, 176, 179–81, 189, 196–98, 200, 208, 210; themes in, 22, 58, 166, 167–69, 187–88; and transcendence of hero quest, 207–8; trickster in, 195; tripartite structure of, 168, 175, 185–86, 203–4; and vernacular culture in, 58, 178, 196, 201; voice in, 184

Coming Home (film), 17, 253 (n. 2)

communism, 25, 28, 56; MIGs of, 254 (n. 6); in novels, 170, 173, 181, 183–84, 187, 195–96, 203

Connecting Times (Harris, Norman), 9, 185

Conrad, Joseph, *Heart of Darkness*, 47

conscientious objectors, 225; Ali as, 43–44; in *Coming Home*, 166; in MLK Jr. speech, 251 (n. 4); in *Tragic Magic*, 48, 57, 120–24, 130–31, 135, 140, 155–56, 161, 214

Contemporary Black Biography, 17

Coogler, Ryan, *Black Panther*, 213–14

Cooke, Benjamin, 104, 105

cool, as survival strategy, 153

cool jazz, 144; of Lester Young, 153, 154

cool pose, 153

Cool Pose (Majors, et. al), 153

coon: as plantation stereotype, 50, 86; types of, 49

Cose, Ellis, 146; *The Envy of the World*, 151–52

Couch, William, Jr., 31

Count Basie Band, 134

Counter-Intelligence Program (COINTELPRO), 26, 27

Crane, Stephen, *Red Badge of Courage*, 31, 223–24

Creek, Mardena, 45–46

Crisis Magazine (NAACP), 22

critical realism, 8

cultural memory: African, 55, 99; American, 125; of Blacks, 3, 126, 135, 170, 180, 187, 194, 197–99, 203; in *Captain Blackman*, 60, 61, 70, 77; in *Coming Home*, 170, 174, 180, 187, 194, 197–99, 203; definition of, 6, 126; in *De Mojo Blues*, 119; and heroic models, 125; racism and, 6, 61; retained in soul, 126; and rise of common quest, 6; and ritual colors, 102–3; and survival, 129; and Thailand, 197, 198; in *Tragic Magic*, 126, 135; and voodoo, 99

"cultural other," 8

Culture of Fear, The (Glassner), 9, 45

"culture of violence," 45, 240 (n. 6)

D

Da 5 Bloods (Lee, Spike) (film), 224, 225

Dalby, David, "The African Element in American English," 1, 6

Dance of the Infidels (Brown, Wesley), 15, 16

Daniels, George, 38

dapping (dapline), 119, 136, 249 (n. 13); definition of, 104–5, 116, 250 (n. 14)

Dash, Julie, 104; *Daughters of the Dust*, 246 (n. 4), 250 (n. 14)

Dau Tranh! (Schuyler), 216

Daughters of the Dust (Dash) (book) (film), 246 (n. 4), 250 (n. 14)

Davis, Angela, 84

Davis, Benjamin O., Sr., 22

Davis, George: *Black Life in Corporate America*, 17, 18; career of, 17–18; *Melting Points*, 17; *Spiritual Intelligence*, 18; Spiritual Intelligence Project, 18. See also *Coming Home* (Davis)

Davis, Miles, 125, 160; "So What," 144, 164; "Walkin'," 136, 161

Davis, Ossie, 33

Davis, Sammy, Jr., 24

Davis, Zeinabu, 33, 243 (n. 7)

de Jongh, James L., 11

De Mojo Blues (Flowers), 3, 14, 39, 53–56, 92, 104–5; on Blacks in Vietnam, 89–91; critical realism in, 8, 88; dapping for unity in, 104, 116, 117, 118; double-consciousness in, 110; dreamstate in, 113, 215; dual personality in, 110; flashback in, 112, 118; griot in, 108; healer in, 93, 107–9, 215; hero in, 52, 57–58, 94–97, 100, 101, 109, 114; identity in, 117; High John de Conquer persona in, 58, 97, 107–9, 114, 118–19; hoodoo in, 10, 96, 101, 106, 109, 111, 114, 249 (n. 11); Hoodooman in, 13, 97, 113, 114–15, 116; mask of cool in, 109–10; mojo/mojo bag as knowledge in, 97, 98, 100, 106, 112–15, 117, 118, 120; Moses myth in, 96, 106; and orishas, 101–3, 107, 109–11, 115; power of history in, 91, 98, 108, 114, 118; power paths in, 115–18; reconnecting or re-membering in, 94, 99, 101, 108, 116;

ritual colors in, 102–3, 109; "Shine and the Titanic," in, 118; signification in, 96, 106; signifying in, 112; suppression in, 99; survival in, 113, 114–15, 118–19; symbology in, 99, 103, 106, 107, 112–13, 118; time changes in, 94, 114; trickster in, 99–101, 109, 115; tripartite structure of, 96–97, 112; and vernacular culture, 58; visions in, 112, 114; Vodoun/voodoo in, 10, 13, 87–88, 93–96, 99–102, 109–13, 215, 249 (n. 11); Voodooman in, 118

Deadwood Dick, 21

Del Vecchio, John M., *The 13th Valley*, 29, 30, 171

Delgrès, Louis, 4

Dellums, Ronald, 44, 244 (n. 21)

Descartes, [René], 175, 176

desertion: by Black soldiers, 22, 35, 42, 57, 68, 168, 206, 209, 215; in *Coming Home*, 57, 201, 202, 205, 207–8, 225, 253 (n. 1); in film, 31, 35; *Memphis-Nam-Sweden* on, 42, 168, 205, 206, 254 (n. 14); in novels, 17, 22, 48, 81, 169–70, 215, 225, 253 (n. 1)

dialectic discourse, 5, 6; and binary thinking, 177; in *Coming Home*, 177–78; rhetorical, 177; in *Tragic Magic*, 151

"Diminuendo and Crescendo in Blue" (Ellington) (song), 154

Dinerstein, Joel, 153; "Lester Young and the Birth of Cool," 154

Directors Guild of America, 33

discourse: Black, 6; dialogic versus dialectic, 177–78

dishonorable discharge, 219; in *De Mojo Blues*, 58, 88, 91, 114, 225

Dispatches (Herr), 29, 30, 46, 49

diunital thinking, 175, 177, 178, 198, 207

Dixon, Ivan, 32

Dixon, Melvin: "The Black Writer's Use of Memory," 1, 2; on identity disruption, 5

Dixon, Thomas, *The Clansman*, 50

Dog Soldiers (Stone, Robert), 47

Doty, William G, 62

double-consciousness, 5, 10, 86, 110, 174, 178–79, 182, 187, 195–98

"double V" symbol, 23–24, 144

Douglass, Frederick, 20, 51

Doyle, Mary Ellen, 188

Du Bois, W. E. B.: and Black and White heroism, 48–49, 51, 208; and double-consciousness, 5, 10, 86, 110, 178–79; *The Souls of Black Folk*, 86; on treatment of Black soldiers, 22; on White heroism victimizing Blacks, 48

dualism, 194, 253 (n. 5)

E

Early, Gerald, 146, 252 (n. 14)

Ebony (magazine), 12, 244 (n. 19)

Edgerton, Robert, 245 (n. 27), 247 (n. 2)

Egejuru, Phanuel A., 255 (n. 17)

Ehrhart, William D., 148

Eisenhower, Dwight D., 69

Elbow, Peter, 177–78

Ellington, Duke, 125–27, 138; "Afro-Eurasian Eclipse," 128; arts integration by, 140; *Black, Brown and Beige*, 140; "Blutopia," 164; cool jazz style of, 128, 144, 153; "Diminuendo and Crescendo in Blue," 154; and *Tragic Magic*, 139, 140, 141, 154, 164

Ellison, Ralph: "Battle Royal," 163, 246 (n. 6);

"Flying Home," 196, 203, 205; influences on, 143; *Invisible Man*, 1, 57, 82, 122–28, 163, 195, 206–7, 251 (n. 6), 254 (n. 11); as jazz musician, 123; jazz tradition theme of, 139

emancipation, 6, 21, 52

Emancipation Proclamation, 71, 140

Envy of the World, The (Cose), 151–52

epics: African, 80, 98, 211–12; hero in, 74, 76, 84

Epic of Sundiata, 80, 98, 212

Essence (magazine), 12, 18

Estabrook, Prince, 66, 67

"Ethics of Living Jim Crow, The" (Wright, Richard), 252 (n. 13)

Euro-American imagination, 47–48

Euro-American myth, 55–56, 188, 189; hero in, 124

Eurocentric culture, 176; hero champion of, 212; and mythology, 95; on peoples of color, 46; and self and power, 212

Evers, Medgar, 26

"extended self," 213

F

Fabre, Geneviève, 180; *History and Memory in African-American Culture*, 6

Fallen Angels (Myers, Walter Dean) (YA novel), 223, 224

Fanfare for Life (Williams, Kimo) (symphony), 225

Fanti people, 62, 245 (n. 3)

FBI, 26–27, 183

fictional narratives: in African American tradition, 7; by Black writers, 5; and film, 36; of George Davis, 16–18; racism in, 47;

of Wesley Brown, 15–16

Fields of Fire (Webb), 29, 47

Fighting on Two Fronts (Westheider), 248 (n. 6), 249 (nn. 12–13), 254 (n. 8)

films: archetypal of Black experience in Vietnam, 35–37; Black, definition of, 33; Black directors in, 33, 34, 213; blackface in, 51; Black performers in, 31, 33; Black screenwriters, 34, 213; Black stereotypes in, 50; and Black Vietnam War, 32, 34, 36; earliest Black, 33; and industry racism, 33; soundtracks, 35–36. *See also names of individual films and filmmakers*

Fire Next Time, The (Baldwin), 152

Fitzgerald, Ella, 141, 142, 150

Flame in the Icebox (Morrison), 221

flashbacks, 13, 34, 112, 118, 137, 222

Flowers, A. R.: African myths adapted by, 213; *Another Good Loving Blues*, 13; *Brer Rabbit Retold*, 14; career of, 13; *Cleveland Lee's Beale Street Band*, 13; as griot, 13; on hoodoo and voodoo, 249 (n. 11); *I See the Promised Land*, 14; *Mojo Rising*, 13–14; *Rootwork the Rootsblog*, 14; signification by, 13; sorcerer as hero of, 100–102; themes used by, 13, 39, 101, 225; Vodoun symbols used by, 13, 95, 101, 112. See also *De Mojo Blues* (Flowers)

flying: bondage symbology in, 193, 194, 202, 215; as symbolic Middle Passage, 192

"Flying Home" (Ellison), 196, 203–5

F. N. G. (Bodey), 29

Foley, Barbara, 69, 188

Foner, Jack, 38

Ford, Clyde, 94, 100; *The Hero with an African Face*, 55–56, 96, 211–12, 246 (n. 8); on orishas, 101, 102, 103, 107

Forrest, Nathan Bedford, 68

Forten, James, 20

Fowler, Carolyn, *Black Arts and Black Aesthetics*, 241 (n. 10)

fragging: and Black soldiers, 1, 58, 90, 91, 114, 117, 215, 245 (n. 27); definitions of, 247 (n. 2)

Franklin, Clyde, 190, 191

Franklin, John Hope, *From Slavery to Freedom*, 23

Franklin, Wendell, 243 (n. 7); *The Bus Is Coming*, 33

Freejack soldiers, 68

French, Albert, *Patches of Fire*, 223

French Army, 67

French Flying Corps, 67

From Trickster to Badman (Roberts), 53, 54

Full Metal Jacket [Kubrick] (film), 47

Funderburg, Lisa, 216

G

Garvey, Marcus, 51; Back to Africa Movement, 103

Gates, Henry Louis, Jr.: on Black language, 10; "The Blackness of Blackness," 89; "repetition and revision" trope used by, 9, 83, 122, 132; on "revising text," 122; on signifyin(g)/signifying, 132, 172, 250 (n. 1), 251 (n. 9); *The Signifying Monkey*, 10, 11, 77–78, 135, 250 (n. 1); and Smitherman, 132; on "speakerly text," 15, 129, 178; on "toast," 77; on trickster as topos, 77

Gaye, Marvin, 28

Georgakas, Dan, 68, 69

Georgia, Georgia (Angelou) (film), 34–36, 243 (n. 10)

Gerima, Haile, *Ashes and Embers*, 35–37

Ghana, 36, 249 (n. 9); Akan people of, 62, 245 (n. 3)

G.I. Diary (Parks, David), 39, 42

Giap, Vo Nguyen, 28

Giddens, Gary, 144

Gillespie, Dizzy, "Ooh, Shoo Bee Doo Bee," 160

Gilmore, F. Frank, *Problem*, 22

Ginsburg, Allen: as jazz poet, 252 (n. 14); *100 Years of Lynching*, 155

Glassner, Barry, 45, 46; *The Culture of Fear*, 9

Glover, Danny: in *Bat*21*, 33, 254 (n. 12); *Buffalo Soldiers*, 71

Goff, Stanley, *Brothers*, 37

Going After Cacciato (O'Brien, Tim), 29, 46

Goldberg, Matt, 213

Golus, Carrie, 15

Gordon's War (film), 33

Gould, Jack, 31–32

Grant, Vernon: *The Adventures of Point-Man Palmer in Vietnam*, 218, 219; 50th Officer Course Classbook, 219; reviews of works by, 219

graphic novels: by Bond, 217–18; by Flowers, 14; by Grant, 218–19

Gray, Herman, "Black Masculinity and Visual Culture," 125, 188

Great Migration, 6, 128

Green, John, 22

Green Berets, The (Moore, Robin), 46

Green Eyes (ABC TV film), 32

Greenlee, Sam, *The Spook Who Sat by the Door*, 222

"Greetings (This Is Uncle Sam)," (song) 25, 255 (n. 1)

Griffin, Farah Jasmine, 137

Griffith, D. W., *The Birth of a Nation*, 50, 51

Grimes, William, 11

griots: as African memory personified, 60; as *Captain Blackman* character, 65; definition of, 13, 60; D'Jimo as, 108; Flowers as, 13, 14; heroic struggle and, 98, 108; Kouyate as, 59, 60, 108

Griot, The (Pugh), 211, 220

Grooms, Anthony, *Bombingham*, 221, 222

Guidry, Richard, *The War in I Corps*, 221

Gullah Islands, 246 (n. 4), 250 (n. 14)

Gullah Jack, 100, 114

H

Hackworth, David, "The Point Man," 248 (n. 4); *The Price of Honor*, 248 (n. 4)

Hall, Prince, 20

Hambleton, Iceal, 32, 33

Hamburger Hill (film), 32

Hamer, Fannie Lou, 141

Hanshaw, Shirley, "'What's Goin' On?'," 243 (n. 4)

Harlem Renaissance, 7, 16, 22, 214, 216

harmony: Afrocentric, 56, 177, 213; community, 55–56, 58, 97, 213; with nature, 197; in *Tragic Magic*, 122

Harper, Frances E. W., *Iola Leroy*, 20

Harrington, Colin, 16

Harris, Norman, 10, 103, 174; *Connecting Times*, 9, 185, 186, 196

Harris, Trudier, 54, 82

Harvard, 17, 18, 23; in *Coming Home*, 166, 175, 178–79, 186–87, 192–94, 197–99, 201, 209,

215; in *Fighting on Two Fronts*, 254 (n. 8)

Harvey, William, 38

Hasford, Gustav, *Short Timers*, 47

Heinemann, Larry, *Close Quarters*, 46

Heller, Joseph, *Catch 22*, 31

Hendrix, Jimi, 28

Henry, John, 51–52

Hentoff, Nat, 128

Herald-Journal (newspaper), 12

hero (concept): Blackman as epic, 74; definition of, 61, 211; and group identity, 213; High John as, 52, 58, 97, 107; and orishas, 101–3, 107, 109–11, 115; questing, 212

Hero with an African Face, The (Ford), 55–56, 96, 211–12, 246 (n. 8)

heroes (historic and from literature): Audie Murphy, 148; Benjamin Banneker, 51; Black, 8, 55; Crispus Attucks, 51, 67; Daniel Boone, 52, 61; Davy Crockett, 61, 147, 212; Father Divine, 51; Frederick Douglass, 20, 51; Gabriel Prosser, 51; Harriet Tubman, 51; in "Jack/John" tales, 52; John Henry, 51–52; John Wayne type of, 52, 123–25, 140, 146–49, 212, 214, 252 (n. 12, 146); Marcus Garvey, 51, 103; Nat Turner, 51, 114; Paul Bunyan, 212; Paul Robeson, 51, 255 (n. 16); Randolph Scott, 140, 146; Robin Hood, 148; Shine, 55; and Signifyin(g) monkey, 55; Sojourner Truth, 51; Staggerlee, 54–55; in *Tragic Magic*, 124. *See also* Black heroism; White heroes

heroism: alone, in Western culture, 57; and "bad man," 51, 54, 55; Black, 20; as ideal, 51, 124, 140; tricksters in, 52, 61; White, 48, 212

Herr, Michael, *Dispatches*, 29, 30, 46, 49

Herzog, Tobey, 146, 147

High John de Conquer (also High John the Conqueror), 2, 55; and devil, 52, 250 (n. 16); as first slave, 52, 107; as healer, 108; as hero, 52, 58, 97, 107; as power, 52; root of, 97, 106, 107, 108; symbolizes survival, 107–8; and Tucept character, 58, 97, 106–8, 115

History and Memory in African-American Culture (O'Meally), 6

Holiday, Billie, 15, 36

Hollingsworth, Dell, 145, 252 (n. 14)

Home to Harlem (McKay), 22, 253 (n. 19)

Home News (newspaper), 15

hoodoo, 10, 96, 101, 106, 109, 111, 114, 249 (n. 11)

Hoodooman, 13, 97, 113, 114–15, 116

Hoover, J. Edgar, 26–27

Horton, John, 151

Hounon, Mamaissii Vivian Dansi, 89, 95–96; on Hoodoo and voodoo, 249 (n. 11)

Hudson-Weems, Clenora, 174

Hughes, Langston, "The Negro Speaks of Rivers," 250 (n. 17)

Hurston, Zora Neale: *Dust Tracks on a Road*, 142; *Moses, Man of the Mountain*, 96, 249 (n. 10); *Their Eyes Were Watching God*, 13, 205, 209

Hynes, William, 62

hyperbole, 173

I

I See the Promised Land (Flowers), 14

identity, 139; biracial, 5, 20, 216, 217; Black experience in Vietnam and, 3; and Black heroism, 134, 185–86, 205, 210; Black male, 253 (n. 18); in *Coming Home*, 57, 166–69, 173, 178, 180–86, 195, 201–2, 206–10, 213; double-consciousness and, 5; and "nigrescence," 3; search for, 22, 57; and Vietnamese, 3

identity crisis, of Black war veteran, 37, 140, 156

Ifill, Gwen, 141

imagination: in *Beloved*, 5; Black character stereotypes from, 49; "comic" characters in, 49; Euro-American, 47; and memory, 5; in song, 79

improvisation: Ellison uses, 128; as heroic, 252 (n. 14); and identity, 128; Murray on flexibility in, 127; and survival, 121, 127, 139; in *Tragic Magic*, 129

Indian wars, Buffalo Soldiers in, 21, 64, 70–71, 174

IndieWire, 34

integration, 5, 9; in military, 23, 25

Interracial Civil Rights Group, 218

Invisible Man (Ellison), 1, 57, 122–23, 127–28, 163, 195, 206–7, 251 (n. 6), 254 (n. 11); Black phallic symbol in, 82

Iola Leroy (Harper), 20

Iraq, 9, 45

irony, 23, 67, 71, 216

J

Jackson, Blyden, 249 (n. 10); *Operation Burning Candle*, 222

Jackson, Gale, 95

Jackson-Lowman, Huberta, 3–4

Jade (King-Gamble), 224

Jahn, Johnheinz, 70

"Jane Crow," 6

Japanese underground (Beheiren), 42, 208, 209, 254 (n. 14)

Jason, Philip K.: *Fourteen Landing Zones*, 47, 239 (n. 1); "Sexism and Racism in Vietnam War Fiction," 47

Jason's Lyric (McHenry) (film), 34

jazz: addiction to, 144, 160–61; and African American cultural memory, 125; bebop style of, 135, 138, 144–46, 153, 160, 252 (n. 12), 252 (n. 14); cool, 144; influence of, 134; *jasi* word origin for, 160; as metaphor, 139; as motif, 10, 125; "music as text," 134; as power, 125; rhetorical strategies of, 126; scatting in, 141, 150; and swing, 144; "telling the story" in, 15, 124, 129; in *Tragic Magic*, 134, 135. *See also names of individual musicians and singers*

Jazz (Morrison), 134, 136, 137

jazz/blues aesthetic, 122; of Black males, 125; and Black musicians, 125; of Ginsburg, 252 (n. 14); music as cool talk in, 133; Randle's "music as text" as, 134–35; rhetorical strategies in, 126; in *Tragic Magic*, 126

Jazz Cadence of American Culture, The (O'Meally), 124

"Jazz Is a Dance" (Murray, Albert), 121

jazz poets, 252 (n. 14)

jazzerly metaphorical language: in *Home to Harlem*, 253 (n. 19); in *Tragic Magic*, 10, 58, 126–28, 134–37, 153, 161–62, 165

jazzerly text, 15, 57, 122, 133

Jim Crow, 16, 128, 204, 222, 252 (n. 13)

"John Wayne syndrome," 125, 140, 148–52, 158, 165; in *The Alamo*, 146, 147; in *Sands of Iwo Jima*, 149; in *Stagecoach*, 149; and *Tragic Magic*, 147; and violence, 212

Johnson, Charles: interprets *maafa*, 5; *Middle Passage*, 5, 175, 193, 194, 253 (n. 5), 254 (n. 10)

Johnson, James Weldon, *The Autobiography of an Ex-Coloured Man*, 200

Johnson, Lyndon B., 46

Jolls, Shirley, *Black Marines against the Brass*, 38

Jones, Gayl, 77

Jones, Patricia Spears, 16

Jones Men, The (Smith, Vern), 222

journalism, Vietnam War, 239–40 (n. 1)

Jubilee (Alexander), 21

"Junglegrave," (Anderson, S. E.) (poem), 19, 36

Junne, George H., Jr., 27

K

Kalu, Anthonia, 117

Karenga, Maulana Ron, 27

Kelley, Robin G., 125

Kennedy, John F., 26, 148, 198

Kennedy, Robert F., 26, 27

Killens, John Oliver, 13; *And Then We Heard the Thunder*, 23–24

King, Boston, 20

King, Martin Luther, Jr., 14, 130, 218; assassination of, 26, 27, 38, 44; "Beyond Vietnam: A Time to Break Silence," 31, 44, 245 (n. 22), 251 (n. 4); in Williams's *The King God Didn't Save*, 12, 81

King God Didn't Save, The (Williams, John A.), 12, 81

King-Gamble, Marcia, *Jade*, 224

Kinnard, Douglas, 28, 247 (n. 1)

Kirkus Reviews, 81

Korean War, 65, 75–76, 222; Buffalo Soldiers in, 71

Kouyate, D'Jimo, 108

Kouyate, Mamadou, 59, 60

Kovic, Ron, 47

Ku Klux Klan, 38, 50, 145

[Kubrick, Stanley], *Full Metal Jacket*, 47

Kuhn, Thomas, 9, 241 (n. 11)

L

Lacy, Steve, 126

language. *See* Black Idiom; improvisation; vernacular culture

Laos, 32, 46, 248 (n. 5)

Laotian Fragments (Pratt), 46

Lawson, Jacqueline E.: "She's a Pretty Woman for a Gook," 47; on soldiers as "old kids," 157–58

Leake, George, 145, 252 (n. 14)

Lee, Carol D., 129

Lee, Spike: *Bamboozled*, 16; *Da5 Bloods*, 224, 225

Lester, Julius, 52, 107

"Lester Young and the Birth of Cool" (Dinerstein), 153, 154

Levine, Lawrence, 78, 80, 212, 250 (n. 16); *Black Culture and Black Consciousness*, 52, 53; on jazz as power, 125; on slave trickster, 63

Lewis, John, 44

Lewis, T. G. (artist), 217

Lewis, W. R. B., *The American Adam*, 45

Lifton, Robert, 147

Lillian Smith Award for Fiction, 221

Lim, Edward, *Masque of Honor*, 171

liminality: Baker defines, 62, 195; and middle passage, 194, 195; and trickster, 150, 157, 165, 195

Lincoln Abraham, 20

Ling, Amy, 16

Literary Griot, The (journal), 61

Literary Griot, The (Traore), 207

"Literary sense-making," 60

Little, Lloyd, *Parthian Shot*, 29

Lock, [Graham], 164

Loeb, Jeff, 241 (n. 8)

Lomperis, Timothy, 43

Los Angeles Times (newspaper), 34

Los Angeles Tribune (newspaper), 12

Lott, Eric, 145

Love, Nat, 21

Luckett, Perry D., 29–30

Lynch, Charles, 124, 126

Lynch, John, 22

Lyons, Daniel J., as *Good Men Die* editor, 41–42, 216

M

maafa, 4, 5, 83

Mailer, Norman, *Why Are We in Vietnam?*, 46

Major, Clarence, *All-Night Visitors*, 8, 223

Majors, Richard, *Cool Pose*, 153

Malcolm X, 26, 36, 44, 155

"Man Who Killed a Shadow, The," (Wright, Richard), 186

"Man Who Lived Underground, The" (Wright, Richard), 253 (n. 18)

Manchester Union Leader (newspaper), 40

Mandelbaum, Michael, 35

Marable, Manning, 36, 43; *The Black Male*, 167

"Marching Off to War" (Bell, William) (song), 25

Masque of Honor (Lim and Pearl), 171

Mathews, Gilda, 17

Mbiti, John S., 56, 177

McHenry, Doug, *Jason's Lyric*, 34

McKay, Claude, *Home to Harlem*, 22, 253 (n. 19)

Med Press Review (magazine), 12

Medal of Honor, Captain Blackman's, 74, 76, 81

Meditation in Green (Wright, Steven), 46

Melting Points (Davis, George), 17

memory, 6, 7, 126, 196; in *Coming Home*, 174–75, 193; in "Flying Home," 203; griots as personified, 60; as metaphor, 180; and Middle Passage, 193; Morrison on, 5, 108, 174; oral, 176; in oral narration, 37, 77; and proverbs, 3; racial, 10, 174, 185–87; and rememory, 108, 174–75; sites of, 197, 199. *See also* cultural memory; griots

metaphors: bombing as, 192; "castration," 192; "City on a Hill," 45; in *Coming Home*, 174, 195, 199; identity as, 139; improvisation as, 139; memory as, 180; regeneration through violence as, 45; *Stagolee* as, 54; survival as, 139; in *Tragic Magic*, 143; war as dehumanization, 167

"metaphorical castration," 192

MIA (missing in action), 219, 222

M.I.A. (Amos), 219

middle passage (metaphorical/symbolic): as liminal phase, 194, 195; Scott on dualism of, 194; space as paradoxical, 180; and trickster, 195

Middle Passage (sea voyage): and African Diaspora, 1, 59, 60, 83, 193, 245 (n. 1);

African folkways survived, 95, 100, 126; as Black Holocaust, 4, 6, 83–84, 97, 126; brutality during, 83–84; and deliverance monuments, 4; and *maafa*, 4, 5, 83; metaphorical, 180, 193; and racial consciousness, 6, 182, 197; and slavery, 6, 83–84

Middle Passage (Johnson), 5, 175, 193, 194, 254 (n. 10); binary thinking in, 253 (n. 5)

Miller, Dorie, 24

misogyny, 47, 48, 184, 190

modernism, 7, 12

Mojo Rising (Flowers), 13–14

Monk, Thelonious, 15, 125–26, 252 (n. 15); tunes of, 155

Moonspinners (Whittington), 223

Moore, Michael, 9, 46, 241 (n. 7); *Bowling for Columbine*, 8, 240 (n. 6); on "culture of violence," 45, 240 (n. 6); *Stupid White Men*, 8

Moore, Robin, *The Green Berets*, 46

Morrison, C. T., *Flame in the Icebox*, 221

Morrison, Toni: *Beloved*, 5, 136, 174, 240 (n. 3), 246 (n. 4); binary construction of, 253 (n. 5); *The Bluest Eye*, 133, 36; *Jazz*, 134, 136, 137; and musicality of text, 121, 133, 136; on racism, 19; on "rememory," 108, 174–75; *Sula*, 82, 175, 253 (n. 5); and Toni Morrison Society, 4, 249 (n. 3); tricksters in novels of, 81–82; "Unspeakable Things Unspoken," 19, 121, 133; *World Magazine* interview with, 240 (n. 3)

Mosley, Walter, "The Black Man: Hero," 1

mulattoes: stereotypes, 50, 86; strike force in *Captain Blackman*, 82, 84, 85, 86; tragic, 50

Mulira, Jessie, 100

Muller, Gilbert, 65, 69–70

Multicultural Review (magazine), 12

Munro, C. Lynn, 68

Murray, Albert, 139; on improvisation, 127, 143; "Jazz Is a Dance," 121

Murray, Pauli, *Proud Shoes*, 20–21

music: Black response to the Vietnam War through, 243 (n. 4); and cool talk, 133; and soundtracks, 35–36; vernacular language inseparable from, 134. *See also* blues; jazz

Muyumba, Francois, 201

Mwindo Epic, 212

Myers, Linda James, 56, 169; on "extended self," 213; on "nigrescence," 3; on "optimal" world view, 177; on sub-optimal world view, 175, 185

Myers, Walter Dean: *Fallen Angels*, 223, 224; *Patrol*, 223, 224

myth: African "Tree of Life," 246 (n. 8); of America, 45, 46; American warrior, 46; of Ananse the Spider, 56

N

NAACP, 22

Nation, The (magazine), 12, 168, 184

National Literary Hall of Fame, 11

National Museum of African American History and Culture, 4, 240 (n. 5)

National Revue (magazine), 40

Native Son (Wright, Richard), 82, 191, 254 (n. 9)

NBC television, 12, 33

Negro History Week, 51

"Negro Speaks of Rivers, The" (Hughes),

allegory in, 250 (n. 17)

Negroes: and *Coming Home*'s Thai people, 198; Du Bois on double-consciousness of American, 86, 179; Hurston's allegory on American, 249 (n. 10); racism and, 71, 192; as recruits, 69; reenlistment of, 26; stereotypes for, 49; troops in war, 22, 26; as war fatalities, 26, 218; white control over, 50, 72. *See also* "nigger," stereotype; *and U.S. military branches by name*

"Negro-ness" (Blackness), 9

Nettleford, Rex, 128

New Black Aesthetic," 10, 215

New Jersey State Council on the Arts Award, 11

New York Daily Mirror (newspaper), 40

New York Times, 3, 31; Davis on staff at, 17; and John A. Williams, 10–12; Rand review in, 167

New York Times Book Review, 3, 17

Newsweek (magazine), 12, 241 (n. 9), 244 (n. 20)

"nigger": and Ali's attitude, 2; as brute, 50; as "cappin" remark, 146; in *Captain Blackman*, 71, 81, 85–86; in *Coming Home*, 155, 178, 188, 192; as derogatory term, 22, 38, 71, 81, 91, 94, 188, 192; Du Bois on, 22; in Jim Crow setting, 252 (n. 13); and "metaphorical castration," 192; and sexual fears, 192; and soldiers, 23, 71; as term in American West, 71; as "toast" theme, 246 (n. 10); in vernacular, 49–50, 86, 107; in Vietcong messages, 38; in Vietnam, 188, 192; as Weiss film title, 31, 252 (n. 16)

"nigger hater," 91

"nigguh," 246 (n. 10)

"nigrescence," 3

Nixon, Richard M., 90, 247 (n. 1), 253 (n. 3), 256 (n. 2)

NMAAHC (National Museum of African American History and Culture), 4, 240 (n. 5)

"no such thing as a black prisoner of war," 68

No Vietnamese Ever Called Me Nigger (Weiss) (film), 31, 252 (n. 16)

nonfiction: by Black writers, 5, 37–42, 44; by Philippa Schuyler, 28, 39–43, 169, 216, 217, 224

Nora, Pierre, 197

North Vietnamese, 38, 41, 181, 196, 248 (n. 5); General Giap of, 28

nostos, 253 (n. 1)

novelistic conventions, 94; critical realism, 7, 8; naturalism, 7, 8; neorealism, 7, 8, 12, 168

novels: African American, 5, 7–8, 219; American, 7; double consciousness in, 7; myth, legend, and ritual in, 7; neglected, 2–3; neorealism in, 7; "nigrescence" rite of passage in, 3; on Vietnam War by Black writers, 47, 90–94, 97, 106, 116–20, 147, 169–71, 221, 223, 239–40 (n. 1); on Vietnam War by women, 224. *See also names of individual novels*

O

O'Brien, John, 11

O'Brien, Tim, 47; *Going After Cacciato*, 29, 46

O'Meally, Robert, 180; *History and Memory in African-American Culture*, 6; *The Jazz Cadence of American Culture*, 124

Obama, Barack, 4, 240 (n. 5)

Ogunyemi, Chikwenye Okonjo, 204

"Old Music" (Taylor, Chris), 256 (n. 2)

one drop of Black blood, 50, 61

One They Called Quiet, The (Bolar), 221

100 Years of Lynching (Ginsburg), 155

Operation Burning Candle (Jackson, Blyden), 222

Oprah Winfrey Show, The, 8–9, 240 (n. 6), 241 (n. 7)

oral narratives: African folk, 98; *Bloods*, 37; fictional, 174; as oral history, 43; toast as, 55; Vietnam-related, 5, 29, 37–38, 44, 174; and Wallace Terry, 148

orisha, 101–3, 107, 109–11, 115

Ostendorf, Berndt, 194

Other, 194; "cultural other," 8; and "Othering," 9; peoples of color as, 46, 188

P

parable, 70; "Platonic," 253 (n. 5)

Parker, Charlie (Bird, Birdland), 15, 125, 126; as bebopper, 135, 144–45, 153, 160, 161; and "Celebrating Bird" video, 135; "Cherokee" style of, 135; improvisation of, 144; "Koko," 135, 144–45, 149; "Ooh, Shoo Bee Doo Bee," 160; "Ornithology," 135; personal life of, 145; and *Tragic Magic*, 138

Parks, David, *G.I. Diary*, 39, 42

Parks, Gordon, 39

parodies, 132–33

Patches of Fire (French), 223

Patrol (Myers, Walter Dean), 223, 224

PBS (television), 16, 141

Peabody Prize, 32

Pearl, Jack, *Masque of Honor*, 171

Peers, William R., 47

Pelton, Robert, 62, 81

Pentagon, 12, 25, 85

Pentagon Papers, The (Sheehan), 217, 253 (n. 3)

Peters, Erskine, *African Openings to the Tree of Life*, 89

phallicism: Calibanic, 223; and symbols, 82, 107, 227

phallus. *See* "black phallus"

Phyllis Wheatley Award for Invaluable Contributions to African American Letters and Culture, 11

Pickett, Bill, 21

Pickett, Wilson, 201

Piece of This Country, A (Taylor, Thomas), 29, 30

Pittsburgh Courier (newspaper), 12, 216

Plains Wars, 21, 64; Buffalo Soldiers in, 71

Plato, 175, 176, 188, 199; world view of, 197

Platonic parable, 253 (n. 5)

Platoon (Stone) (film), 29, 32

Playing the Changes (Werner), 138, 139

plays: by Black writers, 2, 11, 12, 16, 31–32, 39, 243 (n. 10); Vietnam-related, 2, 32

poetry: awards for, 11; by Black writers, 5, 11, 12, 34, 36, 44, 45, 250 (n. 17), 251 (n. 7); performance, 13, 252 (n. 14); Vietnam-related, 29, 31–32

point man, Black soldiers as, 30, 39, 90, 106, 221, 248 (n. 4)

"Point Man, The" (Hackworth), 248 (n. 4)

Politico (online magazine), 241 (n. 7)

Poor, Salem, 20

Post, The (film), 169, 253 (n. 3)

postmodernism: in Black fiction, 7–8, 46, 58; in Vietnam fiction, 46; and White experience in Vietnam, 46

post–traumatic stress disorder. *See* PTSD

POW (prisoner of war), 221, 222; "black," 68

Powell, Colin, 40

power (*Nommo*), 70, 141

Pratt, John Clark, *Laotian Fragments*, 46

Presidential Commission on Race, 23

Prewitt, J. Everett, 256 (n. 8); *A Long Way Back*, 219; *Something about Ann*, 219–20

Price of Honor, The (Hackworth), 248 (n. 4)

Problem (Gilmore), 22

profanity, 10, 46. *See also individual words and phrases*

Project 100,000, 25

Proud Shoes (Murray, Pauli), 20–21

proverbs: African, 3, 59, 98, 119, 211; Bakongan, 59; and memory, 3–4

PTSD, 36, 118, 150, 223, 224; in *Captain Blackman*, 213; in *Coming Home*, 213; in *De Mojo Blues*, 90, 213; in *Jason's Lyric*, 34; in *Tragic Magic*, 15, 123, 213

Publishers Weekly (magazine), 3, 222

Pugh, Charles, *The Griot*, 211, 220

Puhr, Kathleen, 46, 47

Push Comes to Shove (Brown, Wesley), 16

Q

Quarterly Black Review (magazine), 12

Quartermaster Rangers, (Bolar), 222

"Quiet as it's kept," 132–33

racial consciousness, 6, 182, 197

racism: and biracial persons, 5, 20, 216, 217; and Buffalo Soldiers, 21, 64, 70–71, 174; and colonialism, 36, 48; external threats of, 145; institutionalized, 6, 192; and military discrimination, 38, 104; Morrison on, 4; and one-drop theory of dehumanization, 50, 61; ongoing struggle with, 5; in Vietnam novels, 29–30, 44, 47; in Vietnam War, 43, 44, 47, 244 (n. 19), 104

R

Railroad Bill (Bill Slater), 2; legend of heroic, 53–54
Ramparts Magazine, 25
Rand, Peter, 167
Randle, Gloria T., 134
rape: in Civil War, 72, 83; during enslavement, 83–84; on Middle Passage slave ships, 83, 84; symbolic, 83; and trickster, 84; in Vietnam, 37, 48; as weapon, 84
(re)call and response, 137, 139, 144
Reconstruction, 6, 16, 21
Red Badge of Courage (Crane), 31, 223–24
Redeemer Nation (Tuveson), 45–46
Reed, Ishmael, 13
reenlistment: in *Captain Blackman*, 26, 61, 66, 214, 225; in *Coming Home*, 57; in *De Mojo Blues*, 94, 225; of Flowers, 94
Regeneration through Violence (Slotkin), 45, 247 (n. 14)
re-membering: of Black cultural memory, 3, 4, 108; of Black roots, 205; in *Coming Home*, 180, 196, 203, 210; and identity, 4; and *maafa*, 4, 5, 83; in practicing *sankofa*, 2; and racism, 3
"rememory," 108, 174–75
rhetoric: dialectic discourse as, 77; as jazzerly strategies, 126; pseudo-revolutionary, 156.

See also metaphors; Signifying Monkey toast; tropes
Ribman, Ronald, *The Final War of Olly Winter*, 31
Rice, Alan J., 126
Richard Wright-Jacques Roumain Award, 11
Richards, Dona Marimba, 175; "The African Aesthetic and National Consciousness," 59
Roberts, John W., 61, 74, 76; *From Trickster to Badman*, 53, 54
Robeson, Paul, 51, 255 (n. 16)
Roosevelt, Eleanor, 204
Roosevelt, Theodore, racist remark by, 71
Ross, Ted, 135
Rumor of War, A (Caputo), 46, 47
Runner Mack (Beckham), 8, 223

S

Saigon, 28, 104, 241 (n. 9), 252 (n. 17)
Salem, Peter, 20, 66, 67
Samuels, Wilfred D., 174
Sanders, Robert, *Brothers*, 19, 37
Sands, Diana, 35, 243 (n. 10)
sankofa, 2
Schroeder, Daniel, 71
Schroeder, Patricia, 13
Schuyler, George S.: *Black No More*, 216, 255 (n. 1); and wife Josephine Cogdell, 216
Schuyler, Philippa, 224; biracial, 216, 217; as childhood genius, 216; *Dau Tranh!*, 216–17; death of, 39, 41–42, 43; *Good Men Die*, 28, 39–42, 169, 216
Scott, Daniel M., III, 194, 253 (n. 5)
Scott, Nathan B., 72
Seale, Bobby, 54

Selective Service Act, 22, 43; 1940 revision to, 23

self, and community, 139, 211

self-image, Euro-American male, 188–89

Senna, Danzy, 255 (n. 1)

"Sexism and Racism in Vietnam War Fiction" (Jason), 47

sexual stereotype, in *Coming Home*, 190, 191

shapeshifters, 54, 62, 87

"She's a Pretty Woman for a Gook" (Lawson), 47

Sheehan, Neil, *Pentagon Papers, The*, 217, 253 (n. 3)

Shine, as Black hero, 2, 24, 55, 79–80, 119

"Shine and the Titanic": in *Captain Blackman*, 79; in *De Mojo Blues*, 118; legend of, 79; as toast, 24, 55, 79, 80, 119; and Signifying Monkey, 79, 80

short timer, 47, 157, 245 (n. 24)

Short Timers (Hasford), 47

signification, 9, 13; "cappin" in, 146, 246 (n. 9); definitions of, 122, 246 (n. 9), 250 (n. 1); Smitherman on, 77, 80, 81, 129–30, 132, 246 (n. 9); and "we, us, they and them," 132, 133

signifyin(g)/signifying, 9, 172: as Black idiom, 129, 250 (n. 1); as "buzz talk," 138; "cappin" as, 130; in *Captain Blackman*, 78, 80–81, 83, 84, 86; in *Coming Home*, 173, 255 (n. 15); as cultural phenomenon, 122; in *De Mojo Blues*, 112; definition of, 122, 126, 129, 250 (n. 1); as empowerment, 122; as hyperbole, 173; as indirection, 129, 173; lyrical speech of, 129, 162, 164; as metaphoric and ironic, 133; "musivocal"/ speakerly text, 15, 129, 133, 178; as parody, 132; as pastiche, 132–33, 146; repetition

and revision in, 122; as revenge, 80; Rice defines, 126; as scatting, 141, 150; Smitherman on light and heavy types of, 77, 80–81, 129, 130, 132, 246 (n. 9); and "speakerly text" of Gates, 129; in *Tragic Magic*, 122, 129–34, 138, 143–44, 150, 158, 162

Signifying Monkey, The (Gates), 10, 11, 55, 77–78, 135, 250 (n. 1)

Signifying Monkey toast, 55, 80; in *Captain Blackman*, 77–79; in *Coming Home*, 172–73

Sims-Holt, Grace, 98

simultaneous existence, 6

Sisson, Jack (Tack), 20

Sixties Project, 218, 255 (n. 5)

Slater, Bill (Railroad Bill), 2; legend of heroic, 53–54

slavery: abolishment of, 21; chattel, 21, 190, 192, 208

Slotkin, Richard, *Regeneration through Violence*, 2, 45, 247 (n. 14)

Smith, Jeanne Rosier, 81–82

Smith, Vern, *The Jones Men*, 222

Smith, Walter B., 69

Smitherman, Geneva, 122; on Black Idiom, 10, 129; on Black Semantics, 10, 53; on signification, 77, 80, 81, 129–30, 132, 246 (n. 9); on signifying types, 77, 81, 130, 246 (n. 9); *Talkin' and Testifyin'*, 10, 53, 63, 246 (n. 9); on toast, 246–47 (n. 10); "Word from the Hood," 153

socialized ambivalence, 5, 6, 7

"Soldier Boy" (song), 25

Soldier Boy, Soldier (Anderson, T. J.) (opera), 121, 220

soldiers, Vietnam War writings by, 239–40 (n. 1)

Soldiers of Freedom (Wright, Kai), 20, 21

solidarity rituals: Black liberation as, 103; Black power handshake in, 104–5; clothing as, 250 (n. 16); dapping, 38, 103–5, 250 (n. 15); power moves for, 105; power salutes, 90

Souls of Black Folk, The (Du Bois), 86

South Vietnam, 28, 41, 196, 241 (n. 9); as ally, 159, 248 (n. 5); forces failed, 247 (n. 1); and Montagnards, 105

Southern Christian Leadership Conference, 218

"spade," 30

Spanish-American War, Black soldiers in, 21, 22, 24, 71

Spanish Civil War, 64

speakerly text, 15, 129, 133, 178

Spiritual Intelligence (Davis, George), 18

Spook Who Sat by the Door, The (Greenlee): as film, 22, 256 (n. 11); as novel, 222

Staggerlee (Stagolee, Stackerlee) (toast), 54, 55

Stagolee Shot Billy (Brown, Cecil), 54

Stapp, Andy, *Black Marines against the Brass*, 38

Stepto, Robert, 9, 180, 198, 200, 207; *From behind the Veil*, 185–86

stereotypes: Black "brutes," 50; Black "bucks," 50; blackface, 51; for Black females, 50; and Black male identity, 167, 190, 191; "comic" characters in, 49; "coon," 49; dumb darkey, 79, 86; Euro-American, 47; in film, 50; from imagination, 49; "mammy," 50, 79; in minstrelsy, 16, 49, 118; and one drop of Black blood, 50, 61; sexual, 190, 191; in song, 79; "tragic

mulatto," 79; in Vietnam War novels, 47, 170–71; of WWI Black soldiers, 80

Stern, Saul, 25–26

Stone, Oliver, *Platoon*, 29, 32

Stone, Robert, *Dog Soldiers*, 47

stream-of-consciousness technique, 169, 223

"street committee" ("Street Institution"), 124, 137

Student Nonviolent Coordinating Committee, 218, 244 (n. 21)

Sula (Morrison), 82, 175, 253 (n. 5)

survival, Black, 37, 91, 131; and Ananse, 60, 61; Black Idiom and, 129; and blues, 139; and buddy system, 157; cool as, 109, 110, 153; cool jazz style for, 128, 133, 144, 153–54; cool pose as, 125, 133, 153; and cultural memory, 2, 7, 8, 13, 61, 98, 119, 129, 170, 187; in *De Mojo Blues*, 113, 114–15, 118–19; as group, 29; High John symbolizes, 107; improvisation for, 127, 139, 162; jazz addiction for, 125, 160–61; as metaphor, 107, 139; and power, 14, 112, 115, 118; psychological, 109, 119; racial solidarity as, 30, 38; re-membering for, 127; rituals of solidarity and, 100, 104–7; by signifying, 77–80; strategies, 5, 7, 39, 77, 120, 153–54, 162, 214; and "toast," 77; and trickster, 64, 77

Sussman, Alison Carb, 17, 18

symbolism: Black phallus, 69, 82–83, 130, 246 (n. 6); in *Coming Home*, 192–94, 197, 198, 200

Symphony for the Sons of 'Nam (Williams, Kimo) (symphony), 225

T

Tal, Kali, 218

Talalay, Kathryn, 42; *Composition in Black and White*, 216

Talkin' and Testifyin' (Smitherman), 10, 53, 63, 246 (n. 9)

Tara Books, 14

Tavis Smiley Show, 55

Taylor, Chris, "Old Music: Freda Payne—Bring the Boys Home," 256 (n. 2)

Taylor, Clyde, *Vietnam and Black America: An Anthology of Protest and Resistance*, 44, 45

Taylor, Thomas, *A Piece of This Country*, 29, 30

TeacherServe, 54

Terry, Wallace: *Bloods*, 30, 37, 43, 148; publisher rejections of, 43; on racism in Vietnam War, 43, 244 (n. 19)

Terry Whitmore, for Example (Brodie) (film), 31, 42

Thailand: air bases in, 168; Black pilots in, 254 (n. 6); in *Coming Home*, 169–71, 176, 179–81, 189, 196–98, 200, 210

Their Eyes Were Watching God (Hurston), 13, 205, 209

Things Fall Apart (Achebe), 180, 207, 254 (n. 7), 255 (n. 17)

13th Valley, The (Del Vecchio), 29, 30, 171

Thomas, Kevin, 34

Thompson, Robert Farris, 195

Thornton, Jerome, 205

time: conflation of, 246 (n. 4); mythic, 64; and simultaneous existence, 63

TIME (magazine), 37

toast (theme): and Black heroism, 55, 247

(n. 10); definition of, 54, 55, 246 (n. 10); performance of, 80; and survival, 77. *See also* "Shine and the Titanic"; Signifying Monkey toast; Staggerlee (Stagolee, Stackerlee) (toast)

Toffoli, Marissa, *Words with Writers* blog, 14

"tom," as Negro character, 49, 50

Tombolo massacre, 68–69, 75

Toms, Coons, Mulattoes, Mammies, & Bucks (Bogle), 49–50

Toni Morrison Society, 4, 240 (n. 3)

topos, 77

Tragic Magic (Brown), 3, 125; aggregation, 154, 161, 176; Black survival in, 120; Black woman in, 48; blues tone and melody in, 139, 141; buzz talk in, 138; call-and-response in, 130, 137–39, 164; "code of the streets" in, 214; cultural memory in, 126, 135; flashbacks in, 137; heroic quest in, 154; heroism in, 57, 124, 140, 151, 165–66, 214; identity in, 158, 163–66, 215; improvisational dream as life coda in, 163–65; jazz and survival in, 160, 134, 135, 214; jazz as Black expressive culture in, 139; jazzerly metaphorical language in, 10, 58, 126–28, 134–38, 153, 161–62, 165; jazzerly text of, 15, 57, 122, 133, 137, 165; jazz tradition in text of, 10, 137, 138; liminality in, 159; neorealism in, 12; prison experience as war experience in, 157–62, 166; resembles *Invisible Man*, 163; rite of passage in, 164; *rites of Black (w)hole* in, 154, 156–57, 162, 213, 254 (n. 15); on separation, 157; signifying in, 131, 144, 158, 162; signifyin(g) monkey in, 122, 129–30, 132, 134, 138, 143, 150; style and appearance in, 151, 152; tension in, 140; "tragic magic" theme of, 165; trickster in, 150; tripartite structure in, 154; vernacular influenced, 142, 143–44

Traore, Ousseynou, 207; *The Literary Griot*, 61

Traylor, Eleanor, 126

tricksters, 81, 246 (n. 10); African versus American, 61–63; amorality of, 82, 84; Black phallic, 223; as Black value source, 61; cap of, 112; and colors, 102, 109; cultural memory and Ansansean motif of, 245 (n. 1); definition of, 52, 56, 63, 64, 83; as Diasporan African myth, 10, 52, 56, 58, 60–64, 87, 99, 245 (n. 1); as Eshu, 102, 115; as fatalistic of, 61; and heroic bad man, 51, 54; and hero model, 51, 52, 61, 109; as Jethro, 102; as liminal, 150, 157, 165, 195; and middle passage, 195; and "moral hard man," 51; and ritual colors, 102–3; signification of, 77, 78, 84, 87; and slavery, 63; Sula as, 82; symbolism of, 52, 63, 64, 66, 76, 82, 84, 102–3, 107; as topos, 77

Trimmer, Joseph, 205

tropes: "Black (w)hole" as, 156, 213, 253 (n. 18), 254–55 (n. 15); paradigm shift as, 241 (n. 11); "repetition and revision," 9, 83, 122, 132

Tuck, David, 26

Tucker, Mark, 128

Turner, Nathaniel, 14

Turner, Victor, 200

Tuskegee Airmen, 203, 204; Davis of, 22

Tuskegee Institute, 204

Tuveson, Ernest Lee, *Redeemer Nation*, 45–46

U

Union Army (Civil War), Black soldiers in, 20–21, 64, 140

United Press Features (news), 40

"Unspeakable Things Unspoken" (Morrison), 19, 121, 133

U.S. Air Force, 22, 32; Black pilots in, 17, 23, 33, 223; Blacks in *Coming Home*, 166–69, 179, 186, 192, 202, 209, 215

U.S. Army: Air Command, 203; and Audie Murphy heroism, 148; Black salutes in, 76; Black soldiers in, 43, 69; in John Wayne movies, 147–50

U.S. Marine Corps: Black soldiers in, 38, 43; in John Wayne movies, 147–50

U.S. Navy: Black sailors in, 22, 24; hero Miller in, 24; Williams in, 12

U.S. Supreme Court, 43, 218, 255 (n. 6)

V

Van de Burg, William R., 48–55

Van Sertima, Ivan, 66, 81, 83; "Trickster, the Revolutionary Hero," 64

Verharen, Charles C., "African-Centeredness and the New Black Millennium," 167

vernacular culture, 58–59, 193, 203; and Ananse myth, 60, 77; Black, 8, 54, 62, 73, 87, 122, 124, 129, 141, 143; Black dapping as, 38–39, 104; and Black heroes, 51; and bonding rituals, 38–39; and "dancin' the talk," 80; expressions of camaraderie, 38; and folk tradition, 38; and "jazzerly" text, 57, 143; music of, 122, 129, 141; *Nommo* in, 141; "Quiet as it's kept," 132; sayings in, 132; scatting in, 141, 150

vernacular theory, 10, 58, 60, 215; and

trickster tradition as Black value source, 61

Vietcong (also Viet Cong): Ali quote on, 2; as enemy, 28, 159, 247 (n. 1), 248 (n. 5); in film, 32–34, 149–50; guerilla warfare in novels, 48, 65, 91, 147, 149, 194–95, 221–22; leaflet drops by, 38; psychological victory of, 28; in tunnels, 25, 91

Vietnam: *ao dai* dress of, 41; and Vietnamese identifying with Black soldiers, 3; war writings by Vietnamese, 239–40 (n. 1). *See also* North Vietnamese; South Vietnam; Vietcong (also Viet Cong)

Vietnam (Bond) (graphic novel/comic), 217–18, 219

Vietnam and Black America (Taylor, Clyde) (anthology), 44, 45

Vietnam War: air versus ground war in, 193, 254 (n. 12); and anti-War movement, 255 (n. 5); autobiographies about, 39, 206, 223, 254 (n. 14); banned music in, 256 (n. 2); Black enlistments in, 24; Black experience in, 3, 29, 89; Black fatalities and casualties, 26, 28, 218; Black films on, 31–37; Black nationalism in, 155–56; Black pilots in, 204; Black soldiers in, 26, 37, 39, 43, 57, 66, 90, 202, 223; Black volunteers for, 248 (n. 6); Black writers' works about, 2–3, 43, 90–94, 97, 106, 116–20, 147, 169, 221–23, 239–40 (n. 1); bombing in, 170, 193, 244 (n. 14); booby traps in, 40; casualty count of, 2; criticism of, 41; devastation in, 193, 197; divisiveness of, 2; draft in, 2, 43, 254 (n. 7); duration of, 2, 241 (n. 9); euphemisms about, 40; films about, 31, 34–37, 243 (n.

10); fragging in, 245 (n. 27); imperialism in, 70, 244 (n. 20); integration in, 25; "jazz high" for survival in, 160; journalists in, 43; music of era of, 25, 28; My Lai Massacre, in, 47; Nixon's strategies for, 90, 247 (n. 1), 256 (n. 2); 29; opposition to, 218; photography in, 252 (n. 17); point man in, 30, 39, 90, 106, 221, 248 (n. 4); protesting and immolation in, 252 (n. 17); protests against, 249 (n. 7); PTSD in, 90; publishers avoided works on, 42–43; racism in, 43, 44, 47, 244 (n. 19), 104; rape and violence in, 47; and reenlistment, 26, 57, 61, 66, 94, 214, 225; returning home from, 87, 89–90, 94, 96–97, 123, 222; as rite of passage, 106, 137; "search and destroy mission" in, 91, 92, 248 (n. 5); short timer in, 47, 157, 160, 245 (n. 24); solidarity in, 249 (n. 12), 250 (n. 15); on television, 35; Tet Offensive in, 27–28, 46; trickster in, 63, 102, 115; unit cohesion in, 249 (n. 12); U.S. Air Force in, 17, 22, 23, 33, 223; U.S. Air Force in *Coming Home*, 168–70, 179, 182, 186, 192, 202, 209, 215; U.S. Army in, 26, 39; U.S. Marine Corps in, 43; U.S. Navy in, 12, 22, 24; veterans as authors, 10; Vietcong ambushes in, 147, 149; weaponry in, 40; White writers' works on, 3, 29–32, 43, 46, 48–49, 60, 171; women in, 41–42

Vietnamization, 247 (n. 1)

Village Voice, (newspaper), 12

Vodoun, 249 (n. 8); creation myth in, 101; in *De Mojo Blues*, 10, 13, 87–88, 93–96, 99–102, 109–13, 215, 249 (n. 11); as healing, 215; and heroic quest, 95–96;

ritual in, 95; slavery and, 95, 100; symbols in, 112; from West Africa, 95. *See also* hoodoo; voodoo

voice: artistic, 124; character, 64, 138, 184, 214; inner, 123; and revoice, 185, 187, 203; and speakerly text as jazzerly, 133, 138, 141–43; vernacular, 178

voodoo, 10; and cultural memory, 99; and hoodoo, 249 (n. 11); Hurston on Jewish Exodus and, 249 (n. 10); psychological base of, 100; spiritual system of, 93, 94

W

Wakin, Edward, 254 (n. 6)

Walking Dead, The (Whitmore) (film), 33, 34

War of 1812: Black soldiers in, 64, 74; Freejacks in, 68

War in I Corps, The (Guidry), 221

Ward, Jerry, Jr., 5

"Warring Fictions," (Young), 20

Wars We Took to Vietnam, The (Bates), 25, 171

Washington Post, 12, 17; in *The Post*, 169, 253 (n. 3); on MIA, 219

Watkins, Mel, 17; *Coming Home* "Introduction" by, 168

Watson, Glegg, *Black Life in Corporate America*, 17, 18

Wayne, John: *Alamo*, 146, 147; as hero type, 52, 123–25, 212, 214, 252 (n. 12, 146); movie hero roles of, 147, 149; as "mythical figure," 147; "syndrome" of, 125, 140, 148–52, 158, 165

weaponry, 24, 40, 85

Webb, James, *Fields of Fire*, 29, 47

Weiss, David Loeb, *No Vietnamese Ever Called Me Nigger*, 31, 252 (n. 16)

Werner, Craig Hansen, *Playing the Changes*, 138, 139

Westheider, James: on dapping, 104–5, 249 (n. 13); *Fighting on Two Fronts*, 248 (n. 6), 249 (nn. 12–13), 254 (n. 8); on solidarity, 103, 250 (n. 15)

"'What's Goin' On?'" (Hanshaw), 243 (n. 4)

Whitaker, Forest, 32, 34

White, Deborah Gray, *Ar'n't I a Woman?*, 83

White heroes, 2, 48–49, 212

White writers: on Blacks in Vietnam War, 3, 29–32, 43, 46, 48, 60, 171; early literary, 49; publishing problems of, 43

Whitmore, Preston, II, *The Walking Dead*, 33, 34

Whitmore, Terry, 207; *Memphis-Nam-Sweden* autobiography, 42, 168, 205, 206, 254 (n. 14); on Beheiren, 42, 209; as Black deserter, 31, 42, 57, 168, 206; *Terry Whitmore, for Example* film/documentary, 31, 42

Whittington, Ruben Benjamin, *Moonspinners*, 223

Why Are We in Vietnam? (Mailer), 46

Williams, John A.: career of, 10–12, 81, 86; genres worked in, 11, 12; *The King God Didn't Save*, 12, 81; "melodramatic" style of, 69; as "metahistorical novel" of, 69; as modern griot, 60–61; *New York Times* on, 10–12; nonfiction works of, 12; as trickster, 83; uses trickster in novels, 52, 82. See also *Captain Blackman* (Williams)

Williams, Kimo: *Buffalo Soldiers*, 225; *Fanfare for Life*, 225; *Symphony for the Sons of 'Nam*, 225

Williams, Thomas D., *Cohesion*, 48, 221,

249 (n. 12)

"Willow Weep for Me" (Ammons), 134

Willson, David, editor of *Vietnam Generation*, 219

Wilson, August, 141

Wilson, D. B., *Betrayed*, 221

Wilson, Nancy, 141, 142, 251 (n. 4)

Winfield, Paul, 32, 33

Wirtz, James J., 28

women, Black: in Vietnam War novels, 48; Schuyler's writings on Vietnam, 28, 39, 41–43, 169, 216, 217, 224; Vietnam War writing by, 239–40 (n. 1)

Woodson, Carter G., 11, 51

"Word from the Hood" (Smitherman), 153

Words with Writers blog, 14

Workings of the Spirit (Baker), 179

"World, the," 17

World Magazine, Morrison interview in, 240 (n. 3)

World War I: Black soldiers in, 22, 67, 72; in *Captain Blackman*, 10, 64, 67, 72, 74–76, 79; *Home to Harlem* about, 22, 253 (n. 19); "Shine" toast in, 79

World War II, 253 (n. 19); *And Then We Heard the Thunder* about, 23–24; bebop started in, 144; Black heroes in, 24, 67; Black pilots in, 203–5; Black soldiers in, 10, 12, 23–24, 64, 67–69, 72, 148; *Captain Blackman* in, 64, 67, 72, 75–76; "double V" symbol of, 23–24, 144; integrated units in, 23, 69; movies about, 146–48; novels about, 23–24, 64, 136, 203–4; racial atrocities in, 68, 72; racial discrimination in, 23, 69; segregated forces in, 69, 144, 204–5; Tombolo massacre in, 68–69, 75; Tuskegee Airmen in, 22, 203, 204; veterans as authors, 10

Wright, John, 123

Wright, Kai, *Soldiers of Freedom*, 20–22, 24, 27, 40

Wright, Richard, 12, 255 (n. 16); and black (w) hole, 154, 156–57, 162, 213, 254 (n. 150); "The Ethics of Living Jim Crow," 252 (n. 13); "The Man Who Killed a Shadow," 186; "The Man Who Lived Underground," 253 (n. 18); *Native Son*, 82, 191, 254 (n. 9)

Wright, Steven, *Meditation in Green*, 46

Y

Yette, Samuel, 44, 244 (n. 20)

Yoruba (people), 89, 110, 111

"You Talk Like You Got Books in Your Jaws" (Brown, Wesley), 142

Young, Elizabeth, 20

Young, Lester, 153, 154

Z

zoot suits, 145